Rick Steves'

BUDAPEST

Rick Steves & Cameron Hewitt

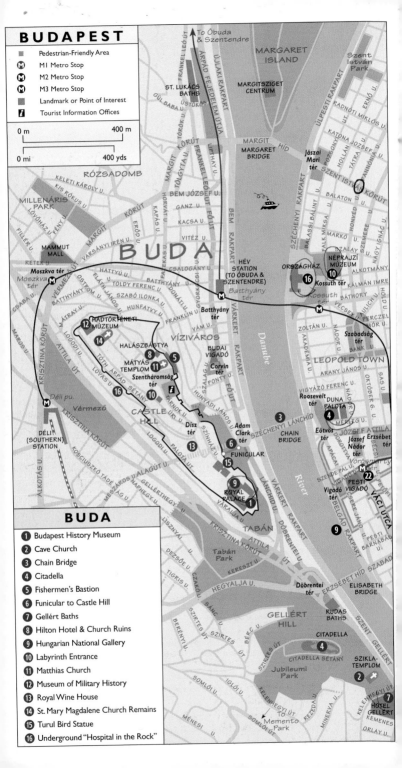

BUDAPEST

- Pedestrian-Friendly Area
- Ⓜ M1 Metro Stop
- Ⓜ M2 Metro Stop
- Ⓜ M3 Metro Stop
- Landmark or Point of Interest
- ⓘ Tourist Information Offices

0 m   400 m

0 mi   400 yds

BUDA

1. Budapest History Museum
2. Cave Church
3. Chain Bridge
4. Citadella
5. Fishermen's Bastion
6. Funicular to Castle Hill
7. Gellért Baths
8. Hilton Hotel & Church Ruins
9. Hungarian National Gallery
10. Labyrinth Entrance
11. Matthias Church
12. Museum of Military History
13. Royal Wine House
14. St. Mary Magdalene Church Remains
15. Turul Bird Statue
16. Underground "Hospital in the Rock"

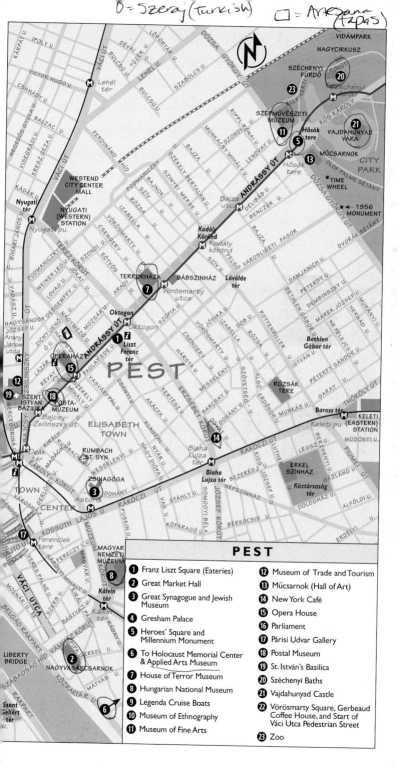

O = Szeraj (Turkish) □ = Arkosana (Tapas)

PEST

1 Franz Liszt Square (Eateries)
2 Great Market Hall
3 Great Synagogue and Jewish Museum
4 Gresham Palace
5 Heroes' Square and Millennium Monument
6 To Holocaust Memorial Center & Applied Arts Museum
7 House of Terror Museum
8 Hungarian National Museum
9 Legenda Cruise Boats
10 Museum of Ethnography
11 Museum of Fine Arts

12 Museum of Trade and Tourism
13 Műcsarnok (Hall of Art)
14 New York Café
15 Opera House
16 Parliament
17 Párisi Udvar Gallery
18 Postal Museum
19 St. István's Basilica
20 Széchenyi Baths
21 Vajdahunyad Castle
22 Vörösmarty Square, Gerbeaud Coffee House, and Start of Váci Utca Pedestrian Street
23 Zoo

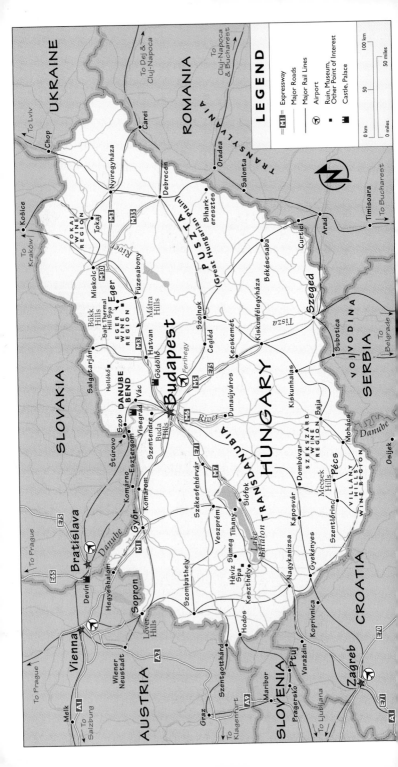

Rick Steves'

BUDAPEST

AVALON
TRAVEL

CONTENTS

DAY TRIPS FROM BUDAPEST

BEYOND BUDAPEST

HUNGARY:
PAST AND PRESENT   389

APPENDIX   407

INDEX   427

INTRODUCTION

Budapest (locals say "BOO-daw-pesht") is a unique metropolis at the heart of a unique nation. Here you'll find experiences like nothing else in Europe: Feel your stress ebb away as you soak in hundred-degree water, surrounded by opulent Baroque domes...and by Speedo- and bikini-clad Hungarians. Ogle some of Europe's most richly decorated interiors, which faintly echo a proud little nation's bygone glory days. Open your ears to a first-rate performance at one of the world's top opera houses—at bargain prices. Ponder the region's bleak communist era as you stroll amidst giant Soviet-style statues designed to evoke fear and obedience. Try to wrap your head around Hungary's colorful history...and your tongue around some of its notoriously difficult words. Dive into a bowl of goulash, the famous paprika-flavored peasant soup with a kick. Go for an after-dinner stroll along the Danube, immersed in a grand city that's bathed in floodlights.

Budapest excites good travelers...and exasperates bad ones. I love this city for its flaws as much as for its persistent personality. As a tour guide, for years I've introduced travelers to Budapest: walked them step-by-step through the byzantine entry procedure at the thermal baths; handed them a glass of local wine with an unpronounceable name and an unforgettable flavor; and taught them to greet their new Hungarian friends with a robust *"Jó napot kívánok!"* I've watched them struggle to understand—and gradually succumb to the charms of—this fascinating but beguiling place. And I took careful notes. This book represents the lessons I've learned on my own and with them, organized to help you experience Budapest with the wisdom of a return visitor.

INTRODUCTION

About This Book

Think of *Rick Steves' Budapest* as a personal tour guide in your pocket. Better yet, it's actually two tour guides in your pocket: The co-author of this book is Cameron Hewitt, who writes and edits guidebooks and leads tours in Hungary for my travel company, Rick Steves' Europe Through the Back Door. Inspired by Hungary's epic past, charming people, and delightfully spicy cuisine, Cameron has spent the last decade closely tracking the exciting changes in this part of the world. Together, Cameron and I keep this book up-to-date and accurate (though for simplicity we've shed our respective egos to become "I" in this book).

Here's what you'll find in the following chapters:

Hungary offers an introduction to this mesmerizing land, including a crash course in its notoriously difficult language.

Orientation includes a "verbal map" of the city, tourist information, specifics on public transportation, local tour options, and other helpful hints. The "Planning Your Time" section suggests a day-to-day schedule for how to best use your limited time.

Sights provides a succinct overview of Budapest's most important sights, arranged by neighborhood, with ratings:

▲▲▲—Don't miss.

▲▲—Try hard to see.

▲—Worthwhile if you can make it.

No rating—Worth knowing about.

The **Thermal Baths** chapter offers step-by-step instructions for enjoying Budapest's quintessential activity like a local.

The **Self-Guided Walks** cover Budapest's Castle Hill (its historic center), Leopold Town (the banking and business district), Pest Town Center (the down-and-dirty downtown urban zone), Andrássy út (the main boulevard, lined with fine architecture and great sightseeing), and Heroes' Square and City Park (the city's playground, including a Who's Who lesson in Hungarian history).

The **Self-Guided Tours** lead you through two of Budapest's most compelling sights from its troubled 20th century: the House of Terror Museum and Memento Park. Additional self-guided tours of many other attractions are included in some of the walks and in the Sights chapter.

Sleeping describes my favorite hotels, from budget deals to cushy splurges.

Eating outlines one of Hungary's top attractions—its delicious cuisine—and serves up a range of recommendations, from inexpensive take-away joints to fancy sit-down restaurants.

Budapest with Children includes my top recommendations for keeping your kids (and you) happy in Budapest.

Shopping gives you tips for shopping painlessly and enjoyably, without letting it overwhelm your vacation or ruin your budget.

	Map Legend				
⤶	Viewpoint	✈	Airport		Pedestrian Zone
➤	Entry Point	Ⓣ	Taxi Stand	o⊦⊦⊦⊦⊦⊦o	Funicular
🅸	Tourist Info	Ⓜ	Metro Stop	------	Railway
WC	Restroom	Ⓣ	Tram Stop	⊢—⊣	Tram Line
⛫	Castle	Ⓑ	Bus Stop	⊪⊪⊪⊪⊪	Stairs
⛪	Church	⛴	Boat Stop	-------	Trail
☪	Mosque	Ⓟ	Parking	)▨▨▨(	Tunnel

Use this legend to help you navigate the maps in this book.

Entertainment & Nightlife is your guide to fun, from a low-key stroll along the Danube embankment to Budapest's most cutting-edge nightspots...and everything in between (opera, tourist concerts, music pubs, river cruises, and more).

Transportation Connections lays the groundwork for your smooth arrival and departure, covering connections by train, bus, plane, car, and Danube riverboat.

Day Trips from Budapest covers nearby sights: the opulent Gödöllő Palace, the folk village of Hollókő, and the "Danube Bend" river towns of Szentendre, Visegrád, and Esztergom.

The **Beyond Budapest** section includes in-depth chapters on Hungary's best attractions outside of Budapest: the towns of **Eger, Pécs,** and **Sopron.** I've also thrown in the nearby Slovak capital of **Bratislava.**

Hungary: Past and Present is an overview of this nation's epic and illustrious history, and a survey of contemporary Hungary.

The **appendix** is a traveler's tool kit, with a handy packing checklist, recommended books and films, instructions on how to use the telephone, useful phone numbers, a climate chart, festival list, hotel reservation form, and Hungarian survival phrases.

Throughout this book, when you see a ✪ in a listing, it means that the sight is covered in much more detail in one of my walks or tours (a page number will tell you where to look to find more information).

Browse through this book and select your favorite sights. Then have a great trip! Traveling like a temporary local, and taking advantage of the information here, you'll enjoy the absolute most of every mile, minute, and dollar. As you travel the route I know and love, I'm happy that you'll be meeting some of my favorite Hungarians.

PLANNING

Trip Costs

Traveling in Budapest (and throughout Hungary) is a good value. While Budapest has Westernized at an astonishing rate since the Iron Curtain fell, it's still cheaper than most Western European capitals.

Five components make up your trip cost: airfare, surface transportation, room and board, sightseeing and entertainment, and shopping and miscellany.

Airfare: A basic round-trip flight from the US to Budapest costs $800–1,500, depending on where you fly from and when (cheaper in winter). If you're going beyond Hungary, consider saving time and money by flying "open jaw" (into one city and out of another—for example, into Budapest and out of Prague).

Surface Transportation: For a typical one-week visit, figure about $100. That includes $20 for a week-long Budapest transit pass, $70 for side-trips to other Hungarian towns (e.g., about $30 round-trip to Eger and $40 round-trip to Pécs), plus an extra $10 for miscellaneous taxi rides. Add around $15 per person for each transfer between the airport and downtown Budapest (cheaper but slower if you take public transportation). If you rent a car for a few days of side-tripping, figure nearly $100 per day (cheaper per day for longer rentals).

Room and Board: You can thrive in Budapest on an average of $100 a day per person for room and board. A $100-a-day budget per person allows $10 for lunch, $25 for dinner, and $65 for lodging (based on two people splitting the cost of a $130 double room that includes breakfast). If you're on a tighter budget, settle for a $100 double room to bring the per-person average down to $85 per day. Students and tightwads do it on $40 a day ($20 per hostel bed, $20 for meals). If you're traveling beyond Budapest, accommodations cost much less in smaller Hungarian towns and cities (a comfortable double typically costs no more than $90, bringing your budget down to $80 per day per person for two people traveling together).

Sightseeing and Entertainment: Figure on paying about $8–14 for major sights (House of Terror, Memento Park, touring the Parliament or Opera House), $3–6 for minor ones, and $15–20 for splurge experiences (e.g., soaking in a thermal bath, taking a nighttime boat cruise on the Danube, going to a tourist concert or opera). You can hire your own private guide for four hours for around $120—a great value when divided between two or more people. An overall average of $20–35 a day works for most. Don't skimp here. After all, this category is the driving force behind your trip—you came to sightsee, enjoy, and experience Budapest.

Major Holidays and Weekends

Popular places are even busier on weekends...and inundated on three-day weekends, when hotels, trains, and buses can get booked up before, during, and after the actual holiday. Holidays bring many businesses to a grinding halt. Reserve your accommodations and transportation well in advance if you'll be traveling on New Year's Day, 1848 Revolution Day (March 15), Good Friday through Easter Monday (April 10–13 in 2009, April 2–5 in 2010), Labor Day (May 1), Pentecost and Whitmonday (May 31–June 1 in 2009, May 23–24 in 2010), St. István's Day (Aug 20), Budapest's Formula 1 races (Aug 24–26 in 2009, likely similar dates in 2010), 1956 Uprising Day (Oct 23), All Saints' Day (November 1), and the Christmas holidays (Dec 24–26). The busy convention months of September and October are also tight.

Many businesses, as well as many museums, close on Good Friday, Easter, and New Year's Day. On Christmas, virtually everything closes down. Museums are also generally closed December 24 and 26; smaller shops are usually closed December 26. Also check the list of festivals and holidays on page 420 in the appendix.

Shopping and Miscellany: Figure $1–2 per postcard, coffee, beer, or ice-cream cone. Shopping can vary in cost from nearly nothing to a small fortune. Good budget travelers find that this category has little to do with assembling a trip full of lifelong and wonderful memories.

When to Go

The "tourist season" runs roughly from May through September. Book ahead for the holidays that occur throughout the year (see "Major Holidays and Weekends" sidebar, above).

Summer (July and August) has its advantages: very long days, the busiest schedule of tourist fun and special festivals, and virtually no business travelers to compete with for hotel rooms. However, because Hungary has a practically Mediterranean climate, summer temperatures can skyrocket to the 80s or 90s (choose a hotel with air-conditioning). And many cultural events (such as the opera) are on summer vacation.

In spring and fall—May, June, September, and early October—travelers enjoy fewer tourist crowds and milder weather. This is my favorite time to visit Budapest. However, it's also prime convention time (especially September), when hotels tend to fill up and charge their top rates.

Winter travelers find concert season in full swing, with absolutely no tourist crowds, but some accommodations and sights are

INTRODUCTION

Know Before You Go

Your trip is more likely to go smoothly if you plan ahead. Check this list of things to arrange while you're still at home.

Be sure that your **passport** is valid at least six months after your ticketed date of return to the US. If you need to get or renew a passport, it can take up to two months (for more on passports, see www.travel.state.gov).

Book your rooms in advance, especially if you'll be traveling at busy convention times (Sept–Oct) or during any major holidays (see "Major Holidays and Weekends," previous page).

Call your **debit and credit card companies** to let them know which countries you'll be visiting, so that they'll accept (and not deny) your international charges. Confirm your daily withdrawal limit, and consider asking to have it raised so you can take out more cash at each ATM stop. Ask about international transaction fees.

If you'll be **renting a car** in Hungary, you'll need your driver's license. It's recommended—but not required—that you also carry an International Driving Permit (IDP), available at your local AAA office ($15 plus the cost of two passport-type photos, www.aaa.com).

Since **airline carry-on restrictions** are always changing, visit the Transportation Security Administration's website (www.tsa.gov/travelers) for an up-to-date list of what you can bring on the plane with you, and what you have to check. Remember to arrive with plenty of time to get through security. Some airlines may restrict you to only one carry-on (no extras like a purse or daypack); check your airline's website.

either closed or run on a limited schedule. Confirm your sight-seeing plans locally, especially when traveling off-season. The weather can be cold and dreary, and night will draw the shades on your sightseeing before dinnertime. You might find the climate chart in the appendix helpful.

Sightseeing Priorities

Depending on the length of your trip, here are my recommended priorities.

3 days:	Budapest
5 days, add:	Eger and one more day in Budapest
7 days, add:	Pécs and another day in Budapest, or choose a day trip
10 days, add:	Bratislava, Sopron, and additional day trips
More days, add:	More time in Budapest and more day trips

For more tips, see "Planning Your Time" on page 36 in the Orientation chapter.

INTRODUCTION

Travel Smart

Your trip to Budapest is like a complex play—easier to follow and really appreciate on a second viewing. While no one does the same trip twice to gain that advantage, reading this book in its entirety before your trip, then re-reading it as you travel, accomplishes much the same thing. A walk through the communist relics at Memento Park, for instance, is more meaningful if you've read up on the Soviet era the night before.

As a practical matter (to avoid redundancy), many cultural or historical details are explained for one sight and not repeated for another—even if they would increase your understanding and appreciation of that second sight.

Design an itinerary that enables you to visit the various sights at the best possible times. As you read this book, make note of festivals, seasonal closures, and the days that sights are closed. For example, most Hungarian museums close on Mondays. Saturdays are virtually weekdays with earlier closing hours. Sundays have the same pros and cons as they do for travelers in the US: Sightseeing attractions are generally open; shops, banks, and markets are closed; public-transportation options are fewer; and city traffic is light. Rowdy evenings are rare on Sundays.

Be sure to mix intense and relaxed periods in your itinerary. Every trip (and every traveler) needs at least a few slack days. Pace yourself. Assume you will return.

If traveling beyond Budapest, visit local tourist information offices as you go. Upon arrival in a new town, lay the groundwork for a smooth departure; write down the schedule for the train, bus, or boat you'll take when you depart.

To maximize rootedness, minimize one-night stands. If you're venturing outside Budapest, it's worth a long drive after dinner to be settled into a town for two nights.

Plan ahead for laundry and picnics. Get online at Internet cafés or your hotel to research transportation connections, confirm events, check the weather, and get directions to your next hotel. Buy a phone card (or carry a mobile phone) and use it to make reservations, reconfirm hotels, and double-check hours of sights. For more information on phones, see page 412.

Connect with the culture. Set up your own quest for the best thermal bath, bowl of goulash, nostalgic Golden Age interior, atmospheric café, or whatever. Enjoy the hospitality of the Hungarian people. Slow down and be open to unexpected experiences. Ask questions—most locals are eager to point you toward their idea of the right direction. Keep a notepad in your pocket for organizing your thoughts. Wear your money belt. Learn the local currency, and how to estimate rough prices in dollars. Those who expect to travel smart, do.

Attitude Adjustment

Americans sometimes approach Hungary—for so long part of the "Evil Empire"—expecting grouchy service, crumbling communist infrastructure, and grimy, depressing landscapes. But those who visit are pleasantly surprised at the color, friendliness, safety, and ease of travel here. Many Hungarians speak excellent English and are forever scrambling to impress their guests. Any remaining rough edges simply add to the charm and carbonate the experience.

The East–West stuff still fascinates us, but to locals, the Soviet regime is old news, Cold War espionage is the stuff of movies, and oppressive monuments to Stalin are a distant memory. Two decades after the fall of the Iron Curtain, Hungarians think about communism only when tourists bring it up. Freedom is a generation old, and—for better or for worse—McDonald's, MTV, and mobile phones are every bit as entrenched here as anywhere else in Europe.

When Hungary and seven other former Soviet Bloc countries joined the European Union in 2004—followed by two more in 2007—the geographical center of Europe shifted from Brussels to Prague. The Hungarians have put the communist days behind them and have embraced the EU: Hungary has already waived passport checks along its borders with fellow EU members (see "Practicalities," next), and is on track to adopt the euro currency in the next few years. Now more than ever, Hungarians bristle at the idea that they live in "Eastern" Europe (which implies a connection to Russia); to them, it's *Central* Europe. They're looking to the future...and hope you will, too.

PRACTICALITIES

Red Tape: You need a passport—but no visa or shots—to travel in Hungary. Pack a photocopy of your passport in your luggage in case the original is lost or stolen.

Borders: Hungary has officially joined the open-borders Schengen Agreement. This means that there are no passport checks when traveling between Hungary and the 24 other Schengen countries (including neighbors Slovakia, Austria, and Slovenia). At airports, by car, or by train, you'll simply zip through the border without stopping. (Because Hungary's southern and eastern neighbors—Croatia, Serbia, Romania, and Ukraine—have not yet joined Schengen, you'll still need to present your passport when entering any of those places.) Even as borders fade, when you change countries, you must still change telephone cards, postage stamps, and underpants.

Just the FAQs, Please

Whom do I call in case of emergency?
The all-purpose emergency number in Hungary is 112. You can also call 107 for police, 104 for ambulance, or 105 for fire.

What if my credit card is stolen?
Act immediately. See "Damage Control for Lost Cards," page 12, for instructions.

How do I make a phone call to, within, and from Hungary?
For detailed dialing instructions, refer to page 415.

How can I get tourist information about Hungary?
This book is probably all the information you'll need for your trip. See page 407 for info on Budapest's not-too-useful tourist information offices (called TourInform in Hungary, abbreviated **TI** in this book). The Hungarian National Tourist Office can be helpful (see page 407).

What's the best way to pack?
Light. For a recommended packing list, see page 423.

Does Rick have other resources that could help me?
For info on Rick's guidebooks, public television series, public radio show, website, guided tours, travel bags, accessories, and railpasses, see page 407.

Are there any updates to this guidebook?
Check www.ricksteves.com/update for changes to the most recent edition of this book.

Can you recommend any good books or movies for my trip?
For suggestions, see page 410.

Do you have information on train travel, flights, and driving?
See the Transportation Connections chapter on page 260.

How much do I tip?
Relatively little. For tips on tipping, see page 13.

Will I get a student or senior discount?
While discounts are not listed in this book, youths (under 18) and students (with International Student Identity Cards) often get discounts—but only by asking. To get a student ID card, visit www.statravel.com or www.isic.org.

How can I get a VAT refund on major purchases?
See the details on page 14.

Does Hungary use the metric system?
Yes. A liter is about a quart, four to a gallon. A kilometer is six-tenths of a mile. I figure kilometers to miles by cutting them in half and adding back 10 percent of the original (120 km: 60 + 12 = 72 miles, 300 km: 150 + 30 = 180 miles). For more metric conversions, see page 421.

Time: In Hungary—and in this book—you'll use the 24-hour clock. It's the same through 12:00 noon, then keep going—13:00, 14:00, and so on. For anything after 12, subtract 12 and add p.m. (14:00 is 2:00 p.m.). Hungary is generally six/nine hours ahead of the East/West Coasts of the US. The exceptions are the beginning and end of Daylight Saving Time: Hungary and Europe "spring forward" the last Sunday in March (two weeks after most of North America), and "fall back" the last Sunday in October (one week before North America). For a handy online time converter, try www.timeanddate.com/worldclock.

Business Hours: Most stores are open Monday through Friday (roughly 10:00–18:00), with a late night on Thursday (until 20:00 or 21:00). On Saturdays, shops are usually open from 10:00 to 13:00 or 14:00. Most things close down on Sunday (except large shopping malls).

Medical Help: If you get sick, do as the locals do and go to a pharmacist. They can help you with almost any ailment. If you need more in-depth attention, ask your hotel for the nearest hospital. For specifics in Budapest, see page 42.

Watt's Up? Europe's electrical system is different from North America's in two ways: the shape of the plug (two round prongs) and the voltage of the current (220 volts instead of 110 volts). For your North American plug to work in Europe, you'll need an adapter, sold inexpensively at travel stores in the US. As for the voltage, most newer electronics and travel appliances (such as hair dryers, laptops, and battery chargers) automatically convert the voltage—if you see a range of voltages printed on the item or its plug (such as "110–220"), it'll work in Europe. Otherwise, you can buy a converter separately in the US (about $20).

News: Americans keep in touch in Europe with the *International Herald Tribune* (published almost daily throughout Europe). Budapest also publishes two English-language newspapers, but the articles are of more local than international interest (see page 43 in Orientation). Every Tuesday, the European editions of *Time* and *Newsweek* hit the stands with articles of particular interest to travelers. Sports addicts can get their daily fix from *USA Today*. Good websites include www.iht.com, http://news.bbc .co.uk, and www.europeantimes.com. Many hotels have CNN or BBC television channels available.

MONEY

Cash from ATMs

Throughout Europe, cash machines (ATMs) are the standard way for travelers to get local currency. As an emergency backup, you could bring several hundred US dollars in hard cash.

Exchange Rates

Hungary still uses its traditional currency, the **forint** (abbreviated Ft, or sometimes as HUF).

200 Ft = about $1

To figure dollars, divide by two and drop the last two digits. For example, 1,000 Ft = about $5, 5,000 Ft = about $25, and 10,000 Ft = about $50. Note that the exchange rate has fluctuated wildly in recent years, and these are just rough estimates. To get the latest rates and print a cheat sheet, see www.oanda.com.

While Hungary is on track to adopt the Europe-wide **euro** currency, it likely won't happen until 2012 at the earliest. However, you might already see some prices (especially hotel rates in Budapest) listed in euros for the convenience of international visitors. Even when you see prices listed in euros, locals usually prefer payment in forints.

Hungary's neighbors Slovakia (its capital Bratislava is included in this book), Austria, and Slovenia all use the euro:

1 euro (€) = about $1.40

To roughly convert prices in euros to dollars, add 40 percent: €20 is about $28, €50 is about $70, and so on.

So, that 1,500-Ft canister of paprika costs $7.50, that €25 meal in Bratislava is about $35, and that 13,000-Ft taxi ride through Budapest is...uh-oh.

In Hungary, ATMs are called *bankjegy-automata* (BONK-yedge OW-toh-maw-taw). Most Hungarians also recognize the international term *Bankomat*. To use an ATM to withdraw money from your account, you'll need a debit card (ideally with a Visa or MasterCard logo for maximum usability), plus a PIN code. Know your PIN code in numbers; there are only numbers—no letters—on European keypads. It's smart to bring two cards, in case one gets demagnetized or eaten by a temperamental machine.

Before you go, verify with your bank that your cards will work overseas, and alert them that you'll be making withdrawals in Europe; otherwise, the bank may not approve transactions if it perceives unusual spending patterns. Also ask about international fees; see "Credit and Debit Cards," next page.

When using an ATM, try to take out large sums of money to reduce your per-transaction bank fees. If the machine refuses your request, try again and select a smaller amount (some cash machines limit the amount that you can withdraw—don't take it personally). If that doesn't work, try a different machine. Bank machines often dispense high-denomination bills, which can be difficult to break. My strategy: Request an odd amount of money from the ATM (such as 38,000 Ft instead of 40,000 Ft); or, if that doesn't work, go as soon as possible to a bank or a large store (such as a supermarket) to break the big bills.

Avoid using currency exchange booths, which generally offer lousy rates and/or charge excessive fees. One exception is if you are traveling between countries that have different currencies (say, from Hungary to Slovakia or Croatia). Coins can't be exchanged once you leave the country, so try to spend them before you cross the border. But bills are easy to convert to the "new" country's currency. Regular banks have the best rates. Post offices and train stations usually change money if you can't get to a bank. Traveler's checks are a waste of time (long waits at slow banks) and a waste of money (in fees).

Keep your cash safe. Thieves target tourists. Use a money belt—a pouch with a strap that you buckle around your waist like a belt, and wear under your clothes. A money belt provides peace of mind, allowing you to carry lots of cash safely. Don't waste time every few days tracking down a cash machine—withdraw a week's worth of money, stuff it in your money belt, and travel!

Credit and Debit Cards

For purchases, Visa and MasterCard are more commonly accepted than American Express. Just like at home, credit and debit cards work easily at larger hotels, restaurants, and shops, but smaller businesses prefer payment in local currency (in small bills—break large bills at a bank or larger store). If a receipt shows your credit-card number, don't toss it out thoughtlessly.

Fees: Most credit and debit cards—whether used for purchases or ATM withdrawals—now charge additional, tacked-on "international transaction" fees of up to 3 percent; some also take an extra $5 per transaction. To avoid unpleasant surprises, call your bank or credit-card company before your trip to ask about these fees. If the fees are too high, consider getting a card just for your trip: Capital One (www.capitalone.com) and most credit unions have low-to-no international transaction fees.

If merchants offer to convert your purchase price into dollars (called dynamic currency conversion), refuse this "service." You'll pay even more in fees for the expensive convenience of seeing your charge in dollars.

Damage Control for Lost Cards

If you lose your credit, debit, or ATM card, you can stop people from using it by reporting the loss immediately to the respective global customer-assistance centers. Call these 24-hour US numbers collect: Visa (410/581-9994), MasterCard (636/722-7111), and American Express (623/492-8427).

At a minimum, you'll need to know the name of the financial institution that issued you the card, along with the type of card (classic, platinum, or whatever). Providing the following information will allow for a quicker cancellation of your missing card: full card number, whether you are the primary or secondary cardholder, the cardholder's name exactly as printed on the card, billing address, home phone number, circumstances of the loss or theft, and identification verification (your birth date, your mother's maiden name, or your Social Security number—memorize this, don't carry a copy). If you are the secondary cardholder, you'll also need to provide the primary cardholder's identification-verification details. You can generally receive a temporary card within two or three business days in Europe.

If you promptly report your card lost or stolen, you typically won't be responsible for any unauthorized transactions on your account, although many banks charge a liability fee of $50.

Tipping

A decade ago, tipping was unheard of in Hungary. But then came the tourists. Today, while tipping is on the rise, it still isn't as automatic or as generous as in the United States. And, as in the US, the proper amount depends on your resources, tipping philosophy, and the circumstances. The following guidelines should help you out.

Restaurants: Tipping is an issue only at restaurants that have table service. If you order your food at a counter, don't tip.

At table-service restaurants in Budapest, most servers expect about a 10 percent tip (though a bit less is fine, if it rounds to a convenient total). More than 10 percent is not necessary, and 15 percent verges on extravagant. For example, for a 3,650-Ft bill, I'd hand over 4,000 Ft (that's a 350-Ft tip, or a bit more than 9 percent—perfectly acceptable). Increasingly, some tourist-oriented Budapest restaurants are tacking a 10–12 percent service charge onto the bill (noted as "service," *borravaló, felszolgálási díj,* or *szervízdíj*)—in these cases, an additional tip is not necessary. (More commonly, menus and bills remind you that the tip is *not* included.) If you're not sure whether your bill includes the tip, just ask. You can tip a bit less (5–8 percent) outside Budapest, where Western tipping customs haven't quite arrived.

Taxis: To tip the cabbie, round up about 10 percent (for a 1,350-Ft fare, pay 1,500 Ft). If the cabbie hauls your bags and zips you to the airport to help you catch your flight, you might want to toss in a little more. But if you feel like you're being driven in circles or otherwise ripped off, skip the tip.

Special Services: It's thoughtful to tip 200–400 Ft to someone who shows you a special sight and who is paid in no other way. Tour guides at public sites sometimes hold out their hand for tips after they give their spiel; if I've already paid for the tour, I don't tip extra, though some tourists do give a small tip, particularly for a job well done. I don't tip at hotels, but if you do, give the porter 100 or 200 Ft for carrying bags, and, at the end of your stay, leave 400 or 500 Ft for the maid if the room was kept clean. In general, if someone in the service industry does a super job for you, a small tip (200–400 Ft) is appropriate...but not required.

When in doubt, ask. If you're not sure whether (or how much) to tip for a service, ask your hotelier or the TI; they'll fill you in on how it's done on their turf.

Getting a VAT Refund

Wrapped into the purchase price of your Hungarian souvenirs is a Value-Added Tax (VAT) of about 20 percent. If you purchase more than 45,000 Ft (about $225) worth of goods at a store that participates in the VAT-refund scheme, you're entitled to get most of that tax back. Getting your refund is usually straightforward and, if you buy a substantial amount of souvenirs, well worth the hassle. If you're lucky, the merchant will subtract the tax when you make your purchase. (This is more likely to occur if the store ships the goods to your home.) Otherwise, you'll need to:

Get the paperwork. Have the merchant completely fill out the necessary refund document, called a "Tax-Free Shopping Cheque." You'll have to present your passport at the store.

Get your stamp at the border or airport. Process your cheque(s) at your last stop in the EU (e.g., at the airport) with the customs agent who deals with VAT refunds. It's best to keep your purchases in your carry-on for viewing, but if they're too large or dangerous (such as knives) to carry on, track down the proper customs agent to inspect them before you check your bag. You're not supposed to use your purchased goods before you leave. If you show up at customs wearing your new communist-kitsch T-shirt, officials might look the other way—or deny you a refund.

Collect your refund. You'll need to return your stamped document to the retailer or its representative. Many merchants work with a service, such as Global Refund (www.globalrefund.com) or Premier Tax Free (www.premiertaxfree.com), which have offices at major airports, ports, or border crossings. These services, which extract a 4 percent fee, can refund your money immediately in your currency of choice or credit your card (within two billing cycles). If the retailer handles VAT refunds directly, it's up to you to contact the merchant for your refund. You can mail the documents from home, or quicker, from your point of departure (using a stamped, addressed envelope you've prepared or one that's been provided by the merchant)—and then wait. It could take months.

Customs for American Shoppers

You are allowed to take home $800 worth of items per person duty-free, once every 30 days. The next $1,000 is taxed at a flat 3 percent. After that, you pay the individual item's duty rate. You can also bring in duty-free a liter of alcohol (slightly more than a standard-size bottle of wine; you must be at least 21), 200 cigarettes, and up to 100 non-Cuban cigars. You may take home vacuum-packed cheeses; dried herbs, spices (such as paprika), or mushrooms; and canned fruits or vegetables, including jams and vegetable spreads. Meats (even vacuum-packed or canned) and fresh fruits or vegetables are not permitted. Note that you'll need to carefully pack any bottles of wine and other liquid-containing items in your checked luggage, due to limits on liquids in carry-ons. To check customs rules and duty rates before you go, visit www.cbp.gov, and click on "Travel," then "Know Before You Go."

SIGHTSEEING

Many of Budapest's museums are dusty and a bit old-fashioned. But with a bit of patience and imagination, and a solid background in the topic (provided by this book's descriptions, self-guided tours, in-depth sidebars, and Hungary: Past and Present chapter), Budapest's museums come to life and become genuinely enthralling.

Sightseeing can be hard work. Use these tips to make your visits to Budapest's big sights meaningful, fun, fast, and painless.

Plan Ahead

Set up an itinerary that allows you to fit in all your must-see sights. For a one-stop look at opening hours, see "Budapest at a Glance" on page 56 (also see "Daily Reminder" on page 37). Most sights keep stable hours, but you can easily confirm the latest by checking with the local TI.

Don't put off visiting a must-see sight—you never know when a place will close unexpectedly for a holiday, strike, or restoration. If you'll be visiting during a holiday (listed on page 5), find out if a particular sight will be open by phoning ahead or visiting its website.

When possible, visit key museums first thing (when your energy is best) and save other activities for the afternoon. Hit the highlights first, then go back to other things if you have the stamina and time.

Going at the right time can also help you avoid crowds. This book offers specific tips on a few of Budapest's most crowded sights.

Read ahead. To get the most out of the self-guided tours and sight descriptions in this book, read them the night before your visit. When you arrive at the sight, use the overview map to get the lay of the land and the basic tour route.

At the Sight

All sights have rules, and if you know about these in advance, they're no big deal.

Some sights (including the Parliament, Great Synagogue, and Holocaust Memorial Center) have metal detectors that will slow your entry.

At churches—which often offer interesting art and a cool, welcome seat—a modest dress code (no bare shoulders or shorts) is encouraged.

Most museums require you to check daypacks and coats. They'll be kept safely. If you have something you can't bear to part with, stash it in a pocket or purse. If you don't want to check a small backpack, carry it under your arm like a purse as you enter. From a guard's point of view, a backpack is generally a problem while a purse is not.

Photography is sometimes banned at sights. At other places, you'll have to buy a pricey "photo ticket" for permission. If cameras are allowed, flashes or tripods are usually not. Even without a flash, a handheld camera will take a decent picture (or buy postcards or posters at the museum bookstore).

Some museums have special exhibits in addition to their permanent collection. These usually come at an extra cost (though in some cases, you can skip the temporary exhibit and see just the main collection for the normal price).

Once inside, you'll generally follow a confusing one-way tour route through a maze of rooms with squeaky parquet floors, monitored by grumpy grannies who listlessly point you in the right direction.

While most museums label exhibits in English, most don't post full descriptions; you'll have to buy a book or borrow laminated translations. In some cases, neither option is available.

Audioguides with recorded descriptions of the collection are still relatively rare at Budapest museums, and aren't included with your admission fee. If you bring along your own pair of headphones and a Y-jack, two people can sometimes share one audioguide and save.

Expect changes—items can be on tour, on loan, out sick, or shifted at the whim of the curator. To adapt, pick up any available free floor plans as you enter, and ask museum staff if you can't find a particular painting.

Key sights and museums have bookstores selling postcards

How Was Your Trip?

Were your travels fun, smooth, and meaningful? If you'd like to share your tips, concerns, and discoveries, please fill out the survey at www.ricksteves.com/feedback. I value your feedback. Thanks in advance—it helps a lot.

and souvenirs. Before you leave, scan the postcards and thumb through the biggest guidebook (or skim its index) to be sure you haven't overlooked something that you'd like to see.

Most big sights have an on-site café or cafeteria (usually a good place to rest and have a snack or light meal). The WCs are free and generally clean.

Most sights stop admitting people 30–60 minutes before closing time, and some rooms close early (generally about 45 minutes before the sight's posted closing time). Guards usher people out, so don't save the best for last.

Every sight and museum offers more than what is covered in this book. Use the self-guided tours in this book as an introduction—not the final word.

TRANSPORTATION

Transportation concerns within Budapest include the Metro (subway), trams, buses, and taxis, all of which are covered in the Orientation chapter (see "Getting Around Budapest" on page 44). If you have a car, stow it. You don't want to drive in Budapest. For information on connecting from Budapest to outlying Hungarian towns, or to other big cities in the region, see the Day Trips and Transportation Connections chapters.

TRAVELING AS A TEMPORARY LOCAL

We travel all the way to Europe to enjoy differences—to become temporary locals. You'll experience frustrations. Certain truths that we find "God-given" or "self-evident," such as cold beer, ice in drinks, bottomless cups of coffee, hot showers, cigarette smoke being irritating, and bigger being better, are suddenly not so true. One of the benefits of travel is the eye-opening realization that there are logical, civil, and even better alternatives. A willingness to go local ensures that you'll enjoy a full dose of local hospitality.

Fortunately for you, hospitality is a Hungarian forte. The warmth of the Hungarians seems to have only been enhanced during the communist era: Tangible resources were in short supply, so an open door and a genial conversation were all that people had to offer. Even so, some people—hardened by decades of being spied on by neighbors and standing in long lines to buy food for their family—seem brusque at first. In my experience, all it takes is a smile and a little effort to befriend these residents of the former "Evil Empire."

If there is a negative aspect to the image Europeans have of Americans, it's that we are big, loud, aggressive, impolite, rich, superficially friendly, and a bit naive. Most Hungarians place a high value on speaking quietly in public places, such as restaurants and trains. Listen to others in these situations—the place can be packed, but the decibel level is low. Try to remember this nuance, and soften your speaking voice as a way of respecting their culture.

While Europeans look bemusedly at some of our Yankee excesses—and worriedly at others—they nearly always afford us individual travelers all the warmth we deserve. While updating my guidebooks, I hear over and over again that my readers are considerate and fun to have as guests. Thank you for traveling as temporary locals who are sensitive to the culture. It's fun to follow you in my travels.

Judging from all the happy feedback I receive from travelers, it's safe to assume you'll enjoy a great, affordable vacation—with the finesse of an independent, experienced traveler.

Thanks, and *jó utat*—happy travels!

BACK DOOR TRAVEL PHILOSOPHY
From *Rick Steves' Europe Through the Back Door*

Travel is intensified living—maximum thrills per minute and one of the last great sources of legal adventure. Travel is freedom. It's recess, and we need it.

Experiencing the real Europe requires catching it by surprise, going casual..."Through the Back Door."

Affording travel is a matter of priorities. (Make do with the old car.) You can travel—simply, safely, and comfortably—nearly anywhere in Europe for $120 a day plus transportation costs (allow more for bigger cities). In many ways, spending more money only builds a thicker wall between you and what you came to see. Europe is a cultural carnival, and, time after time, you'll find that its best acts are free and the best seats are the cheap ones.

A tight budget forces you to travel close to the ground, meeting and communicating with the people, not relying on service with a purchased smile. Never sacrifice sleep, nutrition, safety, or cleanliness in the name of budget. Simply enjoy the local-style alternatives to expensive hotels and restaurants.

Extroverts have more fun. If your trip is low on magic moments, kick yourself and make things happen. If you don't enjoy a place, maybe you don't know enough about it. Seek the truth. Recognize tourist traps. Give a culture the benefit of your open mind. See things as different but not better or worse. Any culture has much to share.

Of course, travel, like the world, is a series of hills and valleys. Be fanatically positive and militantly optimistic. If something's not to your liking, change your liking. Travel is addictive. It can make you a happier American as well as a citizen of the world. Our Earth is home to six and a half billion equally important people. It's humbling to travel and find that people don't envy Americans. Europeans like us, but, with all due respect, they wouldn't trade passports.

Globe-trotting destroys ethnocentricity. It helps you understand and appreciate different cultures. Regrettably, there are forces in our society that want you dumbed down for their convenience. Don't let it happen. Thoughtful travel engages you with the world—more important than ever these days. Travel changes people. It broadens perspectives and teaches new ways to measure quality of life. Rather than fear the diversity on this planet, travelers celebrate it. Many travelers toss aside their hometown blinders. Their prized souvenirs are the strands of different cultures they decide to knit into their own character. The world is a cultural yarn shop, and Back Door travelers are weaving the ultimate tapestry. Join in!

HUNGARY

Magyarország

Hungary is an island of Asian-descended Magyars in a sea of Slavs. Even though the Hungarians have thoroughly integrated with their Slavic and German neighbors in the millennium-plus since they arrived, there's still something about the place that's distinctly Magyar (MUD-jar). Here in quirky, idiosyncratic Hungary, everything's a little different from the rest of Europe—in terms of history, language, culture, customs, and cuisine—but it's hard to put your finger on exactly how.

Travelers to Hungary notice many endearing peculiarities. Hungarians list a person's family name first, and the given name is last—just as in many other Eastern cultures (think of Kim Jong Il). So the composer known as "Franz Liszt" in German is "Liszt Ferenc" in his homeland. (To help reduce confusion, many Hungarian business cards list the surname in capital letters.) Hungarians have a charming habit of using the English word "hello" for both "hi" and "bye," just like the Italians use "ciao." You might overhear a Hungarian end a telephone conversation with a cheery "Hello!" Hungarians even drove on the left until 1941.

Just a century ago, this country controlled half of one of Europe's grandest realms: the Austro-Hungarian Empire. Today, perhaps clinging to their former greatness, many Hungarians remain old-fashioned and nostalgic. With their dusty museums and bushy moustaches, they love to remember the good old days. Buildings all over the country are marked with plaques boasting *MŰEMLÉK* ("historical monument").

Thanks to this focus on tradition, the Hungarians you'll encounter are generally polite, formal, and professional. Hungarians have class. Everything here is done with a proud flourish. People in the service industry seem to wear their uniforms as a badge of honor rather than a burden. When a waiter comes to

your table in a restaurant, he'll say, *"Tessék parancsolni"*—literally, "Please command, sir." The standard greeting, *"Jó napot kívánok,"* means "I wish you a good day." Women sometimes hear the even more formal greeting, *"Kezét csókolom"*—"I kiss your hand." And when your train or bus makes a stop, you won't be alerted by a mindless, blaring beep or hoot—but instead, peppy music. (You'll be humming these contagious little ditties all day.) Perhaps thanks to this artful blending of elegance and formality, Hungarians have a cultural affinity for the French.

Hungarians are also orderly and tidy...in their own sometimes unexpected ways. Yes, Hungary has as much litter and graffiti—and as many crumbling buildings—as any other formerly communist country, but you'll find great reason within the chaos. The Hungarian railroad has a long list of discounted fares—for seniors, kids, dogs...and, until recently, monkeys. Just in case. (It could happen.) My favorite town name in Hungary: Hatvan. This means "Sixty" in Hungarian...and it's exactly 60 kilometers from Budapest. You can't argue with that kind of logic.

This tradition of left-brained thinking hasn't produced many great Hungarian painters or poets who are known outside their homeland. But the Hungarians, who are renowned for their ingenuity, have made tremendous contributions to science, technology, business, and industry. Hungarians of note include Edward Teller (instrumental in creating the A-bomb), John von Neumann (a pioneer of computer science), Andy Grove (who, as András Gróf, immigrated to the US and founded Intel), and George Soros (the billionaire investor famous—or notorious—for supporting

HUNGARY

Hungary Almanac

Official Name: Magyar Köztársaság (Hungarian Republic), or simply Magyarország.

Snapshot History: Settled by the Central Asian Magyars in A.D. 896, Hungary became Catholic in the year 1000, and went on to become Christian Europe's front line in fighting against the Ottomans (Muslims from today's Turkey) in the 16th–17th centuries. After serving as co-capital of the vast Austro-Hungarian Empire and losing World Wars I and II, Hungary became a Soviet satellite until achieving independence in 1989.

Population: Hungary's 10 million people (similar to Michigan) are 92 percent ethnic Hungarians who speak Hungarian. One in 50 is Roma (Gypsy). Half the populace is Catholic, with 20 percent Protestant and 25 percent listed as "other" or unaffiliated. Of the world's approximately 12 million ethnic Hungarians, one in six lives outside Hungary (mostly in areas of Romania, Slovakia, Serbia, and Croatia that were once part of Hungary).

Latitude and Longitude: 47°N and 20°E; similar latitude to Seattle, Paris, and Vienna.

Area: 36,000 square miles, similar to Indiana or Maine.

Geography: Hungary is situated in the Carpathian Basin, bound on the north by the Carpathian Mountains and on the south by the Dinaric Mountains. Though it's surrounded by mountains, Hungary itself is relatively flat, with some gently rolling hills. The Great Hungarian Plain—which begins on the east bank of the Danube in Budapest—stretches all the way to Asia. Hungary's two main rivers—the Danube and Tisza—run north–south through the country, neatly dividing it into three regions.

Biggest Cities: Budapest (the capital on the Danube, 1.7 million), Debrecen (in the east, 205,000), and Miskolc (in the north, 180,000).

---

left-wing causes). A popular local joke claims that Hungarians are so clever that they can enter a revolving door behind you and exit in front of you.

Perhaps the most famous Hungarian "scientist" invented something you probably have in a box in your basement: Ernő Rubik, creator of the famous cube. Hungarians' enjoyment of a good mind-bending puzzle is also evident in their fascination with chess, which you'll see played in cafés, parks, and baths.

Like their Viennese neighbors, Hungarians know how to enjoy the good life. Favorite activities include splashing and soaking in their many thermal baths (see the Thermal Baths chapter). "Taking the waters," Hungarian-style, deserves to be your top priority while you're here. Though public baths can sound intimidating, they're a delight. In this book I recommend my two favorite

Economy: The Gross Domestic Product is $191 billion (a third of Poland's), but the GDP per capita is $19,300 (about 20 percent more than Poland's). Thanks to its progressive "goulash communism," Hungary had a head start on many other former Soviet Bloc countries and is now thriving, privatized...and largely foreign-owned. In the 1990s, many communist-era workers (especially women) lost their jobs. Today, the workforce is small (only 57 percent of eligible workers) but highly skilled. Grains, metals, and machinery are major products, and nearly a third of trade is with Germany.

Currency: 200 forints (Ft, or HUF) = about $1.

Government: The single-house National Assembly (386 seats) is the only ruling branch directly elected by popular vote. The legislators in turn select the figurehead president (currently the right-of-center László Sólyom) and the ruling prime minister (Socialist Ferenc Gyurcsány—see page 406).

Flag: Three horizontal bands, top to bottom: red (representing strength), white (faithfulness), and green (hope). It's identical to the Italian flag, but flipped 90 degrees counterclockwise. It often includes the Hungarian coat of arms: horizontal red-and-white stripes (on the left); the patriarchal, or double-barred, cross (on the right); and the Hungarian crown (on top).

The Average János: The typical Hungarian eats a pound of lard a week (they cook with it). The average family has three members, and they spend almost three-fourths of their income on (costly) housing. According to a recent condom-company survey, the average Hungarian has sex 131 times a year (behind only France and Greece), making them Europe's third-greatest liars.

baths in Budapest, a fine one in Eger, and another just outside of Eger. For each one, I've included careful instructions to help you enjoy the warm-water fun like a pro. (To allay your first fear: Yes, you can wear your swimsuit the entire time.)

Hungarians are also reviving an elegant, Vienna-style café culture that was dismantled by the communists. Whiling away the afternoon at a genteel coffeehouse, as you nurse a drink or a delicate dessert, is a favorite pastime. (For the best options in Budapest, see "Budapest's Café Culture" on page 234 in the Eating chapter.)

Classical music is revered in Hungary, perhaps as nowhere else outside Austria. Aside from scientists and businessmen, the best-known Hungarians are composers: Béla Bartók, Zoltán Kodály, and Franz Liszt. (For more on these figures, see "Hungarian Music" on page 252.)

While one in five Hungarians lives in Budapest, the countryside plays an important role in Hungary's economy—this has always been a highly agricultural region. You'll pass through fields of wheat and corn, but the grains are secondary to Hungarians' (and tourists') true love: wine. Hungarian winemaking standards plummeted under the communists, but many vintner families are now reclaiming their land, returning to their precise traditional methods, and making wines worth being proud of once more. (For details, see "Hungarian Wines" on page 223.)

Somehow Hungary, at the crossroads of Europe, has managed to become cosmopolitan while remaining perfectly Hungarian. In the countryside, where less mixing has occurred, traditional Magyar culture is more evident. But in the cities, the Hungarians—like Hungary itself—are a cross-section of Central European cultures: Magyars, Germans, Czechs, Slovaks, Poles, Serbs, Jews, Ottomans, Romanians, Roma (Gypsies), and many others. Still, no matter how many generations removed they are from Magyar stock, there's something different about a Hungarian—and not just the language. Look a Hungarian in the eye, and you'll see a glimmer of the marauding Magyar, stomping in from the Central Asian plains a thousand years ago.

Hungarian Language

Even though Hungary is surrounded by Slavs, Hungarian is not at all related to Slavic languages (such as Polish, Czech, or Croatian). In fact, Hungarian isn't related to *any* European language, except for very distant relatives Finnish and Estonian. It isn't even an Indo-European language. English is more closely related to Hindi, Russian, and French than it is to Hungarian.

Hungarian is agglutinative, which means that you start with a simple root word and then start tacking on suffixes to create meaning—sometimes resulting in a pileup of extra sounds at the end of a very long word. The emphasis always goes on the first syllable, and the following syllables are droned downhill in a kind of a monotone—giving the language a distinctive cadence that Hungary's neighbors love to tease about.

While the language is overwhelming for tourists, one easy word is *"Szia"* (SEE-yaw), which means both hello and goodbye (like "ciao" or "aloha"). Confusingly, sometimes Hungarians simply say the English word "hello" to mean either "hi" or "bye." Another handy word that Hungarians (and people throughout Central Europe) will understand is *Servus* (SEHR-voos, spelled *Szervusz* in Hungarian)—the old-fashioned greeting from the days of the Austro-Hungarian Empire. If you draw a blank on how to say hello in the local language, just offer a cheery, *"Servus!"*

Hungarian pronunciation is straightforward, once you

remember a few key rules. The trickiest: *s* alone is pronounced "sh," while *sz* is pronounced "s." This explains why you'll hear in-the-know travelers pronouncing Budapest as "BOO-daw-pesht." You might catch the *busz* up to Castle Hill—pronounced "boose." And "Franz Liszt" is easier to pronounce than it looks: It sounds just like "list." To review:

s sounds like "sh" as in "shirt"

sz sounds like "s" as in "saint"

Hungarian has a set of unusual palatal sounds that don't quite have a counterpart in English. To make these sounds, gently press the thick part of your tongue to the roof or your mouth (instead of using the tip of your tongue behind your teeth, as we do in English):

gy sounds like "dg" as in "hedge"

ny sounds like "ny" as in "canyon" (not "nee")

ty sounds like "tch" as in "itch"

cs sounds like "ch" as in "church"

As for vowels: The letter *a* almost sounds like o (aw, as in "hot"); but with an accent *(á),* it brightens up to the more standard "ah." Likewise, while *e* sounds like "eh," *é* sounds like "ay." An accent *(á, é, í, ó, ú)* indicates that you linger on that vowel, but not necessarily that you stress that syllable. Like German, Hungarian has umlauts *(ö, ü),* meaning you purse your lips when you say that vowel: roughly, *ö* sounds like "ur" and *ü* sounds like "ew." A long umlaut *(ő, ű)* is the same sound, but you hold it a little longer. Words ending in *k* are often plural.

Here are a few other letters than sound different in Hungarian than in English:

c and **cz** both sound like "ts" as in "cats"

zs sounds like "zh" as in "leisure"

j and **ly** both sound like "y" as in "yellow"

Okay, maybe it's not *so* simple. But you'll get the hang of it... and Hungarians will appreciate your efforts.

For a complete list of Hungarian survival phrases, see page 425 in the appendix.

HUNGARY

BUDAPEST

ORIENTATION

Europe's most underrated big city, Budapest is as challenging as it is enchanting. The sprawling Hungarian capital on the banks of the Danube is, in so many ways, the capital of Central Europe. It's a city of nuance and paradox—cosmopolitan, complicated, and tricky for the first-timer to get a handle on. Like a full-bodied Hungarian wine, Budapest can overwhelm visitors...even as it intoxicates them with delights. After more than a dozen visits over the last decade, I can't get enough of this place. The longer I stay, the more I want to see. Every time I check an item off my "to do" list, I have to add two more. For a traveler, it's a wonderful dilemma to have.

Think of Budapest like that favorite Hungarian pastime, chess: It's simple to learn...but takes a lifetime to master. This chapter is your first lesson. Then it's your move.

Budapest: A Verbal Map

Budapest is huge, with nearly two million people. Like Vienna, the city was built as the head of a much larger empire than it currently governs—which can make it feel a bit too grandiose for the capital of a small country. But the city is surprisingly easy to manage once you get the lay of the land and learn the excellent

Budapest Neighborhoods

NOT TO SCALE

TO ÓBUDA

MARGARET ISLAND

XIII SZÉCHENYI BATHS→

NYUGATI (WESTERN) TRAIN STN.

CITY PARK

III

MARG. BR.

GREAT

HOUSE OF TERROR

HEROES' SQUARE

N

II

DANUBE

PARLIAMENT

VI

OKTOGON

MOSZKVA TÉR

VÍZI-VÁROS

OPERA

XIV

I

LEOPOLD TOWN

VII

PEST

DÉLI (SOUTHERN) TRAIN STN.

CASTLE HILL

TOWN CENTER

GREAT SYNAGOGUE

CHAIN BRIDGE

V

SMALL ←BLVD.

KELETI (EASTERN) TRAIN STN.

HEGY. ÚT

ELIS. BR.

ELISABETH TOWN

VIII

BUDA

LIB. BR.

ÜLLŐI ÚT

GELLÉRT HILL

GREAT MARKET HALL

IX

GELLÉRT BATHS

RIVER

TO MEMENTO PARK

TO AIRPORT

DCH

ORIENTATION

public transportation network. Those who are comfortable with the Metro, trams, and buses have the city by the tail (see "Getting Around Budapest," page 44).

The city is split down the center by the Danube River. On the west side of the Danube is hilly **Buda,** and on the east is flat **Pest** (pronounced "pesht"). A third part of the city, **Óbuda,** sits to the north of Buda.

Buda and Pest are connected by a series of characteristic bridges. From north to south, there's the low-profile **Margaret Bridge** (Margit híd, crosses Margaret Island), the famous **Chain Bridge** (Széchenyi lánchíd), the white and modern **Elisabeth Bridge** (Erzsébet híd), and the green **Liberty Bridge**

Snapshot History of Budapest

When describing the story of this grand metropolis, it's tempting to fall back on the trusty onion metaphor: Budapest, which has been adored and destroyed by many different groups across the centuries, is layered with a rich history...sometimes stinky, sometimes sweet. The Hungary: Past and Present chapter—and many other tidbits throughout this book—will help you peel back those layers, step by step. But here's the quick version:

Budapest is hot—literally. The city sits on a thin layer of earth above thermal springs, which power its many baths. Even the word Pest comes from a Slavic word for "oven." Two thousand years ago, the Romans had a settlement (called Aquincum) on the northern edge of today's Budapest. Several centuries later, in A.D. 896, a mysterious nomadic group called the Magyars arrived from the steppes of Central Asia and took over the Carpathian Basin (roughly today's Hungary). After running roughshod over Europe for a time, the Magyars—the ancestors of today's Hungarians—settled down, adopted Christianity, and became fully European. The twin towns of Buda and Pest emerged as the leading cities of Hungary.

In the 16th century, the Ottomans invaded and occupied the region for nearly a century and a half. The Habsburgs (monarchs of neighboring Austria) finally forced them out, but Buda and Pest were in ruins. The cities were rebuilt in a more Austrian style.

After many decades of Hungarian uprisings, the Compromise

(Szabadság híd). These bridges are fun to cross by foot, but it's faster to go under the river (on the M2/red Metro line), or to cross over it by tram or bus. (Four more bridges lie beyond the tourist zone: the Petőfi and Lágymányosi Bridges to the south, and Árpád and Megyeri Bridges to the north.)

Budapest uses a **district** system (like Paris and Vienna). There are 23 districts (*kerület*), identified by Roman numerals. For example, Castle Hill is in district I and City Park is in district XIV. Notice that the district number does not necessarily indicate how central a location is: Districts II and III are to the north of Buda, where few tourists go, while the heart of Pest is district V. Addresses often start with the district number (as a Roman numeral). Budapest's four-digit postal codes also give you a clue as to the district: The first digit (always 1) represents Budapest, then a two-digit number represents the district (such as "05" for district V), then a final digit gives more specific information about the location.

As you navigate Budapest, remember these key Hungarian terms: **tér** (pronounced "tehr," square), **utca** (OOT-zaw, street), **út**

of 1867 granted Hungary an equal stake in the Austro-Hungarian Empire. Six years later, the cities of Buda, Pest, and Óbuda united to form the capital city of Budapest, which governed a huge chunk of Eastern Europe. For the next few decades, Budapest boomed, and Hungarian culture enjoyed a Golden Age. The expansion reached its peak with a flurry of construction surrounding the year 1896—Hungary's 1,000th birthday.

But with Hungary's defeat in World War I, the city's fortunes reversed. World War II left Budapest in ruins...and in the hands of the Soviets. A bold uprising in 1956 was brutally dealt with, but before long a milder "goulash communism" emerged in Hungary. Budapest, though still oppressed, was a place where other Eastern Europeans could come to experiment with "Western evils"...from Big Macs to Nikes.

Since communism's graceful exit in 1989, Budapest has once again been forced to re-invent itself. The city clings to its past prominence even as it looks ahead to a future that promises to be much brighter than its dismal 20th century.

Through it all, Budapest—atmospherically shot through with the crumbling elegance of former greatness—remains the heart and soul of Central Europe. It's a rich cultural stew made up of Hungarians, Germans, Slavs, and Jews, with a dash of Turkish paprika—simmered for centuries in a thermal bath. Each group has left its mark, but through it all, something has remained that is distinctly...Budapest.

ORIENTATION

(oot, boulevard), **körút** (KUR-root, ring road), **híd** (heed, bridge), and **város** (VAH-rohsh, town). To better match what you'll see locally, in this book I've mostly used these Hungarian terms (instead of the English equivalents).

Let's take a tour through the places where you'll be spending your time, neighborhood by neighborhood. This section—like all of the sightseeing, sleeping, eating, and other advice in this book—is divided between Buda and Pest. (It might help to think of these as two separate cities...which, after all, they once were.)

Buda

The Buda side is dominated by two hills: **Castle Hill,** topped by the green dome of the Royal Palace and the spiny Neo-Gothic spire of the Matthias Church; and to the south, the taller, wooded **Gellért Hill,** capped by a 150-year-old fortress and the Liberation Monument.

The **Castle District,** atop Castle Hill (in district I), is historic but fairly dull. It's packed with tourists by day, and dead at night. More lively is the pleasant **Víziváros** (VEE-zee-vah-rohsh)

ORIENTATION

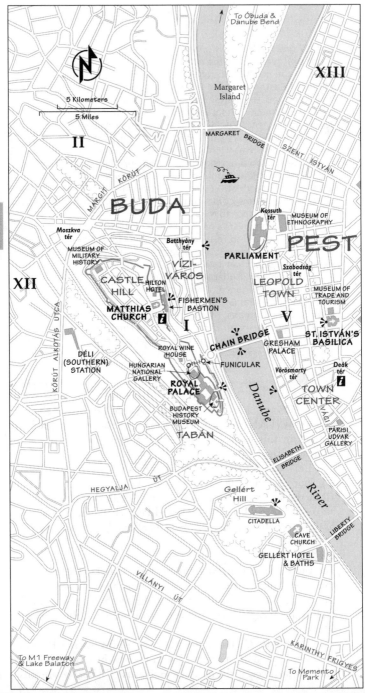

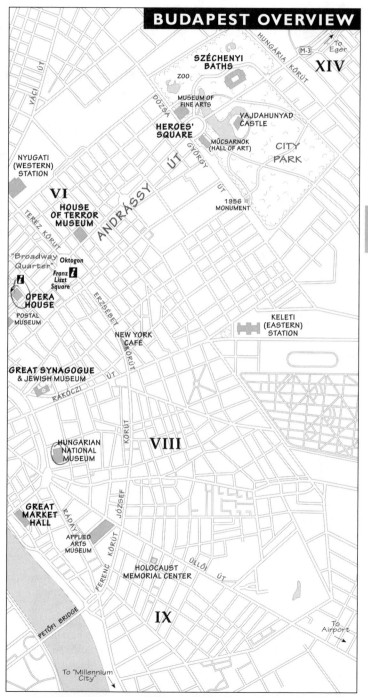

BUDAPEST OVERVIEW

SZÉCHENYI BATHS

ZOO

MUSEUM OF FINE ARTS

HEROES' SQUARE

VAJDAHUNYAD CASTLE

MŰCSARNOK (HALL OF ART)

CITY PARK

HUNGARIA KÖRÚT

To Eger

M-3

XIV

DÓZSA GYÖRGY ÚT

1956 MONUMENT

NYUGATI (WESTERN) STATION

VI

HOUSE OF TERROR MUSEUM

ANDRÁSSY ÚT

TERÉZ KÖRÚT

"Broadway Quarter"

Oktogon

Franz Liszt Square

OPERA HOUSE

POSTAL MUSEUM

ERZSÉBET KÖRÚT

NEW YORK CAFÉ

KELETI (EASTERN) STATION

GREAT SYNAGOGUE & JEWISH MUSEUM

RÁKÓCZI ÚT

HUNGARIAN NATIONAL MUSEUM

JÓZSEF KÖRÚT

VIII

GREAT MARKET HALL

RÁDAY

APPLIED ARTS MUSEUM

FERENC KÖRÚT

HOLOCAUST MEMORIAL CENTER

ÜLLŐI ÚT

To Airport

IX

PETŐFI BRIDGE

To "Millennium City"

ORIENTATION

neighborhood, or "Water Town," which is squeezed between the castle and the river. The square called Batthyány tér, roughly at the north end of Víziváros, is a hub for the neighborhood, with a handy Metro stop (M2/red line), tram  stops, market hall, and eateries. Just north of Castle Hill (and Víziváros) is **Moszkva tér,** or "Moscow Square," another transit hub for Buda, with a Metro station (M2/red line), several tram stops, and the giant Mammut shopping mall.

Tucked to the south of **Gellért Hill** is another fine residential district. Here you'll find the Gellért Hotel, with its famous thermal baths.

Central Buda is surrounded by a ring road, and the busy Hegyalja út rumbles through the middle of the tourists' Buda (between Castle and Gellért Hills). Behind Castle and Gellért Hills is a low-lying neighborhood of little interest to tourists (except for the Déli/Southern train station), and beyond that rise the **Buda Hills,** a scenic and upscale place to live.

Pest

Pest—the real-world commercial heart of the city—feels more gritty, urban, and exciting than Buda, and is where most tourists

 spend the majority of their time.

"Downtown" Pest (district V), just across the river from Castle Hill, is divided into two sections:

The more genteel northern half, called **Leopold Town** (Lipótváros), surrounds the giant red-domed, riverside Parliament building. This is the governmental, business, and banking district, with several fine monuments and grand buildings. Leopold Town is sleepy after hours.

The southern half, the grittier and more urban-feeling **Town Center** (Belváros, literally "Inner Town"), is a thriving shopping, dining, nightlife, and residential zone that bustles day and night. The main pedestrian artery through the Town Center is the famous (and overrated) Váci utca shopping street, which runs parallel to the fine and scenic Danube promenade one block inland. At the southern end of the Town Center is the vast Great Market Hall, with the Ráday utca "restaurant row" just beyond.

The Town Center is hemmed in by the first of Pest's four concentric **ring roads** *(körút)*. The innermost ring is called the Kiskörút, or "Small Boulevard." The next ring, several blocks farther out, is called the Nagykörút, or "Great Boulevard." These ring roads change names every few blocks, but they are always called *körút*. Historically, the Nagykörút is subdivided into sections named for Habsburg monarchs, such as Erzsébetkörút ("Elisabeth Boulevard"); each of these sections also defines a neighborhood, such as Erzsébetváros ("Elisabeth Town"). Beyond the Nagykörút are two more ring roads—the Hungária körút highway, and the partially unfinished M-0 expressway—that few tourists see.

Arterial **boulevards**, called *út*, stretch from central Pest into the suburbs like spokes on a wheel. One of these boulevards, **Andrássy út**, provides a useful spine for reaching some of outer Pest's best sights, restaurants, and accommodations. It begins at the Small Boulevard (near Deák tér) and extends past several key sights (including the Opera and the House of Terror museum) and dining zones (such as the "Broadway Quarter" and Franz Liszt Square) out to **City Park**. The park has its own collection of attractions, including the monumental Heroes' Square and Budapest's top experience: soaking in the Széchenyi Baths.

Various key sights lie along the **Small Boulevard** ring road (connected by trams #47 and #49), including (from north to south) the Great Synagogue (marking the start of the former Jewish Quarter, also called Elisabeth Town or Erzsébetváros, and now a run-down but hopping nightlife zone with cool so-called "ruin pubs"), the National Museum, and the Great Market Hall mentioned above; just over the Liberty Bridge, in Buda, are the Gellért Baths.

Several other points of interest are spread far and wide along the **Great Boulevard** ring road (circled by trams #4 and #6). From north to south, it passes Margaret Island (the city's playground, in the middle of the Danube); the Nyugati/Western train station; the prominent Oktogon intersection, where it crosses Andrássy út; the opulent New York Café, with the Keleti/Eastern train station just up the street; and the intersection with Üllői út, near the Holocaust Memorial Center and the Applied Arts Museum.

Outer Budapest

The city doesn't end there. This book also includes tips for the Óbuda district north of central Buda; sights on the outskirts of town (but accessible on the suburban transit network), including Memento Park, Gödöllő Palace, and the small riverside town of Szentendre; and more.

Planning Your Time

Visitors attempting to "do" Budapest in just one day leave dazed, exhausted...and yearning for more. Two days are the bare minimum, and force you to tackle the city at a breakneck pace (and you still won't see everything). Three days work, but assume you'll go fast and/or skip some things. Four days are ideal, and a fifth day (or even sixth) gives you time for various day-trip options.

Budapest is quite decentralized, making efficient sightseeing tricky. You'll have to zig and zag, refer to your map constantly, rely on public transit, and strategize to maximize your sightseeing time.

Each of this book's self-guided walks acts as a sightseeing spine for a particular neighborhood or area: Buda's Castle Hill, Pest's Leopold Town, Pest's Town Center, Pest's Andrássy út, and Pest's Heroes' Square and City Park. The walks offer an orientation overview, with several optional, in-depth sightseeing opportunities along the way. If you're ambitious, you can do several of these walks in a single day—but you'll have to skip most of the museums. To take your time and dip into each of sight, spread the walks over several days.

When divvying your time between Buda and Pest, consider that (aside from the Gellért Baths) Buda's sightseeing is mostly concentrated on Castle Hill, and can easily be seen in less than a day, while Pest deserves as much time as you're willing to give it. Start by getting your bearings in Pest (where you'll likely spend most of your time), then head for relatively laid-back Buda when you need a break from the big city.

Here are some possible plans, depending on the length of your trip. Note that these very ambitious itineraries assume you want to sightsee at a speedy (some would say unreasonable) pace. I've left your evenings open for your choice of activities: enjoying good restaurants, taking in an opera or concert, snuggling on a romantic floodlit river cruise, exploring the city's unique "ruin pubs," or simply strolling the Danube embankments and bridges. (Your options are outlined in the Entertainment & Nightlife chapter.)

Budapest in Two Days

Your time will be full but memorable. Spend Day 1 in Pest. Start with the Leopold Town Walk, then the Pest Town Center Walk. From the Great Market Hall (at the end of that walk), circle around the Small Boulevard to Deák tér and consider the Andrássy út and Heroes' Square/City Park walks. Or, if you're exhausted already, just take the M1/yellow Metro line to Hősök tere, ogle the Heroes' Square statues and Vajdahunyad Castle, and reward yourself with a soak at Széchenyi Baths. (Note that this leaves virtually no time for entering any museums—though you might be able to fit in one

Daily Reminder

Monday: Most of Budapest's museums are closed on Mondays. But you can still take advantage of these sights and activities: both major baths, Memento Park, Great Synagogue, Matthias Church and Budapest History Museum on Castle Hill, St. István's Basilica, Hungarian Museum of Trade and Tourism, Parliament tour, Great Market Hall, Opera House tour, City Park (and Zoo), Danube cruises, concerts, and bus, walking, and bike tours. Monday is also a great day to do the Leopold Town and Pest Town Center walks, since their major sights are virtually unaffected.

Tuesday: The Budapest History Museum (on Castle Hill) and Hungarian Museum of Trade and Tourism (in Leopold Town) are closed today.

Wednesday: All major sights are open.

Thursday: Some shops and the Műcsarnok (Hall of Art) are open later (until 20:00 or 21:00).

Friday: All major sights are open. The Great Synagogue and Rumbach Street Synagogue close early (usually at 14:00 or 15:00).

Saturday: The Great Synagogue and Rumbach Street Synagogue are closed today. Most shops, including the Great Market Hall, close early (usually 13:00 or 14:00). The Petőfi Csarnok flea market is hopping (8:00–14:00).

Sunday: The Great Market Hall is closed today, as are most shops, though large shopping malls remain open. The Petőfi Csarnok flea market is open (8:00–14:00).

or two big sights, such as the Parliament, Opera House, Great Synagogue, or House of Terror. Choose carefully.)

On the morning of Day 2, tackle any Pest sights you didn't have time for yesterday (or take the bus out to Memento Park). After lunch, ride bus #16 from Deák tér to Castle Hill and follow the Castle Hill Walk. Head back to Pest for some final sightseeing and dinner.

Budapest in Three or Four Days

Your first day is for getting your bearings in Pest. Choose between touring the Parliament or the Opera House; for the Parliament, buy your tickets in the morning before starting your day. Then do the Leopold Town Walk, followed by the Andrássy út and Heroes' Square/City Park walks, ending with a soak at the Széchenyi Baths.

On Day 2, delve deeper into Pest, starting with the Pest Town Center Walk. After visiting the Great Market Hall, consider crossing the Liberty Bridge for a soak at the Gellért Baths (if you want more spa time), or circle around the Small Boulevard to see

Budapest Essentials

English	Hungarian	Pronounced
Pest's Main Pedestrian Street	Váci utca	VAHT-see OOT-zaw
Pest's Main Square	Vörösmarty tér	VOO-roosh-mar-tee tehr
Pest's Grand Boulevard	Andrássy út	AWN-drah-shee oot
City Park	Városliget	VAH-rohsh-lee-geht
(Buda) Castle	(Budai) Vár	BOO-die vahr
Castle Hill	Várhegy	VAHR-hayj
Chain Bridge	Széchenyi lánchíd	SAY-chehn-yee LAHNTS-heed
Liberty Bridge (green, a.k.a. Franz Josef Bridge)	Szabadság híd	SAW-bawd-shahg heed
Elisabeth Bridge (white, modern)	Erzsébet híd	EHR-zay-beht heed
Margaret Bridge (crosses Margaret Island)	Margit híd	MAWR-geet heed
Danube River	Duna	DOO-naw
Eastern Train Station	Keleti pályaudvar	KEH-leh-tee PAH-yuh-uhd-vawr
Western Train Station	Nyugati pályaudvar	NYOO-gaw-tee PAH-yuh-uhd-vawr
Southern Train Station	Déli pályaudvar	DAY-lee PAH-yuh-uhd-vawr
Suburban Train System	HÉV	hayv

the National Museum and/or Great Synagogue.

On Day 3, use the morning to see any remaining sights, then ride the 11:00 bus out to Memento Park. On returning, grab a quick lunch and take bus #16 from Deák tér to Castle Hill, where you'll do the Castle Hill Walk.

With a fourth day, spread the Day 1 tours over more time, and circle back to any sights you've missed so far.

If you've got five or more days, consider some of these tempting destinations...

Beyond Budapest

Eger, at the heart of a popular wine region and packed with off-beat sights, is the best day trip from Budapest (2.25 hours by train each way). **Pécs,** with a gorgeous colorful streetscape and engaging sightseeing, is a close second (3 hours by train). Roughly between Budapest and Vienna, the small town of **Sopron** (historic and charming) and the Slovak capital of **Bratislava** (big, bustling, and on the move) are both worthy stopovers. Each of these is covered in its own chapter. While any of these could be done as long day trips from Budapest, it's much more satisfying to spend the night (especially in Eger and Pécs).

The Day Trips from Budapest chapter covers excursions that, frankly, are less appealing than the farther-flung towns mentioned above—but easier to do in a day from Budapest: The **Danube Bend** comprises three towns north of Budapest: the charming, Balkan-flavored artists' colony of **Szentendre;** the castle at **Visegrád;** and Hungary's most impressive church at **Esztergom.** (The Danube Bend is also doable by car on the way to Bratislava or Vienna.) To the east are **Gödöllő Palace** (dripping with Habsburg history, and a very easy side-trip from Budapest) and the more distant village of **Hollókő,** an open-air folk museum come to life (by car, these two can be combined into a single rewarding day...and you'll be back in Budapest in time for dinner).

OVERVIEW

Tourist Information

Budapest has several TIs (www.budapestinfo.hu, tel. 1/438-8080). The main branch is a few steps from the M2 and M3 Metro station at **Deák tér** (daily 8:00–20:00, Sütő utca 2, near the McDonald's, district V). Other locations include **Franz Liszt Square,** a block south of the Oktogon on Andrássy út (June–Sept daily 10:00–19:00; Oct–April Mon–Fri 10:00–18:00, closed Sat–Sun; May Mon–Fri 10:00–18:00, Sat 10:00–16:00, closed Sun; Liszt Ferenc tér 11, district VII, M1: Oktogon, tel. 1/322-4098); on top of **Castle Hill,** across from Matthias Church (daily May–Oct 9:00–19:00, Nov–April 10:00–18:00, Szentháromság tér, district I, tel. 1/488-0475); and in both Terminals 1 and 2B at the **airport** (daily 9:00–22:00). The helpfulness of Budapest's TIs can vary, but they do produce some free, useful publications, including a good city map, the *Budapest Panorama* events guide, and the information-packed *Budapest Guide* booklet. At all of the TIs, you can also collect a pile of other free brochures (for sights, bus tours, and more) and buy a Budapest Card.

Budapest Card: This card includes free use of all public transportation and 10–50 percent discounts on many major museums and other attractions (6,300 Ft/48 hours, 7,500 Ft/72 hours, includes handy 100-page booklet with maps, updated hours, and brief museum descriptions). Unfortunately, it's hard to imagine a

Tonight We're Gonna Party Like It's 1896

Visitors to Budapest need only remember one date: 1896. For the millennial celebration of their ancestors' arrival in Europe, Hungarians threw a huge blowout party. In the thousand years between 896 and 1896, the Magyars had gone from being a nomadic Central Asian tribe that terrorized the Continent to sharing the throne of one of the most successful empires Europe had ever seen.

On the morning of New Year's Day, 1896, church bells clanged endlessly though the streets of Buda and Pest. In June of that year, Emperor Franz Josef and Empress Sisi were two of the 5.7 million people who came to enjoy the Hungarian National Exhibition at City Park. At Vérmező Park (behind Castle Hill), whole oxen were grilled on the spit to feed commoners.

Much as the year 2000 saw a fit of new construction worldwide, Budapest used its millennial celebration as an excuse to build monuments and buildings appropriate for the co-capital of a huge empire, including:

- **Heroes' Square** and the **Millennium Monument**
- **Vajdahunyad Castle** (in City Park)
- The riverside **Parliament** building (96 meters tall, with 96 steps at the main entry)
- **St. István's Basilica** (also 96 meters tall)
- The M1 (yellow) Metro line, a.k.a. *Földalatti* ("Underground")—the first subway on the Continent
- The **Great Market Hall** (and four other market halls)
- **Andrássy út** and most of the fine buildings lining it
- The **Opera House**
- A complete rebuilding of **Matthias Church** (on Castle Hill)
- The **Fishermen's Bastion** decorative terrace (by Matthias Church)
- The green **Liberty Bridge** (then called Franz Josef Bridge, in honor of the ruling Habsburg emperor)

Ninety-six is the key number in Hungary—even the national anthem (when sung in the proper tempo) takes 96 seconds. But after all this fuss, it's too bad that the date was wrong: A commission—convened to establish the exact year of the Magyars' debut—determined it happened in 895. But city leaders knew they'd never make an 1895 deadline, and requested the finding be changed to 896.

scenario where the card might save even a very busy sightseer more than a dollar or two. Most travelers will do better simply buying a transit pass (1,500 Ft/24 hours, 3,700 Ft/72 hours) and paying full price for each sight as you go. But if you like the convenience of a Budapest Card, you can buy it all over the city—at TIs, travel agencies, major Metro stations, sights, and many hotels. Be sure to sign and date your card before you use it.

Discover Budapest: Ben Frieday, an American in love with Budapest (and one of its women), runs this agency, which specializes in answering questions Americans (especially backpackers) have about Budapest. There are two locations in central Budapest: at Deák tér (Sütő utca 2, in the courtyard between the McDonald's and TI, marked "Yellow Zebra," district V, M1/M2/M3: Deák tér) and near Andrássy út (behind the Opera House at Lázár utca 16, district VI, M1: Opera; this branch also has a small secondhand English bookstore). At either branch, you can use the Internet (200 Ft/15 min) or rent a bike (both offices open May–Oct daily 9:30–19:30, shorter hours off-season, tel. 1/266-8777 or 1/269-3843, www.discoverbudapest.com). Ben also runs Yellow Zebra bike tours, Absolute Walking Tours, and City Segway Tours (all described later in this chapter).

Arrival in Budapest

For a comprehensive rundown on Budapest's train stations, bus stations, airport, driving tips, and boat connections, see the Transportation Connections chapter.

Helpful Hints

Rip-Offs: Budapest feels—and is—safe, especially for a city of its size. There's little risk of violent crime here. And, while people routinely try to rip me off in Prague, I've never had a problem in Budapest. Still, some of my readers have reported falling victim to scams and con artists here. As in any big city, it's especially important to beware of pickpockets in crowded and touristy places, particularly on the Metro and in trams. Wear a money belt and watch your valuables closely. Keep your wits about you and refuse to be bullied or distracted. Any deal that seems too good to be true...probably is.

Restaurants on the Váci utca shopping street are notorious for overcharging tourists. Here or anywhere in Budapest, don't eat at a restaurant that doesn't list prices on the menu, and always check your bill carefully.

If you're a male in a touristy area and a gorgeous local girl takes a liking to you, avoid her. She's a *konzumlány* ("consumption girl"), and the foreplay going on here will climax in your grand rip-off. You'll wind up at her "favorite bar," with astronomical prices enforced by a burly bouncer.

Budapest's biggest crooks? Unscrupulous cabbies. (For tips on outsmarting them, see "Getting Around Budapest—By Taxi," page 49). Bottom line: Locals *always* call for a cab, rather than hail one on the street or at a taxi stand. If you're not comfortable making the call yourself, ask your hotel or restaurant to call for you.

Emergency Numbers: The default emergency telephone number in Hungary is 112. You can also dial 107 for police, 104 for ambulance, or 105 for fire.

Medical Help: In Hungary, pharmacies (*gyógyszertár* or *patika*) are the first place to go to pick up a basic remedy (one handy location listed below). If your health concern is more serious, ask your hotel for advice. Embassies can recommend English-speaking doctors (see contact information on page 418). Near Buda's Moszkva tér, **FirstMed Centers** is a private, pricey, English-speaking clinic (by appointment or urgent care, call first, Hattyú utca 14, 5th floor, district I, M2: Moszkva tér, tel. 1/224-9090, www.firstmedcenters.com). Hospitals *(kórház)* are scattered around the city. Ambulances usually head for the Országos Baleseti Intézet, just south of Pest's Keleti/Eastern train station (Fiumei út 17, district VIII).

Pharmacies: The helpful **Dorottya Gyógyszertár** pharmacy is dead-center in Pest, between Vörösmarty and Roosevelt squares. Because they cater to clientele from nearby international hotels, they have a useful directory that lists the Hungarian equivalent of US prescription medicines (Mon–Fri 8:00–20:00, likely closed Sat–Sun, Dorottya utca 13, district V, M1: Vörösmarty tér, tel. 1/317-2374). Each district has one pharmacy that stays open 24 hours (these should be noted outside the entrance to any pharmacy).

Train Tickets: Ticket-buying lines can be long at train stations, particularly for long-distance international trains. If you want to pre-buy your ticket, **MÁV** (Hungarian Railways) has a very convenient ticket office right in the heart of downtown Pest. They generally speak English and sell tickets for no additional fee (Mon–Fri 9:00–18:00, closed Sat–Sun, just up from the Chain Bridge and across from Erzsébet tér at József Attila utca 16, district V, M1: Vörösmarty tér).

Internet Access: If you have your own laptop, most hotels have Wi-Fi or cable Internet in the rooms (usually free, sometimes for a fee). Internet cafés are everywhere—just look for signs or ask your hotel. In Pest, I like **Discover Budapest/Yellow Zebra,** with fast access and good prices (200 Ft/15 min; for locations, hours, and contact information, see "Discover Budapest" listing on the previous page).

Post Offices: These are marked with a smart green *posta* logo (usually open Mon–Fri 8:00–18:00, Sat 8:00–12:00, closed Sun).

Laundry: Budapest doesn't have a handy coin-op, self-serve launderette. But two places in Pest can do your laundry for a reasonable price. Your best option is **Laundromat-Mosómata,** just behind the Opera House (2,000 Ft to wash and dry a big load, generally takes 3–5 hours, Mon–Fri 9:00–19:00, Sat–Sun 10:00–16:00; walk straight behind the Opera House and turn right on Ó utca, then look left for signs at #24–26, district VI, M1: Opera; mobile 0620-392-5702). Another option—closer to the Town Center, but with more difficult communication— is **Patyolat Gyorstisztító.** They say it's "self-service," but usually you can just drop off your clothes with the monolingual laundry ladies in the morning and pick them up in the afternoon (borrow the English information sheet, allow 2,500 Ft to wash and dry a load, Mon–Fri 7:00–19:00, Sat 7:00–13:00, closed Sun, just up from Váci utca at the corner of Vármegye utca and Városház utca, district V, M3: Ferenciek tere).

English Bookstores: The **Central European University Bookshop** offers the best selection anywhere of scholarly books about this region (and beyond). They also sell guidebooks, literary fiction, and some popular American magazines—all in English (Mon–Fri 10:00–19:00, Sat 10:00–14:00, closed Sun, just down the street in front of St. István's Basilica at Zrínyi utca 12, district V, tel. 1/327-3096). **Tree Hugger Dan,** which bills itself as a "local bookstore with a global conscience," is a hole-in-the-wall crammed with a wide variety of English books, from literary fiction to leisure-reading paperbacks. They also host literary events and run a café with the "only free-trade coffee in Hungary." The main office (where they also buy used books) is just off Andrássy út, between the House of Terror and Oktogon (Mon–Fri 10:00–19:00, Sat 10:00–17:00, Sun 10:00–16:00, Csengery utca 48, district VII, M1: Vörösmarty utca, tel. 1/322-0774). A smaller second branch is part of the Discover Budapest office just behind the Opera House (see page 76). **Red Bus Bookstore** has a great selection of used books in English (also buys used books, Mon–Fri 11:00–18:00, Sat 10:00–14:00, closed Sun, Semmelweis utca 14, district V, M2: Astoria, tel. 1/337-7453).

Local Guidebook: András Török's fun, idiosyncratic *Budapest: A Critical Guide* is the best guidebook by a local writer. Its quirky walking tours do a nice job of capturing the city's spirit (available in English at some souvenir stands and bookshops, around 3,000 Ft).

English Newspapers: Newsstands sell two weekly English newspapers: the *Budapest Sun* (399 Ft, often free at hotels and TIs) and the *Budapest Times* (600 Ft, more business-oriented).

Bike Rental: You can rent a bike at **Yellow Zebra,** part of Discover Budapest (2,500 Ft/all day, 3,500 Ft/24 hrs; for locations, hours, and contact information, see "Discover Budapest" listing on page 41).

Drivers: Friendly, English-speaking **Gábor Balázs** can drive you around the city or into the surrounding countryside (3,500 Ft/hr, 3-hr minimum in city, 4-hr minimum in countryside—good for a Danube Bend excursion, mobile 0620-936-4317, balazs.gabor@upcmail.hu). **József Király** runs a 10-car company, Artoli (20,000 Ft/4 hrs within town, 40,000 Ft/8 hrs to Danube Bend, these prices for up to 4 people—more for bigger groups, tel. 1/240-4050, mobile 0620-369-8890, artoli @t-online.hu). Note that these are drivers, not tour guides. For tour guides, see page 50.

Best Views: Budapest is a city of marvelous vistas. Some of the best are from the Citadella fortress (high on Gellért Hill), the promenade in front of the Royal Palace and the Fishermen's Bastion on top of Castle Hill, and the embankments or many bridges spanning the Danube (especially the Chain Bridge). Don't forget the view from the tour boats on the Danube—lovely at night.

Getting Around Budapest

Budapest is huge. Connecting your sightseeing by foot is tedious and unnecessary. It's crucial to get comfortable with the excellent public transportation system—an ingenious network of Metro lines, trams, and buses that can take you virtually anywhere you want to go.

The same tickets work for the entire system. Buy them at kiosks, Metro ticket windows, or machines. The new machines are slick and easy (with English instructions). The old orange ones are tricky: Put in the appropriate amount of money, then wait for your ticket or press the button. As it can be frustrating to find a ticket machine (especially when you see your tram or bus approaching), I generally invest in a multi-day ticket to have the freedom of hopping on at will.

Your options are:

• **Single ticket** (*vonaljegy,* for a ride of up to an hour on any means of transit; transfers are allowed only within the Metro system)—290 Ft (or 400 Ft if bought from the driver);

• **Short single Metro ride** (*Metrószakaszjegy,* 3 stops or fewer

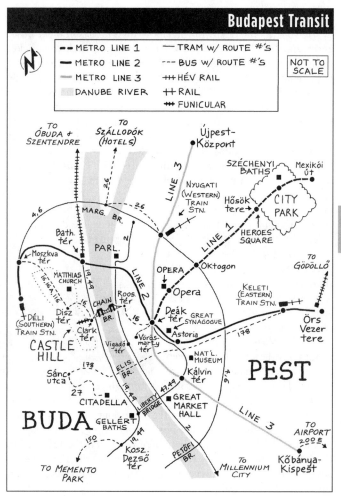

Budapest Transit

- - METRO LINE 1
— METRO LINE 2
— METRO LINE 3
DANUBE RIVER
— TRAM w/ ROUTE #'s
--- BUS w/ ROUTE #'s
+++ HÉV RAIL
++ RAIL
+++ FUNICULAR

NOT TO SCALE

TO ÓBUDA & SZENTENDRE

TO SZÁLLODÓK (HOTELS)

Újpest-Központ

SZÉCHENYI BATHS

Mexikói Út

LINE 3

NYUGATI (WESTERN) TRAIN STN.

Hősök tere

CITY PARK

HEROES' SQUARE

MARG. BR.

Bath. tér

PARL.

Moszkva tér

MATTHIAS CHURCH

OPERA

Oktogon

LINE 1

TO GÖDÖLLŐ

LINE 2

Opera

KELETI (EASTERN) TRAIN STN.

Roos. tér

CHAIN BR.

Deák tér

GREAT SYNAGOGUE

Örs Vezer tere

DÉLI (SOUTHERN) TRAIN STN.

Disz tér

Clark tér

Astoria

Vigadó tér

Vörösmarty tér

NAT'L. MUSEUM

CASTLE HILL

ELIS. BR.

PEST

Sánc utca

Kálvin tér

LIBERTY BRIDGE

GREAT MARKET HALL

CITADELLA

BUDA

GELLÉRT BATHS

LINE 3

TO AIRPORT 200 E

Kosz. Dezső tér

PETŐFI BR.

Kőbánya-Kispest

TO MEMENTO PARK

TO MILLENNIUM CITY

ORIENTATION

on the Metro)—240 Ft;

• **Transfer ticket** (*átszállójegy*—allowing up to 90 minutes, including one transfer)—450 Ft;

• **Pack of 10 single tickets** (*10 darabos gyűjtőjegy*), which can be shared—2,600 Ft (that's 260 Ft per ticket, saving you 30 Ft per ticket);

• Unlimited multi-day tickets, including a **one-day ticket** (*napijegy,* 1,500 Ft/24 hours), **three-day ticket** (*turistajegy,* 3,700 Ft/72 hours), and **weekly ticket** (*hetijegy,* 4,400 Ft/7 days, requires a photo); or

• The **Budapest Card,** which combines a multi-day ticket with sightseeing discounts (but it's generally a bad value—see page 39).

Always validate single-ride tickets as you enter the bus, tram, or Metro station (stick it in the elbow-high box). On older buses and trams that have little red validation boxes, stick your ticket in the black slot, then pull the slot toward you to punch holes in your ticket. The multi-day tickets need be validated only once. The stern-looking people with blue-and-green armbands waiting as you enter or exit the Metro want to see your validated ticket. Cheaters are fined 6,000 Ft on the spot, and you'll be surprised how often you're checked (inspectors are most commonly seen at train stations and along the touristy M1/yellow line). All public transit runs from 4:30 in the morning until 23:10. *Végállomás* means "end of the line." A useful route-planning website is www.bkv.hu.

By Metro

Riding Budapest's Metro, you really feel like you're down in the efficient guts of the city. There are three working lines:

• **M1 (yellow)**—The first Metro line on the Continent, this shallow line runs under Andrássy út from the center to City Park (see "Millennium Underground of 1896," page 152).

• **M2 (red)**—Built during the communist days, it's 115 feet deep and designed to double as a bomb shelter. This line has undergone a thorough renovation, leaving its stations new and shiny. The only line going under the Danube to Buda (for now), M2 connects the Déli/Southern train station, Moszkva tér (where you catch bus #16, #16A, or #116 to the top of Castle Hill), Batthyány tér (where you catch the HÉV train to Óbuda or Szentendre), Kossuth tér (behind the Parliament), Astoria (near the Great Synagogue on the Small Boulevard), and the Keleti/Eastern train station.

• **M3 (blue)**—This line makes a broad, boomerang-shaped swoop north to south on the Pest side. It hasn't been renovated and is noticeably older, but its number will come up soon. Key stops include the Nyugati/Western train station, Ferenciek tere (in the heart of Pest's Town Center), and Kálvin tér (near the Great Market Hall and many recommended hotels).

• **M4 (green; not yet running)**—Currently under construction, the "Big Dig" for this brand-new line is the reason for some of the torn-up streets you might see in town. It will go from southern Buda to the Gellért Baths, under the Danube to the Great Market Hall and Kálvin tér (where it will cross the M3/blue line), then up to Keleti/Eastern train station (where it will cross the M2/red line). As stations on this line are finished, they'll open to the

public, but the whole line won't be done for several years (www
.metro4.hu).

The three original lines—M1, M2, and M3—cross only once:
at the **Deák tér** stop (often signed as *Deák Ferenc tér*) in the heart
of Pest, near where Andrássy út begins.

Most M2 and M3 Metro stations are at intersections of ring
roads and other major thoroughfares. You'll usually exit the Metro
into a confusing underpass packed with kiosks, fast-food stands,
and makeshift markets. Directional signs help you find the right
exit. Or do the prairie-dog routine: Surface to get your bearings,
then head back underground to find the correct stairs up to your
destination.

The Metro stops themselves are usually very well-marked,
with a list of upcoming stops on the wall behind the tracks. Digital
clocks either count down to the next train's arrival, or count up
from the previous train's departure; either way, you'll rarely wait
more than five minutes.

You'll ride very long, steep, fast-moving escalators to access
the M2 and M3 lines. Hang on tight, enjoy the gale as trains below

shoot through the tunnels...and
don't make yourself dizzy by trying to read the Burger King ads.

The city is due to upgrade the
M3/blue line soon. They usually
do work in "low season" for business, but peak season for tourists:
July and August. If a particular
stretch of Metro line is closed,
buses run the same route instead. This can extend the length of
your journey—allow plenty of time. For the latest on which stations are closed, ask your hotel or the TI, or check www.bkv.hu.

By HÉV

Budapest's suburban rail system, or HÉV (pronounced "hayv,"
stands for Helyiérdekű Vasút, literally "Railway of Local Interest"),
branches off to the outskirts and beyond. Of the four lines, tourists
are likely to use only two: the **Szentendre line,** which begins at
Batthyány tér in Buda's Víziváros neighborhood (at the M2/red line
stop of the same name) and heads through Óbuda to the charming
Danube Bend town of Szentendre; and the **Gödöllő line,** which
begins at Örs vezér tere (in outer Pest, at the end of the M2/red
line) and heads to the town of Gödöllő, with its Habsburg palace.
(Szentendre and Gödöllő are both described in the Day Trips from
Budapest chapter.)

The HÉV is covered by standard transit tickets and passes
for rides within the city of Budapest (such as to Óbuda). But if

going beyond—such as to Szentendre or Gödöllő—you'll have to pay more. Tell the ticket-seller (or punch into the machine) where you're going, and you'll be issued the proper ticket. If you have a transit pass, you pay only the difference.

By Tram

Budapest's trams are handy and frequent, taking you virtually anywhere the Metro doesn't. Here are some trams you might use (note that all of these run in both directions):

Tram #2: Follows Pest's Danube embankment, parallel to Váci utca. From north to south, it begins at the Great Boulevard (near Margaret Bridge) and passes the Parliament, Roosevelt tér and the Chain Bridge, Vigadó tér, and the Great Market Hall. From there, it continues southward to the Petőfi Bridge, then all the way to the new "Millennium City" complex near Lágmányosi Bridge. (Note that this route might also be operated by tram #2A.)

Trams #19 and #41: Run along Buda's Danube embankment from Batthyány tér (with an M2/red Metro station, and HÉV trains to Óbuda and Szentendre). From Batthyány tér, these trams run (north to south) through Víziváros to Adam Clark tér (the bottom of the Castle Hill funicular), then under Elisabeth Bridge and around the base of Gellért Hill to the Gellért Hotel and Baths.

Trams #4 and #6: Zip around Pest's Great Boulevard ring road (Nagykörút), connecting Nyugati/Western train station and the Oktogon with the southern tip of Margaret Island and Buda's Moszkva tér (with M2/red Metro station).

Trams #47 and #49: Connect the Gellért Baths in Buda with Pest's Small Boulevard ring road (Kiskörút), with stops at the Great Market Hall, the National Museum, the Great Synagogue (Astoria stop), and Deák tér (end of the line).

Note: Because of ongoing construction along the Small Boulevard (near the Great Market Hall and Kálvin tér), trams #2, #47, and #49 might not be running their normal routes. In these cases, the trams are replaced by buses that follow similar routes. Look for a bus with the same number, ending in *V* (for *villamospótló*, "tram substitute"; for example, #47–49V).

By Bus

I use the Metro and trams for most of my Budapest commuting. But some buses are useful for shortcuts within the city, or for reaching outlying sights. Note that the transit company draws a distinction between gas-powered "buses" and electric "trolley

buses" (which are powered by overhead cables). Unless otherwise noted, you can assume the following are standard buses.

Buses **#16, #16A,** and **#116:** All head up to the top of Castle Hill (get off at Dísz tér, near the Royal Palace). You can catch any of these three at Moszkva tér (on M2/red Metro line). When coming from the other direction, bus #16 makes several handy stops in Pest (Deák tér, Roosevelt tér), then crosses the Chain Bridge for more stops in Buda (including Adam Clark tér, at Buda end of Chain Bridge).

Trolley buses **#70** and **#78:** Zip from near the Opera House (intersection of Andrássy út and Nagymező utca) to the Parliament (Kossuth tér).

Bus **#178:** Goes from Keleti/Eastern train station to central Pest (Astoria and Ferenciek tere Metro stops), then over the Elisabeth Bridge to Buda.

Bus **#26:** Begins at Nyugati/Western train station and heads around the Great Boulevard to Margaret Island, making several stops along the island.

Bus **#27:** Runs from Sánc utca (along Hegyalja út) up to just below the Citadella fortress atop Gellért Hill.

Bus **#150:** Goes from Kosztolányi Dezső tér (several blocks beyond Gellért Hotel and Baths, in Buda) to Memento Park.

Bus **#200E:** Connects all three terminals at Ferihegy Airport to the Kőbánya-Kispest M3/blue Metro station.

Buses **#54** and **#55:** Head from Boráros tér (at the Pest end of the Petőfi Bridge) to the Ecseri Flea Market.

By Taxi

Budapest's public transportation is good enough that you probably won't need to take many taxis. But if you do, you're likely to run into a dishonest driver. Arm yourself with knowledge: Cabbies are not allowed to charge more than a drop rate of 300 Ft, and then 240 Ft per kilometer. (The prices go up at night, between 22:00 and 6:00 in the morning: 420 Ft drop, 350 Ft per kilometer.) The big companies charge even less than these rates. Prices are per ride, not per passenger. A 10 percent tip is expected. A typical ride within central Budapest shouldn't run more than 2,000 Ft. Despite what some slimy cabbies may tell you, there's no legitimate extra charge for crossing the river.

Instead of hailing a taxi on the street, do as the locals do and call a cab from a reputable company—it's cheaper and you're more likely to get an honest driver. Try **City Taxi** (tel. 1/211-1111), **Taxi 6x6** (tel. 1/266-6666), or **Főtaxi** (1/222-2222). Most dispatchers speak English, but if you're uncomfortable calling, you can ask your hotel or restaurant to call for you. (Request that they call a "City Taxi"—otherwise, they might call a pricier company to get a bigger kickback.)

Many cabs you'd hail on the streets are there only to prey on rich, green tourists. Avoid unmarked taxis and cabs waiting at tourist spots and train stations. If you do wave down a cab on the street, choose one that's marked with an official company logo and telephone number, and has a yellow license plate (if the plate's not yellow, it's not official). Ask for a rough estimate before you get in—if it doesn't sound reasonable, walk away. If you wind up being dramatically overcharged for a ride, simply pay what you think is fair and go inside. If the driver follows you (unlikely), your hotel receptionist will defend you.

On a recent trip to Budapest, I arrived late at night at the Keleti/Eastern train station. The lone, unmarked taxi out front wanted 4,000 Ft for the ride to my hotel. Following my own advice, I called a legitimate company and ordered a taxi from the English-speaking dispatcher. A few minutes later, an honest cabbie picked me up and whisked me to my hotel...for 1,500 Ft.

TOURS

By Foot
Private Guides—Budapest has an abundance of enthusiastic, hardworking young guides who speak perfect English and enjoy showing off their city. Given the reasonable fees and efficient use of your time, hiring your own personal expert is an excellent value. I have two favorites, either of whom can do half-day or full-day tours, and can also drive you into the countryside. **Péter Pölczman** is an exceptional guide who really

puts you in touch with the Budapest you came to see (€90/4–5 hrs, €120/8 hrs, mobile 0620-926-0557, polczman@freestart.hu or peter.polczman@guideclub.net). **Andrea Makkay** is also great, with a professional and polished approach (€95/4 hrs, €160/8 hrs, mobile 0620-962-9363, www.privateguidebudapest.com, amakkay @t-online.hu—arrange details by email; if Andrea is busy, she might arrange to send you with another guide). Both Péter and Andrea were a big help in writing this book.

Walking Tours—A youthful, backpacker-oriented company, **Absolute Walking Tours,** is run by Oregonian Ben Frieday. These tours are loose and informal, but informative. You can choose from a number of different itineraries, which include the following: The Absolute Walk gives you a good overview of Budapest

ORIENTATION

(4,000 Ft, mid-May–Sept daily at 9:30 and 13:30, Oct–mid-May daily at 10:30, 3.5 hours). The Hammer and Sickle Tour includes a guided visit to Memento Park (you take the regular direct bus to Memento Park with other passengers), then a quick visit to a mini-museum of communist artifacts (6,500 Ft, 4/week, 3 hours). Absolute Hungro Gastro, focused on Hungarian cuisine and wine, gives you information on traditional recipes and ingredients, and a chance to taste several specialties at a local restaurant (7,000 Ft, 2/week, 1/week in winter, 3 hours). In the evening, consider the Absolute Night Stroll, which includes a one-hour cruise on the Danube (5,000 Ft, mid-April–Sept only, 4/week, 2.5 hours); or the rowdier Pub Crawl, which sometimes continues late into the night (4,500 Ft, departs 20:30, 4/week, at least 3 hours). History buffs appreciate the 1956 Uprising Walk, which visits some of the sites of those bloody but inspirational events five decades ago (6,500 Ft, 2/week, 3 hours).

All tours depart from the blocky, green-domed Lutheran church at Deák tér, near the Metro station (tel. 1/266-8777, www .absolutetours.com). Travelers with this book get a 500-Ft discount on any tour, as does anyone with a student ID card.

By Boat

Danube Boat Tours—Cruising the Danube, while touristy, is fun and convenient. The most established company, **Legenda,** is a class act that runs new, glassed-in panoramic boats day and night. I've negotiated a special discount with Legenda for my readers (but you must book direct and ask for the Rick Steves price). By **day,** the one-hour cruise costs 2,300 Ft for Rick Steves readers, or pay 2,900 Ft to also include a one-hour walking tour around Margaret Island (8/day May–Aug, 7/day April and Sept, 4/day March and Oct, 1/day Nov–Feb). By **night,** the one-hour cruise (with no Margaret Island visit) costs 3,700 Ft for Rick Steves readers (3/day May–Aug, 4/day March–April and Sept–Oct, 1/day Nov–Feb). All cruises include two drinks and headphone commentary. By night, TV monitors show the interiors of the great buildings as you float by. The Legenda dock is in front of the Marriott on the Pest embankment (find pedestrian access under tram tracks just downriver from Vigadó tér, district V, M1: Vörösmarty tér, tel. 1/317-2203, www.legenda .hu). Competing river-cruise companies are nearby, but given the discount, Legenda offers the best value.

Margaret Island Shuttle—If you just want to get out on the water, but don't care for a full tour with commentary, consider Mahart's cheap hop from Vigadó tér to Margaret Island (590 Ft one-way, 890 Ft round-trip, 4/day, 45 min, June–Aug daily, Sept and May Sat–Sun only, none Oct–April, boat dock directly in front of Vigadó tér). Mahart's standard sightseeing cruises pale in comparison to Legenda's.

On Wheels

Bike Tours—A sister company of Absolute Walking Tours, **Yellow Zebra,** wheels by Budapest's major sights on a 3.5-hour tour (5,000 Ft, mid-March–mid-Oct daily at 11:00, also at 16:00 July–Aug, no tours off-season, meet at Deák tér, tel. 1/266-8777, www.yellowzebrabikes.com).

City Segway Tours—In addition to walking and bike tours, Discover Budapest also offers tours of the city by Segway (stand-up electric scooter). Although expensive, it's a unique way to see Budapest while trying out a Segway (14,500 Ft, daily at 10:00, also daily at 18:30 April–Oct, 2.5–3 hours with 30- to 45-min training beforehand, 6 people per group, must reserve and pre-pay at www .citysegwaytours.com or call the office when in Budapest—tel. 1/269-3843).

Bus Tours—Several different companies run essentially the same bus tours that glide past all the big sights (figure around 3,500 Ft for a 2-hr tour). A hop-on, hop-off bus tour by **City-Circle Sightseeing** makes 12 stops as it cruises around town on a two-hour loop (4,500 Ft for a 24-hr ticket). Most companies also offer a wide variety of other tours, including dinner boat cruises and trips to the Danube Bend. Pick up fliers about all these tours at the TI or in your hotel lobby.

SIGHTS

The sights listed in this chapter are arranged by neighborhood for handy sightseeing. When you see a ✪ in a listing, it means the sight is covered in much more depth in one of my walks or self-guided tours. This is why Budapest's most important attractions get the least coverage in this chapter—we'll explore them later in the book. For tips on sightseeing, see page 15 in the Introduction.

Budapest boomed in the late 19th century, after it became the co-capital of the vast Habsburg Empire. Most of its finest build-ings (and top sights) date from this age. To appreciate an opulent interior—a Budapest experience worth ▲▲▲— I strongly recommend touring either the Parliament or the Opera House, depending on your interests. The Opera tour is more crowd-pleasing, while the Parliament tour is a bit drier (with a focus on history and parliamentary process)— but the spaces are even grander. Seeing both is also a fine option. "Honorable mentions" go to the interiors of St. István's Basilica, the Great Synagogue, New York Café, and both the Széchenyi and the Gellért Baths. This diversity—government and the arts, Christian and Jewish, coffee-drinkers and bathers—demonstrates how the shared prosperity of the late 19th century made it a Golden Age for a broad cross-section of Budapest society.

Remember, most sights in town offer a discount if you buy a Budapest Card (though the card is a bad value for most travelers—described on page 39). If you have a Budapest Card, always ask about discounts when you buy your ticket.

BUDA

Nearly all of Buda's top sights are concentrated on or near its two riverside hills: Castle Hill and Gellért Hill.

Castle Hill (Várhegy)

✪ Most of these sights are covered in detail in the Castle Hill Walk on page 97. If a sight is covered in the walk, I've listed only its essentials here.

Royal Palace and Nearby

Royal Palace (Királyi Palota)—While imposing and grand-seeming from afar, the palace perched atop Castle Hill is essentially a shoddily rebuilt shell. But the terrace out front offers glorious Pest panoramas, there are signs of life in some of its nooks and crannies (such as a playful fountain depicting King Matthias' hunting party), and the complex houses two museums (described below).

▲Hungarian National Gallery (Magyar Nemzeti Galéria)—The best place in Hungary to appreciate the works of home-grown artists, this art museum offers a peek into the often-morose Hungarian worldview. The collection includes a remarkable group of 15th-century, wood-carved altars from Slovakia (then "Upper Hungary"); piles of gloomy canvases dating from the dark days after the failed 1848 Revolution; several works by two great Hungarian Realist painters, Mihály Munkácsy and László Paál; and paintings (including the huge *Theater at Taormina*) by the troubled, enigmatic, and recently in-vogue Post-Impressionist Tivadar Csontváry Kosztka.

Cost and Hours: 800 Ft, may be more for special exhibitions, 1,500 Ft extra to take photos, Tue–Sun 10:00–18:00, closed Mon, required bag check for large bags, café, in the Royal Palace—enter from terrace by Eugene of Savoy statue, district I, tel. 1/201-9082, www.mng.hu.

For a self-guided tour of the Hungarian National Gallery, ✪ see page 103 of the Castle Hill Walk.

Budapest History Museum (Budapesti Történeti Múzeum)—This earnest but dusty collection strains to bring the history of this city to life. The dimly lit fragments of 14th-century sculptures, depicting early Magyars, allow you to see how Asian those original Hungarians truly looked. The "Budapest in the Modern Times" exhibit deliberately but effectively traces the union

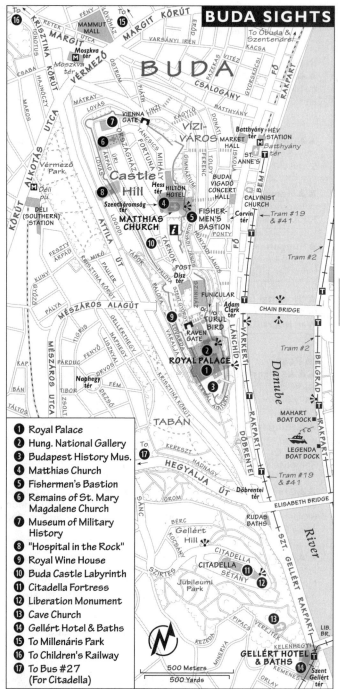

BUDA SIGHTS

1. Royal Palace
2. Hung. National Gallery
3. Budapest History Mus.
4. Matthias Church
5. Fishermen's Bastion
6. Remains of St. Mary Magdalene Church
7. Museum of Military History
8. "Hospital in the Rock"
9. Royal Wine House
10. Buda Castle Labyrinth
11. Citadella Fortress
12. Liberation Monument
13. Cave Church
14. Gellért Hotel & Baths
15. To Millenáris Park
16. To Children's Railway
17. To Bus #27 (For Citadella)

500 Meters
500 Yards

SIGHTS

Budapest at a Glance

In Buda

▲▲**Matthias Church** Landmark Neo-Gothic church with gilded history-book interior and revered 16th-century statue of Mary and Jesus. **Hours:** Mon–Sat 9:00–17:00, Sun 13:00–17:00, sometimes closed Sat after 13:00 for weddings. See page 58.

▲▲**Gellért Baths** Touristy baths in historic Buda hotel. **Hours:** May–Sept daily 6:00–19:00; Oct–April Mon–Fri 6:00–19:00, Sat-Sun 6:00–17:00. See page 62.

▲▲**Memento Park** Larger-than-life communist statues all collected in one park, on the outskirts of town. **Hours:** Daily 10:00–sunset. See page 86.

▲**Hungarian National Gallery** Top works by Hungarian artists, housed in the Royal Palace. **Hours:** Tue–Sun 10:00–18:00, closed Mon. See page 54.

▲**"Hospital in the Rock"** Fascinating underground network of hospital and bomb-shelter corridors from WWII and the Cold War. **Hours:** Tue–Sun 10:00–19:00, closed Mon. See page 59.

In Pest

▲▲▲**Széchenyi Baths** Budapest's steamy soaking scene in City Park—the city's single best attraction. **Hours:** Swimming pool—daily 6:00–22:00, thermal bath—daily 6:00–19:00. See page 79.

▲▲**Hungarian Parliament** Vast riverside government center with remarkable interior. **Hours:** English tours usually daily at 10:00, 12:00, and 14:00, and Mon–Sat sometimes also at 16:00. See page 64.

▲▲**Great Market Hall** Colorful Old World mall with produce, eateries, souvenirs, and great people-watching. **Hours:** Mon 6:00–17:00, Tue–Fri 6:00–18:00, Sat 6:00–15:00, closed Sun. See page 69.

▲▲**Great Synagogue** The world's second-largest, with fancy interior, good museum, and memorial garden. **Hours:** April–Oct Mon–Thu 10:00–17:00, Fri 10:00–15:00, Sun 10:00–18:00; Nov–March Mon–Thu 10:00–15:00, Fri and Sun 10:00–14:00; always closed Sat and Jewish holidays. See page 71.

SIGHTS

▲▲**Hungarian State Opera House** Neo-Renaissance splendor and affordable opera. **Hours:** Lobby/box office open Mon–Sat from 11:00 until show time—generally 19:00; Sun open 3 hours before performance—generally 16:00-19:00, or 10:00-13:00 if there's a matinee; English tours nearly daily at 15:00 and 16:00. See page 76.

▲▲**House of Terror** Harrowing remembrance of Nazis and communist secret police in former headquarters/torture site. **Hours:** Tue–Fri 10:00-18:00, Sat-Sun 10:00-19:30, closed Mon. See page 77.

▲▲**Heroes' Square** Mammoth tribute to Hungary's historic figures, fronted by art museums. **Hours:** Square always open. See page 77.

▲▲**City Park** Budapest's backyard, with Art Nouveau zoo, Transylvanian Vajdahunyad Castle replica, amusement park, and Széchenyi Baths. **Hours:** Park always open. See page 78.

▲**Szabadság Tér** Monumental square with a controversial obelisk honoring Soviet "liberators." **Hours:** Always open. See page 68.

▲**St. István's Basilica** Budapest's largest church, with a saint's withered fist and great city views. **Hours:** Mon–Fri 9:00-17:00, Sat 9:00-13:00, Sun 13:00-17:00, observation deck has shorter hours and is closed Nov–March. See page 68.

▲**Hungarian National Museum** Expansive collection of fragments from Hungary's history. **Hours:** Tue–Sun 10:00-18:00, closed Mon. See page 70.

▲**Postal Museum** Funky, charming tribute to old postal service objects in venerable old Andrássy út mansion. **Hours:** Tue–Sun 10:00-18:00, closed Mon. See page 76.

▲**Holocaust Memorial Center** Excellent memorial and museum honoring Hungarian victims of the Holocaust. **Hours:** Tue–Sun 10:00-18:00, closed Mon. See page 80.

▲**Margaret Island** Budapest's traffic-free urban playground, with spas, ruins, gardens, a game farm, and fountains, set in the middle of the Danube. **Hours:** Park always open. See page 82.

SIGHTS

between Buda and Pest. Rounding out the collection are exhibits on prehistoric residents and a sprawling cellar that unveils fragments from the oh-so-many buildings that have perched on this hill over the centuries.

Cost and Hours: 1,100 Ft, audioguide-850 Ft, some good English descriptions posted; mid-May–mid-Sept daily 10:00–18:00; March–mid-May and mid-Sept–Oct Wed–Mon 10:00–18:00, closed Tue; Nov–Feb Wed–Mon 10:00–16:00, closed Tue; last entry 30 min before closing, district I, tel. 1/487-8800, www.btm.hu.

For more details about the Budapest History Museum, ✪ see page 106 of the Castle Hill Walk.

Matthias Church and Nearby

▲▲Matthias Church (Mátyás-Templom)—Arguably Budapest's finest church inside and out, this historic house of worship—with a frilly Neo-Gothic

spire and gilded Hungarian historical motifs slathered on every interior wall—is Castle Hill's best sight. From the humble Loreto Chapel (with a tranquil statue of the Virgin that helped defeat the Ottomans), to altars devoted to top Hungarian kings, to a replica of the crown of Hungary, every inch of the church oozes history.

Cost, Hours, Location: 700 Ft, includes Museum of Ecclesiastical Art, 12-stop audioguide-400 Ft, Mon–Sat 9:00–17:00, Sun 13:00–17:00, may close Sat after 13:00 for weddings, Szentháromság tér 2, district I, tel. 1/355-5657, www.matyas-templom.hu.

For a self-guided tour of the Matthias Church, ✪ see page 110 of the Castle Hill Walk.

Fishermen's Bastion (Halászbástya)—Seven pointy domes and a double-decker rampart run along the cliff in front of Matthias Church. Evoking the original seven Magyar tribes, and built to celebrate the millennial celebration of their arrival, the Fishermen's Bastion is one of Budapest's top landmarks. This fanciful structure adorns Castle Hill like a decorative frieze or wedding-cake flowers. While

some suckers pay for the views from here, parts of the rampart are free and always open. Or you can enjoy virtually the same view through the windows next to the bastion café for free.

Cost and Hours: 400 Ft, buy ticket at automated machine by bastion entrance or at kiosk near TI in park, daily mid-March–mid-Oct 9:00–23:00; after closing time and off-season, no tickets are sold, but bastion is open and free to enter.

For more details about the Fishermen's Bastion, ✪ see page 111 of the Castle Hill Walk.

North Castle Hill

Remains of St. Mary Magdalene Church—Standing like a lonely afterthought at the northern tip of Castle Hill, St. Mary Magdalene was the crosstown rival of the Matthias Church. After the hill was recaptured from the Ottomans, only one church was needed, so St. Mary sat in ruins. But ultimately they did rebuild the church tower—which today evokes the rich but now-missing cultural tapestry that was once draped over this hill (free, always viewable).

For more details about St. Mary Magdalene Church, ✪ see page 114 of the Castle Hill Walk.

Museum of Military History (Hadtörténeti Múzeum)—This fine museum explains various Hungarian military actions through history in painstaking detail. Watch military uniforms and weaponry evolve from the time of Árpád to today. With enough old uniforms and flags to keep an army-surplus store in stock for a decade, but limited English information, this place might interest military and history buffs (700 Ft; April–Sept Tue–Sun 10:00–18:00, closed Mon; Oct–March Tue–Sun 10:00–16:00, closed Mon; closed mid-Dec–mid-Jan; Tóth Árpád sétány 40, district I, tel. 1/325-1600).

Under Castle Hill

The hill is honeycombed with caves and passages, accessible to tourists in three different ways: Do you want your caves with recent history, wine, or a silly exhibit?

▲**"Hospital in the Rock" Secret Military Hospital and Nuclear Bunker (Sziklakórház és Atombunker)**—Bring your Castle Hill visit into modern times with this engaging new tour. Sprawling beneath Castle Hill is a 25,000-square-foot labyrinthine network of hospital and fallout-shelter corridors built during the mid-20th century. (Hidden access points are actually scattered throughout the tourist zone above ground.) While pricey, this visit is a must for doctors, nurses, and World War II buffs. I enjoy this as a lively interactive experience to balance out an otherwise sedate Castle Hill visit.

At the outbreak of World War II in 1939, the Hungarian

SIGHTS

government began building a secret hospital here in the heart of Budapest, which was heavily used as that war came to Hungary. While designed for 300 patients, eventually it held more than double that number. Later, the forgotten hospital was used for two months to care for those injured in the 1956 Uprising. Then, as nuclear paranoia grew intense in the late 1950s, it was expanded to include a giant bomb shelter and emergency post-nuclear-holocaust hospital.

Today, after decades in mothballs, it's newly open to tourists. On the required tour, your guide will lead you through the tunnels to see room after room of perfectly preserved WWII-era medical supplies and equipment, most still in working order. Wax figures engagingly bring the various hospital rooms to life: giant sick ward, operating room, and so on. On your way to the fallout shelter, you'll pass the decontamination showers, and see primitive radiation detectors and communist propaganda directing comrades how to save themselves in case of capitalist bombs or gas attacks. In the bunker, you'll also tour the various mechanical rooms that ventilated and provided water to this sprawling underground city.

Cost and Hours: 2,000 Ft for 30-min tour of just the hospital, 3,000 Ft for 60-min tour that also includes the bunker—recommended, visits by guided tour only, Tue–Sun 10:00–19:00, English tours at the top of each hour, last tour at 18:00, closed Mon, Lovas utca 4C, district I, mobile 0630-689-8775, www.hospitalintherock.com.

Getting There: To find the hospital (after all, it's hidden), stand with your back to Matthias Church and the Fishermen's Bastion. Walk straight past the plague column and down the little street (Szentháromság utca), then go down the covered steps at the wall. At the bottom of the stairs, turn right on Lovas utca, and walk 50 yards to the well-marked bunker entrance.

Royal Wine House and Wine Cellar Museum (Királyi Borház és Pincemúzeum)—The hillsides of Castle Hill used to be blanketed with vineyards, producing wines that aged in cellars burrowed inside the castle walls. Today a new museum fills

some of those Renaissance-era cellars with a sprawling exhibit devoted to the history of Hungarian winemaking. While the actual content is skimpy, you'll be accompanied by a guide who will explain the exhibits. You'll climb up and down and up and down, along the way walking through some 14th- and 15th-century wine cellars. You'll also see fragments of an early synagogue, including the remains of a ritual bath. A few wax figures illustrate wine-making traditions, and six major Hungarian wine regions are explained. Do this only if you're really interested in wine; it's also a convenient place to do an optional wine-tasting.

Cost and Hours: 900 Ft for museum entry, or just 400 Ft if you also pay for a tasting, daily 12:00–20:00, likely shorter hours off-season, Budavár kerület, district I, tel. 1/267-1100, www.kiralyiborok .com.

Wine Tasting: You can taste regular wine (1,350–4,200 Ft depending on number and quality), sparkling wine (900–3,600 Ft), or pálinka (Hungarian schnapps, 800–2,600 Ft). They also have an extensive wine shop, selling 800- to 20,000-Ft bottles.

Getting There: It's hiding just downhill (away from the Danube) from the former Ministry of War and Dísz tér: Walk down the street and look for the entrance to the rampart garden on your left, then follow *Királyi Borház* signs along the inside of the wall.

Labyrinth of Buda Castle (Budavári Labirintus)—Armchair spelunkers can explore these caverns and see a conceptual exhibit that traces human history. After 18:00, they turn the lights out and give everyone gas lanterns. The exhibit loses something in the dark, but it's nicely spooky and a fun chance to startle amorous Hungarian teens—or be startled by mischievous ones. Even so, this hokey tourist trap pales in comparison to the other "underground" options.

Cost, Hours, Location: 1,500 Ft, daily 9:30–19:30, last entry at 19:00, entrance between Royal Palace and Matthias Church at Úri utca 9, district I, tel. 1/212-0207, www.labirintus.com.

Gellért Hill (Gellérthegy) and Nearby

The hill rising from the Danube just downriver from the castle is Gellért Hill. When King István converted Hungary to Christianity in the year 1000, he brought in Bishop Gellért, a monk from Venice, to tutor his son. But some rebellious Magyars had other ideas. They put the bishop in a barrel, drove long nails in from the outside, and rolled him down this hill...tenderizing him to death. Gellért became the patron saint of Budapest and gave his name to the hill that killed him. Today the hill is a fine place to commune with nature on a hike or jog, followed by a restorative splash in its namesake baths. The following sights are listed roughly from north to south.

Monument Hike—The north slope of Gellért Hill (facing Castle Hill) is good for a low-impact hike. You'll see many monuments, most notably the big memorial to Bishop Gellért himself (you can't miss it as you cross the Elisabeth Bridge on Hegyalja út). A bit farther up, seek out a newer monument to the world's great philosophers—Eastern, Western, and in between—from Gandhi to Plato to Jesus. Nearby is a scenic overlook with a king and a queen holding hands on either side of the Danube.

Citadella—This strategic, hill-capping fortress was built by the Habsburgs after the 1848 Revolution to keep an eye on their Hungarian subjects. There's not much to do up here (no museum or exhibits), but it's a good destination for an uphill hike, and provides the best panoramic view over all of Budapest.

The hill is crowned by the **Liberation Monument,** featuring a woman holding aloft a palm branch. Locals call it "the lady with the big fish" or "the great bottle opener." The heroic Soviet soldier—who once inspired the workers with a huge red star from the base of the monument—is now in Memento Park (see page 192).

Getting There: It's a steep hike up from the river to the Citadella, but bus #27 cuts some time off the trip. Catch the bus along the busy highway Hegyalja út that bisects Buda, at the intersection with Sánc utca (from central Pest, you can get to this stop on bus #78 from Astoria or Ferenciek tere). From Sánc utca, ride bus #27 up to the Búsuló Juhász stop, from which it's still an uphill hike to the fortress.

Cave Church (Sziklatemplom)—Hidden in the hillside on the south end of the hill (across the street from Gellért Hotel) is Budapest's atmospheric cave church—literally burrowed into the rock face. The communists bricked up this church when they came to power, but now it's open for visitors once again (free entry, but closed to sightseers during frequent services).

▲▲Gellért Baths—Located at the famous and once-exclusive Gellért Hotel, right at the Buda end of the Liberty Bridge, this elegant bath complex has long been the city's top choice for a swanky, hedonistic soak. It's also awash in tourists, and the Széchenyi Baths beat it out for pure fun...but the Gellért Baths' mysterious (and gender-segregated) thermal spa rooms, and its giddily fun outdoor wave pool, make it an enticing thermal bath option.

Cost, Hours, Location: 3,400 Ft for personal changing cabin, 3,100 Ft for locker in gender-segregated locker room, cheaper after 16:00; open May–Sept daily 6:00–19:00; Oct–April Mon–Fri

6:00–19:00, Sat–Sun 6:00–17:00; last entry one hour before closing, Kelenhegyi út 4–6, district XI, tel. 1/466-6166, ext. 165, www .gellertbath.com.

○ See the Thermal Baths chapter on page 87.

The Rest of Buda

There's not much of tourist interest in Buda beyond Castle and Gellért Hills.

The **Víziváros** area, or "Water Town," is squeezed between Castle Hill and the Danube. While it's a great home base for sleeping and eating (see those chapters for details), there's little in the way of sightseeing. The riverfront Batthyány tér area, at the northern edge of Víziváros, is both a transportation hub (M2/red Metro line, HÉV suburban railway to Óbuda and Szentendre, and embankment trams) and a shopping and dining center.

To the north of Castle Hill is **Moszkva tér** ("Moscow Square"), a transportation hub (for the M2/red Metro line, several trams, and buses #16, #16A, and #116 to Castle Hill) and shopping center (featuring the giant Mammut supermall, and many smaller shops that cling to it like barnacles to a boat). This unpretentious zone, while light on sightseeing, offers a chance to commune with workaday Budapest. Its one attraction is the new **Millenáris Park,** an inviting play zone for adults and kids that combines grassy fields and modern buildings. Though not worth going out of your way for, this park might be worth a stroll if the weather's nice and you're exploring the neighborhood (a long block behind Mammut mall).

Rózsadomb ("Rose Hill"), rising just north of Moszkva tér, was so named for the rose garden planted on its slopes by a Turkish official four hundred years ago. Today it's an upscale residential zone.

To the south, the district called the **Tabán**—roughly between Castle Hill and Gellért Hill—was once a colorful, ramshackle neighborhood of sailor pubs and brothels. After being virtually wiped out in World War II, now it's home to parks and a dull residential district.

Beyond riverfront Buda, the terrain becomes hilly. This area— the **Buda Hills**—is a pleasant getaway for a hike or stroll through wooded terrain, but still close to the city. One enjoyable way to explore these hills is by hopping a ride on the Children's Railway (see page 240 in the Budapest with Children chapter).

Two other major attractions—the part of town called **Óbuda** ("Old Buda") and **Memento Park**—are on the Buda side of the river but away from the center, and described later in this chapter.

PEST

Most of Pest's top sights cluster in four neighborhoods: **Leopold Town** and the **Town Center** (together forming the city's "downtown," along the Danube); along **Andrássy út;** and at **Heroes' Square and City Park.** Each of these areas is covered by a separate self-guided walk (as noted by ✪ below). But several other excellent sights are not contained in these areas, and are covered in greater depth in this chapter: along the **Small Boulevard** (Kiskörút); along the **Great Boulevard** (Nagykörút); and along the boulevard called **Üllői út.**

Leopold Town (Lipótváros)

✪ Most of these sights are covered in detail in the Leopold Town Walk on page 115. If a sight is covered in the walk, I've listed only its essentials here. These are listed north to south.

▲▲Hungarian Parliament (Országház)

With an impressive facade and an even more extravagant interior, the oversized Hungarian Parliament stakes its claim on the

Danube. A hulking Neo-Gothic base topped by a soaring Neo-Renaissance dome, it's one of the city's top landmarks. Touring the building offers the chance to stroll through one of Budapest's best interiors. On the 45-minute tour, you'll first pass through a security checkpoint, then climb up a 96-step staircase. Stops include the monumental entryway, the Hungarian crown (under the ornate gilded dome—described on page 116), and the legislative chamber of the now-disbanded House of Lords. Your guide will explain the history and symbolism of the building's intricate decorations and offer a lesson in the Hungarian parliamentary system. You'll find out why a really good speech was nicknamed a "Havana" by cigar-aficionado parliamentarians.

Cost, Hours, Location: 2,600 Ft, free for EU citizens; English tours usually daily at 10:00, 12:00, and 14:00; Mon–Sat sometimes also at 16:00—but schedule can change, so confirm in advance; Kossuth tér 1–3, district V, M2: Kossuth tér, tel. 1/441-4904, www.parlament.hu.

Getting Tickets: The ticket office opens each day at 8:00 (tickets sold for same-day tours only). On busy days, ticket-buyers line up, and tours can sell out (especially if a tour group has reserved a large block of tickets, which individuals can't do). If your heart is set on getting in, buy your tickets early (for morning tours, I'd try to arrive by 9:00; the line is longest around 10:30). Behind the Parliament, follow signs to the entry marked "X" (slightly right of center as you face the back of the giant building), and find the line at the fence marked *For Buying Tickets*. Wait for the guard to let you enter door X, pay the cashier, and return to the mob to wait for your tour.

For more details about the Parliament, ✪ see page 116 of the Leopold Town Walk.

SIGHTS

Near the Parliament

Kossuth (Lajos) Tér—This giant square behind the Parliament is peppered with monuments honoring great Hungarian statesmen (Lajos Kossuth, Ferenc Rákóczi, Imre Nagy), artists (Attila József), and anonymous victims of past regimes (you'll see two different memorials to the 1956 Uprising, during which protesters were gunned down on this very square).

For more details about Kossuth tér, ✪ see page 119 of the Leopold Town Walk.

The square is fronted by the...

Museum of Ethnography (Néprajzi Múzeum)—This museum, housed in one of Budapest's majestic venues, feels deserted. Its fine collection of Hungarian folk artifacts (mostly from the late 19th century) takes up only a small corner of the cavernous building. The permanent exhibit, with surprisingly good English explanations, shows off costumes, tools, wagons, boats, beehives, furniture, and ceramics of the many peoples who lived in pre-WWI Hungary (which also included much of today's Slovakia and Romania). The museum also has a collection of artifacts from other European and world cultures, which it cleverly assembles into good temporary exhibits (800 Ft, may be more for special exhibitions, Tue–Sun 10:00–18:00, closed Mon, Kossuth tér 12, district V, M2: Kossuth tér, tel. 1/473-2442, www.neprajz.hu).

Between the Parliament and Town Center

✪ For more details on all of the following sights, see the Leopold Town Walk on page 115.

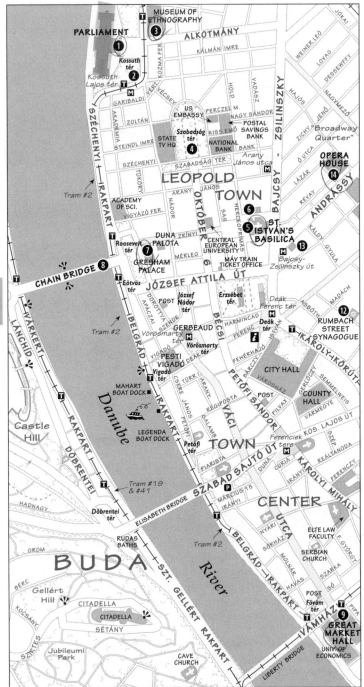

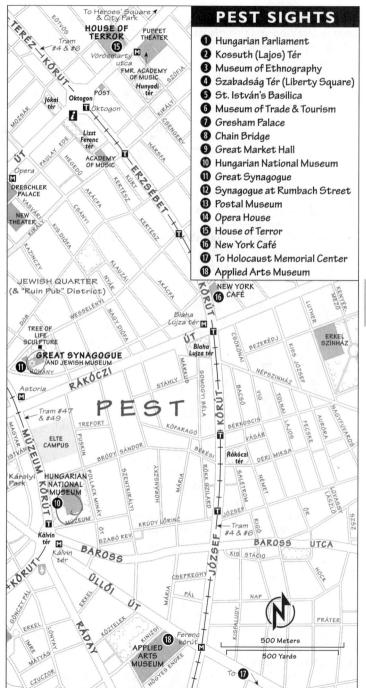

PEST SIGHTS

1. Hungarian Parliament
2. Kossuth (Lajos) Tér
3. Museum of Ethnography
4. Szabadság Tér (Liberty Square)
5. St. István's Basilica
6. Museum of Trade & Tourism
7. Gresham Palace
8. Chain Bridge
9. Great Market Hall
10. Hungarian National Museum
11. Great Synagogue
12. Synagogue at Rumbach Street
13. Postal Museum
14. Opera House
15. House of Terror
16. New York Café
17. To Holocaust Memorial Center
18. Applied Arts Museum

SIGHTS

▲**Szabadság Tér ("Liberty Square")**—One of Budapest's most genteel squares, this space is marked by a controversial mon-

ument to the Soviet soldiers who "liberated" Hungary at the end of World War II, and ringed by both fancy old apartment blocks and important buildings (such as the Hungarian State Television headquarters, the US Embassy, and the National Bank of Hungary). A fine café and fun-
filled playgrounds round out the square's many attractions. More architectural gems—including the quintessentially Art Nouveau Bedő-Ház, and the Postal Savings Bank in the Hungarian national style—are just a block away.

▲**St. István's Basilica (Szent István Bazilika)**—Budapest's biggest church is one of its top landmarks. The grand but some-what gloomy interior celebrates St. István, Hungary's first

Christian king. You can see his withered, blackened, millennium-old fist in a gilded reliquary in the side chapel. Or you can zip up on an elevator (or climb up stairs partway) to an obser-vation deck with views over the rooftops of Pest.

Cost, Hours, Location: Interior—free, treasury—400 Ft, Mon–Fri 9:00–17:00, Sat 9:00–13:00 (but often closed Sat in summer for weddings), Sun 13:00–17:00; Observation deck—500 Ft, daily June–Aug 9:30–18:00, April–May 10:00–16:30, Sept–Oct 10:00–17:30, closed Nov–March; Szent István tér, district V, M1: Bajcsy-Zsilinszky út or M3: Arany János utca.

Hungarian Museum of Trade and Tourism (Magyar Keres-kedelmi és Vendéglátóipari Múzeum)—With an emphasis on Budapest's commerce during its late-19th-century Golden Age, this place offers a whiff of the nostalgic air that permeates Hungarian society. While the tiny permanent collection is noth-ing special, check to see if its generally good temporary exhibits appeal to you (600 Ft, Wed–Mon 11:00–19:00, closed Tue, around to the left as you face St. István's Basilica at Szent István tér 15, district V, M1: Bajcsy-Zsilinszky út or M3: Arany János utca, tel. 1/375-6249, www.mkvm.hu).

▲**Gresham Palace**—This stately old Art Nouveau building, long neglected, has now been renovated to its former splendor.

Overlooking Roosevelt tér, today it houses one of Budapest's top hotels. Even if you're not a guest, ogle its glorious facade and stroll through its luxurious lobby (lobby open 24 hours daily, Roosevelt tér 5–6, district V, www.fourseasons.com/budapest).

▲**Chain Bridge (Lánchíd)**—The city's most beloved bridge stretches from Pest's Roosevelt tér to Buda's Adam Clark tér (named for the bridge's designer). The gift of Count István Széchenyi to the Hungarian people, it was the first permanent link between the two towns that would soon merge to become Budapest.

Pest Town Center (Belváros)

✪ All of these sights are covered in detail in the Pest Town Center Walk on page 132. I've listed only the essentials here.

Váci Utca and Nearby

▲▲**Vörösmarty Tér**—The central square of the Town Center,

dominated by a giant statue of the revered Romantic poet Mihály Vörösmarty and the venerable Gerbeaud coffee shop, is the hub of Pest sightseeing. Within a few steps of here are the main walking street Váci utca (described below), the delightful Danube promenade, the new "Fashion Street" of Deák utca, and much more.

For more details about Vörösmarty tér and the sights that surround it, ✪ see page 133 of the Pest Town Center Walk.

Váci Utca—In Budapest's Golden Age, Váci Street was where well-heeled urbanites would shop, then show off for each other. During the Cold War, it was the first place in the Eastern Bloc where you could buy a Big Mac or Adidas sneakers. And today, it's an overrated, overpriced tourist trap disguised as a pretty street. I'll admit that I have a bad attitude about Váci utca. It's because more visitors get fleeced by dishonest shops, crooked restaurants, and hookers masquerading as lonely hearts here than anywhere else in town. Like moths to a flame, tourists can't seem to avoid this strip. And I can't blame them. Walk Váci utca to satisfy your curiosity. But then venture off it to discover the real Budapest.

To avoid Váci utca entirely, and instead explore more local and more interesting areas nearby, ✪ take the Pest Town Center Walk on page 132.

▲▲**Great Market Hall (Nagyvásárcsarnok)**—"Great" indeed is this gigantic marketplace on three levels: produce, meats, and other foods on the ground floor; souvenirs upstairs; and fish and pickles in the cellar. The Great Market Hall has somehow

succeeded in keeping local shop-
pers happy, even as it's evolved
into one of the city's top tourist
attractions. Goose liver, embroidered tablecloths, golden Tokaji
Aszú wine, pickled peppers,
communist-kitsch T-shirts,
savory *lángos* pastries, patriotic
green-white-and-red flags, kid-
pleasing local candy bars, and

paprika of every level of spiciness...if it's Hungarian, you'll find it
here. Come to shop for souvenirs, to buy a picnic, or just to rattle
around inside this vast, picturesque, Industrial Age hall.

Hours and Location: Mon 6:00–17:00, Tue–Fri 6:00–18:00,
Sat 6:00–15:00, closed Sun, Fővám körút 1–3, district IX, M3:
Kálvin tér.

For a self-guided tour of the Great Market Hall, ✪ see page
143 of the Pest Town Center Walk.

Along the Small Boulevard (Kiskörút)

These two major sights are along the Small Boulevard, between
the Liberty Bridge/Great Market Hall and Deák tér. (Note that
the Great Market Hall, listed above, is also technically along the
Small Boulevard.)

▲Hungarian National Museum
(Magyar Nemzeti Múzeum)

One of Budapest's biggest museums features all manner of
Hungarian historic bric-a-brac, from the Paleolithic age to a

more recent infestation of
dinosaurs (the communists).
Artifacts are explained
by good, if dry, English
descriptions. The first floor
(one flight down from the
entry) focuses on the Carpathian Basin in the pre-
Magyar days, with ancient

items and Roman remains. The basement features a lapidarium,
with medieval tombstones and more Roman ruins. Upstairs, 20
rooms provide a historic overview from the arrival of the Magyars
in 896 up to the 1989 revolution. The museum adds substance to
your understanding of Hungary's story—but it helps to have a
pretty firm foundation first (read the Hungary: Past and Present
chapter, page 389). The most engaging part is room 20, with an
exhibit on the communist era, featuring both pro- and anti-Party

propaganda. The exhibit ends with video footage of the 1989 end of communism—demonstrations, monumental parliament votes, and a final farewell to the last Soviet troops leaving Hungarian soil. Another uprising—the 1848 Revolution against Habsburg rule—was declared from the steps of this impressive Neoclassical building (1,000 Ft, audioguide-750 Ft/hr, Tue–Sun 10:00–18:00, closed Mon, last entry 30 min before closing, near Great Market Hall at Múzeum körút 14–16, district VIII, M3: Kálvin tér, tel. 1/327-7773, www.hnm.hu).

▲▲Great Synagogue (Zsinagóga)

Also called the "Dohány Street Synagogue," Budapest's gorgeous synagogue is the biggest in Europe and the second biggest in the

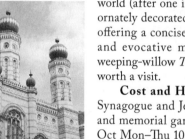

world (after one in New York City). With its ornately decorated interior, attached museum offering a concise lesson in the Jewish faith, and evocative memorial garden (with its weeping-willow *Tree of Life* sculpture), it's well worth a visit.

Cost and Hours: 1,600 Ft for Great Synagogue and Jewish Museum, *Tree of Life* and memorial garden are always free; April–Oct Mon–Thu 10:00–17:00, Fri 10:00–15:00, Sun 10:00–18:00; Nov–March Mon–Thu 10:00–15:00, Fri and Sun 10:00–14:00; always closed Sat and Jewish holidays, last entry 30 minutes before closing, Dohány utca 2, district VII, M2: Astoria plus a five-minute walk, tel. 01/344-5131, www.aviv.hu.

Tours: Aviv Travel, with a well-marked kiosk just outside the synagogue entrance, leads tours of the synagogue, museum, and related sights. You have three options: A quick 45-minute tour combines the Great Synagogue and the *Tree of Life* (1,900 Ft). A longer 80-minute tour covers the above, plus a guided visit to the synagogue's museum (2,250 Ft). And the deluxe 90-minute version covers the Great Synagogue, *Tree of Life,* and the nearby synagogue on Rumbach Street, but not the museum (2,600 Ft). Since these tours include admission, you're paying a small price for the guiding—making this an affordable way to really understand the place (tours leave every 30 min April–Oct Mon–Thu and Sun 10:30–16:30, Nov–March until 13:30; year-round Fri at 10:30, 11:30, 12:30, and 13:00; no Sat tours).

❷ Self-Guided Tour: While the tours described above are worthwhile, the following commentary covers the basics.

First, go through the security checkpoint at the entrance. You can buy tickets for the synagogue interior and the museum at the end of the courtyard on the right. Then visit the sights in the

The Jewish Story of Budapest

As the former co-capital of an empire that included millions of Jews, Budapest always had a high concentration of Jewish residents. Before World War II, 5 percent of Hungary's population and 25 percent of Budapest's was Jewish (and the city was dubbed "Judapest" by its snide Viennese neighbors up the river).

In 1783, the progressive Habsburg Emperor Josef II "emancipated" the Jews of his empire, allowing them to live in the city of Pest. Many settled in the area outside the city wall (today marked by the Small Boulevard ring road), in what would become the Jewish Quarter. Desperate to win the acceptance of their Catholic neighbors, some of these Jews worked hard to assimilate—which is why the Great Synagogue they built here feels almost more like a Christian house of worship than a Jewish one. At the same time, many Jews (like other minorities) were compelled to undergo "Magyarization," taking on Hungarian language and culture, and even adopting Hungarian spellings of their names.

The anti-Semitism that infected Europe in the late 19th and early 20th centuries also consumed Budapest. When Hitler was

following order. (Note that you can visit the *Tree of Life* and memorial garden even if you don't buy a ticket for the synagogue. Or, if the synagogue is closed, go around left side to view the monument through a fence.)

1. Great Synagogue: Before going inside, check out the synagogue's striking **facade,** and consider the rich history of the

building and the people it represents: The synagogue was built in 1859 just outside what was then the city wall (where the Small Boulevard ring road is today). This was a time when Pest's Jewish community wished to prove their worth, and to demonstrate how well-integrated they were with the greater community. Building this new synagogue was an important step in impressing their Catholic neighbors. They commissioned non-Jewish architects—who had designed a major synagogue in Vienna—to create

on the rise in Germany, Hungary allied with him, allowing local politicians to postpone the Holocaust here. But Hitler grew impatient and invaded in March of 1944. By May—just two months after the Nazi takeover—trains began heading for Auschwitz; by the middle of July, about 430,000 Hungarian Jews had already been deported.

As the end of the war neared, Hungarian Nazi collaborators resorted to more desperate measures, such as lining up Jews along the Danube and shooting them into the river (now commemorated by a monument near the Parliament—see page 123). To save bullets, they'd sometimes tie several victims together, shoot one of them, and throw him into the freezing Danube—dragging the others in with him. Hungary lost nearly 600,000 Jews to the Holocaust. Today, only half of 1 percent of Hungarians are Jewish, and most of them live in Budapest.

After the Holocaust, the Great Synagogue sat neglected for 40 years. But since the thawing of communism, Hungarian Jews have taken a renewed interest in their heritage. In 1990, this synagogue was painstakingly rebuilt, partly from financial support from Tony Curtis, an American actor of Hungarian-Jewish origin (he and his daughter Jamie Lee Curtis continue to support these causes today). Other people of Hungarian-Jewish descent include big names from every walk of life: Harry Houdini (born Erich Weisz), Elie Wiesel, Joseph Pulitzer, Estée Lauder, Goldie Hawn, Peter Lorre, and Eva and Zsa Zsa Gabor.

an even more impressive one here. The synagogue is loosely based on biblical descriptions of the Temple of Solomon in Jerusalem. This explains the two tall towers, which are not typical of synagogues. The towers—along with the rosette (rose window)—also helped the synagogue resemble Christian churches of the time.

Now step **inside.** (Men will need to cover their heads, and women their shoulders; loaner yarmulkes and scarves are available at the door.) Notice that it really feels like a church with the symbols switched—with a basilica floor plan, three naves, two pulpits, and even a pipe organ. The organ—which Franz Liszt played for the building's inauguration—is a clue that this synagogue belonged to the most progressive of the three branches of Judaism here at the time. (Orthodox Jews would never be able to do the "work" of playing an organ on the Sabbath.) Of the various synagogues in this district, this one belonged to the Neolog Jewish congregation (not strictly "Reform," but certainly less traditional than the Orthodox or so-called "Status Quo Ante" Jews).

The Moorish-flavored decor—which looks almost Oriental—is a sign of the Historicist style of the time, which borrowed eclectic elements from past styles. Specifically, it evokes how Jewish culture flourished among the Sephardic Jews of Iberia.

In the ark, behind the burgundy curtain, are kept 25 original Torah scrolls. Catholic priests hid these scrolls during World War II (burying them temporarily in a cemetery). The synagogue itself, while damaged, avoided being completely destroyed in that war. While it might have been luck, or divine intervention, it was likely also because the occupying Nazis protected it for their own uses: They put radio antennas in the  two towers, stabled horses in the nave, and (according to some reports) might have even had a base for their Gestapo in the balcony above the main entrance.

The two-tiered balconies on the sides were originally for women, who worshipped separately from the men. (These galleries are accessed by separate staircases, from outside.) Today, men and women can sing together in the choir, but they still sit apart: men in the two inner rows, and women in the two outer rows. (Women sit in the balconies only on important holy days.) The service is still said in Hebrew.

• *When you're finished in here, exit through the main doors, turn right, and go down the passageway to the right (across from the security check-point, past the gift shop).*

2. *Tree of Life* and Memorial Garden: As you walk alongside the Great Synagogue, notice the small **park** on your left. This was used as a cemetery for the first time during the 1945 Nazi occupation,  when Budapest's Jews (those who had not already been shipped to Auschwitz or executed) were sealed in a ghetto behind the synagogue for two months. You can see only a few scant headstones (all dated 1945), but thousands of people were buried in mass graves here.

Behind the synagogue is the *Tree of Life*, sculpted by renowned artist Imre Varga (see page 84). The willow makes an upside-down menorah, and each of the 4,000 metal leaves is etched with the name of a Holocaust victim.

In the center of the courtyard is a symbolic **grave of Raoul Wallenberg.** He was a humanitarian and diplomat who came

here from Sweden to do what he could to rescue Hungary's Jews from the Nazis. By giving Swedish passports to Jews and admitting them to safe hospitals, he succeeded in rescuing tens of thousands of people from certain death. (Shortly after the Soviets arrived, Wallenberg was arrested, accused of being a US spy, sent to a gulag...and never seen alive again. Russian authorities recently acknowledged he was executed, but have not revealed the details.) The grave is also etched with the names of other "righteous Gentiles" who went above and beyond to save Jews. The small stones are typical of Jewish cemeteries (evoking the age-old tradition of placing pebbles over desert graves to cover the body and prevent animals from disturbing it). Surrounding the grave are four rose-colored pillars with the names of other non-Jews who saved individuals or families. In the big stained-glass window that stands near the grave, the fire symbolizes the Holocaust (the Hebrew word is *Shoah,* literally "catastrophe"), and the curling snake represents fascism.

• *Go back out the way you entered. Back at the security checkpoint, turn right, go inside the building, and climb the stairs to the...*

3. Jewish Museum (Zsidó Múzeum): This small but informative museum illuminates the Jewish faith, with artifacts and succinct but engaging English explanations. You'll find descriptions of rituals and holidays, from Rosh Hashanah and Yom Kippur to Passover and Chanukah. The exhibit also explains ancient symbols (prayer shawls, the mezuzah, etc.) and traces the Jewish lifeline from birth to marriage to death. The final room holds a small exhibit about the Holocaust, with lots of old photos and newspaper clippings. Stairs lead down to a small Holocaust memorial. (For more information about this tragic chapter of the Hungarian Jewish experience, don't miss the outstanding Holocaust Memorial Center—see page 80.)

Near the Great Synagogue

Synagogue at Rumbach Street—This synagogue, just two blocks from the Great Synagogue, has recently reopened its doors to visitors. Its colorful but faded Moorish-style interior survives from the Golden Age of Jewish culture in Budapest. The late-19th-century building was designed by the great Viennese architect Otto Wagner. It was deserted for years, and rumor has it that Yoko Ono nearly bought it as a studio space—but backed out when she realized its proximity to the tram tracks would cause unacceptable background noise. The synagogue might close for further renovation, but if it's open (ask at Great Synagogue) and you enjoyed the Great Synagogue, it's worth a look (500 Ft, Mon–Thu and Sun 10:00–17:00, Fri 10:00–14:00, closed Sat, from the *Tree of Life* it's two blocks down Rumbach utca toward Andrássy út, district VII, M2: Astoria).

Andrássy Út

✪ All of these sights are covered in detail in the Andrássy Út Walk on page 148. I've listed only the essentials here.

▲**Postal Museum (Postamúzeum)**—This endearing little museum collects dusty knickknacks from Austria-Hungary's finely tuned postal system. Come here not for the lesson about Habsburg Empire mailmen, but for the rare chance to explore a Golden Age apartment, pungent with nostalgia for times past.

Cost, Hours, Location: 500 Ft, Tue–Sun 10:00–18:00, closed Mon, loaner English information in each room, just up the street from St. István's Basilica at Andrássy út 3, look for easy-to-miss sign and dial 10 to get upstairs, district VI, M1: Bajcsy-Zsilinszky út, tel. 1/269-6838, www.postamuzeum.hu.

For more details about the Postal Museum, ✪ see page 152 of the Andrássy Út Walk.

▲▲**Hungarian State Opera House (Magyar Állami Operaház)**—This sumptuous temple to music is one of Europe's finest opera houses. Built in the late 19th century by patriotic Hungarians striving to thrust their capital onto the European stage, it also boasts one of Budapest's very best interiors.

You can drop in anytime the box office is open to ogle the ostentatious **lobby** (Mon–Sat from 11:00 until show time—generally 19:00; Sun open 3 hours before the performance—generally 16:00–19:00, or 10:00–13:00 if there's a matinee; Andrássy út 22, district VI, M1: Opera).

The 45-minute **tours** of the Opera House are a must for music-lovers, and enjoyable to anyone. With an English-speaking guide (who spouts plenty of fun if silly legends), you'll see the main entryway, the snooty lounge area, some of the cozy but plush boxes, and the lavish auditorium. You'll find out why secret lovers would meet in the cigar lounge, how the Opera House is designed to keep the big spenders away from the nosebleed-seats rabble, and how to tell the difference between real marble and fake marble (2,600 Ft, 500 Ft to take photos, tours nearly daily at 15:00 and

16:00, tickets are easy to get—just show up right before the tour, buy ticket in opera shop—enter the main lobby and go left, shop open Mon–Fri 10:30–12:45 & 13:30–17:00, Sat–Sun 13:30–17:00, open later during performances, tel. 1/332-8197).

For more details about the Opera House, ✪ see page 154 of the Andrássy Út Walk.

▲▲**House of Terror (Terror Háza)**—The building at Andrássy út 60 was home to the vilest parts of two destructive regimes: first

the Arrow Cross (the Gestapo-like enforcers of Nazi-occupied Hungary), then the ÁVO and ÁVH secret police (the insidious KGB-type wing of the Soviet satellite government). Now re-envisioned as the "House of Terror," this building uses high-tech, highly conceptual, bombastic exhibits to document (if not proselytize about) the ugliest moments in Hungary's difficult 20th century. Enlightening and well-presented, it rivals Memento Park as Budapest's best attraction about the communist age.

Cost, Hours, Location: 1,500 Ft, 400 Ft more for special exhibitions, audioguide-1,300 Ft, Tue–Fri 10:00–18:00, Sat–Sun 10:00–19:30, closed Mon, last entry 90 min before closing, Andrássy út 60, district VI, M1: Vörösmarty utca—*not* the Vörösmarty tér stop, tel. 1/374-2600, www.terrorhaza.hu.

✪ See House of Terror Tour on page 159.

Heroes' Square and City Park

✪ All of these sights are covered in detail in the Heroes' Square and City Park Walk on page 176. I've listed only the essentials here. To reach this area, take the M1/yellow Metro line to Hősök tere (district XIV).

▲▲**Heroes' Square (Hősök Tere)**—Built in 1896 to celebrate the 1,000th anniversary of the Magyars' arrival in Hungary, this vast square culminates at a bold Millennium Monument. Standing

stoically in its colonnades are 14 Hungarian leaders who represent the whole span of this nation's colorful and illustrious history. In front, at the base of a high pillar, are the seven original Magyar chieftains, the Hungarian War Memorial, and young Hungarian skateboarders of the 21st century. It's an ideal place to appreciate Budapest's greatness and to learn a little about its story. The square is also flanked by a pair of museums (described below).

For a self-guided tour of Heroes' Square, ✪ see page 177 in the Heroes' Square and City Park Walk.

Museum of Fine Arts (Szépművészeti Múzeum)—This collection of Habsburg art—mostly Germanic, Dutch, Belgian, and Spanish rather than Hungarian—is Budapest's best chance to appreciate some European masters (1,200 Ft, may be more for special exhibitions, audioguide-1,000 Ft, toilets and coat-check downstairs, Tue–Sun 10:00–17:30, closed Mon, last entry 30 min before closing, Dózsa György út 41, tel. 1/469-7100, www.szep muveszeti.hu.

For more details about the Museum of Fine Arts, ✪ see page 185 in the Heroes' Square and City Park Walk.

Műcsarnok ("Hall of Art")—Facing the Museum of Fine Arts from across Heroes' Square, the Műcsarnok shows temporary exhibits by contemporary artists—of interest only to art-lovers. The price varies depending on the exhibits and on which parts you tour. The Ernst Museum wing features up-and-coming artists (usually 1,200 Ft, or 1,400 Ft with Ernst Museum; Tue–Wed and Fri–Sun 10:00–18:00, Thu 12:00–20:00, closed Mon; Ernst Museum open Tue–Sun 11:00–19:00, closed Mon; Dózsa György út 37, tel. 1/460-7000, www.mucsarnok.hu).

For more details about the Hall of Art, ✪ see page 186 in the Heroes' Square and City Park Walk.

▲▲**City Park (Városliget)**—This particularly enjoyable corner of Budapest, which sprawls behind Heroes' Square, is endlessly entertaining. Explore the fantasy castle of Vajdahunyad (described next). Visit the animals and ogle the playful Art Nouveau buildings inside the city's zoo, ride a roller-coaster at the amusement park, or enjoy a circus under the big top (all described in the Budapest with Children chapter, page 237). Go for a stroll, rent a rowboat, eat some cotton candy, or challenge a local  Bobby Fischer to a game of chess. Or (best of all) take a dip in Budapest's ultimate thermal spa, the Széchenyi Baths (described later in this section). This is a fine place to just be on vacation.

For more details about City Park, ✪ see page 188 in the Heroes' Square and City Park Walk.

▲▲**Vajdahunyad Castle (Vajdahunyad Vára)**—An elaborate pavilion that the people of Budapest couldn't bear to tear

down after their millennial celebration ended a century ago, Vajdahunyad Castle has become a fixture of City Park. Divided into four parts—representing four typical, traditional schools of Hungarian architecture—this "little Epcot" is free and always open to explore. It's dominated by a fanciful replica of a Renaissance-era Transylvanian castle. Deeper in the complex, a curlicue-covered Baroque mansion houses (unexpectedly) the **Museum of Hungarian Agriculture** (Magyar Mezőgazdasági Múzeum; 800 Ft; April–Oct Tue–Sun 10:00–17:00, closed Mon; Nov–March Tue–Fri 10:00–16:00, Sat–Sun 10:00–17:00, closed Mon; last entry 30 min before closing, tel. 1/363-2711).

For more details about Vajdahunyad Castle, ✪ see page 189 in the Heroes' Square and City Park Walk.

▲▲▲**Széchenyi Baths (Széchenyi Fürdő)**—My favorite activity in Budapest, the Széchenyi Baths are an ideal way to reward yourself for the hard work of sightseeing and call it a culturally enlightening experience. You'll soak in hundred-degree water, surrounded by portly Hungarians squeezed into tiny swimsuits, while jets and cascades pound away

your tension. Go for a vigorous swim in the lap pool, giggle and bump your way around the whirlpool, submerge yourself to the nostrils in water green with minerals, feel the bubbles from an underwater jet gradually caress their way up your leg, or challenge the locals to a game of Speedo-clad chess. And it's all surrounded by an opulent yellow palace with shiny copper domes. The bright blue-and-white of the sky, the yellow of the buildings, the pale pink of the skin, the turquoise of the water...Budapest simply doesn't get any better.

Cost, Hours, Location: 2,800 Ft for personal changing cabin, 2,400 Ft for locker in gender-segregated locker room, price includes thermal baths, swimming pool, and sauna; swimming pool generally open daily 6:00–22:00, thermal bath daily 6:00–19:00, last entry one hour before closing, Állatkerti körút 11, district XIV, M1: Széchenyi fürdö, tel. 1/363-3210, www.szechenyibath.com.

✪ See the Thermal Baths chapter on page 87.

On the Great Boulevard (Nagykörút)

▲New York Café—My vote for the most over-the-top extravagant coffeehouse in Budapest, if not Europe, this recently restored space ranks up there with the city's most impressive old interiors. While gawking tourists are sternly barred at the door, springing for a pricey cup of coffee here (consider it the admission fee) is worth it simply to soak in all the opulence (daily 9:00–24:00, Erzsébet körút 9–11, district VII, M2: Blaha Lujza tér, tel. 1/886-6167).

For more details about New York Café, ✪ see page 235 in the Eating chapter.

Museums near Üllői Út

These two museums are near the city center, on the boulevard called Üllői út. You could stroll there in about 10 minutes from the Small Boulevard ring road (walking the length of the Ráday utca restaurant street gets you very close), or hop on the M3/blue Metro line to Ferenc körút (just one stop beyond Kálvin tér).

▲Holocaust Memorial Center (Holokauszt Emlékközpont)—This sight honors the nearly 600,000 Hungarian victims of the Nazis...one out of every 10 Holocaust victims. The impres-

sive modern complex (with a beautifully restored 1920s synagogue as its centerpiece) is a museum of the Hungarian Holocaust, a monument to its victims, a space for temporary exhibits, and a research and documentation center of Nazi atrocities. Interesting to anybody, but essential to those interested in the Holocaust, this is Budapest's best sight about that dark time. (For more details, see "The Jewish Story of Budapest" on page 72.)

Cost, Hours, Location: 1,000 Ft, 500-Ft English audioguide repeats posted English information, Tue–Sun 10:00–18:00, closed Mon, Páva utca 39, district IX, M3: Ferenc körút, tel. 1/455-3333, www.hdke.hu.

Getting There: From the Ferenc körút Metro stop, use the exit marked *Holokauszt Emlékközpont* and take the left fork at the exit. Walk straight ahead two long blocks, then turn right down Páva utca.

✪Self-Guided Tour: You'll pass through a security checkpoint to reach the courtyard. Once inside, a black marble wall is etched with the names of victims. Head downstairs to buy your ticket.

The excellent permanent exhibit, called "From Deprivation of Rights to Genocide," traces in English the gradual process of marginalization, exploitation, and dehumanization that befell Hungary's Jews as World War II wore on. The one-way route uses high-tech exhibits, including interactive touch screens and movies, to tell the story. By demonstrating that pervasive anti-Semitism existed here long before World War II, the pointed commentary casts doubt on the widely held belief that Hungary initially allied itself with the Nazis partly to protect its Jews. While the exhibit sometimes acknowledges Roma (Gypsy) victims, its primary focus is on the fate of the Hungarian Jews. Occasionally the exhibit zooms in to tell the story of an individual or single family, following their personal story through those horrific years. One powerful room is devoted to the notorious Auschwitz-Birkenau concentration camp, where some 430,000 Hungarian Jews were sent—most to be executed immediately upon arrival. The finale is the interior of the synagogue, now a touching memorial filled with glass seats, each one etched with the image of a Jewish worshipper who once filled it. Up above, on the mezzanine level, you'll find temporary exhibits and an information center that helps teary-eyed descendants of Hungarian Jews track down the fate of their relatives.

Applied Arts Museum (Iparművészeti Múzeum)—This remarkable late-19th-century building, a fanciful green-roofed castle that seems out of place in an otherwise dreary urban area,

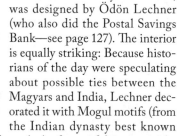

was designed by Ödön Lechner (who also did the Postal Savings Bank—see page 127). The interior is equally striking: Because historians of the day were speculating about possible ties between the Magyars and India, Lechner decorated it with Mogul motifs (from the Indian dynasty best known for the Taj Mahal). Strolling through the forest of dripping-with-white-stucco arches and columns, you might just forget to pay attention to the exhibits. The small permanent collection displays furniture, clothes, ceramics, and other everyday items, with an emphasis on curvy Art Nouveau (all

described in English). This and various temporary exhibits are displayed around a light and airy atrium. If you're visiting the nearby Holocaust Memorial Center, consider dropping by here for a look at the building.

Cost, Hours, Location: 800 Ft for permanent exhibit, several temporary exhibits have separate admission costs—or buy 2,000-Ft combo-ticket for everything, Tue–Sun 10:00–18:00, closed Mon, Üllői út 33–37, district IX, M3: Ferenc körút, tel. 1/456-5100, www.imm.hu.

Getting There: From the Ferenc körút Metro stop, follow signs to *Iparművészeti Múzeum* and bear right up the stairs.

THE DANUBE (DUNA)

The mighty river coursing through the heart of the city defines Budapest. Make time for a stroll along the delightful riverfront embankments of both Buda and Pest. For many visitors, a highlight is taking a touristy but beautiful boat cruise up and down the Danube—especially at night (see "Tours," page 50). Or visit the river's best island...

▲Margaret Island (Margitsziget)

In the Middle Ages, this island in the Danube (just north of the Parliament) was known as the "Isle of Hares." In the 13th century, a desperate King Béla IV swore that if God were to deliver Hungary from the invading Tatars, he would dedicate his youngest daughter Margaret to the Church. Hungary was spared...and Margaret was shipped to a nunnery here. But, the story goes, Margaret embraced her new life as a castaway nun, and later refused her father's efforts to force her into a politically expedient

marriage with a Bohemian king. She became St. Margaret of Hungary, and this island was named for her.

The island remained largely undeveloped until the 19th century, when a Habsburg aristocrat built a hunting palace here and turned it into his playground. It gradually evolved into a lively garden district, connected to Buda and Pest by a paddleboat steamer. Eventually a bath and hotel complex was built (to take advantage of the island's natural thermal springs), and Margaret Island was connected to the rest of the city in 1901 by the Margaret Bridge. In the genteel age of the late 19th century, a small entrance fee was charged to frolic on the island, to keep the rabble away.

Today, Margaret Island remains Budapest's playground. Budapesters come to relax in this huge, leafy park...in the midst of the busy city, but so far away (no cars are allowed on the island—just public buses). The island rivals City Park as the best spot in town for strolling, jogging, biking, and people-watching. Margaret Island is also home to some of Budapest's many baths, one of which (Palatinus Strandfürdő) is like a mini-water park. Rounding out the island's attractions are an iconic old water tower, the remains of Margaret's convent, a rose garden, a game farm, and a "musical fountain" that performs to the strains of Hungarian folk tunes.

Perhaps the best way to enjoy Margaret Island is to rent some wheels. **Bringóhintó** ("Bike Castle"), with branches at both ends of the island, rents all manner of wheeled entertainment (open daily year-round 8:00–dusk, tel. 1/329-2746, www.bringohinto .hu). The main office is a few steps from the bus stop called "Szállodák (Hotels)." For two or more people, consider renting a fun bike cart—a four-wheeled carriage with two sets of pedals, a steering wheel, handbrake, and canopy (bikes—600 Ft/30 min,

1,000 Ft/1 hr, then 200 Ft/hr; bike carts—1,700 Ft/30 min, 2,700 Ft/1 hr; 20,000-Ft deposit or leave your ID). Because they have two locations, you can take bus #26 to the northern end of the island, rent a bike and pay the deposit, bike one-way to the southern tip of the island, and return your bike there to reclaim your deposit. Follow this route (using the helpful map posted inside the bike cart): water tower, monastery ruins, rose garden, past the game farm, along the east side of the island to the dancing fountain; with more time, go along the main road or the west side of the island to check out the baths.

Getting There: Bus #26 begins at Nyugati/Western train station, crosses the Margaret Bridge, then drives up through the middle of the island—allowing visitors to easily get from one end to the other (3–6/hr). **Trams** #4 and #6, which circulate around the Great Boulevard, cross the Margaret Bridge and stop at the southern tip of the island, a short walk from some of the attractions. From Vigadó tér (along the Pest embankment), you can catch a Mahart shuttle **boat** to the island (see page 51).

OUTER BUDAPEST

The following sights, while technically within Budapest, take a little more time to reach.

Óbuda

Budapest was originally three cities: Buda, Pest, and Óbuda. Óbuda ("Old Buda") is the oldest of the three—the first known residents of the region (Celts) settled here, and today it's still littered with ruins from the next occupants (Romans). Despite all the history, the district is disappointing, worth a look only for those interested in Roman ruins or 20th-century Hungarian painting and sculpture. To reach the first three sights listed here, go to Batthyány tér in Buda (M2/red Metro line) and catch the HÉV suburban train north to the Árpád híd stop. The Vasarely Museum is 50 yards from the station. The town square is 100 yards beyond that, and 200 yards later (turn left at the ladies with the umbrellas), you'll find the Imre Varga Collection. Aquincum is three stops farther north on the HÉV line.

Vasarely Museum—This museum features two floors of eye-popping, colorful paintings by Victor Vasarely, the founder of Op Art. The exhibition follows his artistic evolution from his youth as a graphic designer to the playful optical illusions he was most famous for. (If this art gets you pondering Rubik's Cube, it may come as no surprise that Ernő Rubik was a professor of mathematics here in Budapest.) Vasarely, and the movement he pioneered helped to inspire the trippy styles of the 1960s (600 Ft, Tue–Sun 10:00–17:30, Thu until 22:00, closed Mon, Szentlélek tér 6, district III, tel. 1/388-7551, www.vasarely.tvn.hu). This museum is immediately on the right as you leave the Árpád híd HÉV station. Note that Vasarely also has a museum in the city of Pécs (see page 346 in Pécs chapter).

Óbuda Main Square (Fő Tér)—If you keep going past the Vasarely Museum and turn right, you enter Óbuda's cute Main Square. The big, yellow building was the Óbuda Town Hall when this was its own city. Today it's still the office of the district mayor. To the right of the Town Hall, you'll see a whimsical, much-photographed statue of women with umbrellas. Replicas of this sculpture, by local artist Imre Varga, decorate the gardens of wealthy summer homes on Lake Balaton. Varga created many of Budapest's distinctive monuments, including the *Tree of Life* behind the Great Synagogue (see page 74) and a major work that's on display at Memento Park (page 198). His museum is just down the street (turn left at the umbrella ladies).

▲**Imre Varga Collection (Varga Imre Kiállítóház)**—Imre Varga worked from the 1950s through the 1990s. His statues,

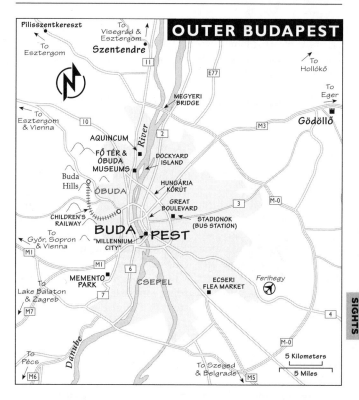

Map: OUTER BUDAPEST

while occasionally religious, mostly commented on life during communist times, when there were three types of artists: banned, tolerated, and supported. Varga was tolerated. His themes included forced marches and mass graves. One headless statue comes with medallions nailed into his chest. (These medallions were Varga's own, from his pre-communist military service. Anyone with such medallions was persecuted by communists in the 1950s...so Varga disposed of his this way.) Varga himself, now in his 80s, drops by each Saturday morning at 10:00 to chat with visitors. He speaks English and he enjoys explaining his art. Don't miss the garden, where you'll see a statue of three prostitutes illustrating "the passing of time" (500 Ft, Tue–Sun 10:00–18:00, closed Mon, Laktanya utca 7, district III, tel. 1/250-0274).

Aquincum Museum—Long before Magyars laid eyes on the Danube, Óbuda was the Roman city of Aquincum. Here you can explore the remains of the 2,000-year-old Roman town and amphitheater. The museum is proud of its centerpiece, a water organ (900 Ft; May–Sept Tue–Sun 9:00–18:00, closed Mon; Oct and late April Tue–Sun 9:00–17:00, closed Mon; closed Nov–mid-April; Szentendrei út 139, district III, HÉV north to Aquincum stop, tel. 1/250-1650, www.aquincum.hu). From the HÉV stop, cross the busy road and turn to the right. Go through the railway underpass, and you'll see the ruins ahead and on the left as you emerge.

▲▲Memento Park (a.k.a. Statue Park)

Little remains of the communist era in Budapest. But to sample those drab and surreal times, head to this motley collection of

statues, which seem to be preaching their Marxist ideology to each other in an open field on the outskirts of town. You'll see the great figures of the Soviet Bloc, both international (Lenin, Marx, and Engels) and Hungarian (local bigwig Béla Kun). And you'll see gigantic, stoic figures representing the Soviet ideals. This stiff dose of Socialist Realist art, while time-consuming to reach, is rewarding for those curious for a taste of history that most Hungarians would rather forget.

Cost, Hours, Location: 1,500 Ft, daily 10:00–sunset, six miles southwest of city center at the corner of Balatoni út and Szabadka út, district XXII, tel. 1/424-7500, www.memento park.hu.

Getting There: A handy bus goes from Deák tér in downtown Pest to the park (year-round daily at 11:00, July–Aug also at 15:00; round-trip takes 1.75 hours total, including a 40-min visit to the park, 3,950-Ft round-trip includes park entry). You can also get there by public transit, but it's more complicated (described on page 193).

○ See Memento Park Tour on page 192.

Beyond Budapest

For information on the village of **Szentendre** and the Royal Palace at **Gödöllő**—both just outside the city limits—see the Day Trips from Budapest chapter.

THERMAL BATHS

Fürdő

Splashing and relaxing in Budapest's thermal baths is the city's top attraction. Though it might sound daunting, bathing with the Magyars is far more accessible than you'd think. The thermal baths I've described in this chapter are basically like your home-town swimming pool—except the water is 100 degrees, there are plenty of jets and bubbles to massage away your stress, and you're surrounded by scantily clad Hungarians.

All this fun goes way back. Hungary's Carpathian Basin is essentially a thin crust covering a vast reservoir of hot water. The

Romans named their settlement near present-day Budapest Aquincum—meaning "abundant waters"—and took advantage of those waters by building many baths. Centuries later, the occupying Ottomans revived the custom. And today, thermal baths are as Hungarian as can be.

Locals brag that if you poke a hole in the ground anywhere in Hungary, you'll find a hot-water spring. Judging from Budapest, they might be right: The city has 123 natural springs and some two-dozen thermal baths *(fürdő)*. The baths, which are all operated by the same government agency, are actually a part of the health-care system. Doctors regularly prescribe treatments that include massage, soaking in baths of various heat and mineral compositions, and swimming laps. For these patients (whom you might see carrying a blue ticket), a visit to the bath is subsidized.

But increasingly, there's a new angle on Hungary's hot water: entertainment. Adventure water parks are springing up all over the country, and even the staid old baths have some enjoyable jets and currents. Overcome your jitters, follow my instructions, and dive in...or miss out on *the* quintessential Budapest experience.

ORIENTATION

American tourists often feel squeamish at the thought of bathing with Speedo-clad, pot-bellied Hungarians. Relax! It's less intimi-

dating than it sounds—and the fun you'll have far outweighs the jitters. I was nervous on my first visit, too. But now I feel like a trip to Hungary just isn't complete without a splish-splash in the bath.

While Hungary has several mostly nude, gender-segregated Turkish baths, the places described in this chapter are less intimidating: Men and women are usually together, and you can keep your swimsuit on the entire time. (Even at mixed baths, there generally are a few clothing-optional, gender-segregated areas, where locals are likely to be nude—or wearing a *kötény,* a loose-fitting loincloth.)

Bring along these items, if you have them: a swimsuit, towel, flip-flops, soap and shampoo for a shower afterwards, a comb or brush, and maybe sunscreen and leisure reading. Hotels typically frown on guests taking their room towels to the baths. Try asking nicely if they have some loaner towels just for this purpose (they'll probably tell you to rent one there...but what they don't know, won't hurt them). At Budapest's baths, you can usually rent a towel, swimsuit (for men, Speedos are always available, trunks sometimes), or sandals.

Each bath complex has multiple pools, used for different purposes. Big pools with cooler water are for serious swimming, while the smaller, hotter thermal baths (*gyógyfürdő,* or simply *gőz*) are for relaxing, enjoying the jets and current pools, and playing chess. The water bubbles up from hot springs at 77° Celsius (170° Fahrenheit), then is mixed with cooler water to achieve the desired temperatures. Most pools

are marked with the water temperature in Celsius (cooler pools are about 30°C/86°F; warmer pools are closer to 36°C/97°F or 38°C/100°F, about like the hot tub back home; and the hottest are

40°C/104°F...yowtch!). Locals hit the cooler pools first, then work their way up to the top temps. While the lap pools are chlorinated, most of the thermal baths are not. Unlike swimming pools in the US—where the water is recycled back into the pool—water here is slowly drained out and replaced with fresh water from the hot springs. Locals figure this means that chemicals aren't necessary.

You'll also usually find a dry sauna, a wet steam room, a cold plunge pool (for a pleasurable jolt when you're feeling overheated), and sunbathing areas (which may be segregated and clothing-optional). Some baths have fun flourishes: bubbles, whirlpools, massage jets, wave pools, and so on.

The most difficult part of visiting a Hungarian bath is the inevitably complicated entrance procedure. This is one of today's best time-travel experiences to communist Eastern Europe. Expect monolingual staff, a complex payment and locker-rental scheme, and lengthy menus of massages and other treatments. I've carefully outlined the specifics for each bath, but be forewarned that they can change from year to year, or even from day to day. Keep track of any receipt or slip of paper you're given, as you may be asked to show it later (for a partial refund or to get your deposit back). Hang in there, go where people direct you, and enjoy this unique cultural experience. Remember, they're used to tourists—so don't be afraid to act like one. If you can make it through those first few confusing minutes, you'll soon be relaxing like a pro.

While enjoying the baths, you can leave your clothing and other belongings in your locked cabin or locker. Although I've found these to be safe, and bath employees assure me that thefts are rare (a cabin is safer than a locker), it's at your own risk. Another option is to leave valuables in a safe (generally costs 500 Ft, ask when you buy ticket). People have been known to steal rental towels from around the pools to collect the deposit—keep an eye on your towels and any other belongings you bring poolside. Many locals bring plastic shopping bags to hold their essentials: towels, leisure reading, and sunscreen.

Be aware that the jets, bubbles, waves, waterfalls, and whirlpools sometimes take turns running. For example, a current pool runs for 10 minutes, then a series of jets starts up and the current pool stops for 10 minutes, then the current pool starts up again, and so on. If a particularly fun feature of the pool doesn't seem to be working, just give it a few minutes.

If you stay less than a designated time (usually three hours), you will usually get a partial refund when you leave—if you get a receipt, take it to the ticket window on your way out and see if they'll give you anything back.

Here are some useful phrases:

English	Hungarian	Pronounced
Bath	*Fürdő*	FEWR-dur
Men	*Férfi*	FAYR-fee
Women	*Női*	NUR-ee
Changing Cabin	*Kabin*	KAH-been
Locker	*Szekrény*	SEHK-rayn
Ticket Office	*Pénztár*	PAYNZ-tar
Thermal Bath	*Gyógyfürdő,*	JODGE-fewr-dur,
	Gőz	gorz

Please trust me, and take the plunge. My readers almost unanimously report that the thermal baths were their top Hungarian experience. If you go into it with an easygoing attitude and a sense of humor, I promise you'll have a blast.

THE BATHS

Budapest's two-dozen baths *(fürdő)* were taken over by the communist government, and they're all still owned by the city. The two baths listed here are the best-known, most representative, and most convenient for first-timers: The Széchenyi Baths are more casual and popular with locals, while the Gellért Baths are touristy, famous, and genteel. To me, Széchenyi is second to none, but some travelers prefer the Gellért experience. As they're quite different, doing both is an excellent option. For more information on all of Budapest's baths, see www.spasbudapest.com.

▲▲▲Széchenyi Baths (Széchenyi Fürdő)

To soak with the locals, head for this bath complex—the big, yellow, copper-domed building in the middle of City Park. Széchenyi (SAY-chehn-yee) is the best of Budapest's many bath experiences—and, thanks to a recent renovation, it feels even classier than the famous Gellért Baths. Relax and enjoy some Hungarian good living. Magyars of all shapes and sizes stuff themselves into tiny swimsuits and strut their stuff. Housewives float blissfully  in the warm water. Intellectuals and Speedo-clad elder statesmen stand in chest-high water around chessboards and ponder their next moves. This is Budapest at its best.

THERMAL BATHS

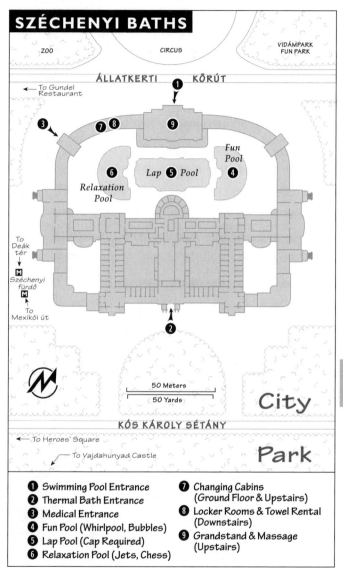

SZÉCHENYI BATHS

ZOO

CIRCUS

VIDÁMPARK
FUN PARK

ÁLLATKERTI KÖRÚT

← To Gundel
Restaurant

Fun
Pool

Lap ⑤ Pool

Relaxation
Pool

To
Deák
tér

Ⓜ Széchenyi
fürdő
Ⓜ

To
Mexikói út

50 Meters

50 Yards

City

KÓS KÁROLY SÉTÁNY

← To Heroes' Square

To Vajdahunyad Castle

Park

❶ Swimming Pool Entrance
❷ Thermal Bath Entrance
❸ Medical Entrance
❹ Fun Pool (Whirlpool, Bubbles)
❺ Lap Pool (Cap Required)
❻ Relaxation Pool (Jets, Chess)
❼ Changing Cabins
  (Ground Floor & Upstairs)
❽ Locker Rooms & Towel Rental
  (Downstairs)
❾ Grandstand & Massage
  (Upstairs)

THERMAL BATHS

Cost: 2,800 Ft for personal changing cabin, 2,400 Ft for locker in gender-segregated locker room, cheaper if you arrive within three hours of closing time, price includes thermal baths, swimming pool, and sauna. Couples can share a changing cabin: One person pays the cabin rate, the other pays the locker rate, but both use the same cabin. There's also a wide array of massages and other special treatments—find the English menu in the lobby (make an appointment as you enter). Once inside the complex, you can rent a swimsuit, towel, or sandals (about 300 Ft apiece with a 2,000- to 4,000-Ft deposit). Renting a small safe for your valuables costs 500 Ft.

Hours: Swimming pool (the best part, outdoors) generally open daily 6:00–22:00, thermal bath (less appealing, indoors) daily 6:00–19:00, last entry one hour before closing.

Location and Entrances: In City Park at Állatkerti körút 11, district XIV, M1: Széchenyi fürdő. The huge bath complex has three entrances. The busiest one—technically the **"thermal bath entrance"**—is the grand main entry, facing south (roughly toward Vajdahunyad Castle). I avoid this entrance—there's often a line during peak times, and it's a bit more confusing to find your way once inside. Instead, I prefer the **"swimming pool entrance,"** facing the zoo on the other side of the complex—it's faster, has shorter lines, and is open later. A third, smaller **"medical entrance,"** to the right as you face the zoo entry (near the Metro stops), provides access to either the thermal bath changing rooms or the swimming pool changing rooms, but can also have long lines.

Massage: The bath complex provides various medical massages. If you're interested in this, you can pay and set up an appointment at the office near the towel-rental desk (2,500–4,000 Ft, might have to wait 15–30 min for your appointment in busy times). For something more hedonistic than medicinal, you can get a Thai massage at the upper level of the complex (above the swimming pool entrance)—just follow the signs (11,000 Ft/1 hour).

Entry Procedure: These instructions assume that you're using the swimming pool entrance (explained previously). First, in the

grand lobby, pay the cashier, and you'll be given a receipt (keep this for later) and a plastic card (red for a changing cabin, blue for a locker). Wave your plastic card over the turnstile to enter the complex. Once inside, rent a towel or swimsuit if needed (do this before you change, as you'll need money). To find the towel/suit rental desk, take the first staircase down on your right as you enter the hallway to the cabins. If you get confused, the attendants (who wear white smocks and occasionally speak a few words of English) can help you find your way.

Once you've got your towel/suit, it's time to change. If you paid for a **locker,** go downstairs to find the appropriate locker room (remember, men are *férfi* and women are *női*), and ask the attendant to assign you a locker. After you change, either you or the attendant will lock it. If you paid for a **cabin,** you'll find them lining the hallway that runs around the outdoor baths courtyard. Show your plastic card to an attendant, who will direct you to a cabin (remember, couples can share a cabin). After changing, find your attendant and have them lock your cabin for you. They'll tell you to remember your cabin number, and give you a little metal disc on a string. Keep this safe (you can secure it around your wrist), as you'll need it to claim your cabin later.

Phew. Now let's have some fun.

Taking the Waters: The bath complex has two parts. Inside is the thermal bath section, a series of mixed-gender indoor pools; each of these is designed for a specific medical treatment. The water here is quite hot—most about 40 degrees Celsius, or 104 Fahrenheit—and some of the pools have very green water, supposedly caused by the many healthy minerals.

But for most visitors, the best part is the swimming pool area outside. Orient yourself to the three pools (facing the main, domed building): The pool to the left is for fun (cooler water—30 degrees Celsius, or 86 Fahrenheit, warmer in winter, lots of jets and bubbles, lively and often crowded, includes circular current pool); the pool on the right is for relaxation (warmer water—38 degrees Celsius, or 100 Fahrenheit, mellow atmosphere, a few massage jets, chess); and the main pool in the center is all business (the coolest water, doing laps, swimming cap required). Stairs to saunas are below the doors to the inside pools. You get extra credit for joining the gang in a chess match.

THERMAL BATHS

Exit Procedure: If you rented a towel or swimsuit, return it to the desk where you got it, and present your receipt to get your deposit back. Then, as you exit the complex, insert your card into the turnstile and another receipt will print out. If you stayed shorter than three hours, the receipt will indicate the amount of your refund *(Visszatérítés: Jár* [amount] *Ft).* Present this and your original receipt at the cashier as you exit to claim your "time-proportional repayment." (If you arrived within three hours of closing time, you already got a discount and won't get a refund.) Then continue your sightseeing...soggy, but relaxed.

▲▲Gellért Baths (Gellért Fürdő)

Using the baths at Gellért (GEH-layrt) Hotel costs a bit more than the Széchenyi Baths, and you won't run into nearly as many locals; this is definitely a more upscale, touristy, spa-like scene. Because most of the warmest pools are in gender-segregated areas, it's not ideal for opposite-sex couples or families who want to spend time together. But if you want a soothing, luxurious bath experience in an elegant setting, this is the place. And if it's fun you're looking for, the Gellért Baths have something that Széchenyi doesn't: a huge, deliriously enjoyable wave pool that'll toss you around like a queasy surfer (summer only).

Cost: 3,400 Ft for personal changing cabin, 3,100 Ft for locker in gender-segregated locker room, cheaper after 16:00. When you buy your ticket, tell them if you want to buy a massage or rent a towel or a swimsuit (600 Ft each with a 4,000-Ft deposit). The 1,000-Ft visitor ticket to see—but not use—the baths is pointless, as you'll see virtually nothing more than what's visible from the ticket window.

Hours and Location: May–Sept daily 6:00–19:00; Oct–April Mon–Fri 6:00–19:00, Sat–Sun 6:00–17:00; last entry one hour before closing. It's on the Buda side of the green Liberty Bridge (trams #47 and #49 from Deák tér in Pest, or trams #19 and #41 along the Buda embankment from Víziváros below the castle). The entrance to the baths is under the white dome opposite the bridge (Kelenhegyi út 4–6, district XI, tel. 1/466-6166, ext. 165).

Entry Procedure: As you enter, a generally English-speaking information desk is dead ahead, with cashiers on either side.

Beyond the cashier on the left is a window where you can deposit valuables in the safe (500 Ft).

In the summer, they sell two different tickets based on which changing area you'll use. With a **thermal bath ticket,** you'll change in a large, gender-segregated area that connects directly to the also-segregated thermal baths (so some people walk nude directly from their cabins to the bath); this means that opposite-sex couples can't share a changing cabin. With a **swimming pool ticket,** you'll go to a mixed area where opposite-sex couples can share a cabin (this area also has gender-segregated locker rooms). Both tickets allow you to move freely between the thermal baths and swimming pool areas once you're inside.

Your entry ticket consists of two parts: a receipt-like slip of paper (which you'll surrender to get into the changing area), and a plastic card used to keep track of how long you're inside (which you'll insert in the turnstile to exit). Keep track of both of these items until you're asked for them.

A dizzying array of **massages** and **treatment options** are also sold at the ticket window. Most are available only with a doctor's note, but anyone can get a "medical massage" (with oil, 2,800 Ft/15 min, 3,800 Ft/30 min) or a "refreshing massage" (with cold soapy water, 2,500 Ft/15 min, 3,500 Ft/30 min)—both are performed in the steam-bath section. Upstairs, you can also get a Thai massage, but you have to arrange that separately.

Pay for everything you want (including massages or towel rentals), enter, and glide through the swanky lobby. The indoor swimming pool is on your right, about halfway down the main

hall. Looking through the window to the pool, visualize the perfectly symmetrical bath complex: The men's thermal bath, changing cabins, and lockers are on the left, while the identical women's facilities are on the right. The two sections meet at this shared pool in the center. If you have a swimming pool ticket, you'll enter from right here: Men/*férfi* go down the stairs on the left, and women/*nöi* on the right (either way, you'll head down a long hallway, then up several flights of stairs and through a maze to the changing areas; for couples sharing a cabin, go to the section corresponding to the person who bought the cabin ticket). If you have a thermal bath ticket, the entrances are a bit farther away: women to the right, closer to the entrance, and men to the left, at the end of the hall. If you paid to rent a towel or swimsuit, pick it up from the attendant on your way.

Taking the Waters: Once you've changed, you can spend your time either indoors or out. Inside, the central, mixed-gender, genteel-feeling hall is home to a cool-water swimming pool (swimming cap required—free loaners available) and a crowded hot-water pool. Back toward the window and main hall are doors to the gender-segregated, clothing-optional massage rooms and thermal baths, with nude or loincloth-wearing bathers stewing in pools at 36 and 38 degrees Celsius (97 and 100 degrees Fahrenheit). Notice that these temperatures perfectly flank that of the human body, allowing you to toggle your temp at will. You'll also find a sauna (near the showers), steam rooms (at the far end of the bath), and a cold plunge pool. If you paid for a massage, report to the massage room in this section when you're ready (no appointments—first-come, first-served; you might wait 30 min or more).

To get outside, head upstairs (which also has a fine view over the main indoor pool). Out here, you'll find several sunbathing areas and a warm thermal pool (up the stairs at the end). But the main attraction is the big, unheated wave pool in the center (generally closed Oct–April, weather-dependent). Not for the squeamish, this pool thrashes fun-loving swimmers around like driftwood. The swells in the deeper area are fun and easy to float on, but the crashing waves at the shallow end are vigorous, if not dangerous. If there are no waves, just wait around a while (you'll hear a garbled message on the loudspeaker five minutes before the tide comes in).

Exit Procedure: When you're finished, return your towel and swimsuit to reclaim your deposit, then insert your card into the machine at the exit turnstile. If you were at the bath for shorter than three hours, and it's not near the end of the day, you'll get some money back when you leave. (If the change isn't automatically dispensed when you go through the exit turnstile, take the printed receipt to the cashier.)

Aaaaahhh.

CASTLE HILL WALK

Várhegy

Once the seat of Hungarian royalty, and now the city's highest-profile tourist zone, Castle Hill is a historic spit of land looming above the Buda bank of the Danube. Scenic from afar, but (frankly) a bit soulless from up close, it's best seen quickly. This walk gives you the lay of the land and leads you to the hill's most worthwhile attractions, including grand sights and monuments (the Matthias Church and Fishermen's Bastion) and fine museums (such as the National Gallery and the WWII-era "Hospital in the Rock"). You'll also appreciate the bird's-eye views that a visit to Castle Hill offers across the Danube to Pest.

ORIENTATION

Overview: Castle Hill is manageable for visitors: The major landmarks are the huge, green-domed Royal Palace at the south end of the hill (housing a pair of museums) and the frilly-spired Matthias Church near the north end (with the hill's best interior). In between are tourist-filled pedestrian streets and dull but historic buildings.

When to Visit: Castle Hill is packed with tour groups in the morning, but it's much less crowded in the afternoon. Since restaurants up here are expensive and low-quality, Castle Hill is an ideal after-lunch activity. If you want a good meal on this side of the river, head to the Víziváros neighborhood just downhill, between the castle and the river (see "Eating," page 218).

Getting There: The Metro and trams won't take you to the top of Castle Hill. Instead, you can hike, taxi, catch a bus, or ride the funicular.

For most visitors, the easiest bet is to hop on **bus #16,** with handy stops in both Pest (at the Deák tér Metro hub, and at Roosevelt tér at the Pest end of the Chain Bridge) and Buda (at Adam Clark tér at the Buda end of the Chain Bridge—across the street from the lower funicular station, and much cheaper than the funicular). Or you can head up from Moszkva tér (on the M2/red Metro line); from here, bus **#16,** as well as buses **#16A** and **#116,** head up the hill (at Moszkva tér, catch the bus just uphill from Metro station—in front of red-brick, castle-looking building). All buses stop at Dísz tér, right in the middle of the hill. From Dísz tér, go past the war-damaged building (the old Ministry of War) and walk five minutes toward the giant green dome, then bear left to find the big Turul bird statue at the start of this walk.

The **funicular** (*sikló*, SHEE-kloh), lifting visitors from the Chain Bridge to the top of Castle Hill, is a Budapest landmark. Built in 1870 to provide cheap transportation to Castle Hill workers, today it's a pricey little tourist trip. Read the fun first-person history in glass cases at the top station (800 Ft one-way, 1,400 Ft round-trip, not covered by transit pass, daily 7:30–22:00, departs every 5  min, closed for maintenance every other Mon). It leaves you right at the Turul bird statue, where this walk begins.

Length of This Walk: Allow about two hours, including quick visits to the National Gallery and Matthias Church; you'll need more time for additional sights (especially the Royal Wine House and/or the "Hospital in the Rock").

Hungarian National Gallery: 800 Ft, Tue–Sun 10:00–18:00, closed Mon, Szent György tér 2, tel. 1/201-9082, www.mng.hu.

Budapest History Museum: 1,100 Ft; mid-May–mid-Sept daily 10:00–18:00; March–mid-May and mid-Sept–Oct Wed–Mon 10:00–18:00, closed Tue; Nov–Feb Wed–Mon 10:00–16:00, closed Tue; Szent György tér 2, tel. 1/487-8800, www.btm.hu.

Matthias Church: 700 Ft, Mon–Sat 9:00–17:00, Sun 13:00–17:00, may close Sat after 13:00 for weddings, Szentháromság tér 2, tel. 1/355-5657, www.matyas-templom.hu.

Starring: Budapest's most historic quarter, with a palace (and a top collection of Hungarian art), a gorgeous church interior, sweeping vistas over city rooftops, and layers of history.

Background

Originally, the main city of Hungary wasn't Buda or Pest, but Esztergom (just up the river—see page 302). In the 13th century, Tatars swept through Eastern Europe, destroying much of Hungary. King Béla IV, who was forced to rebuild his kingdom, re-envisioned Buda as a fortified hilltop town, and moved the capital to this more protected location in the interior of the country. The city has dominated the region ever since.

Over the years, the original Romanesque fortress here was rebuilt and accentuated with a textbook's worth of architectural styles: Gothic, Renaissance, and Baroque. It was one of Europe's biggest palaces by the early 15th century, when King Mátyás (Matthias) Corvinus made the palace even more extravagant, putting Buda—and Hungary—on the map.

Just a few decades later, the invading Ottomans occupied Buda and turned the palace into a military garrison. When the Habsburgs laid siege to the hill for 77 days in 1686, gunpowder stored in the cellar exploded, destroying the palace. The Habsburgs (with a motley, pan-European army that included few Hungarians) took the hill, but Buda was deserted and in ruins. The town was resettled by Austrians, who built a new Baroque palace, hoping that the Habsburg monarch would move in—but none ever did. The useless palace became a garrison, then the viceroy's residence. It was damaged again during the 1848 Revolution, but was repaired and continued to grow right along with Budapest's prominence (for more on the 1848 Revolution, see page 396).

As World War II drew to a close, Budapest became the front line between the Nazis and the approaching Soviets. The labyrinth of natural caves under the hill was even adapted for use as a secret military hospital (now tourable—see "Hospital in the Rock," page 59). The Nazis, who believed the Danube to be a natural border for their empire, destroyed bridges across the river and staged a desperate "last stand" on Castle Hill. The Red Army laid siege to the hill for 100 days. They eventually succeeded in taking Budapest... but the city—and the hill—were devastated. Since then, the Royal Palace and hilltop town have been rebuilt once more, with a mix-and-match style that attempts, with only some success, to evoke the site's grand legacy.

THE WALK BEGINS

• *Orient yourself from the top of the funicular, enjoying the views over the Danube. (We'll get a full visual tour from a better viewpoint later.) At the top of the nearby staircase, notice the giant bird that looks like a vulture. This is the...*

CASTLE HILL WALK

Turul Bird

This mythical bird of Magyar folktales supposedly led the

Hungarian migrations from the steppes of Central Asia in the ninth century. He dropped his sword in the Carpathian Basin, indicating that this was to be the permanent home of the Magyar people. While the Hungarians have long since integrated into Europe, the Turul remains a symbol of Magyar pride. During a surge of nationalism in the 1920s, a movement named after this bird helped revive traditional Hungarian culture. And today, the bird is invoked by right-wing nationalist politicians.

• *We'll circle back this way later. But for now, climb down the stairs by the Turul and walk along the broad terrace in front of the...*

Royal Palace (Királyi Palota)

The imposing palace on Castle Hill barely hints at the colorful story of this hill since the day that the legendary Turul dropped

his sword. It was once the top Renaissance palace in Europe...but that was several centuries and several versions ago (see "Background," page 99). While impressive from afar, the current version of the palace—a histori-

cally inaccurate, post-WWII reconstruction—is a loose rebuilding of previous versions, lacking the style and sense of history that this important site deserves. The most prominent feature of today's

palace—the green dome—didn't even exist in earlier versions. Fortunately, the palace does house some worthwhile museums (described later in this chapter), and boasts the fine terrace you're strolling on, with some of Budapest's best views.

The big **equestrian statue** in front of the palace depicts Eugene of Savoy, a French general who had great success fighting the Hungarians' hated enemies, the Ottomans. (Apparently he wasn't successful enough, as those

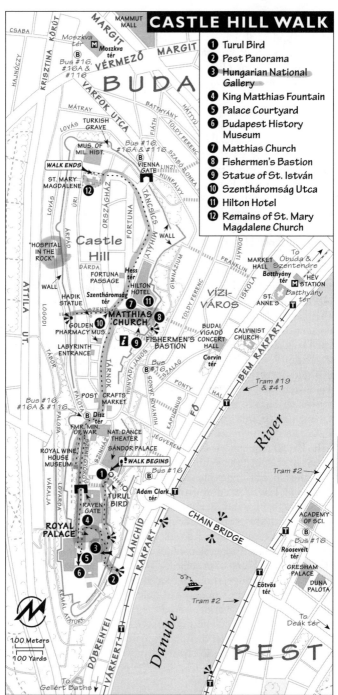

CASTLE HILL WALK

1. Turul Bird
2. Pest Panorama
3. Hungarian National Gallery
4. King Matthias Fountain
5. Palace Courtyard
6. Budapest History Museum
7. Matthias Church
8. Fishermen's Bastion
9. Statue of St. István
10. Szentháromság Utca
11. Hilton Hotel
12. Remains of St. Mary Magdalene Church

Ottomans later occupied this hill—and most of Hungary—for a century and a half.)

• *With the palace at your back, notice the long, skinny promontory sticking out from Castle Hill (on your right). Walk out to the tip of that promontory to enjoy Castle Hill's best...*

Pest Panorama

From here, you can see how topographically different the two halves of Budapest really are. The hill you're on is considered one of the last foothills of the Alps, which ripple from here all the way to France. But immediately across the Danube, everything is oh so flat. Here begins the so-called Great Hungarian Plain, which comprises much of the country—a vast expanse that stretches

all the way to Asia. For this reason, Budapest has historically been thought of as on the bubble between West and East. From the ancient Romans to Adolf Hitler, many past rulers have considered the Danube through Budapest a natural border for Europe.

Scan Pest on the horizon, from left to right. Margaret Island, a popular recreation spot, sits in the middle of the Danube. Following the Pest riverbank, you can't miss the spiny Parliament, with its giant red dome. Straight ahead, you enjoy views of the Chain Bridge, with the newly renovated Art Nouveau Gresham Palace and the 1896-era St. István's Basilica lined up just beyond it. (The Parliament and St. István's are both exactly 96 meters tall, in honor of the auspicious millennium celebration in 1896—see page 40.) The Chain Bridge cuts downtown Pest in two: The left half, or "Leopold Town," is administrative, with government ministries, embassies, banks, and so on; the right half is the commercial center of Pest, with the best riverside promenade. (Each of these is covered by a different self-guided walk in this book.) To the right is the white Elisabeth Bridge, named for the Austrian empress ("Sisi") who loved her Hungarian subjects. Downriver (to the right) is the green Liberty Bridge, formerly named for Elisabeth's hubby Franz Josef. (If you squint, you might be able to see the Turul birds that top the pillars of this bridge.) And the tall hill to the right, named for the martyred St. Gellért (who patiently attempted to convert the rowdy Magyars after their king adopted Christianity), is topped by the Soviet-era Liberation Monument.

• *Head back to the statue on the terrace. Facing Eugene's rear end is the main entrance to the...*

▲Hungarian National Gallery (Magyar Nemzeti Galéria)

Hungarians are the first to admit that they're not known for their artists. But this collection of Hungarian art—with an emphasis on the 19th and 20th centuries, and an excellent collection of medieval altars—offers even non-art-lovers a telling glimpse into the Magyar psyche.

❍ Self-Guided Tour: This once-over-lightly tour touches on the most insightful pieces in this sprawling museum.

From the atrium, head up two flights on the grand staircase.

When you reach the first floor, turn right and walk through a room of gloomy paintings (which we'll return to in a moment). Turn right into the hallway, then an immediate left, to reach the excellent collection of **15th-century winged altars.** The ornately decorated wings could be opened or closed to acknowledge special occasions and holidays. Most of these come from "Upper Hungary," or today's Slovakia—which is more heavily wooded than (Lower) Hungary, making woodcarving a popular way to worship there.

Backtrack to the room of **gloomy paintings** from the 1850s and 1860s. In the two decades between the failed 1848 Revolution

and the Compromise of 1867, the Hungarians were colossally depressed—and these paintings show it. The best-known, dominating the end of the hall, is Viktor Madarász's grim *The Bewailing of László Hunyadi,* which commemorates the death of the Hungarian heir-apparent. (The Hungarians couldn't explicitly condemn their Habsburg oppressors, but invoking this dark event from the Middle Ages had much the same effect.) To the right, *Dobozi* features a Hungarian nobleman who stabs his wife as they're pursued on horseback by Ottomans to prevent her from being raped. While Hungarian culture is generally considered less than upbeat, this is a low point.

Cross through the atrium to another room of depressing canvases (including women valiantly fighting Ottomans at the Siege of Eger, on the right). At the end of this room, we come to a turning point: a painting of St. István (or Vajk, his heathen name) being baptized and accepting European Christianity in the year 1000.

Not surprisingly, this was painted at the time of the Compromise of 1867, when Hungary was ceded authority within the Habsburg Empire. Again, the painter uses a historical story as a tip of the hat to contemporary events.

Continue through the door next to the baptism, then turn left into the hallway and take an immediate right. From here, do a clockwise spin through this wing. The first hall features Hungarian Impressionists, including the appealing *Picnic in May* by Pál Szinyei-Merse. While this scene is innocent today, the thought of men and women socializing freely was scandalous at the time. The next, large room shows off Hungarian artists who took to the countryside, painting landscapes and peasant life in the 1880s and 1890s.

When you're done here, duck into the hall, turn left, then go through the door on your right (past the elevator) into a long hall filled with works by a pair of Hungarian **Realists:** Mihály Munkácsy and László Paál. Mihály Munkácsy, who lived in France alongside the big-name Impressionists and Post-Impressionists, was wealthy and popular, so he was frequently hired to paint portraits. (As a mainstream artist, he was much more successful in

his lifetime than the avant-garde, fringe painters who have since become far better known.) His portrait of the English writer John Milton with his family shows his skill capturing the man's intensity. He did paint the occasional landscape—look for the evocative, Turner-esque *Dusty Road II,* which makes you want to reach up and wipe the grit out of your eyes. Farther along in the room are works by László Paál, who primarily painted murky nature scenes—sun-dappled paths through the forest, pondering the connection between man and nature.

Loop back around to the atrium, then climb up one more flight of stairs. Straight ahead from the landing are three works by **Tivadar Csontváry Kosztka,** the "Hungarian Van Gogh"

(for more on Csontváry, see page 340). Here you see a few of this well-traveled painter's destinations: the giant canvas in the center depicts the theater at Taormina, Sicily; on the left are the water-falls of Schaffhausen, Germany; and on the right is a cedar tree in Lebanon. Colorful, allegorical, and expressionistic, Csontváry has recently become the most in-demand and expensive of Hungarian artists. If you enjoy Csontváry's works and are headed to his home-town of Pécs, don't miss his museum there (see page 340).

If you like, you can climb up one more flight to explore works from the 20th century (including some smaller canvases by Csontváry, depicting scenes in Athens and in Jajce, Bosnia-Herzegovina).

I'd skip the 300-Ft elevator trip to the **dome**—the views are no better than from the promontory out front (included in museum ticket, last entry 30 min before museum closing).

• *Head back out to the Eugene statue and face the palace. Go through the passage to the right of the National Gallery entrance (next to the café). You'll emerge into a courtyard decorated with the...*

King Matthias Fountain

This fountain depicts King Matthias enjoying hunting, one of his favorite pastimes. (Notice the distinctive, floppy-eared Hungarian hound dog, or *vizsla*.) At the bottom of the fountain, the guy on the left is Matthias' scribe, while the woman on the right is Ilonka ("The Beautiful"). While Matthias was on a hunting trip, he wooed Ilonka, who fell desperately in love with him—oblivious to the fact he was the king. When he left suddenly to return to Buda, Ilonka tracked him down and realized who he was. Understanding that his rank meant they could never be together, Ilonka committed suicide. This is typical of many Hungarian legends, which tend to be gloomy and end with suicide.

• *On that cheerful note, go around the right side of the fountain and through the passage, into the...*

Palace Courtyard

This space, while impressive, somehow feels like an empty husk...a too-big office building. The entrance to the Budapest History Museum (described below) is at the far end of the courtyard. But first, duck through the door and down the hallway on your right as you go through the passage (free entry). This hall is lined with minor artifacts from the museum, giving you a free glimpse (and

Mátyás (Matthias) Corvinus: The Last Hungarian King

The Árpád dynasty—descendants of the original Magyar tribes—died out in 1301. For more than 600 years, Hungary would be ruled by foreigners...with one exception.

In the middle of the 15th century, Hungary had bad luck hanging on to its foreign kings: Two of them died unexpectedly within seven years. Meanwhile, homegrown military general János Hunyadi was enjoying great success on the battlefield against the Ottomans. When the five-year-old László V was elected king, Hunyadi was appointed regent and essentially ruled the country.

Hunyadi defeated the Ottomans in the crucial 1456 Battle of Belgrade, which kept them out of Hungary (at least for another 70 years) and made him an even greater hero to the Hungarian people. But soon afterward, Hunyadi died from the plague, which he had contracted during that fateful battle. When the young king also died (at the tender age of 16), the nobles looked for a new leader. At first their sights settled on Hunyadi's eldest son, László. But the Habsburgs—who were trying to project their influence from afar—felt threatened by the Hunyadi family, and László was killed.

At this dark moment, the Hungarians turned to the younger Hunyadi son, Mátyás (or Matthias in English). At the time, Matthias (whose first wife was a Czech princess) was at court in Prague. According to legend, Matthias' mother sent for him with a raven with a ring in its beak. The raven supposedly flew non-stop from Transylvania to Prague. The raven-with-ring motif became part

English descriptions) of the evolution of this site over the centuries, including paintings, drawings, and photographs of the palace in different eras (plus an ATM). If you like what you see here, consider visiting the museum; if not, skip down to the "Walk to Matthias Church" (page 108).

Budapest History Museum (Budapesti Történeti Múzeum)

A good but stodgy museum begging for a makeover, this place celebrates the earlier grandeur of Castle Hill. If Budapest really intrigues you, this is a fine place to explore its history. The core of

of the family crest, as well as the family name: Corvinus (Latin for "raven").

Matthias Corvinus returned to Buda, becoming the first Hungarian-descended king in more than 150 years. Progressive and well-educated in the Humanist tradition, Matthias Corvinus (r. 1458–1490) was the quintessential Renaissance king. A lover of the Italian Renaissance, he patronized the arts and built palaces legendary for their beauty. Also a benefactor of the poor, he dressed up as a commoner and ventured into the streets to see firsthand how the nobles of his realm treated his people.

Matthias was a strong, savvy leader. He created Central Europe's first standing army—30,000 mercenaries known as the Black Army. No longer reliant on the nobility for military support, Good King Matthias was able to drain power from the nobles and make taxation of his subjects more equitable—earning him the nickname the "people's king."

King Matthias was also a shrewd military tactician. Realizing that squabbling with the Ottomans would squander his resources, he made peace with the Ottoman sultan to stabilize Hungary's southern border. Then he swept north, invading Moravia, Bohemia, and even Austria. By 1485, Matthias moved into his new palace in Vienna, and Hungary was enjoying a Golden Age.

Five years later, Matthias died mysteriously at the age of 47, and his empire disintegrated. It is said that when Matthias died, justice died with him. To this day, Hungarians consider him the greatest of all kings, and they sing of his siege of Vienna in their national anthem. They're proud that for a few decades in the middle of half a millennium of foreign oppression, they had a truly Hungarian king—and a great one at that.

the exhibit (on the first two floors) traces the story of the city. On the ground floor (back-right corner, in a darkened room), stroll through the collection of 14th-century sculpture fragments. Many have strong Magyar features—notice that they look Central Asian (similar to Mongolians). One floor up, the good exhibit called "Budapest in the Modern Times" (*Budapest az Újkorban*—through the faux-colonnade) traces the rocky 18th and 19th centuries, with a focus on the gradual movement towards merging Buda and Pest. The top floor has artifacts of Budapest's prehistoric residents. The cellar illustrates just how much this hill has changed over the centuries—and how dull today's version is in comparison. You'll wander through a maze of old palace parts, including the remains of an original Gothic chapel, a knights' hall, and marble remnants (reliefs and fountains) of Matthias Corvinus' lavish Renaissance palace.

Walk to Matthias Church

Leaving the palace courtyard, walk straight up the slight incline, passing under a gate with a raven holding a ring in its mouth (a symbol of King Matthias). As you continue along the line of

flagpoles, the big white building on your right (near the funicular station) is the **Sándor Palace.** This mansion underwent a very costly renovation under the previous Hungarian prime minister, who hoped to make it his residence. But in 2002,

the same year it was finished, he lost his bid for reelection. The spunky new PM refused to move in. By way of compromise, now the president's office is here.

In the field in the middle of this terrace, you'll notice the remains of a medieval monastery and church. Along the left side (past the flagpoles) is the ongoing excavation of the medieval Jewish quarter—more reminders that most of what you see on today's Castle Hill has been destroyed and rebuilt many times over.

After Sándor Palace is the yellow **National Dance Theater,** where Beethoven once performed (for details, see page 251 in the Entertainment & Nightlife chapter). The hulking, war-damaged

building beyond that (at the end of the lawn, partially covered by the huge banner) used to house the **Ministry of War.** Most of the bullet holes are from World War II, while others were left by the Soviets who occupied this hill in

response to the 1956 Uprising (see page 120). The building is a political hot potato—prime real estate, but nobody can decide what to do with it.

Just after the Ministry of War, at the cross street, you reach **Dísz tér** ("Parade Square"), which has a convenient bus stop for connecting to other parts of Budapest (bus #16, #16A, or #116 to Moszkva tér; or bus #16 to the Pest side of the Chain Bridge).

If you walk a few steps down the street to the left, on the left-hand side you'll find an entrance to the rampart garden between the castle walls. A short walk through this area takes you to the **Royal Wine House and Wine Cellar Museum,** where you can tour a network of old wine cellars burrowed under Castle Hill...

and taste some Hungarian wines, if you choose. (For details, see page 60 in the Sights chapter.)

Cross the street in front of the Ministry of War, noticing the handy post office on your left. On the right, behind the yellow wall, is a courtyard with an open-air Hungarian **crafts market.** While it's fun to browse, prices here are high (haggle away). The Great Market Hall has a better selection and its prices are generally lower (see page 143).

Continue straight uphill on **Tárnok utca.** This area often disappoints visitors. After being destroyed by Ottomans, it was rebuilt in sensible Baroque, lacking the romantic time-capsule charm of a medieval old town. But if you poke your head into some courtyards, you'll almost always see some original Gothic arches and other medieval features.

As you continue along, ponder the fact that there are miles of **caves** burrowed under Castle Hill—carved out by water, expanded by the Ottomans, and used by locals during the siege of Buda at the end of World War II. If you'd like to spelunk under Castle Hill, there are two different sightseeing options: a historically oriented, World War II–era tour; or a corny, touristy, but easy cave that's open to the public (both are described on page 59 and page 61 in the Sights chapter).

As you approach the plague column, on your left is the low-profile entrance to the **Golden Pharmacy Museum** (dark-orange building). Consider dipping into this modest three-room collection of historic pharmaceutical bric-a-brac, including a cute old pharmacy counter and an alchemist's lab (500 Ft, borrow English descriptions, Tue–Sun 10:30–17:30, closed Mon, Tárnok utca 18).

• *Continue on Tárnok utca up to the little park with the TI (on your right; pick up their handy* Castle Walks *map).*

Across the street from the park (on the left), the **CBA grocery store** *sells reasonably priced cold drinks, and has a coffee shop upstairs (Mon–Fri 7:00–20:00, Sat 8:00–20:00, Sun 9:00–18:00). Just beyond it, the same store runs a "grill bar" selling cheap and basic sandwiches and sides (to go, or sit at the tables out front).*

Just beyond the park, a warty plague column from 1713 marks **Szentháromság tér** *("Holy Trinity Square"), the main square of old Buda.*

Dominating the square is the...

Matthias Church (Mátyás-Templom)

Budapest's best church has been destroyed and rebuilt several times in the 800 years since it was founded by King Béla IV. Today's version—renovated at great expense in the late 19th century and restored after World War II—is an ornately decorated lesson in Hungarian history. While it's officially named the "Church of

Our Lady," everyone calls it the Matthias Church, for the popular Renaissance king who got married here—twice.

● **Self-Guided Tour:** Examine the **exterior.** While the nucleus of the church is Gothic, most of what you see outside—including the frilly, flamboyant steeple—was added for the 1896 celebrations. At the top of the spire facing the river, notice the raven—the ever-present symbol of King Matthias Corvinus.

The sumptuous **interior** is wallpapered with gilded pages from a Hungarian history textbook. Different eras are represented by symbolic motifs.

For example, the wall immediately to the left of the entry represents the Renaissance, with a giant coat of arms of the beloved King Matthias Corvinus. (The tough guys in armor on either side are members of his mercenary Black Army, the source of his power.) Notice another raven, with a ring in its beak. Meanwhile, the wall across from the entry—with Oriental motifs—commemorates the Ottoman reign of Buda.

Work your way clockwise around the church from the entry. The first chapel (in the back corner, by the closed main doors)—the **Loreto Chapel**—holds the church's prize possession. Peer through the black iron grill to see the 1515 statue of Mary and Jesus. Anticipating Ottoman plundering, locals walled over this precious statue. The occupying Ottomans used the church as their primary mosque—oblivious to the statue plastered over in the niche. Then, a century and a half later, during the siege of Buda in 1686, gunpowder stored in the castle up the street detonated, and the wall crumbled. Mary's triumphant face showed through, terrifying the Ottomans. Supposedly this was the only part of town taken from the Ottomans without a fight.

As you look down the **nave,** notice the banners. They've hung here since the Mass that celebrated Habsburg monarch Franz Josef's coronation at this church on June 8, 1867. In a sly political compromise to curry favor in the Hungarian part of his territory, Franz Josef was "emperor" of Austria, but only "king" of Hungary. (If you see the old German phrase "K+K"—still used today as a boast of royal quality—it refers to this *"König und Kaiser"* arrangement.) So, after F. J. was crowned emperor in Vienna, he came down the Danube and said to the Hungarians, "King me." (For more on the K+K system, see page 278.)

Continue circling around the church. On the left side of the church (toward the main altar from the gift shop) is the altar of St. Imre, the son of the great King (and later Saint) István. This heir to the Hungarian throne was mysteriously killed by a boar while hunting when he was only 19 years old. Though he didn't live long enough to do anything important, he rode his father's coattails to sainthood. The next chapel is the tomb of Béla III, utterly insignificant except that this is one of only two tombs of Hungarian kings that still exist in the country. The rest—including all of the biggies—were defiled by the Ottomans. Up next to the main altar is the chapel of László—St. István's nephew, who stepped in as king of Hungary when the rightful heir, St. Imre, was killed.

Along the left aisle is the entrance to the upstairs gallery, which holds the **Museum of Ecclesiastical Art** (Egyházművé-szeti Gyűjteménye, same ticket and hours as church). The original Hungarian crown is under the Parliament's dome (see page 64)—but a replica is up here, and worth a peek. The church also hosts concerts (Oct–Feb only, maybe a few in shoulder season, none in summer; ticket desk at church entry).

• *Back outside, at the end of the square next to the Matthias Church, is the...*

Fishermen's Bastion (Halászbástya)

This Neo-Romanesque fantasy rampart offers beautiful views over the Danube to Pest. In the Middle Ages, the fish market was just

below here (in today's Víziváros, or "Water Town"), so this part of the rampart actually was guarded by fishermen. The current structure, however, is completely artificial— yet another example of Budapest sprucing itself up for 1896. Its seven pointy towers represent the seven Magyar tribes. The cone-headed arcades are reminiscent of tents the nomadic Magyars called home before they moved west to Europe.

Paying 400 Ft to climb up the bastion makes little sense. Enjoy virtually the same view through the windows (left of café) for free. The café offers a scenic break if you don't mind the tour groups. Note that the grand staircase leading down from the bastion offers a handy shortcut to the Víziváros neighborhood and Batthyány tér (for affordable restaurants there, see page 232 in the Eating chapter).

• *Between the bastion and the church stands a statue of...*

St. István (c. 967–1038)

Hungary's first Christian king tamed the nomadic, pagan Magyars and established strict laws and the concept of private property.

In the late 900s, King Géza of Hungary lost a major battle against the forces of Christian Europe—and realized that he must raise his son Vajk as a Catholic and convert his people, or they would be forcefully driven out of Europe. Vajk took the Christian name István (EESHT-vahn, "Stephen") and was baptized in the year 1000. The reliefs on this statue show the commissioners of the pope crowning St. István, bringing Hungary into the fold of Christendom. This put Hungary on the map as a fully European kingdom, forging alliances that would endure for centuries. Without this pivotal event, Hungarians believe that the Magyar nation would have been lost. A passionate evangelist—more for the survival of his Magyar nation than for the salvation of his people—István beheaded those who wouldn't convert. To make his point perfectly clear, he quartered his reluctant uncle and sent him on four separate, simultaneous tours of the country to show Hungarians that Christianity was a smart choice. Gruesome as he was, István was sainted within 30 years of his death.

• *Directly across from Matthias Church is a charming little street called...*

Szentháromság Utca

Halfway down this street on the right, look for the venerable **Ruszwurm** café—the oldest in Budapest (see page 236 in Eating chapter). At the end of the street is an equestrian statue of the war hero **András Hadik.** If you examine the horse closely, you'll see that his, ahem, undercarriage has been polished to a high shine. Local students rub these for good luck before a big exam.

Continue out to the terrace and appreciate views of the Buda Hills—the "Beverly Hills" of Budapest, draped with orchards, vineyards, and the homes of the wealthiest Budapesters. If you go down the stairs here, then turn right up the street, you'll reach the entrance of the World War II-era **"Hospital in the Rock,"** which you can tour to learn about the Nazi and communist era of Castle Hill (recommended and described on page 59).

• Retrace your steps back to Matthias Church. Some visitors will have had their fill of Castle Hill; if so, you can make a graceful exit down the big staircase below the Fishermen's Bastion.

But if you'd like to extend your walk to the northern part of Castle Hill, turn your attention to the jarringly modern building next to Matthias Church on Fortuna utca...

Hilton Hotel

Built in 1976, the Hilton was the first plush Western hotel in town.

Before 1989, it was a gleaming center of capitalism, offering a cushy refuge for Western travelers and a stark contrast to what was, at the time, a very gloomy city. To minimize the controversy of building upon so much history, architects thoughtfully incorporated the medieval ruins into its modern design. Halfway down the hotel's facade, you'll see fragments of a 13th-century wall, with a monument to King Matthias Corvinus. After the wall, continue along the second half of the Hilton Hotel facade. Turn right

into the gift-shop entry, and then go right again inside the second glass door. Through yet another glass door, stairs on the left lead down to a reconstructed 13th-century Dominican cloister. For an even better look at what was here back then, go back up the stairs and turn left. As you enter the lounge, look out the back windows to see fragments of the 13th-century Dominican church incorporated into the structure of the hotel. If you stood here eight centuries ago, you'd be looking straight down the church's nave. You can even see tomb markers in the floor.

Back out on the street, cross the little park and duck into the entryway of the **Fortuna Passage.** Along the passageway to the courtyard, you can see the original Gothic arches of the house that once stood here. In the Middle Ages, every homeowner had the right to sell wine without paying taxes—but only in the passage of his own home. He'd set up a table here, and his neighbors would come by to taste the latest vintage. These passageways evolved into very social places, like the corner pub.

Leaving the passage, turn left down Fortuna utca and walk to the end of the street, where you'll see (on the right) the low-profile **Vienna Gate.** If you go through it and walk for about 10 days, you'll get to Vienna. (For now, settle for climbing up to the top for a view of some Buda residential neighborhoods.)

• *Now walk left along the hulking, mosaic-roofed National Archive building (with your back to the Danube) until you reach the...*

Remains of St. Mary Magdalene Church

This was once known as the Kapisztrán Templom, named after a hero of the Battle of Belgrade in 1456, an early success in the

struggle to keep the Ottomans out of Europe. (King Matthias' father, János Hunyadi, led the Hungarians in that battle.) The pope was so tickled by the victory that he decreed that all church bells should toll at noon in memory of the battle—and, technically, they still do. (Californians might recognize Kapisztrán's Spanish name: San Juan Capistrano.) This church was destroyed by bombs in World War II, though no worse than Matthias Church. But, since this part of town was depopulated

after the war, there was no longer a need for a second church. The remains of the church were torn down, the steeple was rebuilt as a memorial, and a carillon was added—so that every day at noon, the bells can still toll...and be enjoyed by the monument of János Kapisztrán, just across the square.

• *Our walk is finished, but there are a few more options nearby. You can walk out to the terrace just beyond the big building for another look at the Buda Hills. From here, just to the right*

*(near the flagpole), is the entrance to the **Museum of Military History**, with a mountain of army-surplus artifacts from Hungary's gloriously unsuccessful military history (described on page 59 of the Sights chapter). If you continue around the terrace past the museum, at the northern point of Castle Hill you'll find an old **Turkish grave**, honoring a pasha who once ruled here during Ottoman times.*

If you're ready to leave Castle Hill, you can backtrack to the Fishermen's Bastion and walk down the grand staircase there (into the Víziváros neighborhood). Or you can head out through the Vienna Gate and follow the road downhill. You'll run into bustling Moszkva tér, which has a handy Metro stop (M2/red line) and a huge, modern, popular Mammut shopping complex.

LEOPOLD TOWN WALK

Lipótváros, from the Parliament to the Chain Bridge

The Parliament building, which dominates Pest's skyline, is the centerpiece of a banking and business district that bustles by day but is relatively quiet at night and on weekends. Called Lipótváros ("Leopold Town"), this area is one of Budapest's most genteel quarters, and features some of the best of Budapest's many monuments. This walk also takes in some of the city's most grandiose landmarks: the Parliament, St. István's Basilica, the Gresham Palace, and the Chain Bridge.

Note that you can do the first part of this walk while waiting for your Parliament tour to begin.

ORIENTATION

Getting There: We'll begin on Kossuth tér, behind the Parliament. You can take the M2/red line to the Kossuth tér stop; or, from southern Pest (such as the Great Market Hall, or Vigadó tér near Vörösmarty tér), take tram #2 along the Danube embankment.

Length of This Walk: Allow 90 minutes, not including time to enter the sights.

Parliament: 2,600 Ft, English tours usually daily at 10:00, 12:00, and 14:00, Mon–Sat sometimes also at 16:00, Kossuth tér 1–3, tel. 1/441-4904, www.parlament.hu.

St. István's Basilica: Free, treasury—400 Ft, observation deck—500 Ft, Mon–Fri 9:00–17:00, Sat 9:00–13:00, Sun 13:00–17:00, observation deck has shorter hours and is closed Nov–March, Szent István tér.

Hungarian Museum of Trade and Tourism: 600 Ft, Wed–Mon 11:00–19:00, closed Tue, Szent István tér 15, tel. 1/375-6249, www.mkvm.hu.

Starring: Grand buildings, fine facades, and monuments, monuments, monuments.

THE WALK BEGINS

• *Start in the large square—half-paved, half-grassy—on the non-river side of the gigantic, can't-miss-it, red-domed...*

Hungarian Parliament (Országház)

The Parliament was built from 1885 to 1902 to celebrate the Hungarian millennium year of 1896 (see sidebar on page 40). Its

elegant frilly spires and riverside location were inspired by its counterpart in London (where the architect studied). When completed, the Parliament was a striking and cutting-edge example of the mix-and-match Historicist style of the day—just as Frank Gehry's undulating buildings are examples of today's bold new aesthetic. Like the Hungarian people, this building is at once grandly ambitious and a somewhat motley hodgepodge of various influences—a Neo-Gothic palace topped with a Neo-Renaissance dome, which once had a huge red communist star on top of the tallest spire. Fittingly, it's the city's top icon. The best views of the Parliament are from across the Danube—especially in the late-afternoon sunlight.

The enormous building—with literally miles of stairs—was appropriate for a time when Budapest ruled much of Eastern Europe. But today it feels just plain too big—the legislature only occupies an eighth of the building. Like Britain's Parliament, this building used to be home to a House of Lords and a House of Commons. The Lords are long gone, and their vacated territory is what visitors usually tour (but you sometimes might see the House of Commons, if Parliament is not in session).

The interior—decorated with 84 pounds of gold—is even more glorious than the facade. Apart from all that opulence, it also holds (directly under the dome) the **Hungarian crown.** This quintessential symbol of Hungarian sovereignty is supposedly the original one that Pope

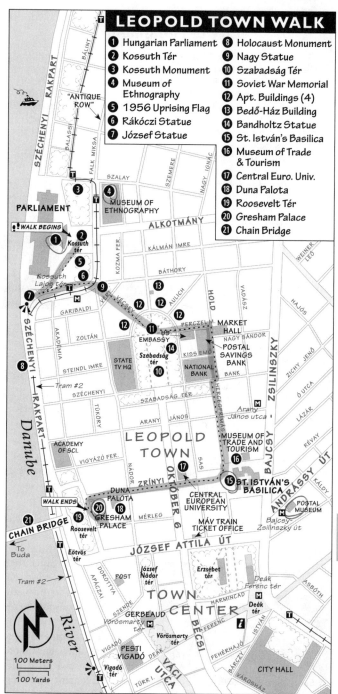

LEOPOLD TOWN WALK

1 Hungarian Parliament
2 Kossuth Tér
3 Kossuth Monument
4 Museum of Ethnography
5 1956 Uprising Flag
6 Rákóczi Statue
7 József Statue
8 Holocaust Monument
9 Nagy Statue
10 Szabadság Tér
11 Soviet War Memorial
12 Apt. Buildings (4)
13 Bedő-Ház Building
14 Bandholtz Statue
15 St. István's Basilica
16 Museum of Trade & Tourism
17 Central Euro. Univ.
18 Duna Palota
19 Roosevelt Tér
20 Gresham Palace
21 Chain Bridge

City of Monuments

There's a reason why Budapest is so monument-crazy. In 1897, German Emperor Wilhelm II came to visit his ally and rival, Habsburg Emperor Franz Josef, here in Budapest. Wilhelm commented on how few monuments graced the city streets, prompting a jealous Franz Josef to fund the immediate creation of 10 new statues around town. The Budapesters' enjoyment of a good monument continues today. Here are a few favorites, scattered around the city:

- **Attila József,** the brooding young poet, on the riverbank by the Parliament (see page 123).

- **Imre Nagy,** the brave anti-communist leader, standing pensively on a bridge just behind Parliament (see page 124).
- **Empty Shoes** lining the Danube riverbank between the Parliament and the Chain Bridge, honoring Jews who stood there before being executed by the Nazis (see page 123).
- **Anonymous,** the first scribe to chronicle the history of the Hungarian people, in City Park's Vajdahunyad Castle (see page 190).
- **George Washington,** minding his own business deep in City Park near Vajdahunyad Castle (see page 190).
- **1956,** a gigantic rusted-metal hull in City Park, honoring the way Hungarians came together to attempt to throw off Soviet rule (see page 187).
- **Heroes' Square,** where 21 Hungarian leaders (and one angel) stand sternly as a Who's Who of Hungarian history (see page 77).
- **Memento Park,** a collection of surviving communist-era statues and monuments that evoke the Red old days (see page 86).

Sylvester II sent to Hungary to crown István on Christmas Day

in the year 1000. Since then the crown has been hidden, stolen, lost, and found again and again...supposedly bending the cross on top in the process. That original, simple crown has been encrusted with jewels and (as a gift from a Byzantine emperor) adorned with a circlet. This makes the crown look like a hybrid of East and West—perhaps appropriately, as for much of history Budapest was seen as the gateway to the Orient. In modern times, the crown actually spent time in Fort Knox, Kentucky, where the US government kept it safe between World War II and 1978, when Jimmy Carter returned it to Hungary.

• *The vast square behind the Parliament is studded with attractions.*

Kossuth Tér

This square is sprinkled with interesting monuments and packed with Hungarian history. Stand by the tall, silver-colored flagpole (which flies a flag only for special occasions), facing **entrance "X"** at the back of the building. Waiting patiently are two lines of visitors ready to tour the Parliament (one line to buy tickets, the other waiting for their tour time). If you'd like to take the tour, get in the line marked *For Buying Tickets* and wait for your turn to buy tickets now (English tours several times daily; for details, see page 65 in the Sights chapter).

Just to the right, notice the big black box that seems to be melting like a candle. The **eternal flame** flickering at the top honors the victims of the 1956 Uprising, many of whom died in this square (explained later).

Turn 90 degrees to the right. At the far end of the grassy park, a statue of the square's namesake, **Lajos Kossuth,** rallies the people of Hungary to arms, as leader of

the 1848 Revolution against the Habsburgs. Below him, on the left, a family gazes adoringly at Kossuth as they send their soldier son off to war; on the right, we see that people of all walks of life joined the (ultimately unsuccessful) rebellion. (For more on Kossuth, see page 185.)

The street that leaves this square behind Kossuth is Falk Miksa utca, Budapest's **"antique row"**—a great place to browse for nostalgic souvenirs (see page 242 in the Shopping chapter).

Walk halfway across the big, empty asphalt lot behind the Parliament. Look back and across the street to see the **Museum of Ethnography.** While its collection of Hungarian folk artifacts is good (closed Mon, see page 65), the building is even more notable.

1956

The year 1956 is etched into the Hungarian psyche. In that year, the people of Budapest staged the first major uprising against the communist regime. It also marked the Eastern Bloc's first time that the Soviets implicitly acknowledged, in brutally putting down the uprising, that the people of Eastern Europe were not "communist by choice."

The seeds of revolution were sown with the death of a tyrant: Josef Stalin passed away on March 5, 1953. Suddenly the choke-hold that Moscow had held on its satellite states loosened. During this time of "de-Stalinization," Hungarian premier Imre Nagy presided over two years of mild reform, before his political opponents (and Moscow) became nervous and demoted him. (For more on Nagy, see page 124.)

In 1955, Austria declared its neutrality in the Cold War. This thrust Hungary to the front line of the Iron Curtain, and raised the stakes both for Hungarians who wanted freedom and for Soviets who wanted to preserve their buffer zone. When Stalin's successor Nikita Khrushchev condemned Stalin's crimes in a "secret speech" to communist leaders in February of 1956, it emboldened the Soviet Bloc's dissidents. A workers' strike in Poznań, Poland, in October inspired Hungarians to follow their example.

On October 23, 1956, the Hungarian uprising began. A student union group gathered in Budapest at 15:00 to articulate a list of 16 demands against the communist regime. Then they marched toward Parliament, their number gradually swelling. One protester defiantly cut the Soviet-style insignia out of the center of the Hungarian flag, which would become the uprising's symbol.

By nightfall, some 200,000 protestors filled Kossuth tér behind Parliament, calling for Imre Nagy, the one communist leader they believed could bring change. Nagy finally appeared around 21:00. Ever the pragmatic politician, he implored patience. Following the speech, a large band of protesters took matters into their own hands, marched to City Park, and tore down the hated Stalin statue that stood there (see page 187).

Another group went to the National Radio building to read their demands on the air. The ÁVH (communist police) refused, and eventually opened fire on the protestors. The peaceful protests evolved into an armed insurrection, as frightened civilians gathered weapons and supplies.

Overnight, Moscow decided to intervene. Budapesters awoke on October 24 to find Red Army troops occupying their city. That morning, Imre Nagy—who had just been promoted again to prime minister—promised reforms and tried to keep a lid on the simmering discontent.

The next day, October 25, a huge crowd gathered on Kossuth tér behind the Parliament to hear from Nagy. In the hubbub, shots rang out, Hungarian and Soviet soldiers opened fire on the (mostly unarmed) crowd, and at least 70 protesters were killed and more than 100 injured.

The Hungarians fought back with an improvised guerilla resistance. They made use of any guns they could get their hands on, as well as Molotov cocktails, to strike against the Soviet occupiers. Many adolescents (the celebrated "Pest Youth") participated. The fighting tore apart the city, and some of the fallen were buried in impromptu graves in city parks.

Political infighting in Moscow paralyzed the Soviet response, and an uneasy ceasefire fell over Budapest. For 10 tense days, it appeared that the Soviets might allow Nagy to push through some reforms. Nagy, a firmly entrenched communist, had always envisioned a less repressive regime...but within limits. While he was at first reluctant to take on the mantle of the uprising's leadership, he gradually began to echo what he was hearing on the streets. He called for free elections, the abolishment of the ÁVH, the withdrawal of Soviet troops, and (crucially) Hungary's secession from the Warsaw Pact.

But when the uprisers attacked and killed ÁVH officers and communist leaders in Budapest, it bolstered the case of the Moscow hardliners. On November 4, the Red Army launched a brutal counterattack in Budapest that left the rebels reeling. At 5:20 that morning, Imre Nagy's voice came over the radio to beg the world for assistance. Later that morning, he sought asylum at the Yugoslav Embassy across the street from City Park. He was never seen alive in public again.

János Kádár—an ally of Nagy's who was palatable to the uprisers, yet firmly loyal to Moscow—was installed as prime minister. The fighting dragged on for about another week, but the uprising was eventually crushed. By the end, 2,500 Hungarians and more than 700 Soviets were dead, and 20,000 Hungarians were injured. Communist authorities arrested more than 15,000 people, of whom at least 200 were executed (including Imre Nagy). Anyone who had participated in the uprising was blackballed; fearing this and other forms of retribution, some 200,000 Hungarians fled to the West.

Though the 1956 Uprising met a tragic end, within a few years Kádár did succeed in softening the regime, and the milder, so-called "goulash communism" emerged. And today, even though the communists are long gone, the legacy of 1956 pervades the Hungarian consciousness. Some Budapest buildings are still pockmarked with bullet holes from '56, and many of Hungarians who fled the country in that year still have not returned. October 23 remains a major Hungarian holiday. In 2006, Budapest commemorated the 50th anniversary of its uprising.

The design was actually the first runner-up for the Parliament building, so they built it here, where it originally housed the Supreme Court.

• *Now continue through the lot to the opposite end. At the edge of the grassy park, find the Hungarian flag with a hole cut out of the center.*

This **flag** commemorates the 1956 Uprising, when protesters removed the communist seal the

Soviets had added to their flag. Two days into that revolt, on October 25, the ÁVH (communist police) and Soviet troops on the rooftop above opened fire on demonstrators gathered in this square—massacring many and leaving no doubt that Moscow would not tolerate dissent. For more on this tragic chapter of Hungarian history, see the "1956" sidebar.

Now imagine this same park in the **fall of 2006,** when it became the site of a new wave of demonstrations—initially impromptu, then carefully choreographed—against Hungary's prime minister,

Ferenc Gyurcsány. Using particularly colorful language in a speech intended only for his own party members, Gyurcsány admitted to lies, deceit, and deception in the way he'd run the government and the recent election. When the tape was leaked to the media, Hungarians showed up here to

(unsuccessfully) demand Gyurcsány's resignation. While a few of the demonstrations turned violent, most remained peaceful. For more about these recent events, see page 406.

In the field behind this flag, you'll see a monument to yet another rebel: **Ferenc Rákóczi,** who valiantly (but unsuccessfully) led the Hungarians in their War of Independence (1703–1711) against the Habsburgs. (For more on this leader, see page 184.)

• *Now walk along the path between the Parliament and the park toward the river. When you reach the tram tracks, turn right and continue past the little guardhouse toward the Danube. You'll see (with his back to you)...*

LEOPOLD TOWN WALK

Attila József (1905–1937)

This beloved modern poet lived a tumultuous, productive, and short life before he killed himself by jumping in front of a train at age 32. József's poems of life, love, and death—mostly written in the 1920s and 1930s—are considered the high point of Hungarian literature. His birthday (April 11) is celebrated as National Hungarian Poetry Day.

Here József re-enacts a scene from one of his best poems, "At the Danube." It's a hot day—his jacket lies in a heap next to him,

his shirtsleeves are rolled up, and he cradles his hat loosely in his left hand. Looking into his profound eyes, you sense the depth of an artist's tortured inner life. "As I sat on the bank of the Danube, I watched a watermelon float by," he begins. "As if flowing out of my heart, murky, wise, and great was the Danube." In the poem, József uses the Danube as a metaphor for life—for the way it has interconnected cities and also times—as he reflects that his ancestors likely pondered the Danube from this same spot...

• *Continue straight down toward the Danube, surveying the panorama from the top of the big staircase over the busy road. From here, you enjoy sweeping views across to Buda, dominated by Castle Hill.*

If you visually trace the Pest riverbank to the left, just before the tree-filled, riverfront park, you can just barely see several low-profile dots lining the embankment. This is a new...

Holocaust Monument

Consisting of 50 pairs of bronze shoes, this monument commemorates the Jews who were killed when the Nazis' puppet government, the Arrow Cross, came to power in Hungary in 1944. While many Jews were sent to concentration camps, the Arrow Cross massacred some of them right here, shooting them and letting their bodies fall into the Danube.

You can't walk to the shoes directly from here (there's no safe crosswalk over the embankment road). For a slightly better view of the Holocaust Monument, you can walk along the tram tracks to another viewpoint just downriver; but to reach the shoes themselves, you'll have to access the embankment from near the Chain Bridge, then walk back up this way along the water (you can do this at the end of this walk).

• *Backtrack past Attila József, cross the tram tracks, and walk along the ugly building (with an entrance to the Metro) up to the back corner of Kossuth tér. Across the street in a little park (at Vértanúk tere), you'll see a monument to...*

Imre Nagy (1896-1958)

The Hungarian politician Imre Nagy (EEM-ray nodge), now thought of as an anti-communist hero, was actually a lifelong com-

munist. In the 1930s, he allegedly worked for the Soviet secret police. In the late 1940s, he quickly moved up the hierarchy of Hungary's communist government, becoming prime minister during a period of reform in 1953. But when his proposed changes alarmed Moscow, Nagy was quickly demoted.

When the 1956 Uprising broke out on October 23, Imre Nagy was drafted (reluctantly, some say) to become the head of the movement to soften the severity of the communist regime. Because he was an insider, it briefly seemed that Nagy might hold the key to finding a middle path between the suffocating totalitarian model of Moscow and the freedom of the West (represented by the bridge he's standing on). Some suspect that Nagy himself didn't fully grasp the dramatic sea change represented by the uprising. When he appeared at the Parliament building on the night of October 23 to speak to the reform-craving crowds for the first time, he began by addressing his countrymen—as communist politicians always did—with, "Dear comrades..." When the audience booed, he amended it: "Dear friends..."

But the optimism was short-lived. The Soviets violently put down the uprising, arrested and sham-tried Nagy, executed him, and buried him face-down in an unmarked grave. The regime forced Hungary to forget about Nagy.

Later, when communism was in its death throes in 1989, the Hungarian people rediscovered Nagy as a hero. His body was located, exhumed, and given a ceremonial funeral at Heroes' Square. And today, thanks to this monument, Nagy keeps a watchful eye on today's lawmakers in the Parliament across the way.

• *Go up the diagonal street behind Nagy, called Vécsey utca. After just one block, you emerge into...*

Szabadság Tér (Liberty Square)

"Liberty Square"—one of Budapest's most inviting public spaces—was so named when a Habsburg barracks here was torn down after

the Hungarians gained some autonomy in the late 19th century.

• *Walk around the stout obelisk to the center of the square. Stand facing the obelisk.*

This is the **Soviet War Memorial,** commemorating "Liberation Day": April 4, 1945, when the Soviets officially forced the Nazis out of Hungary. As a very rare reminder of the Soviet days—you almost never see hammers-and-sickles in the streets of Hungary anymore—it has often been defaced, which is why a fence surrounds it.

In order to erect this monument, the Soviets took down a giant flagpole that flew the Hungarian flag. You might see (in the grassy field facing the memorial) a **tent** and wooden crosses representing a similarly controversial topic: Hungary's massive territorial losses after World War I, through the Treaty of Trianon (described on page 399). The well-worded political statement on the tent explains that protestors want to remove the Soviet monument and reinstate the flag. Ponder for a moment this complex issue: Soviet troops did liberate Hungary from the Nazis. Does their leaders' later oppression of the Hungarians make these soldiers' sacrifice less worthy of being honored?

Ringing the top of Szabadság tér (behind the memorial) are **four ornate apartment buildings,** typical of high-class town-houses from Budapest's Golden Age in the late 1800s. While each one is strikingly different from the next, they are all typical of Historicism—the mix-and-match aesthetic that was popular at the time. Like residential buildings

throughout Pest, the ground floor has particularly high ceilings. But the most desirable location was the second and third floors—up away from the rabble of street life, but with relatively few stairs (in a time before elevators were common). Notice that in each of these building, those are the only floors with balconies.

Here's an optional detour for architecture buffs: If you go up the middle street between these buildings (Honvéd utca, straight ahead from the middle of Szabadság tér), a few doors down on the right you'll find one of Budapest's finest Art Nouveau buildings, **Bedő-Ház.** The curvy green facade is a textbook example of the Hungarian Secession style. Built in 1903, the building was dilapidated for decades before a studs-out restoration in 2007. Inside is a small café and three floors with a modest but interesting exhibit of Art Nouveau items (mostly elegantly delicate furniture, plus some dishes and other household items; 1,000 Ft, Mon–Sat 10:00–17:00, closed Sun, Honvéd utca 3, tel. 1/269-4622).

• *Back in the middle of Szabadság tér, turn with your back to the Soviet memorial and look down to the far end of the square.*

On the right is the giant **Hungarian State Television** building (formerly the stock exchange). This is home to MTV—not

music television, but Magyar television. As a symbol of government-run media, it was one of the few buildings damaged in the 2006 riots. The genteel open-air **café** in the middle of the park is an inviting place for a coffee break. Across the square (on the left), the yellow corner building is the **US Embassy.** This is where Cardinal József Mindszenty holed up for 15 years during the Cold War to evade arrest by the communist authorities (see page 303). A few steps down the left side of the square (and worth a detour for military buffs) stands a statue of **Harry Hill Bandholtz,** a US officer from World War I who prevented treasured Hungarian art from being taken by Romania. This statue stood inside the US Embassy for 40 chilly years (1949–1989), but now it's back out in the open.

• *We're headed for Perczel Mór utca, the street next to the US Embassy—but you'll have to detour a bit to the left (and tiptoe around some barricades) to get there. After one block on Perczel Mór utca, turn right onto...*

Hold Utca

Look for the big yellow *Vásárcsarnok* sign. This **market hall** was built around the same time as the Great Market Hall, but it's smaller and less touristy—worth poking around inside. If you're hungry, consider shopping for a picnic here to eat at Szabadság tér (Mon 6:30–17:00, Tue–Fri 6:30–18:00, Sat 6:30–14:00, closed Sun).

Walking along Hold utca, keep your eyes on the green-and-yellow roofline of the building on the right. This **Postal Savings Bank,** designed by Ödön Lechner in the late 19th century, combines traditional folk motifs with cutting-edge Art Nouveau in an attempt to forge a new, distinct Hungarian national style. A key element of this emerging style was the use of colorful mosaic tiles to decorate the roof. (In its truest form, this style uses pyrogranite ceramic tiles from the famous Zsolnay porcelain factory in the city of Pécs—see page 346.) The beehives along the rooftop are an appropriate symbol for a bank— where people store money as bees store honey. When asked why he lavished such attention on the rooftop, which few people can see, Lechner said, "To please the birds."

Notice that the Postal Savings Bank is attached to the next building with a walkway. This is the **National Bank of Hungary;** on the second floor, fun reliefs trace the history of money.

• *Walk to the end of the giant bank building, then continue two blocks straight ahead up Hercegprimás utca. You'll emerge into a broad plaza in front of Budapest's biggest Catholic church...*

St. István's Basilica (Szent István Bazilika)

The church is only about 100 years old—like most Budapest landmarks, it was built around the millennial celebrations of 1896. Designed by three architects over more than 50 years, St. István's is particularly eclectic. Each one had a favorite style: Neoclassical, Neo-Renaissance, Neo-Baroque. Construction was delayed for a while when the giant dome collapsed midway through.

Though it looks like a major landmark and is packed with tour groups, the church isn't that compelling inside. Step into the dark but recently renovated **interior** and you'll see not Jesus, but St. István (Stephen), Hungary's first Christian king, glowing above the high altar.

The church's main claim to fame is the **"holy right hand"** of **St. István.** The sacred fist—a somewhat grotesque, 1,000-year-old

withered stump—is in a jeweled box in the chapel to the left of the main altar (follow signs for *Szent Jobb Kápolna*, chapel often closed). Pop in a 200-Ft coin for two minutes of light, and ask the guard for tips on taking the best photo. Posted information describes the hand's unlikely journey to this spot.

On your way out, in the back-right corner of the church, you'll find a small exhibit about the building's history.

The church also has a skippable **treasury** and a panoramic **observation deck.** While the views over Budapest's rooftops are pretty distant (and disappointing without a good zoom lens), it offers a good sense of the sprawl of the city. You have various options: You can walk up the entire way (302 steps); or you can take an elevator to midlevel (with WCs), where you can follow signs to another elevator (plus 42 steps) or climb 137 steps to the top.

• *Hiding around the left side of the basilica is the...*

Hungarian Museum of Trade and Tourism (Magyar Kereskedelmi és Vendéglátóipari Múzeum)

This museum takes a nostalgic look at workaday 19th-century Pest commerce. Recently re-opened in a stately former bank building, the museum has a small permanent collection (one room with dusty old artifacts and minimal information), and generally well-presented temporary exhibits offering a peek into the fancy hotels, restaurants, and coffeehouses of the day. Recent topics have included old-fashioned cookbooks, champagne, and the history of ice cream. If these exhibits appeal to you, take a look. The lobby area leading to the collection is lined with new and old advertising posters, including some fun vintage ads for the beloved-by-Hungarians Unicum liquor (see page 223).

• *From here, you have two options. If you'd like to skip ahead to the* **Andrássy Út Walk** *(on page 148), you're very close: Walk around the right side of the basilica, turn right on busy Bajcsy-Zsilinszky út, and you're one block from the start of Andrássy út (across the street, on your left).*

LEOPOLD TOWN WALK

*Or you can complete this walk to Vörösmarty tér, where you can begin the **Pest Town Center Walk**. For this option, walk straight ahead from St. István's main staircase down...*

Zrínyi Utca

Recently pedestrianized Zrínyi utca is a fine people zone, and a handy way to connect St. István's to the river. Plans are in the

works to redevelop other central Pest streets to be as pedestrian-friendly as this one.

At the bottom of the plaza, you'll cross **Sas utca,** home to several good and trendy restaurants (including Café Kör to the right, and Dió and Mokka to the left). Consider window-shopping here and reserving a place for dinner tonight (see page 228 in Eating).

Two blocks down, on the right-hand corner, is **Central European University.** Offering graduate study for Americans and students from all over Central and Eastern Europe, this school is predominantly funded by George Soros, a Hungarian who escaped communism by emigrating to the US, then became a billionaire through shrewd investments. Today Soros is loved by the Left and loathed by the Right as a major contributor to liberal campaigns. But he hasn't forgotten worthy causes back home. In addition to funding this university, he is at the forefront of a movement for Central Europeans to better protect the rights of their huge Roma (Gypsy) population. The university's CEU Bookshop, a few steps up Zrínyi utca toward the basilica, is the best place in town to find academic books about the region in English (listed on page 43).

Continue down Zrínyi utca. After crossing Nádor utca, on the left you'll see **Duna Palota** ("Danube Palace")—a former casino, and today a venue and ticket office for Hungária Koncert's popular tourist shows. If you're up for a crowd-pleasing show of either classical or folk music, drop in here to check your options (see page 250 in the Entertainment & Nightlife chapter).

Zrínyi utca dead-ends at the big traffic circle called **Roosevelt tér.** While the square is named for FDR, who helped defeat the Nazis in World War II, the statues here actually depict Hungarians. The one on the right is István Széchenyi, the early 19th-century nobleman who, among other deeds, built the Chain Bridge and founded the Hungarian Academy of Sciences (both of which face this square). On the left is the statesman Ferenc Deák, who fought for Hungarian autonomy through peaceful means.

• *Turn left and walk a half-block to the entrance (on the left) of the...*

LEOPOLD TOWN WALK

Gresham Palace

The Gresham Palace was Budapest's first building in the popular Historicist style, and also incorporates elements of Art Nouveau.

Budapest boomed at a time when architectural eclecticism—mashing together bits and pieces of different styles—was in vogue. But because much of the city's construction was compressed into a short window of time, even these disparate styles enjoy an unusual harmony. Damaged in World War II, the building was an eyesore for decades. (Legend has it that an aging local actress refused to move out, so developers had to wait for her to pass on before they could reclaim the building.) In 1999, the Gresham Palace was meticulously restored to its former glory. Even if you can't afford to stay here (see page 211 in the Sleeping chapter), saunter into the lobby and absorb the gorgeous details. For example, not only did they have to re-create the unique decorative tiles—they had to rebuild the original machines that made the tiles.

• *Grandly spanning the Danube from this spot is Budapest's best bridge...*

Chain Bridge (Széchenyi Lánchíd)

One of the world's great bridges connects Pest's Roosevelt tér and Buda's Adam Clark tér. This historic, iconic bridge, guarded by lions (symbolizing power), is Budapest's most enjoyable and conve-

nient bridge to cross on foot.

Until the mid-19th century, only pontoon barges spanned the Danube between Buda and Pest. In the winter, the pontoons had to be pulled in, leaving locals to rely on ferries (in good weather) or a frozen river. People often walked across the frozen Danube, only to get stuck on the other side during a thaw, with nothing to do but wait for another cold snap.

Count István Széchenyi was stranded for a week trying to get to his father's funeral. After missing it, Széchenyi commissioned Budapest's first permanent bridge—which was also a major symbolic step toward another of Széchenyi's pet causes, the unification of Buda and Pest. The

Chain Bridge was built by Scotsman Adam Clark between 1842 and 1849, and it immediately became an important symbol of Budapest. Széchenyi—a man of the Enlightenment—charged both commoners and nobles a toll for crossing his bridge, making it an emblem of equality in those tense times. Like all of the city's bridges, the Chain Bridge was destroyed by the Nazis at the end of World War II, but was quickly rebuilt.

• *Our walk is over. From Roosevelt tér, you can catch bus #16 from in front of the Hungarian Academy of Sciences (at the right end of the square) to Castle Hill, or simply walk across the Chain Bridge for great views. For a better look at the Holocaust Monument, you can safely cross from here to the embankment, then follow it back toward the Parliament.*

If you'd like to wind up in the heart of Pest, Vörösmarty tér (and the start of my Pest Town Center Walk—see next chapter) is just two long blocks away: Turn left out of the Gresham Palace, and walk straight on Dorottya utca.

PEST TOWN CENTER WALK

Belváros, from Vörösmarty Tér to the Great Market Hall

Pest's Belváros ("Inner Town") is its gritty urban heart—simultaneously its most beautiful and ugliest district. You'll see fancy facades, some of Pest's best views from the Danube embankment, genteel old coffee houses that offer a whiff of the city's Golden Age, inviting oasis parks tucked between densely populated streets, and a cavernous, colorful market hall filled with Hungarian goodies. But you'll also experience crowds, grime, and pungent smells like nowhere else in Budapest. Remember: This is a city in transition. Local authorities plan to ban traffic from more and more Town Center streets in the coming years. If construction and torn-up pavement (common around here) impede your progress, be thankful that things will be nicer for your next visit. Within a decade, all of those rough edges will be sanded off...and tourists like you will be nostalgic for the "authentic" old days. (If you want the sanitized version today, stick with the other tourists on Váci utca.)

Even if this whole walk doesn't appeal to you, don't miss the spectacular Great Market Hall, described on page 143.

ORIENTATION

Getting There: Take the M1/yellow Metro line to the Vörösmarty tér stop.

Length of this Walk: Allow 90 minutes.

Károlyi Park: Free, open daily May–Aug 8:00–21:00, April and Sept 8:00–19:00, Oct–March 8:00–17:00.

Great Market Hall: Free, Mon 6:00–17:00, Tue–Fri 6:00–18:00, Sat 6:00–15:00, closed Sun, Fővám körút 1–3.

Starring: The urban core of Budapest, a gorgeous riverfront promenade, several of the city's top cafés, and a grand finale at the Great Market Hall.

THE WALK BEGINS

• *Start on the central square of the Town Center, Vörösmarty tér (at the M1 Metro stop of the same name). Face the giant, seated statue in the middle of the square.*

Vörösmarty Tér

As we begin exploring the central part of Pest, consider its humble history. In the mid-1600s, Pest was under Ottoman occupation and nearly deserted. By the 1710s, the Habsburgs had forced out the Ottomans, but this area remained a rough-and-tumble, often-flooded quarter just outside the Pest city walls. Peasants came here to enjoy watching brutal, staged fights between bloodhounds and bears (like cockfights, only bigger and angrier, with more fur and teeth). The rebuilding of Pest was gradual; most of the buildings you'll see on this walk are no older than 200 years.

Today this square—a hub of activity in the Town Center—is named for the 19th-century Romantic poet **Mihály Vörösmarty** (1800–1855), whose statue dominates the little park at the square's center. Writing during the time of reforms in the early 19th century, Vörösmarty was a Romantic whose poetry still stirs the souls of patriotic Hungarians—he's like Byron, Shelley, and Keats rolled into one. One of his  most famous works is a patriotic song whose popularity rivals the national anthem: "Be faithful to your country, all Hungarians." At Vörösmarty's feet, figures representing the Hungarian people hear his words and rise up together. During Vörösmarty's age, the peasant Magyar tongue was, for the very first time, considered worthy of literature. The people began to think of themselves not merely as "subjects of the Habsburg Empire"...but as Hungarians.

• *Facing the statue of Vörösmarty, turn 90 degrees to the left.*

At the north end of the square is the landmark **Gerbeaud** café and pastry shop. Between the World Wars, the well-to-do ladies of Budapest would meet here after shopping their way up Váci utca. Today it's still *the* meeting point in Budapest (for tourists, at least).

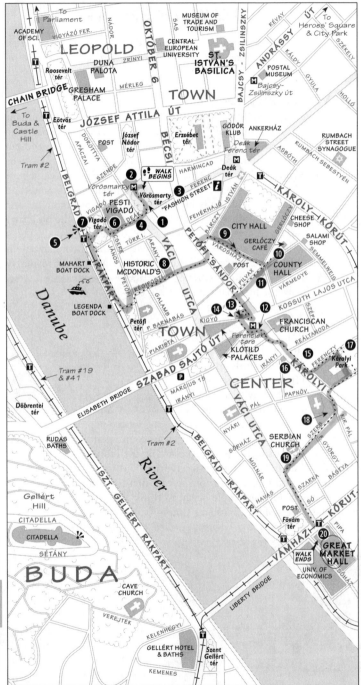

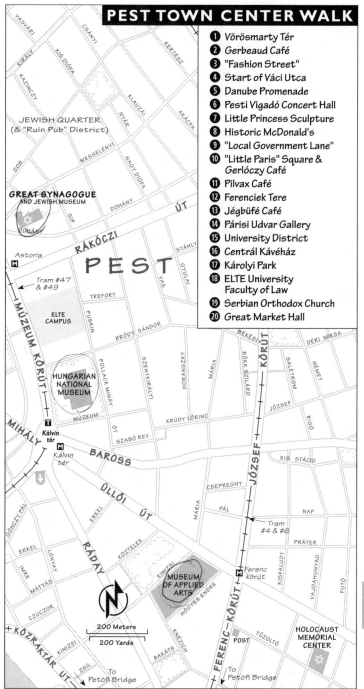

PEST TOWN CENTER WALK

1. Vörösmarty Tér
2. Gerbeaud Café
3. "Fashion Street"
4. Start of Váci Utca
5. Danube Promenade
6. Pesti Vigadó Concert Hall
7. Little Princess Sculpture
8. Historic McDonald's
9. "Local Government Lane"
10. "Little Paris" Square & Gerlóczy Café
11. Pilvax Café
12. Ferenciek Tere
13. Jégbüfé Café
14. Párisi Udvar Gallery
15. University District
16. Centrál Kávéház
17. Károlyi Park
18. ELTE University Faculty of Law
19. Serbian Orthodox Church
20. Great Market Hall

Consider stepping inside to appreciate the elegant old decor, or for a cup of coffee and a slice of cake (but meals here are overpriced—described on page 235). Or you could hold off for now—more appealing cafés await later on this walk.

The yellow **M1 Metro stop** between Vörösmarty and Gerbeaud is the entrance to the shallow *Földalatti*, or "underground"—the first subway on the Continent (built for the Hungarian millennial celebration in 1896). Today, it still carries passengers to Andrássy út sights, running under that street all the way to City Park.

• *Turn another 90 degrees to the left.*

This super-modern **glass building** is the newest addition to Vörösmarty tér. If you think its appearance is jarring, then you should have seen the communist-style eyesore it replaced. Downstairs is upscale shopping; higher up are offices; and at the top are luxury apartments.

• *Turn another 90 degrees to the left, and walk to the beginning of the Váci utca pedestrian street. Look up the street to your left.*

This street (Deák utca) was recently pedestrianized as a **"Fashion Street,"** lined with top-end shops. This is the easiest and most pleasant way to walk to Deák tér (where the three Metro lines converge), and beyond it, through Erzsébet tér to the boulevard called Andrássy út (❂ see the Andrássy Út Walk on page 148).

• *Extending straight ahead from Vörösmarty tér is a broad, bustling, pedestrianized shopping street. Look—but do not walk—down...*

Váci Utca

Dating from 1810–1850, Váci utca (VAHT-see OOT-zah) is one of the oldest streets of Pest. Váci utca means "street to Vác"—a town 25 miles to the north. This has long been the street where the elite of Pest would go shopping, then strut their stuff for their neighbors on an evening promenade. Today, the tourists do the strutting here—and the Hungarians go to American-style shopping malls.

This boulevard—Budapest's tourism artery—was a dreamland for Eastern Bloc residents back in the 1980s. It was here that they fantasized about what it might be like to be free, while drooling over Nikes, Adidas, and Big Macs before any of these "Western evils" were introduced elsewhere in the Warsaw Pact region.

Ironically, this street—once prized by Hungarians and other Eastern Europeans because it felt so Western—is what many Western tourists today mistakenly think is the "real Budapest." Visitors mesmerized by this people-friendly stretch of souvenir stands, Internet cafés, and upscale boutiques are likely to miss

some more interesting and authentic
areas just a block or two away.

Don't fall for this trap. You could
have a fun and fulfilling trip to this
city without setting foot on Váci utca.
In fact, this walk is designed to avoid
Váci utca as much as possible. (If you're
dying to saunter down Váci utca, this
walk concludes at its far end.) Instead,
we'll zigzag through the heart of Pest's
Town Center for a look at the *real* "real
Budapest."

• *Head for the river: Take the street
that runs along the left side of the big glass building at the bottom of
Vörösmarty tér. Cross the street and continue all the way to the railing
and tram tracks. You're right on the most colorful stretch of the...*

Danube Promenade (Dunakorzó)

Some of the best views in Budapest are from this walkway facing
Castle Hill—especially this stretch, between the white Elisabeth

Bridge (left) and the iconic Chain
Bridge (right). This is a favorite place to promenade *(korzó)*,
strolling aimlessly and greeting
friends. Imagine the days before
World War II, when—instead
of mid-century monstrosities
Marriott and InterContinental—
this strip was lined with elegant
grand hotels: Hungaria, Bristol, Carlton.

Take in the views of Buda, across the river (left to right):
Gellért Hill, topped with its distinctive Liberation Monument;
the Royal Palace, capping Castle Hill; and, farther along the hilltop, the colorful tile roof and spiny spire of the Matthias Church,
surrounded by the cone-shaped decorations of the Fishermen's
Bastion.

Dominating this part of the promenade is the Neo-Romantic-
style **Pesti Vigadó**—built in
the 1880s, and today undergoing a thorough renova-
tion. Charmingly, the word
vigadó—used to describe a
concert hall—literally means
"joyous place." In front is a
playful statue of **a girl with
her dog,** which captures the

fun-loving spirit along this drag. At the gap in the railing, notice the platform to catch **tram #2**, which goes frequently in each direction along the promenade—a handy and scenic way to connect riverside sights in Pest. (You can ride it to the right, to the Parliament; or to the left, to the Great Market Hall—where this walk ends.)

• *About 20 yards to the right, find the little statue wearing a jester's hat. She's playing on the railing with the castle behind her.*

The ***Little Princess*** is one of Budapest's symbols and a favorite photo-op for tourists. While many of the city's monuments have interesting back-stories, this one is an exception: It's just whimsical and fun.

• *Now walk down the promenade to the left (toward the white bridge). About 20 yards after the gap in the railing, watch for the easy-to-miss stairs leading down under the tram tracks, to a crosswalk that leads safely across the busy road to the riverbank. Look along the river.*

Lining the **embankment** are several long boats: Some are excursion boats for sightseeing trips up and down the Danube, while others are overpriced (but scenic) restaurants. If you're interested in taking a cruise (especially pleasant at night), you could cross the road here, then walk 100 yards downriver (left) to the Danube Legenda boat dock (described on page 51).

• *Continue walking downstream (left) down the promenade, in front of the blocky, off-white Marriott. When you reach the end of the Marriott complex, at the little parking lot, turn inland (left), cross the street, and walk up the street called Régi Posta utca. Head for the Golden Arches.*

Historic McDonald's

The unassuming McDonald's (on the left) was a landmark in Eastern Europe—the first McDonald's behind the Iron Curtain. Budapest has always been a little more rebellious, independent, and cosmopolitan than other Eastern European cities, whose

citizens flocked here during the communist era. Since you had to wait in a long line—stretching around the block—to get a burger, it wasn't "fast food"...but at least it was "West food." Váci utca also had a "dollar store," where you could buy hard-to-find items as long as you had Western currency. During the Cold War, Budapest was sort of the "Sin City" of the Eastern Bloc. (What happened in Budapest, stayed in Budapest. Unless the secret police were watching...which they always were...uh oh.)

• *After the McDonald's, Régi Posta utca crosses Váci utca.*

If you're curious about what you're missing, take a good look up and down this crowded drag. If you do return later for a stroll along Váci utca, be sure to look up. Along this street and throughout Pest, spectacular facades begin on the second floor, above a plain entryway (in the 1970s, the communist government made ground-floor shop windows uniformly dull). Pan up to see some of Pest's best architecture. These were the townhouses of the aristocracy whose mansions dotted the countryside. You might notice that some of the facades are plain. Many of these used to be more ornate, like the others, but they were destroyed by WWII bombs and rebuilt in a stripped-down style.

Here and elsewhere along Váci utca, you'll see restaurants touting Hungarian fare. Avoid these places. Any restaurant along this street is guaranteed to be at least half as good and twice as expensive as other eateries nearby. (For better options—some just a few steps from Váci utca—see the Eating chapter.)

• *Keep going across Váci utca and straight up Régi Posta utca (past the statue of Hermes). Cross the busy street (Petőfi Sándor utca), then jog a half-block left into the little square. Pause here to appreciate some eclectic and beautiful skinny facades. Turn right and head a few steps up Bárczy utca, then immediately turn right again onto Városház utca, which I think of as...*

"Local Government Lane"

As you walk down this street, the extremely long, pink-and-yellow building on your left is the **City Hall** (Városház). At the end of the block, the green building across the street is the **Pest County Hall.**

• *Don't miss the cute little square tucked between these buildings...*

"Little Paris" Square

On this spot, a local entrepreneur is trying to capture some of the Parisian-style elegance that once pervaded this fine city. The highly recommended **Gerlóczy Café** does a fine job reviving the refined café culture of Budapest's Golden Age. This is a great place for a sit-and-sip coffee stop or a full meal (described on page

226 in the Eating chapter)...though additional coffee stops are coming up soon.

For picnic-shopping, two Paris-style shops flank the café. On the right (at #3), marked *szalámibolt*, is a swanky *charcuterie* selling exclusively French and Italian salamis and pâtés. Up the street to the left of Gerlóczy Café is a fragrant *fromagerie* (or *sajtüzlet*) offering cheeses, wines, and an antipasti bar. Picnickers, go nuts. (Or, to buy Hungarian salami and other local goodies, wait for the Great Market Hall.)

• *Across from Gerlóczy Café, go straight down the street called Pilvax köz. On your left is the...*

Pilvax Café

While no longer an appealing place for coffee, this café is one of Budapest's most historic. On the morning of March 15, 1848, a collection of local intellectuals and artists—who came to be known as the "Pest Youth"—gathered here to listen to their friend Sándor Petőfi read a new poem. Petőfi's call to arms so inspired the group that they decided to revolt against their Habsburg oppressors...right away. Later that day, Petőfi read his poem again on the steps of the National Museum, rebels broke a beloved patriot out of jail at the castle, the group printed their list of 12 demands at a nearby print shop...and the 1848 Revolution had begun. To this day, March 15 remains an important national holiday. On the window, notice the giant red, white, and green ribbon badge—the Hungarian national colors and the symbol of that revolution. For more on 1848, see page 396.

• *Cross the busy street (Petőfi Sándor utca), then take an immediate left and follow the street to the end of the block. Stand at the busy highway and survey the area called...*

Ferenciek Tere

"Franciscan Square"—so named for the church across the highway—is a great place to take in some of Pest's best "diamond in the rough" architecture...fantastic facades that stand grim and caked with soot. Looking to the right (toward the Elisabeth Bridge),

you'll see that the busy street is flanked by twin apartment blocks called the **Klotild Palaces.** This is what happens when a proud city is put through the communist wringer for 40 years. (What would Paris or Rome look like today, if Stalin had somehow reached that far west?) It breaks your heart, even as you marvel at Hungarian resilience.

Imagine this area before 20th-century construction routed a major thoroughfare though it, when people could stroll freely amidst these elaborate facades. Someday, you might not have to imagine. Many of the buildings are slated for renovation, and plans are afoot to route the highway underground to create a traffic-free park here. (It can't happen fast enough.) But for now, breathe in the real Budapest.

Head toward the bridge, noticing (on your right) another artifact of communism: the unique **Jégbüfé.** This communist-era *bisztró* serves stand-up coffee and cakes to urbanites on the go (see page 236 in the Eating chapter).

• *Thirty yards after Jégbüfé, on the right, look for the low-profile entrance (at Kossuth Lajos út 11) to...*

Párisi Udvar Gallery

This "Parisian Courtyard" is the grandest of Pest's many hidden galleries, once used for elegant shopping, now faded and largely unused. Enjoy the delicate woodwork, fine mosaics that glitter evocatively in the low light, and breathtaking stained-glass dome. It's remarkable that such a beautiful space sits ignored, just a couple of blocks from the main shopping street. While many of the storefronts inside are abandoned, a few are still alive and kicking (including a bookstore that sells English guidebooks). This place is a reminder that if you only experience what's on the main streets in Budapest, you'll miss a big  part of the story. (Note that you can also access this gallery from the other end, around the corner at Petőfi Sándor utca 2.)

This gallery is just the beginning. Behind most of Pest's once-grand, now-crumbling facades, you'll find cozy courtyards where residents carry out much of their lives. These courtyards, shared among neighbors and ringed by a common balcony, stay cool through the summer. Poking into some of these courtyards (which are generally open to the public, offering a handy shortcut through city blocks) is an essential Back Door experience for understanding the inner life of the city.

• *Exit the gallery the way you came in, and proceed straight ahead and down the stairs into the pedestrian underpass. Surfacing on the other side, turn left, walk to the end of the block, then turn right and walk along Károlyi Mihály utca through the...*

University District

As you walk up the street, appreciate the pretty corner spires on the buildings. The yellow one marks the university library. We'll see another university building just down the street.

At the end of the block, cross Irányi utca, and you'll be face-to-face with the entrance to **Centrál Kávéház** (on the right-hand corner)— another of Budapest's newly rejuvenated, old-style café/restaurants (see page 226 in the Eating chapter). Step inside to be transported to another time. If you haven't taken a coffee break yet, now's a good time.

• *Continue along Károlyi Mihály utca for another long block, then take the first left up Ferenczy István utca. After the long building, dip through the green fence on the right, into...*

Károlyi Park (Károlyi Kert)

This delightful, flower-filled oasis offers the perfect break from loud and gritty urban Pest. Once the private garden of the aristocratic

Károlyi family from eastern Hungary (whose mansion it's behind), it's now a public park beloved by people who live, work, and go to school in this neighborhood. The park is filled with tulips in the spring, palm trees in the summer, and rich colors in the fall. On a sunny summer day, locals escape here to read books, gossip with neighbors, or simply lie in the sun. Many schools are nearby. Teenagers hang out here after school, while younger kids enjoy the playground. (If you need a break after all that coffee, a pay WC is in the green pavilion in the far-right corner.)

• *Exit the park straight ahead from where you entered, and turn right down Henszimann utca. At the end of the street, you'll come to a church with onion-dome steeples. The big colonnaded building on its left (facing Egyetem tér) is part of...*

ELTE University

Hungary's biggest university, with 30,000 students, has faculties all over the city. This is the law faculty. The name stands for "Eotvös

Lorand Technical University," named for an influential physicist. As in much of the former Soviet Bloc, the university system in Hungary is still heavily subsidized by the government. It's affordable to study here...*if* you can get in (competition is fierce).
• *Facing the university building, turn left, then take the first right down Szerb utca. After one long block, on the right, in the park behind the yellow fence, is a...*

Serbian Orthodox Church

This used to be a strongly Serbian neighborhood—there's still some Cyrillic writing on some of the buildings nearby. To be transported to the far-eastern reaches of Europe, visit this church's interior, heavy with incense and packed with icons (500 Ft).

The Serbs are just one of many foreign groups that have coexisted here. Traditionally, Hungary's territory included most of Slovakia and large parts of Romania, Croatia, and Serbia—and people from all of those places (along with Austrians, Jews, and Roma/Gypsies) flocked to Buda and Pest. And yet, most of the residents of this cosmopolitan city still speak Hungarian. Throughout centuries of foreign invasions and visitors, new arrivals have undergone a slow-but-sure process of "Magyarization"—"becoming" Hungarian (sometimes against their will). This has made Budapest one of the greatest "melting pot" cities in Europe, if not the world.
• *Continue down Szerb utca, until it runs into Váci utca. Turning left, you'll come face-to-face with the...*

Great Market Hall (Nagyvásárcsarnok)

This market hall (along with four others) was built—like so much of Budapest—around the millennial celebration year of 1896 (see page 40).

Appreciate the colorful Zsolnay tiles lining the roof—frostproof and harder than stone, these were an integral part of the Hungarian national style that emerged in the late 19th century. Tunnels connect this hall to the Danube, where goods could be unloaded at the customs house (now Budapest Corvinus University of Economics, formerly Karl Marx University, next door) and easily transported into the market hall.

To the right, the green Liberty Bridge—formerly named for Habsburg Emperor Franz Josef—spans the Danube to the Gellért Baths, in the shadow of Gellért Hill. And to the left, the Small Boulevard (here named Vámház körút) curls around toward Deák tér, passing along the way Kálvin tér, the National Museum, and the Great Synagogue.

You might also witness Budapest's version of the "Big Dig." Since 2007, the Small Boulevard from here up to Kálvin tér has been completely torn up for the construction of the new M4/green Metro line. Its completion will make it even easier to zip around Budapest...but the delays are frustrating to local businesses (and tourists). Here's hoping that, by the time you read this, you'll have

no clue what I'm talking about.

Step inside the market and get your bearings: The cavernous interior features three levels. The ground floor has produce stands, bakeries, butcher stalls, heaps of paprika, goose liver, and salamis. Upstairs are stand-up eateries and souvenirs. And in the basement are a supermarket, a fish market, and piles of pickles.

Main Floor

Before exploring, take this guided stroll along the market's "main drag" (straight ahead from the entry). Notice the floor slopes slightly downhill to the left. Locals say that the vendors along the right wall are (appropriately enough) higher-end, with more specialty items, while the ones along the left wall are cheaper.

At the head of the main drag, notice (on the right) the stall selling all manner of patriotic Hungarian decorations, or **"Hungarica"** (the Magyar version of "Americana"). Many show the larger, pre-World War I shape of Hungary, when it encompassed much of today's Slovakia and Romania and some parts of Serbia, Croatia, Slovenia, and Austria. This symbol, patriotic for many Hungarians, is considered provocative—or even racist—to some Slovaks, Romanians, and others. (For more on the post-WWI breakup of Hungary, see page 399 in the Hungary: Past and Present chapter.)

In the first "block" of stalls, the corner showcase on the left explains how this stall has been in the same family since 1924, and includes photos of three generations. At the end of this set of stalls, in the dairy case, they sell **Túró Rudi** (TOO-roh ROO-

dee), a semi-sweet cottage cheese covered in chocolate (in the red-and-white polka-dot wrapper). This is a favorite treat for young Hungarians—mothers get their kids to behave here by promising to buy them one.

Across the "street," the corner showcase on the right (at the end of this block) displays some favorite **Hungarian spirits:** Tokaji Aszú, colored (and priced) like gold and called "the wine of kings, and the king of wines" (see page 224); Unicum, the secret-recipe herbal liquor beloved by Hungarians and undrinkable to everyone else (see page 223); and the local version of schnapps, *pálinka,* in various fruit flavors.

In the second block, meat is on the right, and produce is on the left. At the end of this section on the left, you have a good opportunity to sample homemade **strudels** *(rétesek)* of various flavors for 200 Ft.

In the third block, you'll see overpriced paprika on both sides. To save a few forints, turn left before entering this block, go down the street, then turn right at the next corner. The **Csárdi és Csárdi**

stall (on the right) actually lets you sample both types of paprika: sweet (*édes,* used for flavor) and hot (*csipós,* used sparingly to add some kick). Note the difference, choose your favorite, and buy some to take home (for more information, see "Paprika Primer" on page 221).

Back on the main paprika drag, just after the stairs on the right, hung high amidst the paprika (at the Kmetty & Kmetty stall), is a photo of **Margaret Thatcher** visiting this market in 1989. She expected atrocious conditions compared to English markets,

but was pleasantly surprised to find this place up to snuff. This was, after all, "goulash communism" (Hungary's pragmatic mix, which allowed a little private enterprise to keep people going). On the steps of this building, she delivered a historic speech about open society, heralding the impending arrival of the market economy.

At the fourth block, on the right, the corner showcase features another favorite Hungarian food: **goose liver** *(libamáj)*—not to be confused with the cheaper and less typical duck liver *(kacsamáj);* see the geese standing above the case. Goose liver comes in various forms: most traditional is packaged whole *(naturel* or *blokk)*, others are pâté *(parfé* or *püré)*. Hungary is, after France, the world's second-biggest producer of foie gras.

In the fifth block, on the left, look for another local favorite: Hungarian *szalámi* (Pick, a brand from the town of Szeged, is a favorite here).

Reaching the sixth block, above the corner showcase on the right, you'll see a poster showing two types of uniquely Hungarian **livestock:** *Mangalica* is a hairy pig that almost went extinct, but became popular again after butchers discovered it makes great ham—and has a lower fat content than other types of pork (look for this on local menus). *Szürkemarha* are gray longhorn cattle. Keeping an eye on all that livestock, but not pictured here, is the distinctive *Puli* (or larger *Komondor)*—a Hungarian sheepdog with tightly curled hair that resembles dreadlocks.

· *Head up the escalator at the back of the market (on the left).*

Upstairs

Along the upstairs back wall are historic photos of the market hall (and pay WCs).

If you're in the mood for some shopping, this is a convenient (if pricey) place to look—with a great selection of souvenirs both traditional (embroidery) and not-so-traditional (commie-kitsch T-shirts). For tips on shopping here, see the Shopping chapter.

The left wall (as you face the front) is lined with fun, cheap, stand-up, Hungarian-style fast-food joints and six-stool pubs. About two-thirds of the way along the hall (after the second bridge), the **Lángos** stand is the best eatery in the market, serving up the deep-fried snack called *lángos*—similar to elephant ears, but savory rather than sweet. The most typical version is *sajtos tejfölös*— with sour cream and cheese. You can also add garlic *(fokhagyma)*. The **Fakanál Étterem** cafeteria above the main entrance is handy but pricey.

· *For a less glamorous look at the market, head down the escalators to the...*

Basement

In addition to the handy supermarket down here, the basement is pungent with tanks of still-swimming carp, catfish, and perch, and piles of pickles (along the left side). Stop at one of the pickle stands and take a look. Hungarians pickle just about anything: peppers and cukes, of course, but also cauliflower, cabbage, beets,

tomatoes, garlic, and so on. They use particularly strong vinegar, which has a powerful flavor but keeps things very crispy. Until recently—before importing fruits and vegetables became more common—most "salads" out of season were pickled items like these. Vendors are usually happy to give you a sample; consider picking up a colorful jar of mixed pickled veggies for your picnic.

• *When your exploration is finished...so is this walk. Exit the hall the way you came in. Near the Great Market Hall, you have several sightseeing options. If you'd like to stroll back to Vörösmarty tér—this time along the fashionable Váci utca—you can walk straight ahead from the market. The green bridge next to the market leads straight to Gellért Hotel, with its famous hot-springs bath, at the foot of Gellért Hill (see the Thermal Baths chapter).*

Convenient trams connect this area to the rest of Budapest (unless they're temporarily interrupted by the "Big Dig"): **Tram #2** *runs from under the Liberty Bridge along the Danube directly back to Vigadó tér (at the promenade by Vörösmarty tér), the Chain Bridge, and the Parliament.* **Trams #47** *and* **#49** *(catch them directly in front of the market) zip to the right around the Small Boulevard to the National Museum (see page 70 in the Sights chapter) and, beyond that, the Great Synagogue (page 71)—or you can simply walk around the Small Boulevard to reach these sights in about 10–15 minutes.*

ANDRÁSSY ÚT WALK

From Deák Tér to Heroes' Square

Connecting downtown Pest to City Park, Andrássy út is Budapest's main boulevard, lined with plane trees, shops, theaters, cafés, and locals living well. Budapesters like to think of Andrássy út as the Champs-Elysées and Broadway rolled into one. While that's a stretch, it is a good place to stroll, get a feel for today's urban Pest, and visit a few top attractions (most notably the Opera House and the House of Terror).

ORIENTATION

Overview: Andrássy út is divided roughly into thirds. The most interesting first section (from Deák tér to the Oktogon) is the focus of this walk. The middle section (between the Oktogon and Kodály körönd) features one major sight, the House of Terror. And the final third (Kodály körönd to Heroes' Square), while pleasant and comparatively low-key, offers fewer sight-seeing opportunities.

Getting There: The walk begins at Deák tér—easy to reach from anywhere in the city, as it's on all three Metro lines. If you're coming from Vörösmarty tér in central Pest, simply hop the M1/yellow Metro line one stop, or walk five minutes up Deák utca. If you want to skip to the start of Andrássy út itself, you can ride the M1 to the Bajcsy-Zsilinszky út stop, and turn to "Millennium Underground of 1896," page 152.

Length of This Walk: Allow an hour, not including time to enter the sights.

Shortcut: The M1/yellow Metro line runs every couple of minutes just under the street—so it's easy to skip several blocks ahead, or to backtrack (stops marked by yellow signs).

Postal Museum: 500 Ft, Tue–Sun 10:00–18:00, closed Mon, Andrássy út 3, tel. 1/269-6838, www.postamuzeum.hu.

Opera House: 2,600 Ft, lobby open Mon–Sat from 11:00 until show time—generally 19:00; Sun open 3 hours before the performance—generally 16:00–19:00, or 10:00–13:00 if there's a matinee; tours in English nearly daily at 15:00 and 16:00; Andrássy út 22, tel. 1/332-8197.

House of Terror: 1,500 Ft, 400 ft more for special exhibits, Tue–Fri 10:00–18:00, Sat–Sun 10:00–19:30, closed Mon, last entry 90 min before closing, Andrássy út 60, tel. 1/374-2600, www.terrorhaza.hu.

Starring: Budapest's most elegant drag, with fine architecture, upscale shopping, great restaurants, and top-notch sightseeing—from quirky (Postal Museum) to opulent (Opera House) to sobering (House of Terror).

THE WALK BEGINS

• *Begin in the middle of the paved square (near the M2 and M3 Metro entrances) called...*

Deák Tér

This modest square seems more important than it is, since it's the place where the three Metro lines intersect. (All Metro tracks lead

to Deák.) The square is named for **Ferenc Deák** (1803–1876), a statesman who pushed for persistent international pressure on the Habsburgs to improve Hungary's status after his rabble-rousing compatriots failed in the 1848 Revolution. (The peace-loving Deák was sort of a Hungarian Jimmy Carter.) It worked. With the Compromise of 1867, Hungary was granted a good measure of autonomy in the empire.

Sitting unassumingly on the square is the blocky, typically austere **Lutheran church,** with its Neoclassical colonnade entry and shallow green dome. (Absolute Walking Tours—described on page 50—meet on this church's front steps.) Looming over the square across the street is the landmark, but sadly neglected, yellow office block called the **Ankerház** (pictured above). Like the square it dominates, this building isn't as important as it might seem.

• *From Deák tér, cross Harmincad street—the one with all the bus stops (including one to Memento Park, explained on page 86)—and head for...*

ANDRÁSSY ÚT WALK

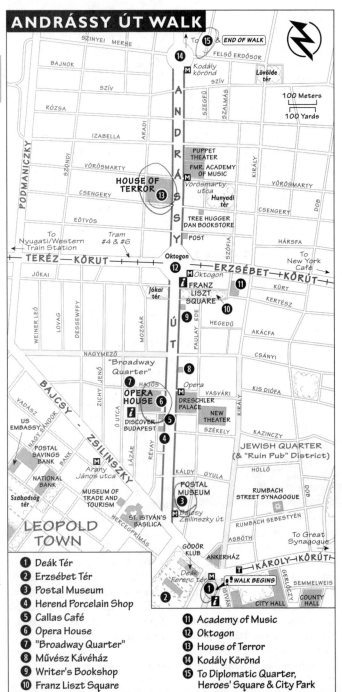

ANDRÁSSY ÚT WALK

1 Deák Tér
2 Erzsébet Tér
3 Postal Museum
4 Herend Porcelain Shop
5 Callas Café
6 Opera House
7 "Broadway Quarter"
8 Művész Kávéház
9 Writer's Bookshop
10 Franz Liszt Square

11 Academy of Music
12 Oktogon
13 House of Terror
14 Kodály Körönd
15 To Diplomatic Quarter, Heroes' Square & City Park

Erzsébet Tér

This pretty, leafy park is named for one of Deák's contemporaries: Elisabeth, the wife of the Habsburg Emperor Franz Josef. While Deák pressed Franz Josef with diplomacy, Empress Elisabeth (a.k.a. Sisi) pressured him at home...Hungarian autonomy was one of her pet issues (for more on this "royal and imperial" couple, see page 278).

The park was long marred by the presence of a gloomy, polluting, communist-era international bus station. A few years ago, locals reclaimed the space as a welcoming public zone. Notice there are two parts to Erzsébet tér: the more traditional park behind the bus-station skeleton, and a sleek, modern new area in front of it. Recently the government planned to build a new national theater in this spot, and they even began to dig the foundation. But when the parliament changed hands, construction was aborted—leaving a giant hole that locals called "The National Ditch."

Eventually they came up with a creative use for the space: an underground parking garage and a unique café/nightclub. Walk

closer to the wall and look down (at the end facing Deák tér): A long, gentle slope digs down to the **Gödör Klub** ("Ditch Club"). On balmy summer nights, outdoor performances take place here, and this whole area is filled with young locals. The incline leads to the indoor, underground part of the café, which houses an art gallery and additional performances. If you walk a little farther through the park, you'll reach the artificial pond that covers part of the ditch. Look closely: Especially at night, you can look through the glass floor of the very shallow pond to see people walking around in the underground nightclub. (For more, see page 255 in the Entertainment & Nightlife chapter.)

• *At the far corner of Erzsébet tér, cross the busy Small Boulevard (here called Bajcsy-Zsilinszky út) to the beginning of Andrássy út. For now, stay on the right side of the boulevard. A few steps up from where the street begins, look for the yellow railings on either side of the street with the low-profile* Földalatti *sign.*

This marks the Bajcsy-Zsilinszky út stop for the...

Millennium Underground of 1896

Built to get the masses conveniently out to Heroes' Square, this fun and extremely handy little Metro line follows Andrássy

út from Vörösmarty tér (Pest's main square) to City Park. It was originally dubbed the "Franz Josef Underground Line"—in honor of the then-emperor—but later simply became known as the Underground *(Földalatti)*. Just 20 steps below street level, it's so shallow that you must follow the signs on the street (listing end points) to gauge the right direction, because there's no underpass for switching platforms. The first underground on the Continent (London's is older), it originally had horse-drawn cars. Trains depart every couple of minutes. Though recently renovated, the M1 line retains its 1896 atmosphere, along with fun black-and-white photos of the age.

• *Immediately next to the Metro stop, look for the red mailboxes flanking the entrance (at #3, dial 10 to get inside) to the...*

Postal Museum (Postamúzeum)

This quirky and unexpectedly enjoyable museum, in a fine old apartment from Budapest's Golden Age, features a collection of

postal artifacts. You'll see post office coats of arms, 100-year-old postal furniture, antique telephone boxes, historic mailman uniforms, and all manner of postal paraphernalia that was cutting-edge a century ago. The precision required to operate a postal network serving a sprawling empire seems like a perfect fit for the left-brained, detail-oriented Hungarians—which might explain why this museum is still beloved today. The exhibits are displayed in an elegant old merchant's mansion with big Murano crystal chandeliers, all the original

ornate woodwork, and creaky parquet floors. The apartment—decorated as it was when built in the 1880s—is at least as interesting as the museum's collection. If it's not too busy, one of the nostalgic women who staff the museum (and seem to be a similar vintage as the apartment) might show you around and lovingly explain the exhibits.

• *Now continue...*

Gyula Andrássy
(1823–1890)

A key player in the 1848 Revolution, Count Gyula (Julius) Andrássy went on to help forge (along with Ferenc Deák) the Dual Monarchy of the Austro-Hungarian Empire. As Budapest boomed, Andrássy also served as an urban planner who championed the idea of building a grand boulevard from downtown to City Park. Andrássy was also the Hungarian prime minister and Austro-Hungarian foreign minister (1871–1879). Eventually he was forced to step down after his unpopular campaign to appropriate Bosnia-Herzegovina (and consequently boost the Slav population of the empire, which destabilized its delicate ethnic balance). But to most Hungarians, Andrássy is best known for his alleged relationship with Empress Sisi, who adored all things Hungarian (see page 278). Her third daughter—believed to be the count's—was known as the Little Hungarian Princess.

Strolling Up Andrássy Út

This grand boulevard—140 feet wide and nearly two miles long—was begun in 1871, when local bigwigs decided that on-the-rise Budapest needed an answer to Paris' Champs-Elysées. But instead of leading to an Arc de Triomphe, Andrássy út culminates at the similarly triumphal Heroes' Square. The boulevard also provided a convenient link between the dense urban center of Pest and the green expanse of City Park—city-dwellers could zip out for a break from the bustle without plodding along congested narrow streets. The boulevard was officially inaugurated with much fanfare in 1885. Because most of the buildings were built within about 15 years, Andrássy út enjoys a pleasant architectural harmony. Historicism—a creative merging of various complementary styles—was all the rage at the time, and many of the structures employ the urban Germanic Neoclassical style known as *Gründerzeit*.

Since being built, this boulevard—and the major intersections along its length—have constantly changed names with the tenor of the times. Originally called simply Radial Boulevard (Súgarút), it was later christened for Count Andrássy, who had strongly promoted its construction (see sidebar). When the Soviets moved in, they renamed it Sztálin út; after the 1956 Uprising, it was briefly called Hungarian Youth Boulevard, before they re-dubbed it People's Republic Boulevard. And finally, with the fall of communism, it regained its historical name: Andrássy út.

Running parallel to Andrássy út, two blocks to the right, is **Király utca,** which is lined with home-improvement shops (a hot commodity in this city, where so many people are fixing up flats long neglected by the communists). This area—formerly the Jewish Quarter, and now more seedy than most parts of central Pest—is also home to the city's distinctive "ruin pubs" (described on page 256 of the Entertainment & Nightlife chapter).

• *Cross to the left side of Andrássy út, where you'll find the next few attractions.*

This first stretch of Andrássy út is being developed as the city's cancan of big-money shops. Watch for exclusive international brands that are opening their doors here (such as Gucci and Louis Vuitton). But there are still some local shops—on the left, at #16, is a **Herend** shop, selling very expensive pieces of Hungary's top porcelain (see page 244 in the Shopping chapter).

Upscale as it might become, Andrássy út remains an artery for the city, often clogged with traffic...except twice a year, when 80,000 bikers take back the street in a demonstration called "critical mass." The street is closed to traffic for a full day, and given over to cyclists, inline skaters, skateboarders, and pedestrians...a tempting taste of what could be.

On the left side of the street, on the corner at #20, look for the **Callas café**—recently re-opened, with sumptuous *Jugendstil* decor (for details, see page 236 in the Eating chapter).

It was along this stretch of Andrássy út that Steven Spielberg filmed much of *Munich,* since the street has fine architecture that can stand in for many great European cities.

• *On the left, just after Callas, is the can't-miss-it...*

Hungarian State Opera House (Magyar Állami Operaház)

The Neo-Renaissance home of the Hungarian State Opera features performances (almost daily except during outdoor music season, late June–late Sept) and delightful tours. The building dates from the 1890s, not long after Budapest had become co-capital of

the Habsburg Empire. The Hungarians wanted to put their city on the map as a legitimate European capital, and that meant they needed an opera house. Emperor Franz Josef provided half the funds...on the condition that it be smaller than the opera house in his hometown of Vienna. And so, Miklós Ybl designed a building that would exceed Vienna's famous Staatsoper in opulence, if not in size. (Franz Josef was reportedly displeased.) It was built using almost entirely Hungarian materials. After being damaged in World War II, it was painstakingly restored in the early 1980s. Today, with lavish marble-and-gold-leaf decor, a gorgeous gilded interior slathered with paintings of Greek myths, and high-quality performances at bargain prices, this is one of Europe's finest opera houses.

You have a few options for seeing this place. To just get a taste, slip in the front door when the box office is open and check out the sumptuous entryway. For the full story (and to get into the remarkable auditorium), take one of the 45-minute guided tours in English (usually every day at 15:00 and 16:00—see page 76). To see the Opera House in action, take in an excellent (and refreshingly affordable) performance—see page 247 in the Entertainment & Nightlife chapter.

• *The Opera House marks the beginning of an emerging dining-and-nightlife zone dubbed the...*

"Broadway Quarter"

The street just behind the Opera House, **Hajós utca,** is newly traffic-free and a budding outdoor-dining zone with a smattering of trendy restaurants...and more soon to appear.

• *Cross to the right side of Andrássy út for the next few sights.*

Across the street from the Opera House, and echoing its shape (although in a different style), is the **Dreschler Palace.** It was co-

designed by Ödön Lechner, a leading architect whose works also include the Postal Savings Bank (see page 127). In this building's late-19th-century heyday, one of Budapest's top cafés filled its gallery. More recently, it housed the Ballet Institute. And not long ago, the beautiful but neglected building was purchased by a luxury hotel chain...but the plans fell through, and it's still waiting for a new tenant. Behind it is the **New Theater** (Új Szinház), one of many popular venues around here for Hungarian-language plays (Paulay Ede utca 35, tel. 1/269-6021, www.ujszinhaz.hu).

A few steps up Andrássy út on the right (at #29) is another fine historic café, **Művész Kávéház.** As it's a hangout for actors and musicians, this is your best chance to rub elbows with actual drama queens and divas (described on page 236).

The next major cross-street, **Nagymező utca,** features a chic cluster of restaurants, bars, and theaters. This is an enjoyable place to stroll on a summer evening. While you might be tempted to attend a show along Budapest's answer to Broadway, if you look closely you'll figure out that this is a truly local area—most of the plays and musicals here are in Hungarian only. So unless you want to hear "Music of the Night" sung in Hungarian, as it was meant to be performed...keep looking. (The Entertainment & Nightlife chapter offers several more accessible alternatives.)

At the end of the next block, on the right (at #45), is the **Writer's Bookshop** (Irok Boltja). During Budapest's late-19th-century glory days, the Japan Café at this spot was the haunt of many of the great artistic minds that populated the city, including architect Ödön Lechner and poet Attila József. Today the management still encourages loitering (and sells some English books).

• *Just after the bookshop is Budapest's outdoor-dining mecca...*

Franz Liszt Square (Liszt Ferenc Tér)

This leafy square is surrounded by hip, expensive cafés and restaurants. (The best is the kitschy communist-themed restaurant **Menza**—see page 229 in the Eating chapter.) This is *the* scene for Budapest's yuppies.

Strangely, neither the statue on this square nor the one facing it, across Andrássy út, is of Franz Liszt. But deeper in the park, you'll find a modern statue of Liszt dramatically playing an imaginary piano. And at the far end of the square is the **Academy of Music** founded by and named for Liszt—a German composer with a Hungarian name, who loved his family's Magyar heritage (though he didn't speak Hungarian) and spent his last five years in Budapest. His Academy of Music, while undergoing a renovation, still teaches students and hosts concerts (see page 251 in the Entertainment & Nightlife chapter; for more on Liszt, see page 252).

• *One block up from Franz Liszt Square is the gigantic crossroads known as the...*

Oktogon

This vast intersection with its corners snipped off—where Andrássy út meets the Great Boulevard ring road (Nagykörút)—was called Mussolini tér during World War II, then November 7 tér in honor of the Bolshevik Revolution. Today kids have nicknamed it American tér for the fast-food joints littering the square and streets nearby. Standing (carefully) in the center of Andrássy út, you can already see the column of Heroes' Square at the end of the boulevard.

From here, if you have time to delve into workaday Budapest, consider a trip on tram #4 or #6, which trundle in both directions around the ring road. If you've got time for a short detour to the most opulent coffee break of your life, head for the **New York Café** (see page 235 in the Eating chapter): Just hop on a tram to the right (tram #6 toward Móricz Zsigmond körtér, or tram #4 toward Fehérvári út), and get off at the Wesselényi utca stop.

• There's one more major sight between here and Heroes' Square. You can either walk two more blocks up Andrássy út, or hop on the Metro and take it one stop to Vörösmarty utca, to reach the...

House of Terror (Terror Háza)

The building at Andrássy út 60 (on the left) has been painted a lifeless blue-gray, and the word "TERROR" is carved into the overhanging eaves. This is the place where two evil regimes tortured their Hungarian subjects. Now a modern museum document- ing the terror of Hungary's "double occupation"—first at the hands of the Nazis, then the Soviets—this is

essential sightseeing for those intrigued by Budapest's dark 20th century, and interesting to anyone. ❂ See House of Terror Tour on page 159.

Two significant buildings stand across the boulevard from the House of Terror (on the right side of Andrássy út, just before the Metro stop): The yellow one, on the corner of Vörösmarty utca (at Andrássy #67), is the **former Academy of Music**—founded by Franz Liszt, and later moved to the building we just saw on his square. It currently holds an exhibit that memorializes the great composer, and occasionally hosts performances. The next building is the **Puppet Theater** (Bábszinház), a venue for top-notch puppet shows. For details on either of these options, see page 251 in the Entertainment & Nightlife chapter.

• While you can hoof it from here to Heroes' Square (visible in the distance, about a 15-minute walk), there's less to see along the rest of Andrássy út. If you prefer, hop on the Metro here and ride it three stops to Hősök tere.

Or, if you continue walking up Andrássy út, after four blocks you'll reach the grand intersection called...

Kodály Körönd

This circular crossroads—which seems to echo the octagonal one we passed through earlier—is named for another great Hungarian composer, Zoltán Kodály (who lived in a mansion here, at #1, now a museum; for more on Kodály, see page 252). During the Nazi occupation, it had the jarring name Hitler tér.

Standing in the four wedge-shaped parks—overshadowed by the stately mansions surrounding them—are statues of four Hungarian heroes who fought against Ottoman invaders. Think of these as rejects from the Millennium Monument at Heroes' Square just up the boulevard. In fact, two of the original statues from Kodály körönd were eventually "promoted" to the colonnade there, and their spots here were taken by two different heroes.

• *After Kodály körönd, Andrássy út enters its final third, the...*

Diplomatic Quarter

Continuing up the street, you'll notice that the buildings lining Andrássy út shrink and pull back from the busy boulevard, huddling behind trees. Instead of bulky four- and five-story apartment blocks, it's a sleepy, leafy residential zone. These villas were formerly occupied by aristocrats, diplomats, and wealthy Jews. Today this is where many foreign states maintain their embassies. If you'd like to skip the final stretch, you can hop on the Metro at Kodály körönd. Or, to complete your stroll, keep going.

• *Andrássy út terminates at Heroes' Square. Turn to page 176 to learn more.*

HOUSE OF TERROR TOUR

Terror Háza

Along one of the prettiest stretches of urban Budapest, in the house at 60 Andrássy Boulevard, some of the most horrific acts in Hungarian history took place. The former headquarters of the darkest sides of two different regimes—the Arrow Cross (Nazi-occupied Hungary's version of the Gestapo) and the ÁVO/ÁVH (communist Hungary's secret police)—is now, fittingly, an excellent museum of that time of terror. The high-tech, conceptual, and sometimes over-the-top exhibits attempt to document the atrocities endured by Hungary during the 20th century. This is a powerful experience, particularly for elderly Hungarians who knew both victims and perpetrators and have personal memories of the terrors that came with Hungary's "double occupation."

ORIENTATION

Cost: 1,500 Ft, 400 Ft more for special exhibitions.

Hours: Tue–Fri 10:00–18:00, Sat–Sun 10:00–19:30, closed Mon, last entry 90 min before closing.

Audioguide and Information: The 1,300-Ft English audioguide is good but almost too thorough, and can be difficult to hear over the din of Hungarian soundtracks in each room. You can't fast-forward through the dense and sometimes long-winded commentary. As an alternative, my self-guided tour (below) covers the key points. A silver plaque in each room provides the basics (in English). For more in-depth information (very similar to what's covered by the audioguide), each room is stocked with free English fliers.

Photography: Not allowed inside.

Location: Andrássy út 60, district VI, tel. 1/374-2600, www .terrorhaza.hu. Outside, an overhang casts the shadow outline of the word "TERROR" onto the building.

Getting There: It's near the Vörösmarty utca stop of the M1/ yellow Metro line. Note that this is Vörösmarty utca, not Vörösmarty tér (which is a different stop).

Length of This Tour: Between 90 minutes and two hours.

Services: Café, good bookshop, and WCs.

Starring: Fascism, communism, and the resilient Hungarian spirit.

Background

In the lead-up to World War II, Hungary initially allied with Hitler—both to retain a degree of self-determination and to try to regain its huge territorial losses after World War I's devastating Treaty of Trianon (see page 399). As the rest of Europe fell into war, Hungary tiptoed between supporting the Nazis and, wherever possible, charting its own course. The Hungarians found themselves in the unenviable position of providing a buffer between Nazi Germany to the west and the Soviet Union to the east. They did just enough to stay in the Nazis' good graces (the Hungarian Second Army invaded the Soviet Union in 1941), while attempting to maintain what autonomy they could.

Hitler finally got fed up with Hungary's less-than-whole-hearted support, and in March of 1944, the Nazi-affiliated Arrow Cross Party was forcibly installed as Hungary's new government. The Arrow Cross immediately set to work exterminating Budapest's Jews (most of whom had survived until then, although they had suffered under the earlier regime's anti-Semitic laws).  The Nazi surrogates deported nearly 440,000 Jewish people to Auschwitz, murdered thousands more on the streets of Budapest, and executed hundreds in the basement of this building. (For more on this ugly time, see "The Jewish Story of Budapest" on page 72.)

The Red Army entered Hungary from the USSR in late August of 1944. After a hard-fought battle (and a devastating siege), they took Budapest on February 13, 1945, and forced the last Nazi soldier out of Hungary on April 4. Although the USSR characterized this as the "liberation" of Hungary, it soon became clear that the Hungarians had merely gone from the Nazi frying pan into the Soviet fire. Here in Budapest, the new communist leaders took over the same building as headquarters for their secret police (the ÁVO, later renamed ÁVH). To keep dissent to a minimum, the secret police terrorized, tried, deported, or executed anyone suspected of being an enemy of the state.

Critics of this museum point out that it doesn't draw a very fine distinction between these two very different phases of the "double occupation." As you tour the exhibits, remember that as similar as their methods might seem, the Nazis and the communists represented opposite extremes of the political spectrum. Hungarians, like so many others in the 20th century, got caught in the crossfire.

THE TOUR BEGINS

• *Buy your ticket (and rent an audioguide, if you wish) and head into the museum.*

Atrium

The atrium features a Soviet T-54 tank, symbolizing the looming threat of violence that helped keep both regimes in power. Tanks

like this one rolled into Hungary to crush the 1956 Uprising. Behind the tank, stretching to the ceiling, is a vast wall covered with 3,200 portraits of people who were murdered by two different regimes—the Nazis and the communists—in this very building.

• *The one-way exhibit begins two floors up, then spirals down to the cellar—just follow signs for* Kiállítás/Exhibition. *To begin, you can either take the elevator (to floor 2), or walk up the red stairwell nearby, decorated with old Socialist Realist sculptures from the communist days (including, near the base of the stairs, two subjects you won't find at Memento Park: Josef Stalin and Mátyás Rákosi, the most severe communist leader of Hungary).*

Once upstairs, the first room gives an overview of the...

Double Occupation (Kettős Megszállás)

The video by the entrance sets the stage for Hungary's 20th century: its territorial losses after World War I; its alliance with, then invasion by, the Nazis; and its "liberation," then occupation, by the USSR (see "Background," on previous page).

The TV screens on the partition in the middle of the room show grainy footage of both sides of the "double occupation": the Nazis on the black side, and the Soviets (appropriately) on the red side. Do a slow counterclockwise loop, starting with the black (Nazi) side. See Hitler speaking and saluting in occupied Hungary, and Nazis goose-stepping down Andrássy út. The giant, ironic quote reads, "Last night I dreamed that the Nazis were gone...and nobody else came."

But come they did. The giant picture of the destroyed Chain Bridge (on the back wall) shows the passing of the torch between the two regimes, and a chilling reminder that these two equally brutal groups, which employed similar means of terror, were sworn enemies: As the Soviets' Red Army approached from the east to liberate Hungary, the Nazis made a last stand in Budapest (Hitler, who considered the Danube a natural border, ordered them never to retreat). The Nazis destroyed all of the bridges across the Danube (some without warning, while they were filled with civilians), then holed up on Castle Hill. The Soviets laid siege for 100 days, gradually devastating the city.

Circling around to the red (Soviet) side, you see Budapest in the aftermath of World War II, and the early days of Soviet rule. The telephones on the wall play Hungarian sound clips from the time.

• *Go through the* **Passage of Hungarian Nazis,** *decorated with the words of a proclamation by the Arrow Cross leader Ferenc Szálasi (there's also a WC). Continue into the room of...*

Hungarian Nazis (Nyilas Terem)

The table is set with Arrow Cross china, bearing a V-for-victory emblem with a laurel wreath. At the head of the table stands an

Arrow Cross uniform. Examine the armband: The red and white stripes are an old Hungarian royal pattern, dating from the days of St. István, and the insignia combines arrows, a cross, and an "H" for Hungary. On the loudspeaker, Arrow Cross leader Ferenc Szálasi preaches about reclaiming a "Greater Hungary" and about fighting against the Jews and the insidious influence of their Bolshevism. On the far wall, the footage of the frozen river shows where many of those Jews ended up: unceremoniously shot into the icy Danube. Listen for the sickening, periodic splash...splash...splash...

• *As you leave the room, the exhibit subtly (perhaps too subtly) turns the page from the Nazi period to the communist one.*

Gulag

After the Red Army drove the Nazis out of Hungary, they quickly set to work punishing people who had backed their enemies. Being sent to a gulag was one particularly hard fate.

The word "gulag" refers to a network of secret Soviet prison

camps, mostly in Siberia. These were hard-labor camps where potential and actual dissidents were sent to be punished, to remove their dangerous influence from society, and to make an example of those who would dare to defy the regime. The Soviets euphemistically told them they were going away for "a little work" *(malenki robot)*. It was an understatement.

On the carpet, a giant map of the USSR shows the locations of some of these camps, where an estimated 600,000–700,000 Hungarian civilians and prisoners of war were sent...about half of whom never returned. And that only represents a tiny fraction of the millions of people from throughout Europe and the USSR thought to have perished in the gulag system. The lighted cones locate specific camps, with artifacts from those places. Video screens show grainy footage of transfer trains clattering through an icy countryside, gruesome scenes from the camps, and testimony of prisoners.

People of Germanic heritage living in Hungary were targeted for deportation, but—due to a strict Moscow-imposed quota system—nobody was immune. Among the gulag victims was the Swedish diplomat Raoul Wallenberg, who had rescued many Hungarian Jews from the Nazis (see page 75). For more on the atrocious conditions in the gulag—and similar work camps here in Hungary—see page 172.

Those who survived their experience with "corrective forced labor" were often not allowed to return to their families, and if they did, were sworn to secrecy...never allowed to tell of the horrors of the gulag until after 1989. The final Hungarian gulag prisoner, András Toma, finally returned from Siberia in 2000, having been interred in a mental hospital for decades after the gulags were dissolved. Two years in a gulag became 53 years in an asylum. The doctors, unfamiliar with his tongue-twisting Hungarian language, assumed he was simply mad.

Changing Clothes (Átöltözés)

This locker room—with rotating figures dressed alternately in Arrow Cross and communist uniforms—satirizes the readiness of many Hungarians to align with whoever was in power. The sped-up video shows turncoat guards changing their uniforms. While it seems absurd that someone's allegiance could shift so quickly, many of these people were told that they'd be executed if they did not switch...or they could "change clothes," admit their mistake in joining the Arrow Cross, and pledge allegiance to the new communist regime. For most, it was an easy choice. Many people (including Cardinal József Mindszenty) were imprisoned by both regimes—and it's entirely plausible that they saw the same guard dressed in both uniforms.

The Fifties ('50-es Évek)

Of course, the transition was not always so straightforward. The insinuation of the communist regime into the fabric of Hungary was a gradual process. From the Red Army's "liberation" in 1945 until 1948, a power struggle raged between pro-democracy factions and the Soviet-backed communist puppet leaders. The voting booths at the beginning of this room symbolize that, at first, the Soviets fostered an illusion of choice for the Hungarian people. Elections were held throughout the Soviet satellite states in the mid-1940s, with the assumption that the communist Hungarian Workers' Party would sweep into power. But in 1945 parliamentary elections, the communists won only 17 percent of the vote. After this, the Soviets gradually eliminated opposition leaders by uncovering "plots," then executing the alleged perpetrators. In the following two elections, they also stacked the deck by allowing workers to vote as often as they liked—often five or six times apiece (using the blue ballot cards you'll see in the voting booths). Even so, in the 1947 election, the communists still had to disqualify 700,000 opposition votes in order to win. (And you thought "hanging chads" were aggravating.)

Once in power, the Hungarian Workers' Party ruled with an iron fist and did away with the charade of elections entirely. Hungary became a "People's Republic" and was reorganized on the Soviet system. Private property was nationalized, the economy became fully socialistic, and the country fell into poverty.

Not that you'd know any of this from the sanitized state-sponsored images of the time. In the voting booths, screens show a loop of communist propaganda from the 1950s. Lining the walls are glossy communist-era paintings, celebrating the peasants of the "people's revolution" (farmers, soldiers, and sailors looking boldly to the future), idyllic scenes of communities coming together, and romanticized depictions of communist leaders (Lenin as the brave sailor; Mátyás Rákosi—the portly, bald communist leader of Hungary—as the kindly grandfather, gladly receiving flowers from a sweet young girl). Imagine the societal schizophrenia bred by the communists' good-cop, bad-cop methods: terrorizing the people even as you pretend you're a bunch of nice guys.

The distorted stage separates these two methods of people-control. The stretched-out images of Stalin, Lenin, and Rákosi imply the falsehood of everything we've just seen; behind it is the dark underbelly of the regime: the constant surveillance that bred paranoia among the people. The cases at the end display documentation for show trials. We'll learn more about these means of terror as we progress.

Soviet "Advisors" (Szovjet Tanácsadók)

These "advisors" were more like supervisors. On the wall plaque is a list of the Soviet ambassadors to Hungary, who wielded terrific influence over the communist leaders here. Yuri Andropov, the ambassador during the 1956 Uprising, helped set up the ÁVH secret police, and later became the Soviet premier. So shocked was Andropov at how quickly the uprising had escalated, that he later advocated for cracking down violently at the first signs of unrest in the empire (think of the Soviet tanks rolling into Czechoslovakia during the 1968 Prague Spring).

The desk displays items from the ambassador's office, and the video screens show footage of the ambassador garnering goodwill by visiting families, factories, and so on. A portrait of Stalin slyly surveys the scene.

In the passage, a TV plays an idyllic propaganda video of happy and productive farmers, with swelling music to rouse the Hungarian patriotic spirit.

Resistance (Ellenállás)

It wasn't all upbeat and shiny. This room—empty aside from three very different kitchen tables—symbolizes the way that resistance to the regime emerged in every walk of life. Each table and chair represents a different social class: countryside peasant, middle-class urbanite, and bourgeoisie. On each table is a propaganda message that was printed by that dissident (and now used as evidence in their interrogation). Notice

that, like the furniture, these messages evolve in sophistication from table to table. A screen facing each table shows footage of an accused person from that class, labeled with how many years *(év)* each one spent in prison.

• *Go down the stairs, and enter the room about...*

Resettlement and Deportation (Kitelepítés)

The creation of small nations from sprawling empires at the end of World War I had also created large minority groups, which could upset the delicate ethnic balance of a new country. Having learned this lesson, the Soviets strove to create homogeneous states without minorities. Ethnic cleansing on a staggering scale—or, in the more pleasant parlance of the time, "mutual population exchange"—took place throughout Central and Eastern Europe in the years following World War II (for example, three million ethnic Germans were forced out of Czechoslovakia). In Hungary, 230,000 Germans were uprooted and deported. Meanwhile, Hungarians who had become ethnically "stranded" in other nations after the Treaty of Trianon were sent to Hungary (100,000 from Slovakia, 140,000 from Romania, and 70,000 from Yugoslavia). Most still have not returned to their ancestral homes.

Notice the doorbell on the plaque at the beginning of the room. Press the white button to hear the jarring sound that hundreds of thousands of people heard in the middle of the night, when authorities showed up at their doorstep to tell them they had to pack up and move. You'd sign an "official agreement of repatriation" (see the deportation paperwork on the wall), then the ÁVO would take you away. You were strictly limited in the number of belongings you could bring with you; the rest was left behind, carefully inventoried, and folded into the wealth of the upwardly mobile Party bureaucrats—represented by the fancy black sedan with plush hammer-and-sickle upholstery draped in black in the middle of the room.

In the hallway at the end of this section (after the WCs), peer into the haunting **torture cell.** Inside you'll see original items used to beat and torture prisoners.

Surrender of Property and Land (Beszolgáltatás)

With the descent of the communist cloak, people were forced to surrender their belongings to the government. Land was redistributed. Even those who came out ahead in this transaction—formerly landless peasants—found that it was a raw deal, as they were now expected to meet often-impossible production quotas. The Soviet authorities terrorized the peasant class in order to pry as many people as possible away from their old-fashioned farming lifestyles (not to mention deeply held Hungarian traditions), and embrace the industrialization of the new regime. Some 72,000 wealthy peasants called *kulaks,* who did not want to turn over

their belongings, ended up on a list to be deported; all told, some 300,000 people were eventually ejected. (Eventually the regime sidestepped the peasant-farmer "middleman" completely, as farms were simply collectivized and run as giant units.)

Of the produce grown in Hungary, a significant amount was sent to other parts of the Soviet Bloc, leading to rampant short-

ages. The Hungarian people had to survive on increasingly sparse rations. Enter the labyrinth of pork-fat bricks, which remind old-timers of the harsh conditions of the 1950s (lard on bread for dinner). Look for the ration coupons, which people had to present before being allowed to buy even these measly staples. The pig hiding out in the maze is another symbol of these tough times. Traditionally, peasants would slaughter a pig in order to sustain themselves through the winter. But the communist authorities could seize that pig for its own uses, leaving the farmers to rely on the (unreliable) government to provide for their families. To avoid this, many farmers would illegally slaughter their pigs in the cellar, instead of out in the open.

ÁVO

The communist secret police (State Security Department, or ÁVO, later called the State Security Authority, or ÁVH) began

Victims and Victimizers

The foot soldiers of the secret police were civilians—workaday people who informed on their friends and neighbors in vast numbers. Anything could be cause for suspicion, even just not clapping quite hard enough at a Hungarian Workers' Party rally. The regime routinely turned families against each other. They were just as likely to compel you to implicate your father or brother as your neighbor or co-worker. Pavlik Morozov, a Soviet boy, was the literal poster child for this, after he informed on his own father. It was common to simultaneously be an informant and be informed upon by someone else.

Imagine being a man or woman on the street in 1950s Budapest. Like most people on this planet, you are basically apolitical—you could care less who's in charge, so long as you can raise your family in peace and prosperity. One day on your way to work, a black van pulls up next to you, and in a blur, you're pulled inside. An intimidating agent asks you to report on your friends' water-cooler conversation—particularly any statements against the regime, no matter how casual. When you hesitate, the agent says, "Your son András is so very bright. It would be a shame if he could not attend university." Or maybe, "You appear to have a promising career in engineering ahead of you. And yet, it is so difficult to find employment in your chosen field. Well, there's always ditch-digging."

The decision about whether to collaborate with the secret police suddenly becomes muddled. (Which would you choose? Are you *sure*?) Some people refused, and endured years or decades of misery. Others capitulated, enjoyed relatively fulfilling lives, but regretted selling out their friends and even their families. In post-communist Hungary, both groups wonder if they made the right choice.

as a means to identify and try war criminals. But the organization quickly mutated into an apparatus for intimidating the common people of Hungary—equivalent to the KGB in the Soviet Union. Before they were finished, the ÁVO/ÁVH imprisoned, abused, or murdered one person from every third Hungarian family. On the wall are pictures of secret police leaders, and a quote: "The ÁVH is the fist of the Party." This organization infiltrated every walk of Hungarian life. Factory workers and farmers, writers and singers, engineers and doctors, teenagers and senior citizens, even Party leaders and ÁVO/ÁVH officers were vulnerable. Their power came from enlisting untold numbers of civilians as informants (see "Victims and Victimizers" sidebar).

Gábor Péter's Office

Gábor Péter was the first director of the ÁVO/ÁVH. Like many former communist leaders, Péter wound up a prisoner himself (notice the prison motif lurking around the edges of the room). It became an almost expected part of the life cycle of a communist bigwig to eventually be fingered as an enemy...the more power you gained, the better an example you became. (In Péter's case, it didn't help that he was Jewish—anti-Semitism didn't leave Hungary with the Arrow Cross.) It was abundantly clear that nobody was safe. Péter went to his grave in 1993 without remorse for his participation in the Soviet regime.

"Justice" (Igazságszolgálatás)

This room explores the concept of "show trials"—high-profile, loudly publicized, and completely choreographed trials of people

who had supposedly subverted the regime. The burden of proof was on the accused, not on the accuser, and coerced confessions were fair game. From 1945 until the 1956 Uprising, more than 71,000 Hungarians were accused of political crimes, and 485 were executed.

The TV screen shows various show trials, including the one for Imre Nagy (leader of the 1956 Uprising—see page 124) and his associates. Nagy was found guilty and executed in 1958.

In some cases—as in Nagy's—the defendants had defied the regime. But in many cases, the accused were innocent. (The authorities simply wanted to make an example of someone—innocence was irrelevant.) For example, if there was a meat shortage, they'd arrest and try guys who worked at the slaughterhouse, ferreting out the workers who "didn't do their best." They might even execute the foreman. Not only did this intimidate all of the others to work harder, it also kept people who had gained some small measure of power in check.

The area behind the stage names the judges of these trials, with photos of some of them. Looking at these people, consider that it was not unusual for judges who had conducted show trials... to later go on trial themselves.

Propaganda

Next you'll pass through another, more upbeat method for controlling the people: bright, cheery communist propaganda. The

motivational film (on the right) extols the value of productivity. Under the screen, find the chalkboard where workers would keep track of the "work competition" *(munkaverseny hiradó)* by noting the best workers and how far above the average productivity they achieved.

The next room shows how advertising became more colorful in the 1970s and 1980s. (Because there was no real competition in the

marketplace, glossy posters were relatively rare.) Look at a few of the posters: Several tout Bambi Narancs, the first Hungarian soft drink (at a time when Coke and Pepsi were a pipe dream). The poster about the Amerikai Bogár warns of the threat of the "American Beetle" (from Kolorádó), which threatened Hungarian crops. When the communists collectivized traditional family farm plots, they removed the trees and hedgerows that separated them—also

removing birds that had kept pest populations in check. When a potato beetle epidemic hit, rather than acknowledging their own fault, the communists blamed an American conspiracy.

"The Hungarian Silver" (A Magyar Ezüst)

This was a nickname for aluminum, which was produced in large quantities from local bauxite (the pile of rocks in the middle of the room). The items that line the walls, made of this communist equivalent of "silver," lampoon the lowbrow aesthetic of that era.

Religion (Felekezetek)

In 1949, nearly seven out of every 10 Hungarians identified themselves as Catholics. Over the next four decades, the num-

ber declined precipitously. The communist regime infiltrated church leadership, and bishops, priests, monks, and nuns filled Hungarian prisons. Many people worshipped in private (hence the glowing cross hidden under the floorboards). Those who were publicly faithful were discrimi-

nated against, closely supervised by the secret police, and often arrested. As things mellowed in the 1960s and 1970s, it was easier to be openly religious, but you were still considered an "enemy of the class." You risked being blacklisted (you might find it difficult to find a job, or your children could be denied an education). Hungarians had to choose between church and success. The loudspeakers at the end of the room, which belched communist propaganda, stand at odds with the vestments.

In the next hallway, you'll see a tribute to **Cardinal József Mindszenty,** who was arrested and beaten by the communists, and later sought refuge in the US embassy for 15 years (see sidebar on page 303).

• *Now you'll head down to the basement in a creepy...*

Elevator

You'll board an elevator that gradually lowers down into the cellar, while you watch a three-minute video of a guard explaining the grotesque execution process.

• *When the door opens, you're in the...*

Prison Cellar (Pincebörtön)

As you exit the elevator, a movie shows this cellar when it was first reclaimed in the 1980s. It's chilling to think of this space's history: In the early 1950s, it was the scene of torture; in 1956, it became a clubhouse of sorts for the local communist youth. It has now been reconstructed circa 1955.

You'll wander through **former cells** used for different purposes. On the right

Gulag and Work Camps

The stories that later emerged from the Soviet gulag system, and the equivalent Hungarian work camps, are unthinkably nauseating. Prisoners lived in makeshift barracks with wide gaps between the boards, allowing freezing winter winds to howl through. They were forced to do backbreaking manual labor (such as quarrying stone), and were punished when they failed to meet their impossible daily quota. Nutrition was laughable—prisoners would become walking skeletons in short order. While the gulag were not formally "death camps," many pris-  oners died of exposure, overwork, accidents, punishment, and disease. Two unlucky prisoners, who had served time both at the Nazi-run Dachau Concentration Camp and at the communist Recsk work camp in Hungary, reported that conditions had been better at Dachau.

It's particularly appalling to think that many innocent people were sent to work camps. One prisoner explained that he was accidentally arrested because his name was similar to a suspect's; however, by the time the mistake was sorted out, it was too late to let him go...so off he went to the camp. Another

side of the hall are a "wet cell" (where the prisoner was forced to sit in water) and a cramped "foxhole cell" (where the prisoner was forced to crouch). On the left side are a "standing cell" (where the prisoner was forced to stand 24 hours a day) and a padded cell. On both sides, you'll also see standard cells with photos of the men who once filled them.

In the large room after the cells, you'll see a stool with a lamp; nearby are the primitive **torture** devices: hot pads and electrical appliances. The bucket and hose were used to revive torture victims who had blacked out. Interrogations would normally happen at night, after food, water, and sleep had been withheld from the prisoner for days. Communist interrogators employed techniques still beloved by some torture connoisseurs today, such as "stress positions"...though waterboarding was still just a glimmer in some young sadist's eye. Simple beatings, however, were commonplace.

After the torture room, in a small room on the right, you'll see a **gallows** that was used for executions, as you just heard described in the elevator.

As you think of the people who were imprisoned and mur-

prisoner was recruited by the secret police to make a list of the people he knew to be dissidents. Instead he made a list of the people he disliked the most, then signed his own name at the bottom. Later, a black van pulled up to him on the street and he was thrown in the back—face-to-face with all of the people he'd turned in.

And yet, for some prisoners, their time in a work camp was strangely enjoyable. They were surrounded by other intelligent people, with nothing to do all day but engage in enlightening conversation while they worked. Think of the Greek myth of Sisyphus, who is condemned to spend eternity rolling a stone up a hill again and again. Some philosophers optimistically believe that the only thing Sisyphus could do...was to resolve to be happy. (One good book about the work camp experience, by George Faludy, has the insightful title *My Happy Days in Hell*.)

One university professor was not actually imprisoned, but became unemployable because he was outspoken. He could find work only as a ditch-digger...and looked forward to going to his job every day, so he could engage in long conversations with his fellow ousted professors, who dug ditches alongside him.

Hungary's work camps were closed soon after Stalin's death in 1953, the regime denied their existence, and the topic was taboo through the 1980s. People whose relatives had perished in these camps could not speak of it for decades. Only after 1989 have these families been allowed to mourn publicly.

dered here, feel the vibration of traffic on Andrássy út just outside—these victims were so close to the "normal" world, yet so far away.

Internment (Internálás)

While the most notorious gulag network was in Siberia, a similar system also emerged in the Soviet satellites, including Hungary, which had its own network of prison camps (including a secret one at a quarry overlooking the village of Recsk, not far from Eger—symbolized by the pile of rocks in the center of the room). In just three years (1945–1948), more than 40,000 people were sent to such camps, and the practice continued until 1953. The subtitled video shows a wealthy woman talking about her own experience being sent to one such camp to "learn how to work."

1956 Uprising ('56 Forradalom)

This room commemorates the 1956 Uprising (see page 120). The Hungarian flag with a hole cut out of the middle (a hastily removed Soviet emblem) and the slogan *Ruszkik Haza!* ("Russkies go home!") are important symbols of that time. The clothes and bicycle recall the "Pest Youth," teenagers and preteens who played a major role in the uprising. The Molotov cocktail—a bottle of flammable liquid hastily tied to a grenade—was a weapon of choice for the uprisers. Screens show the events of '56.

In the next room **(Megtorlás)** stand six symbolic gallows—actually used for executions (though not in this building). Children's voices quietly read aloud the names of some of those killed in the aftermath of 1956. Some 230 were formally executed, while another 15,000 were indicted. (On the gallows, see the legal paperwork for execution.)

Emigration (Kivándorlás)

More than 200,000 Hungarians simply fled the country after the uprising. A wall of postcards commemorates these emigrants, who flocked to every corner of the Western world. Once they reached Austrian refugee camps, these desperate Hungarians could chose where to go—the US offered to fly them anywhere in America to get them started. A video screen shows people leaving Hungary, and arriving at their destination, with the help of the United States. Only 11,000 of them would eventually return to their homeland.

Hall of Tears (Könnyek Terme)

This somber memorial commemorates all of the victims of the communists from 1945 to 1967 (when the final prisoners were released from this building).

Room of Farewell (Búcsú Terme)

This room shows several color video clips that provide a (relatively) happy ending: the festive and exhilarating days in 1991 when the Soviets departed, making way for freedom; the reburial of the Hungarian hero, Imre Nagy; Pope John Paul II's visit to Budapest; and the dedication of this museum. In the film of the Soviets' goodbye, watch for the poignant moment when the final Russian officer crosses the bridge on foot, with a half-hearted salute and a look of relief.

Victimizers (Tettesek)

The chilling finale: walls of photographs of the "victimizers"—members and supporters of the Arrow Cross and ÁVO, many of whom are still living and who were never brought to justice. The Hungarians have a long way to go to reconcile everything they lived through in the 20th century. For many of them, this museum is an important first step.

HEROES' SQUARE AND CITY PARK WALK

Hősök Tere és Városliget

The grand finale of Andrássy út, at the edge of the city center, is also one of Budapest's most entertaining quarters. Here you'll find the grand Heroes' Square, dripping with history (both monumental and recent); the vast tree-filled expanse of City Park, dressed up with fanciful buildings that include a replica Transylvanian castle and an Art Nouveau zoo; and, tucked in the middle of it all, Budapest's finest thermal spa and single best experience: the Széchenyi Baths. If the sightseeing grind gets you down, take a mini-vacation from your busy vacation like the Budapesters do... and escape to City Park.

ORIENTATION

What to Bring: If you'll be taking a dip in the Széchenyi Baths, bring along your swimsuit and a towel from your hotel (or you can rent these items there).

Getting There: If you walk the full length of Andrássy út (✪ see Andrássy Út Walk), you'll run right into Heroes' Square. But most visitors hightail it out here on the M1/yellow Metro line, and hop off at the Hősök tere stop. You'll exit the Metro in the middle of busy Andrássy út. Cross the street three times (making three-quarters of a circle) to work your way to the middle of Heroes' Square, with a great view of the Millennium Monument. (If you're heading directly for the baths, you could ride the M1 line one stop farther, to the Széchenyi fürdő stop.)

Length of This Walk: One hour, not including museum visits.

Museum of Fine Arts: 1,200 Ft, Tue–Sun 10:00–17:30, closed Mon, last entry 30 min before closing, Dózsa György út 41, tel. 1/469-7100, www.szepmuveszeti.hu.

Műcsarnok ("Hall of Art"): 1,200 Ft, or 1,400 Ft with Ernst Museum; Tue–Wed and Fri–Sun 10:00–18:00, Thu 12:00–20:00, closed Mon; Ernst Museum open Tue–Sun 11:00–19:00, closed Mon; Dózsa György út 37, tel. 1/460-7000, www.mucsarnok.hu.

Széchenyi Baths: 2,800 Ft for personal changing cabin, 2,400 Ft for locker, admission includes thermal baths, swimming pool, and sauna; swimming pool generally open daily 6:00–22:00, thermal bath daily 6:00–19:00, Állatkerti körút 11, tel. 1/363-3210, www.szechenyibath.com.

Starring: A lineup of looming Hungarian greats, a Transylvanian castle, Budapest's best baths, and the city's most enticing green patch.

THE WALK BEGINS

• *Stand in the middle of...*

Heroes' Square (Hősök tere)

Like much of Budapest, this Who's Who of Hungarian history at the end of Andrássy út was built to celebrate the country's 1,000th birthday in 1896 (see page 40). More than just the hottest place in town for skateboarding, this is the site of several museums and the gateway to City Park.

• *The giant colonnades and tall column that dominate the square are the...*

Millennium Monument

Step right up to meet the world's most historic Hungarians (who look to me like their language sounds). Take a moment to explore this monument, which offers a step-by-step lesson in the story of the Hungarians. (Or, to skip the history lesson, you can turn to "Museum of Fine Arts" on page 185.)

Central Column: The Magyars

The granddaddy of all Magyars, **Árpád,** stands proudly at the bottom of the pillar, peering down Andrássy út. He's surrounded by six others chieftains; all together, seven Magyar tribes first arrived in the Carpathian Basin (today's Hungary) in the year 896. Remember that these ancestors of today's Hungarians were from Central Asia, and barely resembled the romanticized, more

European-looking figures you see here. (Only one detail of these statues is authentically Hungarian: the bushy moustaches.) Magyar horsemen were known and feared for their speed: They rode sleek Mongolian horses (rather than the powerful beasts shown here), and their use of stirrups—revolutionary in Europe at the time—allowed them to ride fast and turn on a dime, to quickly overrun their battlefield opponents. Bows and spears were their weapons of choice; they'd have little interest in the chain mail and the heavy clubs and battle axes that Romantic sculptors gave them. They used these skills to run roughshod over the Continent, laying waste to Europe.

The 118-foot-tall pillar supports the archangel **Gabriel** as he offers the crown to Árpád's great-great-grandson, István (as we'll learn, he accepted it and Christianized the Magyars).

In front of the pillar is the **Hungarian War Memorial** (fenced in to keep skateboarders from enjoying its perfect slope).

The **sculptures** on the top corners of the two colonnades represent, in order from left to right: Work and Welfare, War, Peace, and the Importance of Packing Light.

Each statue in the two colonnades represents a great Hungarian leader, with a relief below showing a defining moment in his life. Likewise, each one represents a trait or trend in the colorful story of this dynamic people. (For all the details, see the Hungary: Past and Present chapter.)

• *Behind the pillar, look to the...*

First (Left) Colonnade

The first colonnade features rulers from the early glory days of Hungary.

St. István (c. 967–1038)

After decades of terrorizing Europe, the Magyars were finally defeated at the Battle of Augsburg in 955. King Géza realized that unless they could learn to get along with their neighbors, the Magyars' military might would only garner them short-term prosperity. Géza decided to baptize his son, Vajk, gave him the

Christian name István (Stephen), and married him off to a Bavarian princess. On Christmas Day in the year 1000, commissioners of the pope (pictured in the relief below) brought to István the same crown that still sits under the Parliament dome. To historians, this event marks the beginning of the Christian (and therefore European) chapter of Magyar history. (For more on István, see page 112 in the Castle Hill Walk.)

St. László I (c. 1040-1095)

Known as Ladislas in English, László was a powerful knight/king who carried the Christian torch first taken up by his cousin István.

Joining the drive of his fellow European Christian leaders, he led troops into battle to expand his territory into today's Croatia. Don't let the dainty chain-mail skirt fool you... that axe ain't for chopping wood. In the relief below, see László swing the axe against a pagan soldier who had taken Christian women hostage. László won a chunk of Croatia, then lost it...and was sainted anyway (hence the halo). László's story is the first of many we'll hear about territorial expansion and loss—a crucial issue to Hungarian leaders across the centuries (and even today).

Kálmán (c. 1070-1116)

Kálmán (Coloman) traded his uncle László's bloody axe for a stack of books. Known as "the Book-Lover," Kálmán was enlightened before his time, and acclaimed as being the most educated king of his era. He was the first European ruler to prohibit the trial or burning of women as witches (in the relief, see him intervening to save the cowering woman, at the bottom-right corner). He was also the king who retook Croatia yet again, bringing it into the Hungarian sphere of influence through the early 20th century. Kálmán reminds us that the Hungarians pride themselves

on being a highly intellectual people, demonstrated by the many scientists, economists, and other great minds they've produced. (As you walk through City Park in a few minutes, keep an eye out for chess players.)

András II (c. 1177–1235)

András (Andrew) II is associated with the golden charter he holds in his hand (with the golden medallion dangling from it)—the Golden Bull of 1222. This decree granted some measure of power to the nobility, releasing the king's stranglehold and acknowledging that his power was not absolute. This was the trend across Europe at the time (such as the similar Magna Carta, signed in 1215 by England's King John). András demonstrates the importance Hungarians place on self-determination: Like many small Central European nations, Hungary has often been dominated by a foreign power...but shown an uncrushable willingness to fight back. (We'll meet some modern-day Hungarian freedom fighters shortly.) It's no

surprise that so many place names in Hungary include the word Szabadság ("Liberty"). The relief shows that the Hungarians are willing to fight for this ideal for others, as well: András is called "The Jerosolimitan" for his success in the Fifth Crusade, in which his army liberated Jerusalem. Here he is depicted alongside the pope kissing the rescued "true cross."

Despite his achievements, András is far less remembered today than his daughter **Elisabeth** (1207–1231, not depicted here), who was sent away to Germany for a politically expedient marriage. She is the subject of an often-told legend: The pious, kindly Elisabeth was known to sneak scraps of food out of the house to give to poor people on the street. One evening, her cruel confessor saw her leaving the house and stopped her. Seeing her full apron (which was loaded with bread for the poor), he demanded to know what she was carrying. "Roses," she replied. "Show me," he growled. Elisabeth opened her apron, the bread was gone, and rose petals miraculously cascaded out onto the floor. In her short life, Elisabeth went on to found hospitals and carry out other charitable acts, and (unlike her father) became a saint. Elisabeth remains a popular symbol of charity not only in Hungary, but also in Germany. (It's easy to confuse St. Elisabeth with the equally adored Empress Elisabeth, a.k.a. Sisi, the Habsburg monarch, described on page 278.)

Béla IV (1206–1270)

Having governed over one of the most challenging periods of Hungarian history, the defiant-looking Béla—St. Elisabeth's brother—is celebrated as the "Second Founder of the Country" (after István). Béla led Hungary when the Tatars swept in from Central Asia, devastating Buda, most of Hungary, and a vast swath of Central and Eastern Europe. Because his predecessors had squandered away Hungary's holdings, Béla found himself defenseless against the onslaught. In the relief, we see Béla surveying the destruction the Tatars left in their wake. Béla made a deal with God to send his daughter Margaret to a nunnery (on the island

that would someday bear her name—see page 82) in exchange for sparing Hungary from complete destruction. After the Tatars left, he rebuilt his ruined nation. It was Béla who moved Buda to its strategic location atop Castle Hill and built a wall around it, to be better prepared for any future invasion. This was the first of many times that Budapest (and Hungary) was devastated by invaders; later came the Ottomans, the Nazis, and the Soviets. But each time, like Béla, the resilient Hungarian people rolled up their sleeves to rebuild.

Károly Róbert (1288–1342)

Everyone we've met so far was a member of the Árpád dynasty—descendants of the tough guys at the base of the big column. But

when that line died out in 1301, the Hungarian throne was left vacant. The Hungarian nobility turned to "Charles Robert," a Naples-born prince from the French Anjou (or Angevin) dynasty, which had married into Hungarian royalty. (His shield combines the red-and-white stripes of Hungary with the fleur-de-lis of France.) The Hungarians were slow to accept Robert—he had to be crowned four different times to convince everybody, and was actually banned from Buda. (He built his own palace, which still stands, at Visegrád up the Danube—see page 298.) Eventually he managed to win them over and stabilize the country, even capturing new lands for Hungary (see the relief). Károly Róbert represents the many Hungarian people who are not fully, or even partially, Magyar. Today's Hungarians are a cultural cocktail of the various peoples—German, Slavic, Jewish, Roma (Gypsy), and many others—that have lived here and been "Magyarized" to adopt Hungarian language, culture, and names.

Nagy Lajos (1326-1382)

"Louis the Great" built on his father Károly Róbert's successes, and presided over the high-water mark of Hungarian history. He expanded Hungarian territory to its historical maximum—including parts of today's Dalmatia (Croatia), Bulgaria, and Bosnia-Herzegovina—and even attempted to re-take his father's native Naples (pictured in the relief). Hungarians still look back with great pride on these days more than six centuries ago, when they were a vast and mighty kingdom.

• *Now turn your attention to the...*

Second (Right) Colonnade

The gap between the colonnades coincides with some dark times for the Hungarians. The invading **Ottomans** swept up the Balkan Peninsula from today's Turkey, creeping deeper and deeper into Hungarian territory...eventually even taking over Buda and Pest for a century and a half. Hungarian nobility retreated to the farthest corners of its lands, today's Slovakia and Transylvania, and soldiered on.

Salvation came in the form of the **Habsburgs,** rulers of a fast-expanding Austrian Empire, who presented Hungary with a classic "good news, bad news" scenario: They forced out the Ottomans, then claimed Hungary as part of their realm. While the Habsburgs eventually granted the Hungarians some leadership in the empire, the Habsburg era was a time of frustration and rebellion. In fact, at the time of this monument's construction—when Budapest was controlled from Vienna—Habsburg rulers stood in the last five slots of the right-hand colonnade. (The statue of Empress Maria Theresa—pictured at left—now stands in

the lobby of the Museum of Fine Arts, across the street.) But after the monument was damaged in World War II, locals seized on the opportunity to replace the Habsburgs with Hungarians...who were famous for fighting *against* those slots' former occupants.

János Hunyadi (c. 1387–1456)

A military hero who achieved rare success fighting the Ottomans, Hunyadi won the fiercest-fought skir-

mish of the era, the Battle of Belgrade (Nándorfehérvár in Hungarian). The relief depicts a particularly violent encounter in that battle. (The guy holding the cross is János Kapisztran, a.k.a. St. John Capistrano, an Italian friar and Hunyadi's right-hand man.) This victory halted the Ottomans' advance into Hungary for decades. Owing largely to his military prowess, Hunyadi was extremely popular among the people, and became wealthier than even the king.

He led Hungary for a time as regent, when the preschooler king was too young to rule. Although he died of the plague, Hunyadi's reputation allowed his son, Mátyás Corvinus, to step up as ruler...

Mátyás Corvinus (1443–1490)

Perhaps the most beloved of all Hungarian rulers, Mátyás (Matthias) Corvinus was a Renaissance king who revolutionized

the monarchy. He was a clever military tactician and a champion of the downtrodden, known among commoners as "the people's king." The long hair and laurel wreath (instead of a crown) attest to his knowledge and enlightenment. And most importantly, he was the first (and last) Hungarian-blooded king from the death of the Árpád dynasty in 1301 until today. Building on his father's military success against the Ottomans, Matthias achieved a diplomatic peace with them—allowing him to actually expand his territory while other kings of this era were losing it. (He even had time for some vanity building projects—the relief shows him appreciating a model of his namesake church, which still stands atop Castle Hill.)

Matthias' death represented the death of Hungarian sovereignty. After him, Hungary was quickly swallowed up by the Ottomans, then the Habsburgs. For more on King Matthias, see page 106.

Appropriately, Matthias is the final head of state at Heroes'

Square. Reflecting the sea change after his death, the rest of the heroes here are freedom-fighters who rallied against Habsburg influence.

István Bocskai (1557–1606), Gábor Bethlen (1580–1629), and Imre Thököly (1657–1705)

After Matthias, the Ottomans took over most of Hungary. Transylvania, the eastern fringe of the realm, was fragmented and in a state of ever-fluctu-ating semi-independence—sometimes under the firm control of sovereign princes, at other times controlled by the Ottomans. The three Hungarian dukes depicted here helped to unify the Hungarians through this dif-

ficult spell (see the reliefs): Bocskai and Thököly found rare suc-cess on the battlefield against the Habsburgs, while Bethlen made peace with the Czechs and united with them to fight against the Habsburgs.

The last two are arguably the greatest Hungarian heroes of the Habsburg era—the namesakes of streets and squares through-out the country.

Ferenc Rákóczi II (1676–1735)

Although he was a wealthy aristocrat educated in Vienna, Rákóczi (Thököly's stepson) resented Habsburg rule over Hungary. When

his countrymen mobilized into a rag-tag peasant army to stage a War of Independence (1703–1711), Rákóczi reluctantly took charge. (The relief depicts an unpleasant moment in Rákóczi's life, when he realizes just how miserable his army will be.) Allied with the French (who were trying to wrest power from the Habsburgs' western territory, Spain), Rákóczi mounted an attack that caught the Habsburgs off-guard. Moving west from his home region of Transylvania, Rákóczi suc-

ceeded in re-claiming Hungary all the way to the Danube. But the tide turned when, during a pivotal battle, Rákóczi fell from his horse and was presumed dead by his army. His officers retreated and appealed to the Habsburgs for mercy, effectively ending the revolution. Rákóczi left Hungary in disgrace, and rattled around

HEROES' SQUARE WALK

Europe—to like-minded Habsburg enemies Poland, France, the Ottoman Empire—in a desperate attempt to gain diplomatic support for a free Hungary. He died in exile in a small Turkish town, but his persistence still inspires Hungarians today.

Lajos Kossuth (1802–1894)

Kossuth was a nobleman and parliamentarian known for his rebellious spirit. When the winds of change swept across Europe in 1848, the Hungarians began to murmur once again about more independence from the Habsburgs—and Kossuth emerged as the movement's leader (in the relief, he's calling his countrymen to arms). After a bitterly fought revolution, Habsburg Emperor Franz Josef enlisted the help of the Russian czar to put down the Hungarian uprising, shattering Kossuth's dream. (For more on the 1848 Revolution, see page 396.) Kossuth went into exile and traveled the world, tirelessly lobbying foreign governments to support Hungary's bid for independence. He even made his pitch to the US Congress...and today, a bust of Kossuth is one of only three sculptures depicting non-Americans in the US Capitol building. After Kossuth died in exile in 1894, his body was returned to Budapest for an elaborate three-day funeral. The Habsburg Emperor Franz Josef—who knew how to hold a grudge—refused to declare the former revolutionary's death a national holiday, so Catholic church bells did not toll...but Protestant ones did.

The less-than-cheerful ending to this survey of Hungarian history is fitting. Hungarians tend to have a pessimistic view of their past...not to mention their present and future. In the Hungarian psyche, life is a constant struggle, and you get points just for playing your heart out, even if you don't win.

• *A pair of fine museums flank Heroes' Square. As you face the Millennium Monument, to your left is the...*

Museum of Fine Arts (Szépművészeti Múzeum)

This giant collection of mostly European art is the underachieving cousin of the famous Kunsthistorisches Museum in Vienna. Like that collection, it's strong in art from areas in the Habsburgs' cultural orbit: Germanic countries, the Low Countries, and especially Spain. (For the best Hungarian art, head for the National Gallery on Castle Hill—see page 103.) The collection belonged to the noble Eszterházy family, and was later bought and expanded

by the Hungarian government. Future plans for the museum include displaying the four surviving Habsburg statues from the Millennium Monument on the front porch, and building a glass entry to the museum on Heroes' Square (à la the Louvre's pyramid entry).

If you enjoy European art (particularly Spanish Golden Age), consider visiting this museum. After buying your ticket, grab a floor plan and head up the stairs on the right, go to the end of the hall and through the door on the right, and do a clockwise spin through the good stuff: German and Austrian (including some works by Albrecht Dürer); early Dutch and Flemish (including paintings by both Brueghels); and finally Spanish. In the Spanish collection, you'll find works by Murillo, Zubarán, Velázquez, and more. The museum owns five El Grecos, plus several Goyas, including *The Water Carrier.*

• *Across Heroes' Square (to the right as you face the Millennium Monument) is the...*

Műcsarnok ("Hall of Art")

Used for cutting-edge contemporary art exhibits, the Műcsarnok (comparable to a German *"Kunsthalle"*) has five or six temporary exhibits each year. It also houses the Ernst Museum and the

Dorottya Gallery (specializing in up-and-coming new artists). While art-lovers enjoy this place, it's more difficult to appreciate than some other Budapest museums.

The Műcsarnok was also the site of a major event in recent history. On June 16, 1989, several anti-communist heroes who had been executed by the regime were finally given a proper funeral on the steps of this building. The Műcsarnok was draped in black and white cloths, and in front were four actual coffins (including one with the recently exhumed remains of reformist hero Imre Nagy—see page 124), and a fifth, empty coffin to honor others that were lost. The Yugoslav Embassy, which was in the building across the busy ring road from Heroes' Square (on the left-hand corner), was the last place Imre Nagy was seen alive in public.

• Before continuing into the park, consider an optional 15-minute detour down Dózsa György út, a.k.a...

"Parade Street"

The area along the busy street beyond the Műcsarnok was once used for communist parades. While the original communist monuments are long-gone, two new monuments have replaced them.

As you walk behind the Műcsarnok, first you'll see the giant, circular **Time Wheel** (Időkerék).
Notice the sand inside the circle, which acts like a giant hourglass. Unveiled with much fanfare when Hungary joined the European Union on May 1, 2004, the wheel is manually rotated 180 degrees to re-start the hourglass every year. Unfortunately, unexpected condensation has gummed up the mechanism (hardly an auspicious kickoff  for Hungary's EU membership). While most Budapesters laugh it off as an eyesore, it's cheaper to leave it here than to tear it down.

Across the street, notice the shiny, undulating new **ING Bank Headquarters.** ING has invested heavily in Budapest over the last few years, building both this and the shiny new glass mall on Vörösmarty tér.

Continuing along the parking lot, you'll soon see the impressive **1956 Monument,** celebrating the historic uprising against the communists (see page 120). During the early days of the Soviet regime, this was the site of a giant monument to Josef Stalin that towered 80 feet high (Stalin himself was more than 25 feet tall). While dignitaries stood on a platform at Stalin's feet, military parades would march past. From the inaugura-tion of the monument in 1951, the Hungarians saw it as a hated symbol of an unwanted regime. When the 1956 Uprising broke out, the removal of the monument was high on the protestors' list of 16 demands. The night the uprising began, October

23, some rebels decided to check this item off early. They came here to cut off Stalin just below the knees, and toppled him from his platform. (Memento Park has a reconstruction of the monument's base, including Stalin's boots—see page 201.) In 2006, to commemorate the 50th anniversary of the uprising, this new monument was erected. Symbolizing the way Hungarians came together to attempt the impossible, it begins with scattered individuals at the back (rusty and humble), gradually coming together and gaining strength and unity near the front—culminating in a silver ship's prow boldly plying the ground. To fully appreciate the monument, walk up the middle of it from the back to the front. Think about how comforting it is to realize you're not alone, as others like you gradually get closer and closer.

• *Head back to the Műcsarnok at Heroes' Square. The safest way to reach City Park is to begin in front of the Műcsarnok, then use the crosswalk to circle around across the street from the Millennium Monument to reach the bridge directly behind it. (There's no crosswalk from the monument directly to the bridge.)*

Begin walking over the bridge into...

▲▲City Park (Városliget)

Budapest's not-so-central "Central Park" was the site of the overblown 1896 Millennium Exhibition, celebrating Hungary's 1,000th birthday. It's still packed with huge party decorations from that bash: a zoo with quirky Art Nouveau buildings, a replica of a Transylvanian castle, a massive bath/swimming complex, walking paths, and an amusement park. City Park is also filled with unwinding locals.

Orient yourself from the bridge: The huge Vajdahunyad Castle is across the bridge and on your right. Straight into the park and on the left are the big copper domes of the fun, relaxing Széchenyi Baths. And the zoo is past the lake on the left. Three recommended restaurants are at the end of the lake near the zoo (see page 230 in the Eating chapter).

The area in front of the castle, which used to be a boat pond in summer and a skating rink in winter, was drained several years ago for repairs. The city discovered that it's more lucrative to rent it out to big companies (for instance, as a "beach bar" that fills part of the area with sand in the summer, or as a street-basketball tournament venue) than to rent paddleboats. Another faction is pushing to tear up the concrete and turn it into more parkland.

• *Cross the bridge, take the immediate right turn, and follow the path*

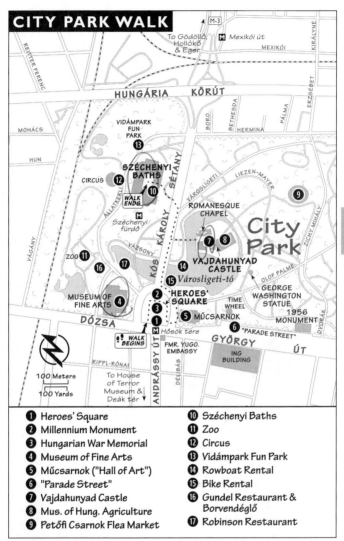

❶ Heroes' Square	❿ Széchenyi Baths
❷ Millennium Monument	⓫ Zoo
❸ Hungarian War Memorial	⓬ Circus
❹ Museum of Fine Arts	⓭ Vidámpark Fun Park
❺ Műcsarnok ("Hall of Art")	⓮ Rowboat Rental
❻ "Parade Street"	⓯ Bike Rental
❼ Vajdahunyad Castle	⓰ Gundel Restaurant & Borvendéglő
❽ Mus. of Hung. Agriculture	
❾ Petőfi Csarnok Flea Market	⓱ Robinson Restaurant

(passing the rowboat rental—700 Ft/30 min, 1,300 Ft/hr) to the entrance of...

Vajdahunyad Castle (Vajdahunyad Vára)

Many of the buildings for Hungary's Millennial National Exhibition were erected with temporary materials, to be torn down at the end of the festival—as was the case for most world fairs at the time. But locals so loved Vajdahunyad Castle that they insisted it stay, so it was rebuilt in brick and stone. The complex actually has four parts, representing the high points of four architectural styles in Hungary: Romanesque chapel, Gothic gate, Renaissance castle, and Baroque palace (free and always open to walk around the grounds).

From this direction, the **Renaissance castle** dominates the view. It's a replica of a famous castle in Transylvania that once belonged to the Hunyadi family (János and Mátyás Corvinus—both of whom we met back on Heroes' Square).

Cross over the bridge and through the **Gothic gateway.** Once inside the complex, on the left you'll see a replica of a 13th-century

Romanesque **Benedictine chapel.** Consecrated as an actual church, this is Budapest's most popular spot for weekend weddings in the summer. Farther ahead on the right, you'll see a big Baroque mansion—which houses the **Museum of Hungarian Agriculture** (Magyar Mezőgazdasági Múzeum). The museum brags that it's Europe's biggest agriculture museum, but most visitors will find the lavish interior more interesting than the exhibits.

Facing the museum entry is a monument to **Anonymous**—specifically, the Anonymous from the court of King Béla IV who penned the first Hungarian history in the Middle Ages.

For an optional detour to yet another monument (of György—er, George—Washington), consider going for a walk in the park. Continue across the bridge at the far end of Vajdahunyad Castle, then turn right along the main path. **George Washington** (funded by Central European immigrants to the US) is about five minutes down, on the left-hand side.

Deeper in the park is the giant **Petőfi Csarnok,** which is used for big rock concerts as well as a weekend flea market (see page 254 in the Entertainment & Nightlife chapter, and page 245 in the Shopping chapter).

• *Time for some fun. Head back out to the busy main road; across the street and a bit to the right, the pretty gardens and copper dome mark the famous...*

▲▲▲Széchenyi Baths (Széchenyi Fürdő)

Budapest's best thermal baths, and (for me) its single best experience, period, the Széchenyi Baths offer a refreshing and culturally enlightening Hungarian experience. Reward yourself with a soak. For all the details, see page 90 in the Thermal Baths chapter.

Attractions Behind Széchenyi Baths

Lining the street behind the baths are three kid-friendly attractions. From the steps of the swimming pool entrance, look through

the fence across the street to see the **zoo's** colorful Art Nouveau elephant house (pictured at left), slathered with Zsolnay tiles outside and mosaics inside. To the right are a **circus** (marked *Nagycirkusz*) and the **Vidámpark fun park,** with rides appealing to travelers both big and small. For more details on these attractions, see the Budapest with Children chapter.

• *Our walk is over. Your options are endless. Soak in the bath, ride a roller coaster, go for a stroll, rent a rowboat, buy some cotton candy...enjoy City Park any way you like.*

If you're ready for some food, cheap snack stands are scattered around the park, and three upscale restaurants are described on page 230 in the Eating chapter.

When you're ready to head home, the M1/yellow Metro line (with effortless connections to the House of Terror, Opera, the Metro hub of Deák tér, or Vörösmarty tér in downtown Pest) has two handy stops here: The entrance to the Széchenyi fürdő stop is at the southwest corner of the yellow bath complex (to the left and a bit around the side as you face the main entry); and the Hősök tere stop is back across the street from Heroes' Square, where we began this walk.

MEMENTO PARK TOUR

a.k.a. Statue Park (Szoborpark)

When regimes fall, so do their monuments. Just think of all those statues of Stalin and Lenin—or Saddam Hussein—crashing to the ground. Throughout Eastern Europe, people couldn't wait to get rid of these reminders of their oppressors. But some clever entrepreneur hoarded Budapest's, and has collected them in a park in the countryside just southwest of the city—where tourists flock to get a taste of the communist era. Though it can be time-consuming to visit, this collection is worth ▲▲▲ for those fascinated by Hungary's commie past.

ORIENTATION

Name-Change Warning: Confusingly, this attraction—which for years had been called Statue Park—was recently re-branded as Memento Park. The names are still occasionally used interchangeably; they refer to the same sight.

Cost: 1,500 Ft.

Hours: Daily 10:00–sunset.

Location: Six miles southwest of the city center at the corner of Balatoni út and Szabadka út, Budapest XXII, tel. 1/424-7500, www.mementopark.hu.

Getting There: The park runs a convenient direct bus from Deák tér in downtown Budapest (where all three Metro lines converge, bus stop is at corner of busy Bajcsy-Zsilinszky út and Harmincad utca, year-round daily at 11:00, July–Aug also at 15:00; round-trip takes 1.75 hours total, including a 40-min visit to the park, 3,950 Ft round-trip including park entry—which means the bus costs the equivalent of 2,450 Ft). The public-transit option is more frequent and less expensive, but also less convenient: First take tram #18, #18A, #19, #49, or #118 from Szent Gellért tér (in front of Gellért Hotel and Baths) to Kosztolányi Dezső tér. From there, catch bus #150 in the direction of Campona and ask for "Memento Park" (stop can be easy to miss—ask fellow passengers for help; 3/hr Mon–Fri, 2/hr Sat–Sun, 25-min trip, covered by one 290-Ft transit ticket or multi-day pass). Other connections are possible, but they're too complicated.

Information: The 600-Ft English guidebook, while poorly translated, is very informative.

Tours: Absolute Walking Tours offers a 6,500-Ft guided visit to Memento Park (see page 51), but the self-guided tour in this chapter covers the essentials.

Starring: Marx, Engels, Lenin, stiff soldiers, passionate patriots... and other ghosts of Hungary's communist past.

Background

Under the communists, creativity was discouraged. The primary purpose of art was to further the goals of the state, with creative

expression only as an afterthought. This **Socialist Realistic** art served two purposes: It was Realistic, breaking with the "decadent" bourgeois art that came before it (Impressionism, Post-Impressionism, and other modern -isms); and Socialistic, encouraging complicity with the brave new world the communists were forging. From 1949 until 1956, Socialist Realism was legally enforced as the sole artistic style of the Soviet Bloc.

As propaganda was an essential weapon in the Soviet arsenal, the regime made ample use of Socialist Realistic art. Aside from a few important figureheads, individuals didn't matter. Everyone was a cog in the machine—strong, stoic, doing their job well and proudly for the good of the people. Individual characteristics and distinguishing features were unimportant; people were represented as automatons serving their nation. Artistic merit was virtually ignored. Most figures are trapped in stiff, unnatural poses that ignore the 3,000 years of artistic evolution since the Egyptians. Sculptures and buildings alike from this era were designed to evoke feelings of power and permanence.

THE TOUR BEGINS

• *As you approach the park, you encounter an imposing red-brick...*

Entry Facade

You're greeted by three of the Communist All-Stars: ❶ **Vladimir Lenin,** a leader of Russia's Bolshevik Revolution; and ❷ **Karl Marx** and **Friedrich Engels,** the German philosophers whose *Communist Manifesto* first articulated the principles behind communism in 1848. (These three figures weren't offensive enough to be destroyed, but very few statues survive anywhere of the biggest "star" of all, the hated Josef Stalin.)

Like the rest of the park, this gate's design is highly conceptual: It looks impressive and monumental...but, like the rotted-out pomp of communism, there's nothing behind it. It's a glossy stage-set with no substance. If you try to go through the main, central part of the gate, you'll run into an always-locked door. Instead, as with the communist system, you have to find another way around (in this case, the side gate to the left). Etched in the door, notice the Hungarian poem "Where seek out tyranny?", published after the 1956 Uprising.

Inside the gate on the left, buy your ticket and head into the park. Surveying the layout, notice that the main road takes you confidently toward...a dead end (the brick wall). Once again, as with life under the communists, you'll have to deviate from this main axis to actually accomplish anything. Even so, notice that the six walkways branching off the main road all loop you right back to where you started—representing the endless futility of communism. The loops are thematically tied together in pairs: roughly, the first figure-eight focuses on Hungarian-Soviet friendship; the second figure-eight celebrates the heroes of communism; and the third figure-eight shows off the idealized concepts of communism.

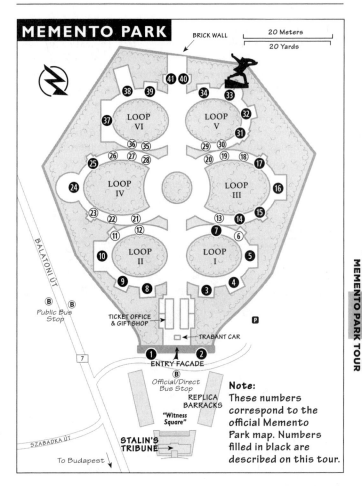

MEMENTO PARK

BRICK WALL

20 Meters
20 Yards

LOOP VI — 37, 38, 39, 36, 35, 25, 26, 27, 28, 24, 23, 22, 21, 11, 12, 10

LOOP V — 41, 40, 34, 33, 32, 31, 29, 30

LOOP IV

LOOP III — 20, 19, 18, 17, 16, 13, 14, 15, 7, 6

LOOP II — 9, 8

LOOP I — 3, 4, 5

TICKET OFFICE & GIFT SHOP

TRABANT CAR

P

BALATONI ÚT

Public Bus Stop

B   B

7

1   ENTRY FACADE   2

B
Official/Direct Bus Stop

REPLICA BARRACKS

"Witness Square"

STALIN'S TRIBUNE →

SZABADKA ÚT

To Budapest ↓

Note:
These numbers correspond to the official Memento Park map. Numbers filled in black are described on this tour.

MEMENTO PARK TOUR

• *Now we'll zigzag back and forth through each of the six loops. The numbers in the following text match the statue labels in the park, the official park map, and my map above.*

Begin with the loop to the right as you enter the park.

Liberation Monuments (Loop I)

All of these statues celebrate the Soviet Red Army's triumphant rescue of Hungary from the Nazis in 1945.

Dominating this loop is a **❸ giant soldier** holding the Soviet flag. This statue once

stood at the base of the Liberation Monument that still overlooks the Danube from Gellért Hill (see page 62). Typical of Socialist Realist art, the soldier has a clenched fist (symbolizing strength) and a face that shows no emotion. After the fall of communism, some critics wanted the entire monument torn down. As a compromise, they covered it with a sheet for a while to exorcise the communist mojo, then unveiled it.

To the left of this soldier, see the ❹ **two comrades** stiffly shaking hands: the Hungarian worker thrilled to meet the Soviet soldier.

Beyond them is a ❺ **long wall,** with a triumphant worker breaking through the left end—too busy doing his job to be very excited. Just another brick in the wall. (The three big blocks protruding from the wall were for hanging commemorative wreaths.)

The big ❼ **panel** came from an apartment building in a conservative Buda Hills neighborhood. Each neighborhood had a similar monument to the liberation: "Everlasting praise for the freedom of the Soviet Union, for its independence, and for its fallen heroes in the battle to liberate Hungary."

• Cross "main street" to a group of statues commemorating the key communist holiday of...

April 4, 1945 (Loop II)

On this date, the Soviets forced the final Nazi soldier out of Hungary. The tall panel nearest the entrance shows a Hungarian woman and a Soviet woman setting free the ❽ **doves of peace.** According to the inscription, "Our freedom and peace is based on the enduring Hungarian-Soviet friendship." (With friends like these....)

The ❾ **woman holding the palm leaf** is reminiscent of the Liberation Monument back on the Danube—who, after all, celebrates the same glorious day.

At the back of the loop, the ❿ **Hungarian**

worker and Soviet soldier (who appear to be doing calisthenics) are absurdly rigid even though they're trying to be dynamic. (Even the statues couldn't muster genuine enthusiasm for communist ideals.)

• *Cross over and head up to the next loop, to pay homage to...*

Heroes of the Workers' Movement (Loop III)

Look for the ⓮ bust of the Bulgarian communist leader **Georgi Dimitrov** (ruled 1946–1949)—one of communist Hungary's many Soviet Bloc comrades. During the 1956 Uprising, protestors put a noose around this bust's neck, and hanged it from a tree. Next is a ⓯ full-size statue of Dimitrov, a gift from "the working people of Sofia." (Talk about a white elephant.)

At the back of this loop are ⓰ three blocky portraits. The middle figure is the granddaddy of Hungarian communism: **Béla Kun** (1886–1938) fought for the Austro-Hungarian Empire in World War I. He was captured by the Russian Army, taken to a prisoner of war camp inside Russia, and became mysteriously smitten with communism. After proving himself too far left even for Lenin, Kun returned to Hungary in 1918 and formed a Hungarian Communist Party at a time when communism was most definitely not in vogue. We'll see more of Kun later in the park.

To the left is one of the park's best-loved, most-photographed, and most artistic statues: ⓱ **Vladimir Lenin,** in his famous "hailing a cab" pose. It once stood at the entrance to the giant industrial complex in Budapest's Csepel district.

• *Cross over—passing the giant red star made of flowers (resembling one that was once planted in the middle of the roundabout at the Buda end of the Chain Bridge)—to meet...*

More Communist Heroes (Loop IV)

This group—which includes a **㉕** statue of an interior minister made a foot shorter at the bottom when the Iron Curtain fell—is dominated by a **㉔** dramatic, unusually emotive sculpture by a genuine artist, **Imre Varga** (described on page 84). Designed to commemorate the 100th anniversary of Béla Kun's birth, this clever statue accomplishes seemingly contradictory feats. On the one hand, it reinforces the communist message: Under the able leadership of Béla Kun (safely overlooking the fray from above), the crusty, bourgeois old regime of the Habsburg Empire (on the left, with the umbrellas and fancy clothes) was converted into the workers' fighting force of the Red Army (on the right, with the bayonets). And yet, those silvery civilians in back seem more appealing than the lunging soldiers in front. And notice the lamppost next to Kun: In Hungarian literature, a lamppost is a metaphor for the gallows—reminding viewers that Kun was ultimately executed by the very communist system he espoused, during Stalin's purges of the late 1930s.

• *Zig and head up again, for a lesson in...*

Communist Concepts (Loop V)

Look for a rusty pair of **❸❶ workers' hands** holding a sphere (which was once adorned with a red star). The sphere represents the hard-won ideals of communism, carefully protected by the hands—but also held out for others to appreciate.

The **❸❷ monument to Hungarian soldiers** (who look like saluting Rockettes) honors those who fought against Francisco Franco in the Spanish Civil War.

Dominating this group is a **❸❸ communist worker** charging into the future, clutching the Soviet flag. Budapesters of the time had a different interpretation: a thermal bath attendant running after a customer who'd forgotten his towel.

To the left is a monument to the communist version of the Boy Scouts: the elementary school-age **❸❹ Little Drummers,** and the older **Pioneers.** While these

organizations existed before the communists, they were slowly infiltrated and turned into propaganda machines by the regime. These kids—with their jaunty red and blue neckerchiefs—were sent to camp to be properly raised as good little communists; today, many of them have forgotten the brainwashing, but still have fond memories of the socializing.

• *Now zag once more to learn about...*

More Communist Concepts (Loop VI)

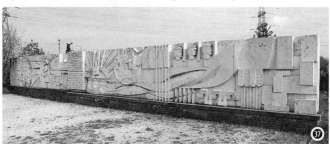

The **❸❼** long, **white wall** at the back of this section tells quite a story (from left to right): The bullet holes lead up to a jumbled, frightful clutter (reminiscent of Pablo Picasso's *Guernica*) representing

World War II. Then comes the bright light of the Soviet system, and by the end everyone's looking boldly to the future (and enjoying a bountiful crop, to boot).

Next is a ❸ **fallen hero** with arm outstretched, about to collapse to the ground—mortally wounded, yet victorious. This monument to "the Martyrs of the Counter-Revolution" commemorates those who died attempting to put down the 1956 Uprising.

Finally you'll see a ❹ **plundered monument** (missing its figures and red star).

• *Now continue down the main drag to, um, a....*

Dead End

Where the main path dead-ends at the wall, it's flanked by statues of two Soviet officers who negotiated with the Nazis to end the WWII siege of Budapest. ❹ **Captain Miklós Steinmetz** (on the right) was killed by a Nazi land mine, while ❹ **Ilja Ostapenko** (on the left) was shot under mysterious circumstances as he returned from a successful summit. Both became heroes for the communist cause. Were they killed by wayward Nazi soldiers, as the Soviets explained—or by their own Red

Army, to create a pair of convenient martyrs? These two statues once flanked the road out of Budapest toward the popular resort area at Lake Balaton. Locals eager to get out of town would hitch-hike "at Ostapenko."

Heading back out to the entry gate, peruse the fun parade of communist kitsch at the **gift shop;** consider picking up the good English guidebook, the CD of *Communism's Greatest Hits,* and maybe a model of a

Trabant (the classic two-stroke commie-mobile). A real **Trabant** is often parked just inside the gate.

• *Now head out across the parking lot, where you'll find...*

Stalin's Tribune

This new section of the complex is a re-creation of the giant grandstand that once stood along Parade Street (the boulevard

next to City Park; the original site is described on page 187 in the Heroes' Square and City Park Walk). Hungarian and Soviet leaders stood here, at the feet of a giant Stalin statue, to survey military and civilian processions. But during the 1956 Uprising, protesters cut Stalin off at the knees...leaving only the boots. (The entire tribune was later dismantled, and Stalin disappeared without a trace.)

• *Flanking the lot in front of the tribune are replica...*

Barracks

These are reminiscent of the ramshackle barracks where political prisoners lived in communist-era work camps (sometimes called gulags; described on page 172 in the House of Terror Tour). These hold special exhibits, often including a good explanation of "Stalin's Boots" (with photos of the original tribune) and the events of 1956. You might also see a short film with former spies discussing their methods and policies.

There are plans to create a "Witness Square" in the lot between the barracks, and possibly even to replace the barracks with permanent museum buildings.

• *Our tour is over. Now, inspired by the bold propaganda of your Hungarian comrades, march proudly into the dawn of a new day.*

SLEEPING

I like to list accommodations that are friendly, clean, comfortable, professional-feeling, centrally located, English-speaking, and family-run. Obviously, a place meeting every criterion is rare, and all of my recommendations fall short of perfection—sometimes miserably. But I've listed the best values for each price category.

September is extremely tight (because of conventions), with October close behind; book as far ahead as possible for these times. The Formula 1 races (one weekend in early Aug) send rates through the roof; for a list of other holidays that might cause increases, see page 420. Most rates drop 10–25 percent in the off-season (generally Nov–March).

In Budapest, most hotels quote their rates in euros (for the convenience of their international guests), and I've followed suit. (Outside of the capital, hotels more often quote rates in forints.) However, most places prefer to be paid in forints (figured at the exchange rate on the day of payment). Unless I note otherwise in the listing, you can assume the hotel accepts credit cards—though smaller places always prefer cash. I've listed prices per room, not per person.

Recent inflation has put Budapest's accommodations rates roughly on par with other European capitals—relatively high. While most hotels listed in this chapter cluster at about €70–115 per double, they range from €14 bunks to €500-plus splurges (maximum plumbing and more). (Rooms outside the capital—such as in Eger, Pécs, and Sopron—are much cheaper.) Hoteliers know what their beds are worth, so generally you get what you pay for. Since my €100 listings are substantially nicer than my €85 listings, I'd spring for the extra expense to have a comfortable home base.

A flurry of new hotel construction over the last few years has flooded the market with top-end rooms. Outside of busy convention times (Sept–Oct), many of these places offer prices that are only a little more than a midrange hotel (these deals are often listed on the hotel's website; I've noted specifics below).

If you're on a tight budget, consider one of Budapest's many hostels (described on page 212). But don't overlook the good-value Bellevue B&B (page 216) and Mária and István (page 213). At any hotel, three or four people can save money by requesting one big room. Traveling alone can be expensive: A single room is often only 20 percent cheaper than a double.

The majority of hotels don't include the 3 percent tourist tax in their rates. Be warned that some big chains also don't include the whopping 20 percent sales tax, which can make your hotel cost nearly a quarter more than you expected. (Independent hotel rates typically do include sales tax.)

Most hotels listed here include a buffet breakfast. Some smaller budget places serve no breakfast at all, while larger chain hotels charge (too much) extra for it; in these cases, I've noted it in the listing. Consider having breakfast instead at one of three good cafés I've recommended in the Eating chapter: Gerlóczy Café (see page 226), Centrál Kávéház (page 226), or Callas (page 236).

Of my recommended hotels, all of the places in Budapest (and virtually all those outside of Budapest) speak English. In the rare instance where they do not, you'll find a note in my listing.

If asked whether they have non-smoking rooms, most hotels will say yes. When pressed, they'll sheepishly admit, "Well, *all* of our rooms are non-smoking"...meaning they air them out after a smoker has stayed there. I've described hotels as "non-smoking" only if they have specially designated rooms for this purpose. Be specific and assertive if you need a strictly non-smoking room.

For environmental reasons, towels are often replaced only when you leave them on the floor. In some cheap hotels, they aren't replaced at all, so hang them up to dry and reuse. You might be tempted to borrow your hotel towel for your visit to the thermal baths (saving the towel-rental cost). Some hotels frown on this, others forbid it, and others will give you a special loaner towel for this purpose.

Before accepting a room, confirm your understanding of the complete price (including taxes). Pay your bill the evening before you leave to avoid the time-wasting crowd at the reception desk in the morning, especially if you need to rush off to catch your train. The only tip my recommended accommodations would like is a friendly, easygoing guest. And, as always, I appreciate feedback on your experiences.

Making Reservations

Given the erratic accommodations values in Hungary—and the quality of the places I've found for this book—I'd recommend that you reserve your rooms in advance, particularly during peak season. Finding accommodations as you travel is possible, but you're more likely to wind up in a poorly located and/or overpriced hotel than if you plan ahead.

To make a reservation, contact hotels directly by email, phone, or fax. Email is the clearest and most economical way to make a reservation. In addition, many hotel websites now have online reservation forms (which can instantly tell you availability, and whether there are any promotional rates). If phoning from the US, be mindful of time zones (see page 10). To ensure you have all the information you need for your reservation, use the form in this book's appendix (also at www.ricksteves.com/reservation). If you don't get a response within a few days, call to follow up.

When you request a room in writing for a certain time period, use the Hungarian style for writing dates: year/month/day. Hoteliers need to know your arrival and departure dates. For example, for a two-night stay in July I would request: "2 nights, arrive 2009.07.16, depart 2009.07.18." Consider carefully how long you'll stay; don't just assume you can extend your reservation for extra days once you arrive.

If the hotel's response tells you its room availability and rates, it's not a confirmation. You must tell them that you want that room at the given rate.

Some travelers make reservations as they travel, calling hotels a few days before their visit. If you prefer the flexibility of traveling without any reservations at all, you'll have greater success snaring rooms if you arrive at your destination early in the day. When you anticipate crowds, call hotels around 9:00 on the day you plan to arrive, when the hotel clerk knows who'll be checking out and just which rooms will be available.

Whether you're reserving from home or on the road, the hoteliers will sometimes request your credit-card number for a deposit. While you can email your credit-card information (I do), some people prefer to share that personal info via phone call, fax, or secure online reservation form (if the hotel has one on its website).

If you must cancel your reservation, it's courteous to do so with as much advance notice as possible (at least three days; simply make a quick phone call or send an email). Hotels lose money if they turn away customers while holding a room for someone who doesn't show up.

Understandably, most hoteliers bill no-shows for one night. Hotels sometimes have strict cancellation policies: For example,

---

Sleep Code

(€1 = $1.40, 200 Ft = about $1, country code: 36, area code: 1)
To help you sort easily through the listings, I've divided the rooms into three categories based on the price for a standard double room with bath in high season:

$$$ Higher Priced—Most rooms €115 or more.
  $$ Moderately Priced—Most rooms between €70–115.
    $ Lower Priced—Most rooms €70 or less.

To give maximum information in a minimum of space, I use the following code to describe the accommodations:

    S = Single room (or price for one person in a double).
    D = Double or twin room.
    T = Triple (typically a double bed plus a single).
    Q = Quad (usually two double beds).
    b = Private bathroom with toilet and shower or tub.

According to this code, a couple staying at a "Db-€100" hotel would pay a total of €100 (about $140) for a double room with a private bathroom. Unless otherwise noted, you can assume credit cards are accepted, prices include breakfast but not the 3 percent tourist tax, and the hotel staff speaks English.

---

you might lose a deposit if you cancel within two weeks of your reserved stay, or you might be billed for the entire visit if you leave early. Ask about cancellation policies before you book. Again, don't let these people down—I promised you'd call and cancel as early as possible if for some reason you won't show up.

Always reconfirm your room reservation a few days in advance from the road. If you'll be arriving after 16:00, let them know.

On the small chance that a hotel loses track of your reservation, bring along a hard copy of their emailed or faxed confirmation.

IN PEST

Most travelers find staying in Pest more convenient than sleeping in Buda. Most sights worth seeing are in Pest, which also has a much higher concentration of Metro and tram stops, making it a snap to get around. Pest feels more lively and local than stodgy, touristy Buda, but it's also much more urban-feeling (if you don't enjoy big cities, sleep in Buda instead). I've arranged my listings by neighborhood, clustered around the most important sightseeing sectors.

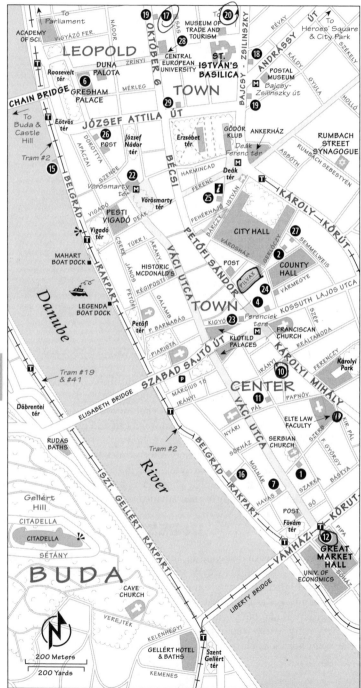

SLEEPING

1 - Cafe Alibi → tasteful coffee shop, breakfast

PEST TOWN CENTER HOTELS AND RESTAURANTS

1 Peregrinus Hotel
2 Gerlóczy Café & Rooms
3 Kálvin-Ház Hotel
4 Leo Panzió Hotel & Főzelékfaló Ételbár
5 Ibis Hotel Budapest Centrum
6 Four Seasons Gresham Palace
7 Domino Hostel
8 Marco Polo Hostel
9 Mária & István Rooms
10 Centrál Kávéház
11 BorLabor Restaurant
12 Great Market Hall
13 Soul Café
14 Café Intenzo
15 Spoon Restaurant
16 Trattoria Toscana & Taverna Dionysos
17 Café Kör
18 Belvárosi Lugas Étterem
19 Duran Szendvics (2)
20 To Hummus Bar
21 New York Café & Deepwater Restaurant
22 Gerbeaud Café
23 Jégbüfé Snack Bar
24 Patyolat G. Laundry
25 Discover Budapest
26 Dorottya Pharmacy
27 Red Bus Bookstore
28 CEU Bookshop
29 MÁV Train Ticket Office

SLEEPING

Pest Town Center (Belváros), near Váci Utca

Sleeping on the very central and convenient Váci utca comes with overly inflated prices. But these less expensive options—just a block or two off Váci utca—offer some of the best values in Budapest.

$$$ Peregrinus Hotel, overpriced despite its good location, has 25 high-ceilinged, spacious, lightly renovated rooms (most of which lack air-conditioning—unusual for this price range). Because it's run by the big ELTE university, many of its guests are visiting professors and lecturers (Sb-€85, Db-€115, Tb-€150, 20 percent cheaper Nov–March, elevator, free Internet access in lobby and cable Internet in rooms, just off Váci utca at Szerb utca 3, district V; 5-min walk to M3: Kálvin tér, or tram #47 or #49 to Fővám tér; tel. 1/266-4911, fax 1/266-4913, www.peregrinushotel .hu, peregrinushotel@elte.hu).

$$ Gerlóczy Café & Rooms, which also serves good meals (see page 226 in the Eating chapter), is the best spot in central Budapest for affordable elegance. The 18 rooms, around a classy old spiral-staircase atrium, recently underwent a thoughtful and stylish renovation. This gem is an exceptional value (Sb-€95, Db-€105, includes great breakfast, some restaurant noise on lower floors until 23:00, air-con, elevator planned soon, free Wi-Fi, 2 blocks from Váci utca, just off Városház utca at Gerlóczy utca 1, district V, M3: Ferenciek tere, tel. 1/501-4000, www.gerloczy.hu, info @gerloczy.hu).

$$ Kálvin-Ház, a long block up from the Great Market Hall, offers 38 big rooms with old-fashioned furnishings and squeaky parquet floors. The new top-floor rooms have a bit less classic character, but are air-conditioned and tidier than the older rooms. All things considered, it's a good value (all rooms cost the same: Sb-€70, Db-€95, apartment-€115, extra bed-€20, 15 percent cheaper Nov–March, elevator, free Internet access and Wi-Fi, Gönczy Pál utca 6, district IX, M3: Kálvin tér, tel. 1/216-4365, fax 1/216-4161, www.kalvinhouse.hu, info@kalvinhouse.hu).

$$ Leo Panzió is a peaceful oasis with 14 modern rooms in a hulking building that's seen better days. The location is central, if you can get past the dingy neighborhood. Once inside, the antique elevator is wonderfully rickety, and the double-paned windows keep out most of the noise from the busy street below. Rooms #1 and #7 overlook a quieter courtyard (Sb-€79, Db-€99, extra bed-€33, includes tax, 15 percent cheaper Nov–March, all rooms have a strange but well-marked little step down in the middle of the room, entirely non-smoking, air-con, free Wi-Fi, hiding upstairs in a giant building at Kossuth Lajos utca 2A—dial 58 at the door to call reception, district V, M3: Ferenciek tere, tel. 1/266-9041, tel. & fax 1/266-9042, www .leopanzio.hu, leo@leopanzio.hu).

$$ Ibis Hotel Budapest Centrum, with 126 rooms, is part of the no-frills chain that's sweeping Europe. Like all other Ibis branches, this place has spongy carpets, cookie-cutter predictability, and utterly no charm. But it's cheap, well-equipped for the price, and beautifully located at the start of the happening Ráday utca restaurant scene, just up the street from the Great Market Hall and Váci utca (Sb/Db-€79 April–Oct, Sb/Db-€65 Nov–March, lousy breakfast-€9/person, air-con, non-smoking rooms, elevator, fee for Internet access and Wi-Fi, Ráday utca 6, district IX, M3: Kálvin tér, tel. 1/456-4100, fax 1/456-4116, www.ibis-centrum.hu, h2078@accor.com).

Near Andrássy Út

Andrássy Boulevard is handy, local-feeling, and endlessly entertaining. It's lined with appealing cafés, restaurants, theaters, and bars—and the living is good. The frequent Metro stations (M1/yellow line) make getting around the city easy from here. Most of the hotels listed here (except Cotton House) are within a two-block walk of this main artery. The Queen Mary and Cotton House, which are often mysteriously empty, are likely to have rooms when other hotels are full. For specific locations, see the map on page 210.

$$$ K+K Hotel Opera is wonderfully situated beside the Opera House in the fun "Broadway Quarter"—probably the handiest home-base location in Budapest. It's a regal splurge, with 206 classy rooms and helpful, professional service. The published rates are sky-high (Sb-€200, Db-€250), but most of the time you can score a better deal (often Sb-€120–140 and Db-€140–160 in summer, Sb/Db-€120 in winter, €25 more for recently renovated "executive" rooms, non-smoking floors, air-con, elevator, free Internet access and cable Internet in rooms, parking garage-€15/day, Révay utca 24, district VI, M1: Opera, tel. 1/269-0222, fax 1/269-0230, www.kkhotels.com, kk.hotel.opera@kkhotels.hu).

$$$ Kapital Inn is an upscale, new-feeling boutique B&B tucked behind the House of Terror. "Gay-owned and straight-friendly," its four rooms are pricey but perfectly stylish—there's not a pillow out of place. Albert, who lived in Boston, gives his B&B a sense of real hospitality (D-€89—a good value if you don't mind sharing a bathroom, Db-€125, 10 percent less Nov–March, air-con, free Internet access and Wi-Fi, pleasant breakfast terrace, no elevator, up several flights of stairs at Aradi utca 30, district VI, M1: Vörösmarty utca, mobile 0630-931-1023, fax 1/266-4634, www.kapitalinn.com, kapitalinn@kapitalinn.com).

$$ Hotel Pest is nicely located a block off Andrássy út (across the street from the Opera House). Its 25 newish, straightforward rooms surround a peaceful atrium with a winter-garden lounge and

ANDRÁSSY ÚT HOTELS AND RESTAURANTS

1 K+K Hotel Opera
2 Kapital Inn
3 Hotel Pest
4 Hotel Queen Mary
5 Cotton House
6 Hotel Medosz
7 easyHotel
8 Menza Rest.
9 Klassz Bistro
10 Balettcipő Rest.
11 Shalimar Rest.
12 Duran Szendvics
13 Főzelékfaló Ételbár
14 Hummus Bar
15 Callas Café
16 Művész Kávéház
17 Laundromat-Mosómata
18 Tree Hugger Dan Bookstore
19 Discover Budapest

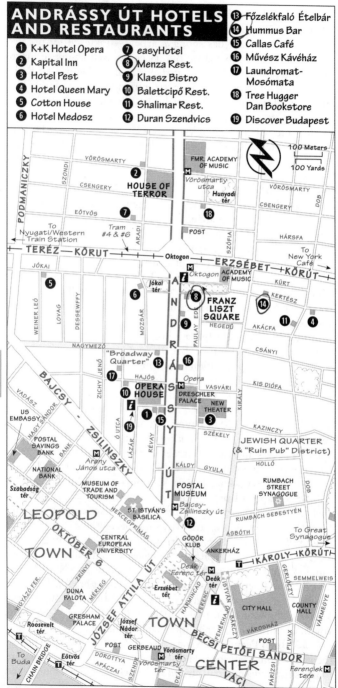

breakfast room. The published rates are a bit too high (Sb-€105, Db-€130), but it's worth considering if you can get a deal (often Sb-€90, Db-€110 in slower times, cheaper Nov–mid-March, air-con, elevator, free cable Internet, Paulay Ede utca 31, district VII, M1: Opera, tel. 1/343-1198, fax 1/351-9164, www.hotelpest.hu, hotelpest@hotelpest.hu).

$$ Hotel Queen Mary (named not for the British monarch, but for the owner's wife) is a good value, with 26 simple and unimaginative but new-feeling rooms. The neighborhood is dingy and gloomy, but it's on the cusp of an emerging dining zone, just two blocks beyond the end of the happening Franz Liszt Square (Sb-€70, Db-€80, Tb-€93, prices soft—ask for discount in slow times or with cash, 30 percent cheaper Nov–March, air-con, elevator, free cable Internet, Kertész utca 34, district VII, between M1: Oktogon and M2: Blaha Lujza tér, tel. 1/413-3510, fax 1/413-3511, www.hotelqueenmary.hu, info@hotelqueenmary.hu).

$$ Cotton House, a bit farther from Andrássy út than the others listed here (near the Nyugati/Western train station), is a fun, blast-from-the-past theme hotel. Its 23 retro rooms are fresh and comfy, with 1930s themes; each room is devoted to a different mobster (Al Capone) or old-time performer (Ella Fitzgerald, Elvis Presley, Frank Sinatra; Sb/Db-€100 with shower, €110 with bathtub, €120 with Jacuzzi, check for deals online, 15 percent less Jan–March, air-con, non-smoking rooms, elevator, fee for Wi-Fi, some street noise on weekends, a few blocks from the Oktogon at Jókai utca 26, district VI, M3: Nyugati pu., tel. 1/354-2600, fax 1/354-1341, www.cottonhouse.hu, info@cottonhouse.hu). The basement jazz club is fun to explore (but may be closed).

$ Hotel Medosz is cheap and dumpy, overlooking a seedy square. But the prices are low and the location is wonderfully central, around the corner from the Oktogon and across busy Andrássy út from the trendy Franz Liszt Square. Beyond the chilling concrete communist facade and gloomy lobby are 67 rooms—old and uninspired but perfectly adequate, comrade (Sb-€55, Db-€65, €10 cheaper Nov–March, elevator, fee for Internet access and Wi-Fi, nearby bars can be noisy—ask for a quieter courtyard room, Jókai tér 9, district VI, M1: Oktogon, tel. 1/374-3000, fax 1/332-4316, www.medoszhotel.hu, info@medoszhotel.hu).

In Opulence, Facing the Chain Bridge

$$$ Four Seasons Gresham Palace is Budapest's top hotel— and one of its most expensive. Stay here only if money is truly no object. You'll sleep in what is arguably Budapest's finest Art Nouveau building. Damaged in World War II, the Gresham Palace sat in disrepair for decades. Today it's sparkling from a recent head-to-toe renovation, and every detail in its lavish public spaces and 179 rooms is perfectly in place. Even if you're not sleeping here, dip into the lobby and café to soak in the elegance (non-view Db-€340–475, Danube-view Db-€540–885, prices don't include 23 percent tax—not a typo, breakfast-€35, air-con, non-smoking rooms, elevator, top-floor spa, Roosevelt tér 5–6, district V, between M1: Vörösmarty tér and M2: Kossuth tér, tel. 1/268-6000, fax 1/268-5000, www.fourseasons.com/budapest, budapest.reservations@fourseasons.com). For more on the building's history, see page 68.

Hostels and Other Cheap Beds

"Official" IYHF hostels are rare in Hungary, but independent hostels prevail. These range from slick, big chains to ramshackle apartments with a few mattresses strewn here and there. Amenities also vary, but you'll generally have access to kitchen facilities, Internet terminals and/or Wi-Fi, and laundry. While many hostels have a few doubles or family rooms available upon request for a little extra money, plan on dorms with 4–20 beds per room. Although these hostels welcome travelers of any age, those over 30 might not enjoy bunking with the backpacker set—so I've also listed some good-value alternatives to the youth hostel scene. (Don't miss the excellent Bellevue B&B, across the river in Buda, and listed on page 216.)

$ Mellow Mood Hostels: Budapest's preeminent hostel chain has plenty of beds, but not much character. Surprisingly institutional for a non-official hostel, the Mellow Mood group is fine for predictable, crank-'em-out bunks (at both branches: cash only, prices include sheets, towel rental-300 Ft, no breakfast, guest kitchen, pay laundry, fee for Internet access). There are two locations. **Domino Hostel**—with four twin rooms and 138 dorm beds in a handy location, right on Váci utca near the Great Market Hall—is more backpacker-oriented (Sb-€40, Db-€60, bunk in shared quad-€20, in 6-bed room-€18, in 8-bed room-€16, more for special events, cheaper Nov–March, 10 percent discount with ISIC card, best prices with advance online booking, lockers in room, Váci utca 77, enter at Havas utca 6, district V, M3: Kálvin tér, tel. 1/235-0492, www.dominohostel.com, info@dominohostel .com). **Marco Polo Hostel,** with a few dorm beds and 36 more twin rooms (with bathrooms) in a less convenient location, attracts a slightly older crowd (similar but slightly higher rates, Nyár utca 6, district VII, M2: Blaha Lujza tér, tel. 1/413-2555, fax 1/413-6058, www.marcopolohostel.com, sales@marcopolohostel.com). Mellow Mood also runs several budget hotels around the city, but they're not a good value.

$ Smaller "Indie" Hostels: Budapest has seemingly dozens of apartments that have been taken over by young entrepreneurs, offering basic, rough-around-the-edges hostel charm. You'll buzz in at the door and climb up a creaky, dank, and smelly staircase to a funky little enclave of fellow backpackers. Most of these places have just three rooms (one double and two small dorms) and feel more like communes than the finely tuned, high-capacity youth hostel machines in many other cities. As each of these fills a niche (party, artsy, communist-themed, etc.), it's hard to recommend just one—read reviews on a hostel site (such as www.hostels.com) and find one that suits your hosteling philosophy. Of the places I've seen, I particularly liked **Aventura Hostel,** a colorful and stylish option in a dreary urban neighborhood near the Nyugati/Western train station. Well-run by Agnes, this homey place is tastefully mod, friendly, clean, and low-key, with imaginatively decorated rooms (3 rooms, bunk in 5- or 8-bed dorm–€14–21, D–€50–60, price depends on season, includes breakfast and sheets, towel rental-500 Ft, free Internet access and Wi-Fi, pay laundry service, massage available, across the busy ring road and a very long block from Nyugati train station at 12 Visegrádi utca—dial 131 at door, district XIII, M3: Nyugati pu., tel. 1/239-0782, www.aventura hostel.com, info@aventurahostel.com). They also rent apartments near Andrássy út (Db-€60–70).

B&B Hostel Alternative: **$ Mária and István,** your chatty Hungarian aunt and uncle, are saving a room for you in their Old

World apartment. For warmth and hospitality at youth-hostel prices, consider bunking in one of their two simple, old-fashioned rooms, which share a bathroom. The smaller room is cheaper and quieter; the bigger room gets some street noise on weekends (S-€20–24, D-€30–36, T-€42–48, price depends on size of room and length of stay—longer is cheaper, no breakfast but guests' kitchen, cash only, elevator plus a few stairs, Ferenc körút 39, district IX, M3: Ferenc körút, tel. & fax 1/216-0768, www .mariaistvan.hu, mariaistvan@t-online.hu). From the Ferenc körút Metro stop, follow signs for the *Ferenc körút 41–45* exit, bear right up the stairs, and walk straight about a block and a half, looking for #39 (on the left, after the post office; dial 19 at the door). Mária and István also rent two apartments that are two Metro stops farther from the center (Db-€50–56, Tb-€60–66, Qb-€68–80, family apartment, both near M3: Nagyvarad tér).

Institutional but Cheap and New: The **$ easyHotel** chain follows a similar model to its parent company, the no-frills easyJet airline: They charge you very little up front, then nickel-and-dime you with optional extras—so you pay only for what you want (pick up the list at entry: TV access-€7.50/24 hrs; cable Internet access-€2/hr, €10/24 hrs; hairdryer-€1/24 hrs; room-cleaning during your stay-€10; and so on). With 59 rooms just a block off the busy Great Boulevard and around the corner from the Oktogon, the location is handy. The rooms feel popped out of a plastic mold, with a nauseating orange-and-gray color scheme, sterile quasi-linoleum floors, and tiny prefab ship's-head bathrooms. But the price is right...if you can resist the extras (Sb/Db-€15–46 depending on demand, no breakfast, 24-hr reception, non-smoking, air-con, elevator, Eötvös utca 25A, district VI, M1: Oktogon, tel. 1/411-1982, www.easyhotel.com, info@budapestoktogon.easyhotel.com).

IN BUDA

Víziváros

The Víziváros neighborhood—or "Water Town"—is the lively part of Buda, squeezed between Castle Hill and the Danube, where fishermen and tanners used to live. Across the river from the Parliament building, it comes with fine views. Víziváros is the most pleasant central area to stay on the Buda side of the Danube. It's expensive and a little less convenient than Pest, but also feels less urban.

The following hotels (except the last one) are in district I, between the Chain Bridge and Buda's busy Margit körút ring road. Trams #19 and #41 zip along the embankment in either direction. Batthyány tér, a few minutes' walk away, is a handy center with lots of restaurants (see page 232 in the Eating chapter), a Metro stop (M2/red line), and the HÉV train to Óbuda and Szentendre. Each of these places comes with professional, helpful staff.

$$$ Hotel Victoria, with 27 business-class rooms—each with a grand river view—is a winner. This tall, narrow place (three rooms on each of nine floors) is run with pride and attention to detail by on-the-ball manager Zoltán and his friendly staff (Sb-€117, Db-€123, extra bed-€46, 30 percent less Nov–March, air-con, elevator, free sauna, free Internet access and Wi-Fi, reserve ahead for €13/day parking garage or park free on street, Bem rakpart 11, tel. 1/457-8080, fax 1/457-8088, www.victoria.hu, victoria@victoria.hu). In 2008, they painstakingly restored the 19th-century Hubay Palace just behind the hotel (entrance next to reception). The hotel plans to use this gorgeous space—which feels like a museum, with inlaid

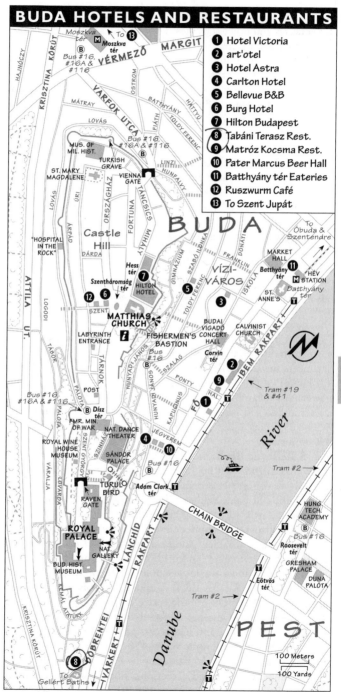

BUDA HOTELS AND RESTAURANTS

1 Hotel Victoria
2 art'otel
3 Hotel Astra
4 Carlton Hotel
5 Bellevue B&B
6 Burg Hotel
7 Hilton Budapest
8 Tabáni Terasz Rest.
9 Matróz Kocsma Rest.
10 Pater Marcus Beer Hall
11 Batthyány tér Eateries
12 Ruszwurm Café
13 To Szent Jupát

SLEEPING

floors, stained-glass windows, and stuccoed walls and ceilings—for concerts and other activities. Drop in and ask to see it, even if you're not staying here.

$$$ art'otel impresses even New York City sophisticates. Every detail—from the breakfast dishes to the carpets to the good-luck blackbird perched in each room—was designed by American artist Donald Sultan. This big, stylish, 165-room hotel is a fun, classy splurge (high rack rates, but usually Sb/Db-€109–165 depending on season, figure Sb/Db-€129 in summer, breakfast-€12/person, Danube view-€20 more, bigger "executive" rooms-€30 more, deluxe "art suites"-€60 more, air-con, non-smoking rooms, elevator, free Internet access in business lounge, fee for Wi-Fi, free sauna and mini-exercise room, Bem rakpart 16–19, tel. 1/487-9487, fax 1/487-9488, www.artotel.hu, budapest @artotel.hu).

$$ Hotel Astra is quiet, old-fashioned, and well-maintained. Its 12 rooms—surrounding a peaceful courtyard—are woody, elegant, and spacious (Sb-€97, Db-€112, sumptuous Sb or Db suite-€139, extra bed-€20, 10 percent less Nov–March, cash only, air-con, fee for Internet access and Wi-Fi, cellar bar with pool table, Vám utca 6, tel. 1/214-1906, fax 1/214-1907, www.hotelastra .hu, hotelastra@euroweb.hu).

$$ Carlton Hotel, with 95 smallish rooms, is all business and no personality. But the location—where the Castle Hill funicular meets the Chain Bridge—is handy for getting to both Castle Hill and Pest (Sb-€95, Db-€110, extra bed-€21, prices 20 percent lower Nov–March, non-smoking rooms, elevator, free Internet access and Wi-Fi, parking garage-€12/day, Apor Péter utca 3, tel. 1/224-0999, fax 1/224-0990, www.carltonhotel.hu, carltonhotel @t-online.hu).

$ Bellevue B&B, hiding in a quiet residential area on the Víziváros hillside just below the Fishermen's Bastion staircase, is easily Budapest's best deal. This gem is run by retired economists Judit and Lajos Szuhay, who lived in Canada for four years and speak flawless English. The breakfast room and some of the five straightforward, comfortable rooms have views across the Danube to the Parliament and Pest. Judit (YOO-deet) and Lajos (LIE-yosh) love to chat, and pride themselves on offering genuine hospitality and a warm welcome (let them know what time you're arriving). As this B&B is understandably popular, book ahead (Sb-€50–65, Db-€60–75, price depends on room size and view, 20–30 percent cheaper mid-Oct–mid-April, cash only, non-smoking, air-con, free Internet access and Wi-Fi; M2: Batthyány tér plus a 10-min uphill walk, or bus #16 from Deák, Roosevelt, or Adam Clark squares to Dónati utca plus a 2-min downhill walk—they'll email you detailed directions; Szabó Ilonka utca 15/B,

mobile 0630-370-8678 or 0630-951-5494, www.bellevuebudapest
.com, judit@bellevuebudapest.com).

$ Hotel Papillon is farther north, in a forgettable residential
area a 10-minute uphill walk past Moszkva tér. It's a cheery little
place with 30 homey, pastel rooms, a garden with a tiny swimming pool, and affordable prices (Sb-€44, older Db-€54, newer
"superior" Db with air-con and balcony-€64 and worth the extra
money, 25 percent less Nov–March, elevator, fee for Internet
access, free Wi-Fi in some parts of hotel, restaurant, tram #4 or
#6 from Moszkva tér to Mechwart liget stop then an uphill walk,
Rózsahegy utca 3, district II, tel. 1/212-4750, fax 1/212-4003,
www.hotelpapillon.hu, rozsahegy@t-online.hu).

Castle Hill

Romantics often like calling Castle Hill home (district I). These
two hotels share Holy Trinity Square (Szentháromság tér) with
Matthias Church. They couldn't be closer to the Castle Hill sights,
but they're in a tourist zone—dead at night, and less convenient to
Pest than other listings.

$$$ Burg Hotel, with 26 rooms, is simply efficient: concrete,
spacious, and comfy, with a professional staff. You'll find more
conveniently located hotels for less money elsewhere, but if you
simply *must* stay in a modern hotel across the street from Matthias
Church, this is it (Sb-€119, Db-€129, Db apartment-€149, extra
bed-€39, 10 percent discount with this book unless they're very
busy, cheaper for 3-night stays, prices 15 percent less Nov–March,
request view room for no extra charge, no elevator, entirely non-
smoking, top-floor rooms are extremely long, family rooms, fee
for Internet access, free Wi-Fi, Szentháromság tér 7–8, tel. 1/212-
0269, fax 1/212-3970, www.burghotelbudapest.com, info@burg
hotelbudapest.com, Lajos).

$$$ Hilton Budapest is a 322-room landmark—the first big
Western hotel in town, back in the gloomy days of communism.
Today, while a bit faded, it still offers a complete escape from
Hungary and a chance to be surrounded by rich tourists mostly
from Japan, Germany, and the United States (very flexible rates,
but usually about Db-€120 in slower times—a great deal, check
for better prices online, best rates are for 3-week advance booking with full nonrefundable prepayment, €30 more for Danube-
view rooms, prices do not include 23 percent tax, breakfast-€27/
person, non-smoking floors, elevator, fee for Wi-Fi, Hess András
tér 1–3 on Castle Hill next to Matthias Church, tel. 1/889-6600,
fax 1/889-6644, www.budapest.hilton.com, reservations.budapest
@hilton.com).

SLEEPING

EATING

Hungarian food is, after French and Italian, perhaps Europe's most delightful—rich, spicy, smooth, and delicious. Best of all, the prices are reasonable, especially if you venture off the main tourist trail. This is affordable sightseeing for your palate.

Restaurants

When restaurant-hunting, choose a spot filled with locals, not the place with the big neon signs boasting, *"We Speak English and Accept Credit Cards."* Most restaurants have an English menu posted (or you can ask to see one). If the place isn't full, you can usually just seat yourself (get a server's attention to be sure your preferred table is OK)—the American-style "hostess," with a carefully managed waiting list, isn't common here.

Once seated, feel free to take your time. In fact, it might be difficult to dine in a hurry. Only a rude waiter will rush you. Hungarian service is polite, but formal; don't expect "Hi, I'm László and I'll be your server—how you folks doin' tonight?" chumminess. At traditional places, your tuxedoed server might bring your food to the table with a formal click of the heels...then go back to the kitchen to apply more wax to his moustache. At any eatery, good service is deliberate (slow to an American).

An *étterem* ("eatery") is a nice sit-down restaurant, while a *vendéglő* is usually more casual (similar to a tavern or an inn). A *söröző* ("beer place") is a pub that sells beer and food, ranging from a small selection of snacks to a full menu. A *kávéház* ("coffeehouse"), or café, is where Budapesters gather to meet friends, get a caffeine fix…and sometimes to have a great meal. (I've listed my favorite cafés—including a few that are also some of Budapest's best eateries—on page 234.) Other cafés serve only light food, or sometimes only desserts. But if you want a wide choice of cakes, look for a *cukrászda* (pastry shop—*cukr* means "sugar").

Ethnic restaurants provide a break from Hungarian fare (in the unlikely event you need one). Budapest has abundant vegetarian, Italian, Indian, Chinese, and other non-Hungarian eateries; I've listed my favorites. Once you leave the capital, the options are fewer, and the food gets even heartier and cheaper.

Occasionally, when you order a main course, it includes only the item itself (with no garnishes, side-dishes, or starches). In these cases, you can order your choice of sides—listed on a separate page of the menu, and paid for separately. If you see a page listing these extras, ask the server if anything is included with your main dish.

Menus usually list drink prices by the tenth of a liter, or deciliter (dl), not by the glass; this is an honest and common practice, but can trip up visitors who aren't in the know.

When the server comes to take your order, he or she might say *"Tessék"* (TEHSH-shayk), or maybe the more formal *"Tessék parancsolni"* (TEHSH-shayk PAW-rawn-chohl-nee)—"Please command, sir." When they bring the food, they will probably say, *"Jó étvágyat!"* (yoh AYT-vah-yawt)—"Bon appétit." When you're ready for the bill, you can simply say, *"Fizetek"* (FEE-zeh-tehk)—"I'll pay."

At any restaurant, it's smart to check the bill and count your change carefully. While most Hungarian restaurants are honest, rip-off joints abound in downtown Budapest's tourist zone—especially along the main walking street, Váci utca. (Frankly, I'd never eat on Váci utca, which practically guarantees bad food and service for high prices.) Avoid any place with a menu that doesn't list prices, and tune in to the fine print (such as the semi-bogus "service" charge that's sadly becoming more common—see "Tipping," next).

Tipping

Hungarians tip less than Americans do. At restaurants with table service, waiters expect a tip of about 10 percent (or a little less; more than 10 percent is too much). Some restaurants automatically add a 10 percent service charge to the bill. (A few more tourist-oriented eateries have nudged

EATING

this up to 12 or even 15 percent, which Hungarian diners consider excessive.) The extra charge should be noted on the menu (if it's not, complain), and appears as a line item after the subtotal on the bill (look for "service," *borravaló, felszolgálási díj,* or *szervízdíj*). In these cases, an additional tip is not necessary. For more on tipping, see page 13.

HUNGARIAN CUISINE

Hungarian cuisine—the undisputed best in Central Europe—delicately blends Magyar peasant cooking (with rich spices) refined by the elegance of French preparation, with a delightful smattering of flavors from the vast, multiethnic Austro-Hungarian Empire (including Germanic, Balkan, Jewish, and Carpathian). Everything is heavily seasoned: with paprika, tomatoes, and peppers of every shape, color, size, and flavor.

When foreigners think of Hungarian cuisine, what comes to mind is goulash. But tourists are often disappointed when "real

Hungarian goulash" isn't the thick stew that they were expecting. The word "goulash" comes from the Hungarian *gulyás leves,* or "shepherd's soup"—a tasty, rustic, nourishing dish originally eaten by cowboys and shepherds on the Great Hungarian Plain. Here in its homeland, it's a clear, spicy broth with chunks of meat, potatoes, and other vegetables. Elsewhere (such as in Hungary's Germanic and Slavic neighbors), the word "goulash" does describe a thick stew.

Aside from the obligatory *gulyás,* make a point of trying another unusual Hungarian specialty: cold fruit soup *(hideg gyümölcs leves).* This sweet, cream-based treat—generally eaten before the meal, even though it tastes more like a dessert—is usually made with *meggy* (sour cherries), but you'll also see versions with *alma* (apples) or *körte* (pears). Other Hungarian soups *(levesek)* include *bableves* (bean soup), *zöldségleves* (vegetable soup), *gombaleves* (mushroom soup), *halászlé* (fish broth with paprika), *húsleves* (meat or chicken soup), and *pörkölt* (a simmered-meat soup similar to goulash but without the potatoes). The ultimate staple of traditional Hungarian home-cooking, but rarely served in restaurants, is *főzelék*—a simple but tasty wheat flour-thickened stew that can be supplemented with various vegetables and meats (served at cheap restaurants around Budapest—see Főzelékfaló Ételbár listing on page 233).

Paprika Primer

The quintessential ingredient in Hungarian cuisine is paprika. In Hungarian, the word *paprika* can mean both peppers (red

or green) and the spice that's made with them. Peppers can be stewed, stuffed, sautéed, baked, grilled, or pickled. For seasoning, red shakers of dried paprika join the salt and pepper on tables.

Locals say paprika is best from the sunny south of Hungary. There are more than 40 varieties of paprika spice, with two main types: hot (*csípős* or *erős*) and sweet (*édesnemes* or simply *édes;* often comes in a white can). Hungarians typically cook with sweet paprika to add flavor and color. Then, at the table, they put out hot paprika so each diner can adjust the heat to their preferred taste. A can of paprika is a handy and tasty souvenir of your trip (see the Shopping chapter).

On menus, anything cooked *paprikás* (PAW-pree-kash) comes smothered in a spicy, creamy red stew. To add even more kick to your food, ask for a jar of the bright-red paste called *Erős Pista* (EH-rewsh PEESH-taw). Literally "Spicy Steve," this Hungarian answer to Tabasco is best used sparingly. Or try *Édes Anna* (AY-desh AW-naw, "Sweet Anna"), a newer variation that's more sweet than spicy.

Hungarians adore all kinds of meat *(hús)*. *Csirke* is chicken, *borjú* is veal, *kacsa* is duck, *liba* is goose, *sertés* is pork, *sonka* is ham, *kolbász* is sausage, *szelet* is schnitzel (*Bécsi szelet* means Wiener schnitzel)—and the list goes on. Meat is often covered with delicious sauces or garnishes, from rich cream sauces to spicy pastes to fruit jam. *Libamáj* is goose liver, which shows up everywhere (for example, anything prepared "Budapest style" is topped with goose liver). Lard is used extensively in cooking, making Hungarian cuisine very rich and filling.

Vegetarians have a tricky time in traditional Hungarian restaurants, many of which offer only a plate of deep-fried vegetables. They haven't quite figured out how to do a good, healthy, leafy salad; a traditional restaurant will generally offer only marinated cucumbers (listed on menus as "cucumber salad"), a plate of sliced-up pickles ("pickled cucumbers"), marinated spicy peppers, or something with cabbage—using lettuce only as a garnish.

Starches *(köretek)*—which you'll sometimes order separately from the meat course—can include *nodeli* (small potato dumplings, a.k.a. *Spätzle*), *galuska* (noodles), *burgonya* (potatoes), *krumpli* (French fries), *krokett* (croquettes), or *rizs* (rice). *Kenyér* (bread) often comes with the meal.

Sometimes your main dish will come with steamed, grilled, or deep-fried vegetables. A common side dish is *káposzta* (cabbage, often prepared like sauerkraut). You may also see *töltött káposzta* (cabbage stuffed with meat) or *töltött paprika* (stuffed peppers). Look for the traditional (and increasingly in-vogue) dish called *lescó* (LEH-chew). Basically the Hungarian answer to ratatouille, this is a mix of tomatoes, peppers, and other vegetables.

Thin, crêpe-like pancakes *(palacsinta)* are sometimes served as a main dish, typically wrapped around meat and vegetables and smothered in creamy sauce. They also appear as desserts, stuffed and/or covered with fruit, jam, chocolate sauce, walnuts, poppy seeds, or whipped cream. Most famous is the *Gundel palacsinta*, named for *the* top-of-the-line Budapest restaurant—stuffed with walnuts and raisins in a rum sauce, topped with chocolate sauce, and flambéed.

Pastries are a big deal in Hungary. In the late 19th century, pastry-making caught on here in an attempt to keep up with the renowned desserts of rival Vienna. Today Hungary's streets are still lined with *cukrászda* (pastry shops) where you can simply point to whichever treat you'd like. Try the *Dobos torta* (a many-layered chocolate-and-caramel cream cake), *somlói galuska* (a dumpling with vanilla, nuts, and chocolate), anything with *gesztenye* (chestnuts),  and *rétes* (strudel with various fillings, including *túrós*, curds). And many *cukrászda* also serve *fagylalt* (ice cream, *fagyi* for short), sold by the *gomboc* (ball).

For an excellent glossary of Hungarian cuisine, see www .chew.hu/encyclopedia.

Drinks

Kávé (KAH-vay) and *tea* (TEH-aw) are coffee and tea. As for water (*víz*, veez) it comes as *szódavíz* (soda water, sometimes just carbonated tap water) or *ásványvíz* (spring water, more expensive).

Hungary is first and foremost wine country. For the complete run-down on Hungarian wines, see the next section.

Hungary isn't particularly well-known for its beer (*sör*, pronounced "shewr"), but Dreher and Borsodi are two of the better brands. *Villagos* is lager; if you prefer something darker, look for *barna* (brown).

Hungary is almost as proud of its spirits as its wines. Unicum is a unique and beloved Hungarian bitter liquor made of 40 different herbs and aged in oak casks. The flavor is powerfully unforgettable—like Jägermeister, but harsher. A swig of Unicum is often gulped before the meal, but it's also used as a cure for an upset stomach (especially if you've eaten too much rich food—not an uncommon problem in Hungary). Unicum has a history as unique and complicated as its flavor. Invented by a Doctor Zwack in the late 18th century, the drink impressed Habsburg emperor Josef II, who supposedly declared: *"Das ist ein Unikum!"* ("This is a specialty!"). The Zwack company went on to thrive during Budapest's late-19th-century Golden Age (when Unicum was the subject of many whimsical Guinness-type ads). But when the communists took over after World War II, the Zwacks fled to America—taking their secret recipe for Unicum with them. The communists continued to market the drink with their own formula, which left Hungarians (literally and figuratively) with a bad taste in their mouths. In a landmark case, the Zwacks sued the communists for infringing on their copyright...and won. In 1991, Péter Zwack—who had been living in exile in Italy—triumphantly returned to Hungary and resurrected the original family recipe. A newer version, called Unicum Next, has a softer, cherry flavor; its ads target the new generation of Hungarian drinkers. To get your own taste of this family saga, look for the round bottle with the red cross on the label (www.zwack.hu).

For a more straightforward spirit, try the local firewater, *pálinka*, a powerful schnapps made from various fruits (most often plum, *szilva;* or apricots, *barack*). Also look for the pear-flavored Vilmos brandy.

If you're drinking with some new Magyar friends, impress them with the standard toast: *Egészségedre* (EH-gehs-shay-geh-dreh; "to your health").

Hungarian Wines

Wine *(bor)* is an essential part of Hungarian cuisine. Grapes have been cultivated here since Roman times, and Hungarian wines had

an excellent reputation (winning raves from the likes of France's King Louis XIV and Ludwig von Beethoven) up until World War II. Under communism, most vineyards were collectivized, and the quality suffered terribly. But since the end of that era, many wine-growing families have reclaimed their property and gone back to their roots (literally). Today they're attempting to resuscitate the reputation of Hungarian wines. They're off to a great start.

Hungary boasts some 20 wine-growing regions. The area around Eger is the most famous, but that's only the beginning. The Villány Hills south of Pécs—with a semi-Mediterranean climate at the same latitude as Bordeaux, France—produce full-bodied reds. The Sopron region near the Austrian border produces both reds and whites. The Szekszárd area, along the Danube in southern Hungary, also produces wines.

Whites *(fehér)* can be sweet *(édes)*, half-dry *(félszáraz)*, or dry *(száraz)*. Whites include the standards (Riesling, Chardonnay), as well as some wines made from more typically Hungarian grapes: **Leányka** ("Little Girl"), a half-dry, fairly heavy, white table wine; **Cserszegi Fűszeres,** a spicy, light white that can be fruity; the half-dry, full-bodied **Hárslevelű** ("Linden Leaf"); and the dry **Furmint** and **Kéknyelű** ("Blue Stalk").

Reds *(vörös)* include the familiar varieties (Cabernet Sauvignon, Cabernet Franc, Merlot, Pinot Noir), and some that are less familiar. **Kekporto** is better known as Blauer Portugieser in German-speaking countries. In Eger, don't miss **Bull's Blood,** a.k.a. Egri Bikavér, a distinctive blend of reds that comes with a fun local legend (described on page 323). The spicy, medium-body **Kékfrankos** ("Blue Frankish") supposedly got its name because when Napoleonic soldiers were here, they could pay

either with valuable blue-colored bank notes, or unstable white ones...and local vintners wanted the blue francs. (Like most wine origin legends, this story is untrue—Kékfránkos wasn't cultivated here until after Napoleon's time.)

Probably the most famous Hungarian wine is **Tokaji Aszú,** a sweet, late-harvest, honey-colored dessert wine made primarily from Furmint grapes. Known as the "wine of kings, and the king of wines," Tokaji Aszú is a D.O.C. product, meaning that to have that name, it must be grown in a particular region. Tokaj is a town in northeastern Hungary (not far from Eger), while Aszú is a "noble rot" grape. The wine's unique, concentrated flavor is made possible by a fungus *(Botrytis cinerea)* that thrives on the grapes in the late fall. The grapes are left on the vine, where they burst and wither like raisins before they are harvested in late October and November. This sucks the water out of the grape, leaving behind a very high sugar content and a deep golden color. Tokaji Aszú wines are numbered, from three to six, indicating how many eight-gallon tubs *(puttony)* of these "noble rot" grapes were added to the base wine—the higher the number, the sweeter the wine. Other variations on Tokaji can be less sweet. (This might sound like another bizarre Hungarian custom, but the French Sauterne and German Beerenauslese wines are also made from "noble rot" grapes. The similarly named French Tokay wine—which derives from the same word—is a different story altogether.)

Finally, note that, except for Bull's Blood and Tokaji Aszú, Hungarian wines are not widely available in the US. Packing home a bottle or two (in your checked luggage) is a unique souvenir.

RESTAURANTS IN BUDAPEST

Thanks to Budapest's ever-evolving culinary scene, there's no shortage of places to dine. A few years ago, I had to scrape the bottom of the barrel to recommend eateries here. Now, I can barely keep track of what's new—and scouting new restaurants is the highlight of my research chores. The broad range of options and healthy sense of one-upmanship among local chefs keeps prices reasonable and quality high. This also means that the foodie scene here is boom-and-bust: A place quickly acquires a huge and enthusiastic following, then soon falls from grace as an even more enticing competitor opens up shop.

While you'll find the Hungarian standards, most big-city restaurants like to dabble in international cuisine. Most of my listings feature an international menu with some Hungarian flourishes. (If you want truly traditional Hungarian fare, you'll actually do a bit better in smaller towns.) The good news: Most Hungarian chefs are so skilled that any cuisine is well-executed here.

Be aware that in the city center—where you'll likely be eating—most restaurants are frequented by tourists and well-heeled local yuppies. Blue-collar Budapesters can't afford to eat out in the areas where you'll be spending your time. If you really want to eat local-style, head for the big shopping malls (like the WestEnd City Center near Nyugati train station, or Mammut near Moszkva tér). There, you can truly dine with the Budapesters...at T.G.I. Friday's and McDonald's, just like back home.

Most Hungarians dine between 19:00 and 21:00, peaking around 20:00; trendy neighborhoods such as Franz Liszt Square and Ráday utca, which attract an after-work crowd, are lively earlier in the evening.

Pest

I've listed these options by neighborhood, for easy reference with your sightseeing.

In Pest's Town Center (Belváros), near Váci Utca

When you ask natives about good places to eat on Váci utca, they just roll their eyes. Budapesters know that only rich tourists who don't know better would throw their money away on the relatively bad food and service along this high-profile pedestrian drag. But wander a few blocks off the tourist route, and you'll discover alternatives with fair prices and better food. For locations, see the map on pages 206–207.

Gerlóczy Café is tucked on a peaceful little square next to the giant City Hall, flanked by gourmet salami and cheese shops.

This classy café features international cuisine with several seating options (out on the square, in the coffee-house interior, upstairs in the non-smoking section, or down in the wine cellar). There's a good permanent menu, special themed menus that change every few months, and new specials that they try out each weekend. The clientele is a mix of tourists and upscale-urban Budapesters, including local politicians and actors from several nearby theaters. With a take-your-time ambience that's arguably more Parisian than Hungarian, this is a particularly inviting spot (2,000–2,500-Ft pastas, 1,700–4,000-Ft main dishes, good breakfasts with egg dishes for under 1,000 Ft, excellent fresh-baked pastries and bread, daily 7:00–23:00, 2 blocks from Váci utca, just off Városház utca at Gerlóczy utca 1, district V, M3: Ferenciek tere, tel. 1/501-4000). They rent good rooms, too (see page 208 in the Sleeping chapter).

Centrál Kávéház, while famous as a grand, old-fashioned café, is also one of Budapest's best spots for a central, characteristic

meal, and offers some good home-style Hungarian dishes you don't often find in restaurants. Since it's across the street from the university library, it's popular with students and professors. Choose between the lively, vast downstairs, or the more refined upstairs dining room—both featuring elegant, early-1900s ambience (1,000-Ft sandwiches, small but filling 1,000- to 1,500-Ft "Zóna" plates until 16:00, larger 2,500- to 4,000-Ft main dishes anytime, daily 8:00–24:00, Károlyi Mihály utca 9, district V, M3: Ferenciek tere, tel. 1/266-2110).

BorLabor ("Wine Lab") features traditional, regional,

updated Hungarian specialties at reasonable prices in a modern, romantic cellar atmosphere (2,000–3,000-Ft main dishes, daily 12:00–24:00, a block north of Váci utca at Veres Pálné utca 7, district V, M3: Ferenciek tere, tel. 1/328-0382).

Great Market Hall: At the far south end of Váci utca, you can eat a quick lunch on the upper floor of the Great Market

Hall (Nagyvásárcsarnok). Fakanál Étterem—the glassed-in, sit-down cafeteria above the main entrance— is overpriced and touristy, but offers good seating (2,000–2,700-Ft main dishes). The stalls along the right side of the building are cheaper, but quality can vary (grab a bar stool or you'll stand while you munch). Locals love the Lángos stand, for deep-fried bread slathered with sour cream and cheese (add garlic for some kick). Produce and

butcher stands line the main floor, and it's easy to miss the big, modern grocery store in the basement (the end nearest Váci utca; Mon 6:00–17:00, Tue–Fri 6:00–18:00, Sat 6:00–15:00, closed Sun, Fővám körút 1–3, district IX, M3: Kálvin tér).

Ráday Utca

Ráday utca is Budapest's "restaurant row." While tourists blow their budgets a few blocks away on Váci utca, Budapesters hang out at this street's trendy, inventive eateries and pubs. As this is a prime pre-dinner drink spot, many places serve no food, only drinks (find out before you sit down). The outdoor seating along here is inviting on a balmy evening. And, while the similar scene at Franz Liszt Square (described on page 229) is becoming more touristy and snooty-upscale, locals still outnumber visitors on Ráday utca. It's worth going out of your way to come here and simply wander, choosing the place that looks best. Just take the M3/blue Metro line to Kálvin tér—a three-minute walk from the Great Market Hall—and stroll south (district IX). Most places are pretty interchangeable; survey your options and take your pick. If you can't decide, consider these:

Soul Café is one of the best-regarded eateries along this drag, with a trendy interior and international fare with some Hungarian options (1,000-Ft sandwiches before 18:00, 1,500–3,000-Ft main dishes anytime, salad options, open daily 12:00–24:00, Ráday utca 11–13, tel. 1/217-6986).

Café Intenzo hides around the corner from the start of Ráday utca, where it meets the busy ring road. Low-key and with a loyal local following, they serve Hungarian and international cuisine in a nondescript interior or out in a pleasant courtyard garden (1,100-Ft sandwiches, 1,200–1,900-Ft pastas, 1,700–3,000-Ft main dishes, daily 10:00–1:00 in the morning, closed Sat–Sun if construction is still going on outside, Kálvin tér 9, tel. 1/219-5243).

Danube Promenade

The riverbank facing the castle is lined with hotel restaurants and permanently moored restaurant boats. You'll find bad service, mediocre food, mostly tourists, and sky-high prices...but the atmosphere and people-watching are marvelous.

Spoon, a boat in front of the InterContinental Hotel next to the Chain Bridge, is your best Danube dining option. This hip, upscale place offers pricey, elaborately prepared international cuisine with an emphasis on seafood, plus some Hungarian standards (3,500–6,000-Ft main dishes). Choose between a dressy candlelit dining room or outdoor tables above decks. The bathrooms—Budapest's most scenic—are a must, even if you don't have to go. If you're going to pay too much to eat along the river, you might as well do it here (daily 12:00–24:00, often booked for special events—call ahead to be sure it's open and to reserve a riverside table, Vigadó tér, dock #3, district V, M1: Vörösmarty tér, tel. 1/411-0933).

For a more affordable and more local experience, head a bit farther south, near the green Liberty Bridge. Along the embankment road called Belgrád Rakpart, you'll find a cluster of fun and lively ethnic restaurants (including good Italian at **Trattoria Toscana,** #13, and a mini-Santorini with Greek fare at **Taverna Dionysos,** #16).

Various companies run **dinner cruises** along the Danube (including Hungária Koncert, which offers a 10 percent discount to Rick Steves readers—see page 250 in the Entertainment & Nightlife chapter). While these can be romantic, the restaurant options in Budapest are too tempting to pass up. Instead, dine at your choice of eateries, then take the Danube Legenda nighttime cruise (see page 51 in the Orientation chapter).

Near St. István's Basilica

The area near St. István's Basilica—a few steps from the start of Andrássy út—has been neatly pedestrianized, and several appealing eateries have popped up here recently. For locations, see the map on pages 206–207.

On Sas Utca, in Front of St. István's Basilica: The street called Sas utca, running along the bottom of the grand plaza in front of St. István's, is lined with a handful of trendy, pricey, well-regarded, and somewhat snobby restaurants (such as Mokka and Dío). For something top-notch but a bit less expensive than the others, head for **Café Kör** ("Circle"). This stylish but unpretentious eatery serves up mostly Hungarian and some Mediterranean fare in a tasteful, tight one-room interior and at a few sidewalk tables. It prides itself on being friendly and providing a good value. Because it's beloved by local foodies, reservations are smart anytime and essential on weekends (2,000–4,000-Ft main dishes, small portions for 30 percent less, good salads, daily specials, cash only, Mon–Sat 10:00–23:00, closed Sun, Sas utca 17, district V, between M3: Arany János utca and M1: Bajcsy-Zsilinszky út, tel. 1/311-0053).

Behind St. István's Basilica: **Belvárosi Lugas Étterem** is your cheap-and-central, no-frills option. *Lugas* is a Hungarian word for a welcoming garden strewn with grape vines, and the cozy dining room—with a dozen tables of happy eaters—captures that spirit. Or sit at the sidewalk tables outside on busy Bajcsy-Zsilinszky boulevard. The food is simply good Hungarian (1,300–2,800-Ft main dishes, order starches separately, daily 12:00–23:30, directly behind and across the street from St. István's Basilica at Bajcsy-Zsilinszky út 15, district VI, M1: Bajcsy-Zsilinszky út, tel. 1/302-5393).

Near Andrássy Út, Between the Oktogon and the Opera

For the locations of these eateries, see the map on page 210.

Franz Liszt Square (Liszt Ferenc Tér): Franz Liszt Square, a leafy park on the most interesting stretch of Andrássy út, boasts a stylish cluster of pricey, pretentious yuppie restaurants, many with outdoor seating (lively on a summer evening). This is the place for Budapesters to see and be seen...but only for those who can afford it (most main dishes hover around 2,500–4,000 Ft). Take the Metro to Oktogon and follow your nose. My favorite Liszt Square

eatery, **Menza** (the old communist word for "School Cafeteria") wins the "Best Design" award. Recycling 1970s furniture and an orange-and-brown color scheme, it's a postmodern parody of an old communist café—half kitschy-retro, half brand-new feeling. When locals come in here, they can only chuckle and say, "Yep. This is how it was." With tasty and well-priced updated Hungarian cuisine, embroidered leather-bound menus, brisk but efficient service, breezy jazz on the soundtrack, and indoor or outdoor seating, it's a memorable spot (1,900–2,600-Ft main dishes, daily 10:00–24:00, halfway up Andrássy út at Liszt Ferenc tér 2, district VII, tel. 1/413-1482,

EATING

www.menza.co.hu). If you like the Franz Liszt Square scene, you'll find more on Kertész utca beyond the end of the square, and in the "Broadway Quarter" near the Opera House (on Hajós utca and Nagymező utca).

Right on Andrássy út: **Klassz** is a trendy but unpretentious bistro with a similarly postmodern "eclectic-mod" aesthetic, both in its decor and its food. Serving up surprisingly affordable international/nouvelle cuisine with Hungarian flair, it's a new favorite among Budapest's value-seeking foodies (1,500–3,000-Ft main dishes, Mon–Sat 11:30–23:00, Sun 11:30–18:00, Andrássy út 41, district VI, between M1: Opera and M1: Oktogon, no reservations possible—try to arrive by 19:00).

Behind the Opera House: **Balettcipő** ("Ballet Slipper"), with indoor and outdoor seating, boasts an affordable, very eclectic, and ever-changing menu that combines Hungarian, Asian, Mexican, Italian, and more (1,500–2,000-Ft main dishes, Mon–Fri 9:00–24:00, Sat–Sun 12:00–24:00, just behind the Opera House at Hajós utca 14, district VI, M1: Opera, tel. 1/269-3114).

Indian: Hungarians seem to have an affinity for Indian cuisines, as both enjoy smoothing together powerful spices. **Shalimar** hides in a stuffy cellar in a dreary neighborhood two blocks beyond the end of Franz Liszt Square. Everything about this place is unexceptional...except the food. This is my number-one place in Central Europe for a break from pork and kraut. I can never resist the *murg makhani*...and I'm never disappointed. The non-smoking section is filled with too-loud Americans, so I sit with the young locals in the smoking section (1,700–2,500-Ft main dishes, half-portions for 40 percent less, daily 12:00–16:00 & 18:00–24:00, reservations smart on weekends, Dob utca 50, district VII, between M1: Oktogon and M2: Blaha Lujza tér, tel. 1/352-0297).

In City Park

These three touristy eateries cluster around the end of the lake behind the Millennium Monument in City Park (district XIV, M1: Hősök tere). All are open for both lunch and dinner. The first one is Budapest's best-known, fanciest splurge; the other two are more reasonable and casual, but still pretty pricey. For locations, see the map on page 189.

Gundel Restaurant has been *the* dining spot for VIPs and celebrities since 1894. The pricey place is an institution—President Bill Clinton ate here. Pope John Paul II didn't, but when his people called out for dinner, they called Gundel. The elegant main room is decorated with fine 19th-century Hungarian paintings and an Art Deco flair, while the more casual garden terrace is leafy and delightful. The Hungarian cuisine flirts with sophisticated international influences (4,000–11,000-Ft main courses, 20,000–

40,000-Ft fixed-price meals). At lunch, choose from the same pricey à la carte items, or opt for a more affordable fixed-price meal (4,000–5,000 Ft). Sunday brunch, with a different theme each week, is popular (6,000 Ft, served 11:30–15:00). Reserve ahead for dinner, and ask to sit either near or far from the live "Gypsy" music (12 percent service charge automatically added to bill, open daily 12:00–15:00 & 18:30–24:00, music nightly, Állatkerti út 2, tel. 1/468-4040, www.gundel.hu). The dress code is formal: Jackets are required for men having dinner in the dining room, but not for lunch, for Sunday brunch, or if you sit outside. (You can borrow a free jacket at the door if you travel like me. Ties and dresses are not required.)

Gundel's **Borvendéglő** ("Wine Cellar") offers similar food in a more casual atmosphere at half the price. With an even more extensive wine list than the main restaurant upstairs, this option is ideal for wine lovers. In addition to full dinners, including some "home-style" dishes (2,000–6,000 Ft, pricier 10,500–13,500-Ft tasting *menus* with wine pairings), they offer wine-and-cheese tastings (4,500–7,500 Ft; Mon–Sat 18:00–23:00, closed Sun, downstairs from Gundel at Állatkerti út 2, tel. 1/468-4041).

Robinson, stranded on an island in City Park's lake, is a hip, playful, mellow theme restaurant. With island-castaway ambience and more outdoor seating than indoor, it's made to order for lazing away a sunny afternoon at the park. The upstairs café terrace has a long menu of 1,000-Ft desserts and ice-cream treats, coffee drinks, and light 2,000–2,500-Ft salads and sandwiches (daily in summer 11:00–23:00, terrace closed Oct–April). The downstairs terrace and elegant, glassed-in dining room feature pricey international and Hungarian cuisine (3,000–6,000-Ft main dishes, daily 12:00–16:00 & 18:00–24:00, reserve ahead and ask for lakefront seating, Városligeti tó, tel. 1/422-0222, www.robinson restaurant.hu).

Buda

Eateries on Castle Hill are generally overpriced and touristy—as with Váci utca, locals never eat here. Instead, they head down the hill into the Víziváros ("Water Town") neighborhood. All of these (except the final one) are in district I.

Víziváros

My first listing is just beyond the southern tip of Castle Hill, near the Elisabeth Bridge. The others are in the heart of Víziváros, right between Castle Hill and the river. For locations, see the map on page 215.

Tabáni Terasz, between the castle and the big, white Elisabeth Bridge, serves tasty Hungarian food to a pleasant mix of locals and tourists. The historic 250-year-old building has several seating options: in a cozy, classy drawing-room interior; on a terrace out front; and in the inner courtyard (2,000–3,500-Ft main dishes, daily 12:00–23:00, by the single-spired yellow church at Apród utca 10, tel. 1/201-1086).

Matróz Kocsma ("Sailor Inn") features specialties from up and down the Danube—mostly Hungarian, but also German, Transylvanian, Serbian, and more. Each dish's place of origin is noted in the menu. Very convenient to most of my recommended Víziváros hotels, this eatery has jaunty nautical decor inside and out (2,200–3,000-Ft main dishes, daily 10:00–24:00, Halász utca 1, tel. 1/212-3817).

Pater Marcus is a well-established beer hall, serving up a hundred types of Belgian beers and Hungarian and international cuisine near the Chain Bridge. The outdoor alley seating is nothing special, but the cellar restaurant will transport you to Brussels (1,800–2,200-Ft main dishes, daily 12:00–24:00, Apor Péter utca 1, tel. 1/212-1612).

Batthyány Tér

This bustling square—the transportation hub for Víziváros—is overlooked by a recently renovated, late-19th-century market hall (today housing a supermarket and various shops). Several worthwhile, affordable eateries cluster around this square (all open long hours daily). Survey your options before settling in. **Nagyi Palacsintázója** ("Granny's Pancakes")—just to the right of the market hall entrance—serves up cheap and tasty crêpes *(palacsinta)* to a local crowd (300–800-Ft sweet or savory crêpes, convenient 800–1,000-Ft combo-meals, communication can be challenging—ask for English menu, open 24 hours daily, Batthyány tér 5). As you face the market hall, go up the street that runs along its left side (Markovits Iván utca) to reach more good eateries: At the end of the block on the right is **Éden Vegetarian Restaurant,** a self-service, point-and-shoot place (main dishes for less than 1,000 Ft, Mon–Thu 8:00–21:00, Fri 8:00–18:00, Sun 11:00–21:00, closed Sat, tel. 1/375-7575). And around the back side of the market hall is **Bratwursthäusle/Kolbászda,** a fun little beer hall/beer garden with specialties and blue-and-white checkerboard decor from Bavaria. Sit outside, or in the woody interior (1,000-Ft sausages, daily 11:00–23:00, Gyorskocsi utca 6, tel. 1/225-3674).

Near Moszkva Tér

Szent Jupát is a reliable choice for large portions of basic, stick-to-your-ribs, traditional Hungarian cuisine (a relative rarity in Budapest). Just a couple of blocks off Moszkva tér (the terminus for buses from the castle), near the corner of the giant Mammut shopping mall, it's a good place to head for an extremely filling meal after a busy day of Castle Hill sightseeing. Choose between the woody interior or the covered terrace beer garden out back (1,500–2,800 splittable main dishes, daily from 12:00 until very late, corner of Retek utca and Dékán utca, district II, M2: Moszkva tér, tel. 1/212-2923).

Snacks and Light Meals

When you're in the mood for something halfway between a restaurant and a picnic meal, look for take-out food stands, bakeries (with sandwiches to go), grocers willing to make you a sandwich, and simple little eateries for fast and easy sit-down restaurant food.

A popular snack is *lángos*—a savory deep-fried doughnut (similar to an elephant ear or Native American fry-bread). Sold at stands on the street, the most typical versions are spread with cheese and sour cream, sometimes also topped with garlic. Some restaurants serve a fancier version (often with meat) as an entrée. The Lángos stand upstairs in the Great Market Hall is a local favorite (see page 143).

All around town, you'll see cheery **open-face sandwich shops,** each displaying a dozen or so tempting little treats in their front windows—thin slices of bread piled with egg salad, veggies, cold cuts, cream spreads, cheese, salmon, affordable caviar, or other toppings for around 200 Ft apiece. Two sandwiches and a drink make a quick and healthy meal for less than $5 (they'll also box things to go for a classy picnic). There are various chains, but **Duran Szendvics** is the dominant operation (convenient location near the start of Andrássy út at Bajcsy-Zsilinszky út 7, district VII, M1: Bajcsy-Zsilinszky út, tel. 1/267-9624; also in Leopold Town at Október 6 utca 15, district V, M3: Arany János utca). These shops are generally open for lunch or an early dinner (Mon–Fri 8:00–18:00, Sat 8:00–14:00, Sun 8:00–12:00).

For quick, inexpensive, and very local grub, head for the chain called **Főzelékfaló Ételbár** (roughly, "Soup Slurper Eating Bar"). This self-service cafeteria dishes up simple fare to businesspeople on their lunch break. *Főzelék*, a simple soup that's thickened with roux (wheat flour mixed into lard or butter) and can be supplemented with various vegetables, is a staple of Hungarian home cooking. Go to the counter, choose your *főzelék* soup (various flavors, 500 Ft), then choose from a variety of basic meat dishes (chicken, pork, meatballs, and more for 500–1,000 Ft apiece; some English spoken, but pointing also works). A filling meal here typically runs 1,000–2,000 Ft (usually open Mon–Fri 10:00–21:30, Sat 12:00–20:00, closed Sun, www.fozelekfalo-bartokhaz.hu). Because of the limited seating, most people get their grub to go. There are two locations in central Pest: One is just off of Andrássy út in the "Broadway Quarter" (Nagymező utca 22, a block north of the Opera House, district VI, M1: Opera), and the other is in a big building along the busy highway at Ferenciek tere (same building as the recommended Leo Panzió hotel, Kossuth Lajos utca 2A, district V, M3: Ferenciek tere). You'll also find them in the WestEnd City Center and Arena Plaza shopping malls (see Shopping chapter).

Hummus Bar, while not authentically Hungarian, is a popular expat-run local chain that offers cheap Middle Eastern vegetarian meals to grateful backpackers and young locals. Their falafel is tasty (500 Ft for a pita-wrapped sandwich, combination plates for 700–1,500 Ft). I'd get it to go and enjoy it on a park bench to avoid the cramped interior (one location just beyond the end of Franz Liszt Square at Kertesz utca 39, district VII, M1: Oktogon, open daily 12:00–24:00; another in Leopold Town at Alkotmány utca 20, district V, M2: Kossuth tér, open Mon–Thu 10:00–22:00, Fri 10:00–24:00, Sat 12:00–24:00, Sun 12:00–22:00; www.hummusbar.hu).

For a fast snack, you'll see **Fornetti** stands everywhere (on street corners and Metro underpasses). This Hungary-based chain, which is becoming wildly popular across Central and Eastern Europe, sells small, tasty, freshly baked phyllo–dough–based pastries by weight. They have both sweet and savory varieties. For a bite on the go, just point to what you want and hold your fingers up for how many you'd like of each type (150 Ft per 100 grams). If you smell something heavenly in the Metro passages…it's probably a Fornetti.

BUDAPEST'S CAFÉ CULTURE

In the late 19th century, a vibrant café culture boomed here in Budapest, just as it did in Vienna and Paris. The *kávéház* ("coffeehouse") was a local institution. By 1900, Budapest had more than 600 cafés. In this crowded and fast-growing cityscape, a neighborhood café allowed urbanites to escape their tiny flats (or to get a jolt of caffeine to power them through a 12-hour workday). Local people (many who'd moved to the city from the countryside) didn't want to pay to heat their homes during the day. So instead, for the price of a cup of coffee, they could come to a café to enjoy warmth, companionship, and loaner newspapers.

Realizing that these neighborhood living rooms were breeding grounds for dissidents, the communists closed the cafés or converted them into *eszpresszós* (with uncomfortable stools instead of easy chairs) or *bisztrós* (stand-up fast-food joints with no chairs at all). Today, nostalgia is bringing back the *kávéház* culture— both as a place to get coffee and food, and as a social institution. While some serve only coffee and cakes, most serve light meals, and some serve full meals (as noted below).

On the Great Boulevard: New York Café makes the others listed here look like Starbucks. Originally built in 1894 as part

of the "New York Palace" (and it really is palatial), this fanciful, over-the-top explosion of Neo-Baroque and Neo-Renaissance epitomizes the "mix and match, but plenty of everything" Historicist style of the day. In the early 20th century, artists, writers, and musicians came here to sip overpriced coffee and bask in opulence. After decades of neglect, Italian investors completely restored it in 2006, and now it welcomes guests once more. Tourists and gawkers are not encouraged—you'll be stopped at the door and asked if you

want a table. If you're up for a coffee break, this place might actually be worth an $8 cup of coffee or an overpriced meal. Read the fun history on the placemat. While it's a few blocks beyond the tourist zone, it's worth the trip out here for the ultimate in turn-of-the-20th-century Budapest elegance (1,000–1,500-Ft coffee and hot chocolate drinks, 1,000–2,000-Ft desserts, 3,000-Ft pastas and sandwiches, 4,000–6,000-Ft main dishes, 5,000-Ft breakfasts served 9:00–12:00, open daily 9:00–24:00, Erzsébet körút 9–11, district VII, tel. 1/886-6167). Sunken down in all that sumptuousness, in the former billiards room, is a separate restaurant called **Deepwater** (5,000-Ft pastas, 7,000-Ft main dishes, dinner only—daily 18:00–23:00). Take the M2/red Metro line to Blaha Lujza tér, and exit toward *Erzsébet körút pártalan oldal/6É Margit híd*. Bear left up the stairs, then turn right, and walk a block. You can also take tram #4 or #6 from the Oktogon (at Andrássy út) around the Great Boulevard to Wesselényi utca.

Two Blocks up from Váci utca: Centrál Kávéház and **Gerlóczy Café,** both listed as restaurants on page 226, nicely recapture Budapest's early-1900s ambience, with elegant cakes and coffees, loaner newspapers on racks, and a management that encourages loitering. After the one listed above, these are Budapest's top two cafés.

On Vörösmarty tér: Gerbeaud (zhehr-BOH) isn't just a café—it's a 150-year-old landmark, the most famous gathering place in Budapest. It's touristy, but central, historic, and great for people-watching (best on a sunny day from

its outdoor tables). I'd avoid the bad-value meals here, and just sip a coffee and nibble a cake (700-Ft coffee drinks, 700–1,100-Ft cakes, 1,500–3,000-Ft salads and sandwiches, daily 9:00–21:00, on Vörösmarty tér, district V, M1: Vörösmarty tér, tel. 1/429-9000). They also have a cellar pub downstairs (hearty but overpriced 2,000–4,000-Ft meals, open only in cool weather).

Near Ferenciek tere: **Jégbüfé** is where Pest urbanites get their quick, cheap, stand-at-a-counter fix of coffee and cakes. And for those feeling nostalgic for the communist days, little has changed at this typical *bisztró*. First, choose what you want at the counter. Then try to explain it to the cashier across the aisle. Finally, take your receipt back to the appropriate part of the counter (figure out the four different zones: coffee, soft drinks, ice cream, cakes), trade your receipt for your goodie, go to the bar, and enjoy it standing up (cakes for under 300 Ft, Mon–Sat 7:00–21:30, Wed until 20:30, Sun 8:00–21:30, Ferenciek tere 10, district V, M3: Ferenciek tere). Now...back to work.

Near the Opera House: **Callas** features ideal outdoor seating facing the Opera House, and one of the finest Art Nouveau interiors in town, with gorgeous *Jugendstil* chandeliers. While their full meals are pricey (2,500–5,000 Ft), this is a wonderful spot on Andrássy út for a coffee break, tasty dessert, or breakfast (ham and eggs plus coffee for 1,800 Ft, 400–600-Ft pastries, Tue–Fri 8:30–24:00, Sat–Sun 10:00–24:00, closed Mon, Andrássy út 20, district VI, M1: Opera, tel. 1/354-0954). Across the street and a block toward the Oktogon, **Művész Kávéház** ("Artists Coffee House") is a classic café with 19th-century elegance, a hoity-toity high-ceilinged interior, outdoor seating on Andrássy út, and a wide variety of cakes. True to its name, this institution in the "Broadway Quarter" is a favorite after-rehearsal haunt of famous-to-Hungarians actors and musicians (500–700-Ft cakes, 1,000-Ft sandwiches, daily 9:00–23:45, Andrássy út 29, district VI, M1: Opera, tel. 1/352-1337).

In Buda, atop Castle Hill: **Ruszwurm** lays claim to being Budapest's oldest café (since 1827). Tiny but classy, with classic Biedermeier furnishings, it carries on its venerable reputation with pride. Its dead-central location—a block in front of St. Matthias' Church in the heart of the castle district—means that it's become a popular tourist spot. However, it remains dear to locals' hearts. Especially after the 10:00 Sunday-morning Mass at the church, you'll still see gussied-up locals chatting here (500-Ft coffees, 300–600-Ft desserts, daily 10:00–19:00, Szentháromság utca 7, district I, tel. 1/375-5284).

BUDAPEST WITH CHILDREN

Despite its reputation as a big, gloomy metropolis, Budapest is surprisingly kid-friendly. Many of the city's best experiences—such as splashing around in a warm-water whirlpool at Széchenyi Baths, or ogling giant monuments from the communist days at Memento Park—bring out the kid in any traveler.

The key to a successful family trip to Budapest is making everyone happy, including the parents. Consider these tips:

• Don't overdo it. Tackle only one or two key sights a day, and mix in a healthy dose of fun activities.

• Budapest's hotels often give price breaks for kids. (Air-conditioning can be worth the splurge.)

• Eat dinner early (around 18:00) to miss the romantic crowd. Skip the fancy or famous places, which are too formal for kids to really enjoy. Look instead for relaxed cafés, or even fast-food restaurants where kids can move around. Eating al fresco is great with kids. Picnic lunches and dinners work well.

• Public WCs can be hard to find. Try shopping malls, museums, cafés, and restaurants, particularly fast-food places.

• Follow this book's crowd-beating tips to a T—kids hate lines even more than you do.

• If you're taking the train outside of the city, ask about family or child discounts.

For ideas beyond what's covered in this chapter, look for these two **books** (available at some local bookstores): *Benjamin in Budapest* is a fun, colorful, thorough "city guide for children" with lots of ideas (around 4,000 Ft, www.benjaminguides.com). Bob Dent's *Budapest for Children* is out of print, but you might find it locally (see English-language bookstores on page 43 in the Orientation chapter).

Thermal Baths

The top attraction for kids is the same for adults: thermal baths

(❂ see the Thermal Baths chapter on page 87). **Széchenyi Baths**—with colorful outdoor pools and mostly mixed-gender areas—are fun for families (though children under 14 are not allowed in the indoor thermal pools). **Gellért Baths'** sprawling outdoor area and fun wave pool offer the best thermal bath thrills for kids in Budapest; unfortunately, major sections of Gellért (such as the thermal bath rooms) are gender-segregated, interfering with family togetherness. At both of these baths, children over two years old pay full price. There are also fun-for-kids thermal baths in and near Eger (see page 320).

Playgrounds

Local parents filled me in on their favorite playgrounds. Many of these are in parks described elsewhere in this book, and are fun for moms and dads, too.

Szabadság Tér—A pair of inviting playgrounds flank the bottom (south) end of this square, which is ringed with some of Budapest's grandest buildings. The café in the middle of the park is perfect for parents to sit out in the sun and sip a coffee. (This square is described in detail on page 125 of the Leopold Town Walk.)

City Park—In addition to the attractions listed below, City Park is scattered with enjoyable playgrounds.

Millenáris Park—This highly conceptual park is tucked behind the Mammut shopping center (near M2: Moszkva tér). In addition to a fun playground, entertaining exhibits called "House of the Future" and "Palace of Miracles" might appeal to older kids.

Gellért Hill—Kids with hill-climbing stamina might enjoy the trails that twist up this peak overlooking the Danube to great views.

Parks

On a sunny day, there's no better place to have fun than City Park or Margaret Island.

City Park

The fun, dynamic statues at Heroes' Square help bring Hungarian history to life. The fairy-tale Vajdahunyad Castle—a striking ensemble of Hungarian buildings—also captures young imaginations. You can rent bikes, bike carts, and rowboats for the lake (look for rental kiosks between Heroes' Square and Vajdahunyad Castle). Or just spread out a picnic blanket and enjoy the park like a local. With a little more energy, tackle one of the following attractions. (For more on this area, ✪ see the Heroes' Square and City Park Walk.)

Zoo (Állatkert)—This modest but enjoyable zoo is entertaining, with a "safari park," butterfly house, petting zoo, baby rhino,

and more. It also has redeeming sightseeing value: Many of its structures are playful bits of turn-of-the-20th-century Art Nouveau. (To reach the beautiful Art Nouveau elephant house, turn right inside the main entry, then right again at the fork, and look for the white-and-turquoise tower.) Sometimes on summer weekends, kids can feed the animals (1,700 Ft; May–Aug Mon–Thu 9:00–17:30, Fri–Sun 9:00–18:00; April and Sept Mon–Thu 9:00–16:30, Fri–Sun 9:00–17:00; Oct and March Mon–Thu 9:00–16:00, Fri–Sun 9:00–16:30; Nov–Feb daily 9:00–15:00; these are last entry times—zoo stays open one hour later; Állatkerti körút 6–12, district XIV, tel. 1/364-0109, www.zoobudapest.com).

Circus (Nagycirkusz)—This old-fashioned big-top act includes clowns, gymnasts, and animals (adults-1,500–2,500 Ft, kids-1,200–2,000 Ft, show schedule changes depending on season but 2–3 shows per day on weekends, directly across from swimming pool entrance at Széchenyi Baths, www.maciva.hu).

CHILDREN

Fun Park (Vidámpark)—An amusement park filled with thrill rides and fun-seeking Hungarians, Vidámpark includes modern rides as well as a rickety old wooden roller coaster and a beautifully restored century-old merry-go-round, plus a section with attractions for young riders. While none of it will thrill American kids who've been to Six Flags, it's good Hungarian fun (buy a wristband that covers almost anything, price based on height: kids under 3 feet tall are free, 3 feet to 4.5 feet–2,300 Ft, over 4.5 feet–3,700 Ft, get park map in English as you enter, in summer daily 10:00–20:00, shorter hours off-season, closed early Nov–March, Állatkerti körút 14–16, www.vidampark.hu).

Játék Mester Playhouse—Wedged down a narrow path between the back end of the zoo and the circus (just across from Széchenyi Baths entry), this is a fun indoor play area where kids can climb around and meet Hungarian rugrats (weekdays: 1,000 Ft per child, or 500 Ft with zoo ticket; weekends: 1,400 Ft, or 700 with zoo ticket; adults free, limited to 80 kids at a time, daily 9:00–20:00, www.jatek-mester.hu).

Margaret Island
This delightful island in the Danube is filled with diversions, including baths/swimming pools, a small petting zoo, great bike trails, and fun bike-cart rentals. For details, see page 82.

Károlyi Park
Right in the heart of Pest's Town Center, this inviting garden is a favorite place for local urbanites to simply relax with their children. Small but beautifully landscaped, it's a popular after-school hangout for local kids. For a full description, see page 142 in the Pest Town Center Walk.

Children's Railway (Gyermekvasút)
This unusual attraction in the Buda Hills is a holdover from the communist days, when kids were primed from an early age to eagerly work for the betterment of their society. While the commies are long gone, their railway's kid-friendly message of "work is fun!" is full steam ahead—and the line is still manned entirely by children (aside from driving the engines, of course). Children get a kick out of seeing fellow kids selling tickets, acting as conductor, and so on.

The only drawback is that it's on the outskirts of town and requires a few transit changes, but if you (and your kids) have a spirit of adventure, it's a fun ride through the Buda Hills. The easiest trip is this: From Buda's Moszkva tér (on the M2/red Metro line), hop on tram #18 or #56 to the Fogaskerekű Vasút stop (or simply walk 10 min along the busy road called Szilágyi Erzsébet fasor away from the Danube). Here you can switch to the rack railway *(fogaskerekű vasút),* which climbs up in about 15 minutes to the end of the line at Széchenyi-hegy. From this stop, it's a short walk to the starting station of the Children's Railway line, which putters seven miles in about 40 minutes through the hills (part of a national park) to the other end at Hűvösvölgy. Near this station is a stop for tram #56 back to Moszkva tér (public transit covered by normal tickets; Children's Railway tickets: free for kids under 6, 300 Ft one-way for kids 6–14, 600 for adults, or 3,000 Ft for "family ticket" for two adults and three kids or one adult and 4 kids; train runs about hourly, sometimes 2/hr on summer weekends; May–Aug daily 9:00–19:00; Sept–April Tue–Sun 9:00–17:00, closed Mon; old-fashioned steam engine runs occasionally for an extra charge, confirm schedules on website: www .gyermekvasut.hu).

Note that the trams listed above (#18 and #56) have been affected by recent construction, and might not be running as normal.

Other Activities

Memento Park, with its gigantic statues, captures kids' imaginations—and offers a good springboard for a lesson about the communist days. (Teenagers might enjoy learning more at the **House of Terror**—though this engaging exhibit is too powerful for most young children.)

The **Puppet Theater** (Bábszinház) offers frequent morning and afternoon performances. The playful "children's" shows feature light folk tales (800 Ft weekdays, 1,000 Ft weekends), while the "youth/adult" shows can include weightier opera performances (1,000 Ft weekdays, 1,400 Ft weekends). While the performances are typically not in English, the puppets still entertain (across Andrássy út from the House of Terror, Andrássy út 69, district VI, M1: Vörösmarty utca, tel. 1/342-2702, www .budapest-babszinhaz.hu).

Kids might also enjoy the touristy, crowd-pleasing Hungarian folk music and dancing shows presented by **Hungária Koncert** (see page 250 in the Entertainment & Nightlife chapter).

The **Labyrinth of Buda Castle,** while a bit too hokey for serious adults, might entertain children with the opportunity to explore the caves beneath Castle Hill. It's especially enjoyable after 18:00, when it's lit only by lanterns (see page 61 in the Sights chapter).

CHILDREN

SHOPPING

While it's not quite a shopper's mecca, Budapest does offer some enjoyable opportunities to hunt for that perfect Hungarian souvenir.

For a look at local life and a chance to buy some mementos, Budapest's single best shopping venue is the **Great Market Hall** (described in detail on page 143 in the Pest Town Center Walk). In addition to all the colorful produce downstairs, the upstairs gallery is full of fiercely competitive souvenir vendors. There's also a **folk-art market on Castle Hill** (near the bus stop at Dísz tér), but it's generally more touristy and a little more expensive. And, while **Váci utca** has been Budapest's main shopping thoroughfare for generations, today it features the city's highest prices and worst values.

Although Budapest isn't a top destination to browse for fashion or big-ticket items, several city-center streets are being redeveloped as pedestrian malls. So far, you'll find most of the top shops on or near **Deák utca** (connecting Vörösmarty tér and Deák tér), or along **Andrássy út.**

To see how Hungarian urbanites renovate their crumbling commie flats, don't miss the home-improvement shops that line **Király utca,** which runs parallel to Andrássy út (two blocks south). For a taste of the good old days—which somehow just feels right, here in nostalgic Budapest—wander up the city's **"antique row,"** Falk Miksa utca, just north of the Parliament (described later in this chapter).

Budapesters do most of their shopping in big, American-style **shopping malls**—three of which (WestEnd City Center,

Mammut, and Arena Plaza) are downtown and described later in this chapter.

Budapest has several excellent **English bookstores.** For details, see page 43 in the Orientation chapter.

Hours: Smaller shops tend to be open Mon–Fri 10:00–18:00 (sometimes later—until 20:00 or 21:00—on Thu), Sat 10:00–13:00 or 14:00, closed Sun. Big malls have longer hours.

Bargaining: At touristy markets (but not established shops), haggling is common for pricier items (more than about 4,000 Ft)—but you'll likely only get the merchant to come down about 10 percent (maybe down to 20 percent for multiple items). If you pay with a credit card, you're less likely to snare a discount.

VAT Refunds and Customs Regulations: For tips on getting a VAT (value-added tax) refund, and getting your purchases through customs, see page 14 in the Introduction.

Souvenir Ideas

The most popular souvenir is that quintessential Hungarian spice: **paprika.** Sold in metal cans, linen bags, or porcelain vases—and

often accompanied by a tiny wooden scoop—it's a nice way to spice up your cooking with memories of your trip. (But remember that only sealed containers will make it through customs on your way back home.) For more, see "Paprika Primer" on page 221. If you want a top-notch Hungarian cookbook, the pricey *Culinaria Hungary* beautifully describes and illustrates Hungary's culinary tradition (though a cheaper paperback edition is available at bookstores in North America).

Special drinks are a fun souvenir, though they're tricky to bring home (you'll have to wrap them very carefully and put them in your checked luggage—not permitted in carry-on; for customs regulations, see page 15). Consider the unique Hungarian spirit **Unicum** (described on page 223), or a bottle of Hungarian **wine** (page 223).

Another popular local item is a hand-embroidered **linen tablecloth.** The colors are often red and green—the national colors of Hungary, of course—but white-on-white designs are also available (and classy). If the thread is thick and the stitching is very even, it was probably done by machine, and therefore is less valuable.

Other handicrafts to look for include **chess sets** (most from Transylvania) and **nesting dolls.** While these dolls have more to do with Russia than with Hungary, you'll see just about every

modern combination available: from classic girl dolls, to *South Park* characters, to Russian heads of state, to infamous terrorists, to American presidents. Tacky...but fun.

Fans of **communist kitsch** can look for ironic T-shirts that poke fun at that bygone era. But remember that the best selection is at the Memento Park gift shop, which also sells communist memorabilia and CDs of commie anthems (see page 200).

Music-lovers can shop for a CD of **Hungarian music** at the Opera House gift shop (see page 252).

Hungarian Porcelain

Hungary has two major porcelain manufacturers. While very pricey, their works might interest collectors.

Herend, arguably the best (and most expensive) of all, produces tableware with intricately detailed color patterns on a white base. They've created porcelain for Queen Victoria, King Maximilian of Mexico, and other historic heads of state. Herend, produced in a town of the same name, is also exported (including to the US). In Budapest, the main shop—with the best selection—is in central Pest, just off Vörösmarty tér (go around the right side of Gerbeaud café, József Nádor tér 11, tel. 1/317-2622, www .herend.com). There are also locations at Castle Hill (in front of the Matthias Church, Szentháromság utca 5, tel. 1/225-1051) and on Andrássy út (at #16, tel. 1/374-0006).

Zsolnay also produces tableware, but it's better known for its decorative tiles, which adorn the facades and roofs of many major Budapest buildings. You can buy Zsolnay pieces at several shops in Budapest (see www.zsolnay.hu for locations). For more about Zsolnay, see the sidebar on page 346 in the chapter on the city of Pécs, where the porcelain originates.

For **antique porcelain,** check the several shops along Pest's "antique row" (described below). However, don't buy porcelain (or any glass) at the Great Market Hall, which includes a high mark-up.

Modern Shopping Malls

Budapest has a range of modern, American-style shopping malls in the city center. The biggest and most convenient options include **WestEnd City Center,** next door to Nyugati/Western train station (daily 8:00–23:00, Váci út 1–3, district VI, M3: Nyugati pu., tel. 1/374-6573, www.westend.hu); **Mammut** ("Mammoth"), two separate malls a few steps from Buda's Moszkva tér (Mon–Sat

10:00–21:00, Sun 10:00–18:00, Lövőház utca 2–6, district II, M2: Moszkva tér, tel. 1/345-8020, www.mammut.hu); and the newer **Arena Plaza**, near Keleti/Eastern train station (Mon–Sat 10:00–21:00, Sun 10:00–19:00, Kerepesi út 9, district XIV, M2: Keleti pu., tel. 1/880-7000, www.arenaplaza.hu).

Pest's "Antique Row": Falk Miksa Utca

Get into the nostalgic spirit of Budapest with a stroll down Falk Miksa utca, which extends from Kossuth tér (behind the Parliament) four blocks north to the Great Boulevard (near the end point of tram #2; also at Jászaí Mari tér stop for trams #4 and #6 around the Great Boulevard). Browse your way up and down this drag, with several hole-in-the-wall shops selling furniture, porcelain, and other antiques (most shops generally open Mon–Fri 10:00–18:00, Sat 10:00–13:00 or 14:00, closed Sun). Look for *antik* or *antikvitás*. At the Great Boulevard end of Falk Miksa utca are a pair of particularly interesting shops. On the left is **BÁV**, the state-run antique shop. On the right, look for **Kieselbach Galéria**, which specializes in top-notch modern and contemporary works by Hungarian artists. In an odd juxtaposition, the hulking building on the east side of the street is the Defense Ministry—sort of the "Hungarian Pentagon."

Flea Markets (Bolhapiac)

The gigantic **Ecseri Flea Market** (sometimes called "Tangó"), on the outskirts of town, is an authentic, down-and-dirty scene, where the fringes of society meet to swap goods (Mon–Fri 8:00–16:00, Sat 6:00–15:00, Sun 8:00–13:00, best on Sat–Sun, mostly under cover, entrance at Nagykörösi út 156, district XIX). The public transit connection is tricky (from Boráros tér, at the Pest end of the Petőfi Bridge, catch bus #54 or #55 and ride it for about 25 min, get off at Autópiac stop); it's easier to take a taxi. This is prime pickpocket territory—keep an eye on your valuables.

For something smaller but much more central, drop by the **Petőfi Csarnok** (or "Pecsa," PEH-chah, for short) concert venue in City Park, which hosts a flea market on weekend mornings (cheap entry fee, Sat–Sun 8:00–14:00, www.bolhapiac.com).

ENTERTAINMENT & NIGHTLIFE

Budapest, the cultural capital of Hungary (and much of Central Europe), is endlessly entertaining. Whether it's opera, folk music and dancing, a twilight stroll or boat trip, live music in a seedy local bar, raving at a nightclub 'til the break-a break-a dawn, or holing up in one of the city's uniquely ramshackle "ruin pubs," Budapest offers something for everybody.

For **event schedules,** pick up the free, monthly *Budapest Panorama,* which makes things easy—listing performances with dates, venues, performers, and contact information for getting tickets (get it at the TI, or search from home at www.budapest panorama.com). The English-language *Budapest Sun* newspaper also has event listings. Other helpful websites include www .wherebudapest.hu (general), www.koncertkalendarium.hu (classical), www.funzine.hu (nightlife), www.pestiest.hu and www .exit.hu (nightlife but only in Hungarian), and www.pestimusor.hu (cutting-edge arts but in only in Hungarian).

To buy **tickets,** I've given strategies for the top options (Opera House and Hungária Koncert), and listed telephone numbers and (where possible) websites for others. Resources such as *Budapest Panorama* usually explain how you can get tickets for specific performances. There are ticket offices around town, but they usually sell for only some (not all) performances. It's possible to search for and buy tickets for many Budapest events at www.kulturinfo.hu and www.jegymester.hu.

What's on can vary by **season.** Some of the best nightclubs and bars are partly or entirely outdoors, so they're far more enjoyable in the summer. Meanwhile, the Hungarian State Opera and other indoor cultural events tend to take a summer break from late June through late September (though that's prime time for outdoor music and Hungária Koncert's touristy shows).

For a list of local **festivals,** which often include excellent live music, see page 420 in the appendix.

BUDAPEST'S MUSIC SCENE

Budapest is a great place to catch a good—and inexpensive—musical performance. In fact, Viennese music lovers often make the three-hour trip here just to take in a fine, cheap opera in a luxurious setting. Options range from a performance at one of the world's great opera houses to light, touristy Hungarian folk concerts. The tourist concerts are the simplest option—you'll see the fliers everywhere—but you owe it to yourself to do a little homework and find something that really appeals to you. See the resources listed earlier, and don't miss the good classical-music schedules at www.koncertkalendarium.hu.

Locals dress up for the more "serious" concerts and opera, but many tourists wear casual clothes—as long as you don't show up in shorts, sneakers, or flip-flops, you'll be fine.

A Night at the Opera

Consider taking in an opera by one of the best companies in Europe, in one of Europe's loveliest opera houses, for bargain

prices. The Hungarian State Opera performs almost nightly, both at the main Opera House (Andrássy út 22, district VI, M1: Opera, see page 76) and in the Erkel Színház theater (not nearly as impressive—described under "Other Venues," later in this chapter). Be careful to get a performance in the Opera House—not the Erkel Színház. Note that there are generally no performances from late June through late September. Most performances are in the original language with Hungarian supertitles.

Ticket prices range 1,000–17,000 Ft, but the best music deal in Europe may be the 400-Ft, obstructed-view tickets (easy to get, as they rarely run out—even when other tickets are sold out). If you buy one of these $2 opera tickets, you'll get a seat in one of two places: If you're sitting at the back of one of the boxes along the side of the theater, you can either sit comfortably, and see nothing; or stand and crane your neck to see about half the stage. If you sit on the top of the side balcony, you can stand near the door for a view of the stage. If the seats in front of you don't fill up, scooting up to an empty seat when the show starts is less than a capital offense. Either way, you'll hear every note along with the big spenders. If

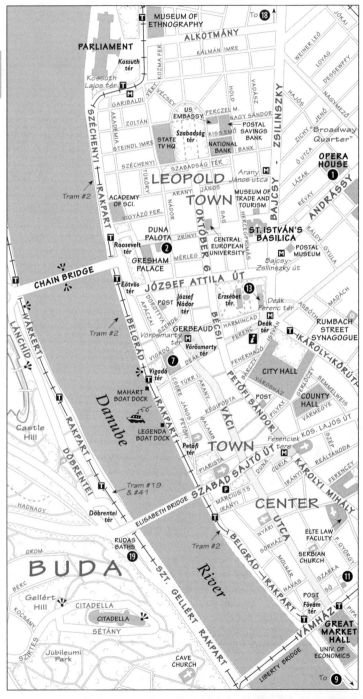

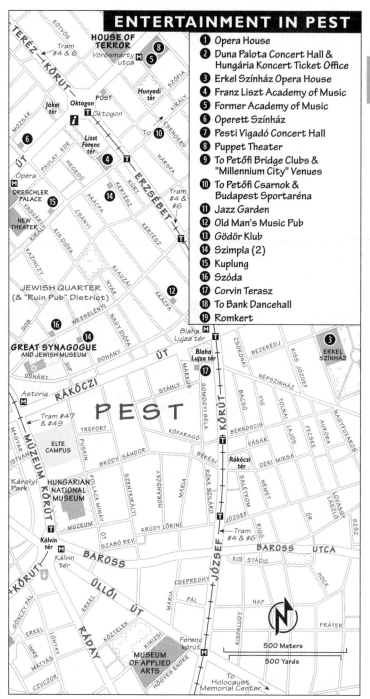

ENTERTAINMENT IN PEST

1. Opera House
2. Duna Palota Concert Hall & Hungária Koncert Ticket Office
3. Erkel Színház Opera House
4. Franz Liszt Academy of Music
5. Former Academy of Music
6. Operett Színház
7. Pesti Vigadó Concert Hall
8. Puppet Theater
9. To Petőfi Bridge Clubs & "Millennium City" Venues
10. To Petőfi Csarnok & Budapest Sportaréna
11. Jazz Garden
12. Old Man's Music Pub
13. Gödör Klub
14. Szimpla (2)
15. Kuplung
16. Szóda
17. Corvin Terasz
18. To Bank Dancehall
19. Romkert

a full evening of opera is too much for you, you can leave early or come late (but buy your ticket ahead of time, since the box office closes when the performance starts).

To get tickets, your best option is to order online (www.opera .hu or www.jegymester.hu), print your e-ticket, and waltz right in. Alternatively, you can call or fax the box office at the main Opera House (tel. 1/353-0170, fax 1/311-9017). In this case, you have to pick up your tickets in person the day before (or, if you fax them your credit-card number, you can pick them up just before the show). Maybe best of all, just drop by in person and see what's available during your visit. There are often a few tickets available at the door, even if it's supposedly "sold out" (box office open and phone answered Mon–Sat from 11:00 until show time—generally 19:00; Sun open 3 hours before the performance—generally 16:00–19:00, or 10:00–13:00 if there's a matinee).

Tourist Concerts by Hungária Koncert

Hungária Koncert offers a wide range of made-for-tourists performances of traditional music. These take place in one of two historic venues: the **Budai Vigadó** ("Buda Concert Hall"—on Corvin tér in Víziváros, between Castle Hill and the Danube, district I—for location, see the map on page 101); or in the former Budapest Ritz, now called the **Duna Palota** ("Danube  Palace"—3 long blocks north of Vörösmarty tér in Pest, behind Roosevelt tér and the Gresham Palace at Zrínyi utca 5, district V, M1: Vörösmarty tér). The most popular options are Hungarian folk music-and-dance shows by various interchangeable troupes (3,600–6,200 Ft, June–Oct Sun–Fri at 20:00, can be at either theater) and classical "greatest hits" by the Danube Symphony Orchestra (with some traditional Hungarian instruments as well; 6,400–8,900 Ft, June–Oct Sat at 20:00, always at Duna Palota). Or you can take in an organ concert (usually mixing Bach and Mozart with Liszt or Bartók) in the Baroque **St. Anne's Church** (3,900 Ft, June–Sept Fri and Sun at 20:00, May Fri only at 20:00, on Batthyány tér at the north end of Víziváros, district I, M2: Batthyány tér). They also offer dinner cruises on the Danube and in-depth tours of the Jewish Quarter.

While highbrow classical music buffs will want a more serious concert, these shows are crowd-pleasers. If you book direct, you'll get a 10 percent Rick Steves discount on anything they offer (must book in person, by phone, or by email—not valid if you buy your tickets on their website or through your hotel). The main office is in the Danube Palace at Zrínyi utca 5 (daily April–Dec 8:00–21:00, Jan–March 8:00–18:00, open later during concerts, tel. 1/317-2754 or 1/317-1377, www.ticket.info.hu, hunkonc@ticket.info.hu).

Other Venues

Budapest has many more grand spaces for enjoying a performance. Notice that *Színház* ("scene house") means "Theater."

As noted earlier, the modern **Erkel Színház** is the State Opera's "second venue" (near the Keleti/Eastern train station at Köztársaság tér 30, district VIII, M2: Keleti pu., tel. 1/333-0540, www.opera.hu).

The **Franz Liszt Academy of Music** (Liszt Ferenc Zene-művészeti Egyetem, a.k.a. Zeneakadémia), on Franz Liszt Square, hosts occasional free concerts by its students and pay concerts by professional groups (fewer performances when school's out July–Aug, performance schedule may be sporadic during planned renovation—call first, Liszt Ferenc tér 8, just off of Andrássy út, district VI, M1: Oktogon, tel. 1/342-0179, www.lfze.hu). The **Former Academy of Music** (Régi Zeneakadémia), up Andrássy út near the House of Terror, also hosts performances (Vörösmarty utca 35, tel. 1/322-9804, www.lfze.hu).

In the heart of the "Broadway Quarter," the **Operett Színház** specializes in operettas and modern musical theater performances, but these are usually in Hungarian (just off of Andrássy út at Nagymező utca 17, district VI, M1: Opera, tel. 1/312-4866, www .operettszinhaz.hu).

The **Pesti Vigadó** ("Pest Concert Hall"), gorgeously restored and sitting proudly on the Pest embankment, will reclaim its status as a fine venue when its interior renovation is complete in the near future (Vigadó tér 1, district V, M1: Vörösmarty tér, tel. 1/266-6177, www.tabulas.hu/vigado).

The **National Dance Theater** (Nemzeti Táncszínház)—with performances ranging from ballet to folk to contemporary—sits on top of Castle Hill, near the upper station for the funicular (Színház utca 1–3, district I, for location, see map on page 101, tel. 1/201-4407, www.dancetheatre.hu).

For something a bit more playful, consider the **Puppet Theater** (Bábszinház), which offers puppet performances that please old and young alike. Shows can include Hungarian folk tales, classical opera, and avant-garde modern puppetry (across Andrássy út from the House of Terror,

Hungarian Music

As a leading city of the music-loving Habsburg Empire, where so many great composers thrived, Budapest has seen a steady parade of great musical talent waltz though its streets. And, for such a small country, Hungary boasts an exceptional musical tradition. The local music is typified by a unique mingling of powdered-wig classical influences and down-home campfire hoedowns. Even the great classical Hungarian composers freely admitted to drawing inspiration from their humble Magyar heritage.

Hungary's traditional music—like its language, cuisine, and everything else—still shows the influence of its Central Asian roots. Almost hauntingly discordant to foreign ears, it makes ample use of stringed instruments, especially violins and the cimbalom (*czembalom,* similar to a hammered dulcimer). These soulful melodies seems to pluck the strings of the Hungarian soul; more than once I've seen Hungarians (especially after sipping some local wine) spontaneously break into a traditional *csárdás* or *verbunkos* dance, with the womenfolk periodically punctuating the proceedings with an excited little yelp. Popular tunes include the lively "Az a Szép" ("He Is Handsome") and the downbeat "Virágom, Virágom" ("My Flower, My Flower").

Another Asian-descended group, the Roma (Gypsies), have also had a strong influence on Hungarian music. Because of the similarities in these two peoples' music, and the convergence of their cultures in the Hungarian countryside, "Hungarian folk" music and "Gypsy" music are virtually indistinguishable to the casual listener. For example, Roma composer Grigoraş Dinicu's "The Lark"—a high-speed violin piece that replicates a bird's chirp—is a favorite show-off song for Hungarian violin virtuosos. The rollicking high spirits that accompany a lively music session is described with the Roma term *mulatság*.

The "big three" Hungarian composers all borrowed tunes from their Magyar ancestors:

Franz Liszt (pronounced "list," 1811–1886) was raised speaking German, but had a Hungarian surname and ancestry, and loved what he considered his homeland of Hungary. This master composer, conductor, pedagogue, and (above all) pianist was prodigiously talented and traveled far and wide to share his skill *("Liszt played here"* signs are plastered on buildings all over Hungary). He died never having mastered the Magyar tongue, but his countrymen embrace him anyway. Liszt composed what's probably the definitive piece of Magyar music, Hungarian Rhapsody No. 2 in D Minor (famously employed by various cartoons, most notably conducted by Bugs Bunny).

Béla Bartók (BAR-tohk, 1881–1945), from Transylvania, was as much an ethnomusicologist as a composer. He collected and cataloged folk songs from the distant corners of the Hungarian realm and beyond. In addition to composing the well-known choral work *Cantata Profana,* he penned two operas (*Bluebeard's Castle* and *The Miraculous Mandarin*). Bartók is particularly well-known to Americans because he fled to New York City during World War II. He never again set foot in Hungary, dying of leukemia before the war ended.

Zoltán Kodály (KOH-die, 1882–1967) was also an ethnomusicologist, who strove to analyze folk music on a scientific basis. Like Bartók, he harvested many songs in the fertile soil of rural and rustic Transylvania, where traditions thrived. But unlike Bartók, Kodály focused on understanding and forging a uniquely Hungarian folk sound. Kodály was also a composer, but he's best-known today as the namesake of the solfège sight-singing method called the "Kodály Method"—the principle behind "do, re, mi…"

Other (non-Hungarian) composers were also inspired by Magyar music. For example, Johannes Brahms (1833–1897), from Germany, composed a series of Hungarian Folk Dances (the most famous is No. 5/Allegro, which the Hungarians have adopted as an anthem of their own).

Traditional Hungarian music was discouraged by the communists because it stoked Magyar patriotism, but it was kept alive by the underground *táncház* ("dance house") movement. Today it thrives once more out in the open. It has become a draw for visitors (touristy Budapest restaurants often have live "Gypsy music"), but it's also popular among locals. Muzsikás is a well-respected band that performs classic folk music with a very old-fashioned sound (www.muzsikas.hu), while the Roma bands Ando Drom (www.andodrom.com) and Besh o droM (www.beshodrom.hu) each have a following of their own.

If you're in the market for some Hungarian music, you'll find music stores around town (including in the Opera House gift shop). For a good local recording, look for the well-regarded Hungaroton label.

Andrássy út 69, district VI, M1: Vörösmarty utca, tel. 1/342-2702, www.budapest-babszinhaz.hu).

The **"Millennium City"** complex, sitting on the Pest riverbank near the Lágymányosi Bridge south of downtown (district IX), is a new, state-of-the-art facility with multiple venues. The **Palace of Arts** (Művészetek Palotája) features art installations as well as musical performances (tel. 1/555-3001, www.mupa .hu). The **National Theater** (Nemzeti Szinház) presents mostly Hungarian-language drama and lectures (tel. 1/476-6868, www .nemzetiszinhaz.hu). While it's an eye-catching cluster of buildings, this complex's inconvenient location makes it less enticing than some of the old-fashioned options in the heart of town (tram #2 heads here from Pest Town Center, or take the HÉV suburban train from Boráros tér near the Petőfi Bridge south to Megálló Lágymányosi-híd, then walk 5 min).

Major rock acts perform at the **Petőfi Csarnok** (in City Park, district XIV, M1: Széchenyi fürdő, tel. 1/363-3730, www.petofi csarnok.hu; also hosts flea market—see page 245 in the Shopping chapter), or at the newly renovated **Budapest Sportaréna** (a.k.a. Papp László Sportaréna; southeast of City Park at intersection of Hungária körút and Kerepesi út, district XIV, M2: Stadionok, www.budapestarena.hu).

NIGHTLIFE

Budapest is a young and lively city, with no shortage of after-hours fun. I've listed these roughly in increasing order of edginess, from "asleep by 10:00 (p.m.)" to "asleep by 10:00 (a.m.)."

Low-Impact Nightlife

This beautiful city is gorgeously lit after dark. Strolling along either the Buda or the Pest **promenade** along the Danube rewards you with wonderful views.

If you need some rejuvenation after a busy day of sightseeing, soak and splash at **Széchenyi Baths.** The indoor thermal baths close down at 19:00, but the outdoor pools—which are the best part anyway—stay open until 22:00 (last entry at 21:00). ✪ See the Thermal Baths chapter on page 87.

Nighttime Danube Cruise

For a different angle on Budapest, consider joining one of these fun, romantic, crowd-pleasing boat trips. Danube Legenda's cruises include two drinks and evocative commentary about the floodlit buildings you pass (for details, see page 51 in the Orientation chapter).

Yuppie Drinking Zones

Young locals meet up for happy hour after work at the many trendy bars in two areas: on **Franz Liszt Square** (Liszt Ferenc tér, on page 229) and along **Ráday utca** (described on page 227 in the Eating chapter). Many of these places also serve food.

For something a bit more genteel—evocative of this city's late-19th-century Golden Age—locals pass their evenings sipping wine or nibbling dessert at a **café** (see "Budapest's Café Culture" on page 234 in the Eating chapter).

Jazz and Blues Clubs

Budapesters (and travelers) in their 30s, 40s, and 50s enjoy these two music clubs, both in central Pest. While they serve food, it's pricey and an afterthought to the entertainment; I'd eat elsewhere and drop by here afterwards for a drink.

Jazz Garden, in a cellar that feels like a nighttime garden (right down to the twinkling stars), feels refined...almost sedate. A favorite venue for the top local jazz acts, it has a mellow yuppie audience that's comfortable for any age (1,000-Ft cover, overpriced food, open Wed–Mon, doors open at 18:00, performances start at 21:00, closes at 1:00 in the morning, closed Tue, Veres Pálné utca 44a, district V, M3: Kálvin tér, tel. 1/266-7364, www.jazz garden.hu).

Old Man's Music Pub is a divey joint that packs 'em in for nightly music performances (generally 21:00–23:00). Cramped, smoky, loud, and rollicking, this place attracts relatively big-name local blues, swing, and rock acts playing for an appreciative audience of Budapesters young and old. After 23:00, the old folks head home and the kids stick around to enjoy the dance hall until dawn (no cover, Akácfa utca 13, district VII, M2: Blaha Lujza tér, tel. 1/322-7645, www.oldmans.hu).

In the "National Ditch"

Gödör Klub ("Ditch Club") fills the foundation for the never-completed new National Theater, in the very center of Pest at Erzsébet tér (next to Deák tér, where the three Metro lines converge). It's a café by day and a music club by night, when the sprawling subterranean art-gallery space (which is faintly visible below the surface of the park's shallow pond) hosts an eclectic range of concerts. In the summer, people fill the long, slanted approach to the club, and hang out on the lawn nearby—creating a fun and engaging local scene (performances most nights, start at 20:00 or 21:00, Erzsébet tér, district V, M1/M2/M3: Deák tér, see Hungarian-only websites www.godorklub .hu or www.vilagveleje.hu). For more on the history of this odd site, see page 151.

"Ruin Pub" Crawl

If you're looking for memorable, lively, smoke-filled, trendy pubs crammed with twentysomething Budapesters and backpackers, explore the dingy streets of the Jewish Quarter, behind the Great Synagogue. (This area is between the Small and Great Boulevards, south of Király utca and north of Rákóczi út.) After World War II, this area was deserted, then resettled by mostly Roma (Gypsies). It remained dilapidated even after the Iron Curtain fell and the rest of Budapest was rejuvenated. Even today, reconstruction here lags behind other parts of the city.

This unusual combination of a very central location and low rents has attracted a funky new breed of bars, dubbed "ruin pubs." The low-profile entryways look abandoned, but once you walk back through a maze of hallways, you'll emerge into large halls and open-air courtyards filled with people huddled around ramshackle tables...rickety-chic.

While dingy and gloomy, this neighborhood is generally considered safe by locals. If you're concerned, figure out the closest Metro stop and quickest route to the pubs to minimize wandering through back streets. Note that most of these have vast outdoor zones, but small interiors—so they're better in good weather.

Szimpla ("Simple") was the first and remains the best of Budapest's "ruin pubs." This place sprawls through an old building that ought to be condemned, and spills out into an equally shoddy courtyard. It oozes nostalgia for young Budapesters who have fond memories of their communist-era childhoods. Even the snacks are communist kitsch, and along with a full range of alcohol, they serve the old commie soft drinks (such as grape-flavored Traubisoda and sour cherry Meggymárka). Although it's on the route of the tourist pub-crawls, Szimpla is still mostly frequented by locals (daily 12:00–4:00 in the morning, Kazinczy utca 14, district VII, M2: Astoria, tel. 1/352-4198, www.szimpla.hu). They have a second, smaller location a few blocks away (Kertész utca 48).

Kuplung is lower-profile and even rougher around the edges (if that's possible). The name means "clutch pedal"...put it into neutral. Tables are scattered around a grand hall that feels like an old hangar with a whale skeleton suspended from the ceiling, and downstairs is a hall for music acts (open nightly into the wee hours, Király utca 46, district VII, M1: Opera, www.kuplung.net). It's virtually impossible to find unless you know what to look for: Make your way to Király utca 46 (two blocks south of the Opera House), go down the parking-lot courtyard (to the right of Caesar's Söröző) toward the *Heineken* sign, then go through the door at the far end (follow the noise). In the summer, the courtyard is also filled with outdoor seating.

Szóda (named for the seltzer bottles that line the wall) is smaller, less edgy, and more polished than the others, so it's not strictly a "ruin pub." But it's still lively and maintains a healthy reverence for the Red old days, with secondhand communist furniture and a sprawling open-air courtyard in good weather (nightly until late, Wesselényi utca 18, district VII, M2: Astoria, tel. 1/461-0007, www.szoda.com).

Nightclubs and Discos

Budapest has a thriving nightlife scene for twentysomethings. In general, places are hopping Wednesday, Thursday, Friday, and Saturday nights, and pretty dead Sunday through Tuesday. In the summer, many Budapesters head to nearby Lake Balaton for the weekend (which has its own share of nightspots)—leaving Budapest's clubs mostly for tourists. To mingle with Hungarians, Thursday nights are best. Many of the places I mention here are outdoor and summer-only—look for the words *kert* (garden), *terasz* (terrace), *udvar* (courtyard), or "beach." Off-season (Oct–April) or in questionable weather, skip the trip. Note that some clubs charge a cover (usually for men only). The current trend is playing 1970s, 1980s, and 1990s retro-hits (a mix of Michael Jackson; Earth, Wind & Fire; mainstream hip-hop; and Madonna of all eras). If a club plays a special type of music, I've noted it here. While this scene is constantly changing, the places listed here are well-established. But before venturing to any specific place, ask around for the latest tips (youth hostels and backpackers are a great source of tips). Look around town (including at some TIs and hotels) for the free weeklies *Funzine* (in English, www.funzine.hu) and *Pesti Est* and *Exit* (in Hungarian, www.pestiest.hu and www.exit.hu).

In Central Pest: The **"ruin pubs"** and **Gödör Klub** (both described earlier) are the top choices. In the summer, various rooftop terraces fill the city center. One of the best is the **Corvin Terasz,** which bills itself as the "underground above the city" (ride up an elevator to the top of the Corvin department store, across from New York Café at Blaha Lujza tér 1–2, enter on Somogyi Béla utca, district VII, M2: Blaha Lujza tér, www.corvinteto.hu). **Bank Dancehall,** near the Nyugati/Western train station, has several floors of dancing with different music (Teréz körút 55, district VI, M3: Nyugati pu., www.bankdancehall.hu).

NIGHTLIFE

In Buda: At the foot of Gellért Hill, **Romkert** is a very posh option, filled with plastic-surgery success stories. This is where Budapest's beautiful people go to see and be seen; it's more popular for its aesthetics than for its music (next to Rudas Baths at Buda end of Elisabeth Bridge, Döbrentei tér 9, district I). Near Moszkva tér, **Jam Pub** often features live performances by has-been bands (otherwise "retro disco," in the second building of the giant Mammut shopping mall, Lövőház utca 1–3, district II, M2: Moszkva tér, www.jampub.hu).

On Margaret Island: Budapest's playground island has two summer-only clubs, both near the southern tip of the island (within a 5-min walk of Margaret Bridge, district XIII): **Cha-Cha-Cha Terasz** (alternative dance music/trip-hop, at the stadium, www.chachacha.hu) and **Holdudvar** (mod and classy, in the courtyard of an old mansion, www.holdudvar.net).

On "Dockyard Island" (Hajógyári Sziget): One of the most happening zones, especially in the summer, is the island in the Danube just north of Margaret Island (near Óbuda, a.k.a. Óbudai Island, district III). Several clubs keep this island throbbing. Some of the best-established are **Mokka Cukka** (alternative), **Bed Beach** (swanky, techno), **Dokk Beach** (funk, R&B, hip-hop), and **Sláger** (pop hits). This is a thriving and sprawling scene, with imported beaches, rental boats, and a meat-market vibe. You can take the HÉV suburban railway from Batthyány tér and get off at the Megálló Filatori gát stop, then walk across the bridge to the island—or just take a taxi from downtown. This island is also the site of Budapest's biggest bash, the **Sziget Festival,** which attracts huge-name, mid-name, and small-name acts for a week each August (www.sziget.hu). This "Hungarian Lollapalooza," typically attended by nearly 400,000 people, is emerging as one of Europe's top parties.

On the Southern Edge of Downtown Budapest, near the Petőfi Bridge (Petőfi Híd): More summer-only options cluster just south of downtown, on either side of the Petőfi Bridge (near Boráros tér, district IX, take tram #2 south from Pest Town Center, or tram #4 or #6 around the Great Boulevard). Floating in the river on the Pest side are the party barge/live music venue called **A38** (www.a38.hu) and **Buddha Beach** (Közraktár utca 9–11). Across on the Buda side, at Goldmann György tér (continue one more stop on tram #4 or #6 to Petőfi híd/budai hídfő) are the **Rio** club (www.rio.hu) and **Zöld Pardon** outdoor dancehall (www.zp.hu), both playing Eurotrash disco music. These places seem to attract a somewhat rowdier crowd (i.e., Brits in town for "stag party" weekends).

Warning: Gentlemen, read and heed my warning about the extremely attractive women nicknamed *konzumlány* who hit on green and goofy tourists in order to lure them into dangerously overpriced bars (see page 41). In general, be highly suspicious if a very attractive local woman fawns all over you. (Sorry, you're not *that* handsome, even here in upside-down Hungary.) Many of the city's strip clubs—whether recommended by *konzumlány* or ones you find on your own—are expert at semi-legally extorting enormous sums of cash from out-of-towners. Even if you're accustomed to visiting strip clubs back home, it's best to steer clear here. (If you're looking for advice on which specific strip clubs are better than others...you bought the wrong book, buddy.)

TRANSPORTATION CONNECTIONS

Budapest is the hub of transportation for all of Hungary; from here, train lines and expressways fan out like spokes on a wheel. This chapter covers arrivals and departures by train, bus, plane, car, and riverboat.

BY TRAIN

Hungary has a good train network, run by MÁV (Magyar Államvasutak). From centrally located Budapest, train lines branch out across Hungary. For connections between outlying cities, you'll often have to go back through Budapest. While Hungary's trains are generally good, many are old and fairly slow; major routes (especially those connecting to international destinations such as Bratislava or Vienna) use faster, newer  InterCity trains (marked with an "IC" or a boxed "R" on schedules). To ride an InterCity train, you must pay extra for a required reservation (which is printed on a separate ticket).

For timetables, the first place to check is Germany's excellent all-Europe site: http://bahn.hafas.de/bin/query.exe/en. You can also check Hungary's own timetable website, at http://elvira.mav-start.hu. For general rail information in Hungary, call 1/461-5400; for information about international trains, call 1/461-5500.

Prices are reasonable (1,500 Ft per 100 kilometers/62 miles). While railpasses can be a good deal in other countries, the low cost of point-to-point tickets in Hungary makes them a lesser value

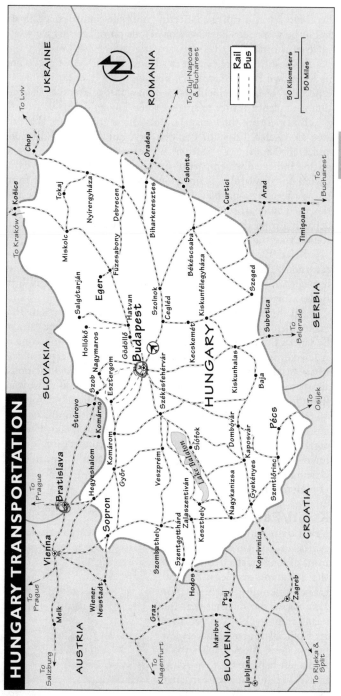

TRANSPORTATION

here. However, if you're connecting multiple countries, a railpass might be worth considering. For details on railpasses, see www .ricksteves.com/rail.

It's best to buy your ticket in advance at the MÁV ticket office in downtown Pest (see page 42). Because ticket lines can be long—especially for international trains—it's smart to arrive at the station with plenty of time to spare if you're buying tickets there.

Budapest has three major train stations (*pályaudvar*, abbreviated *pu.*): Keleti ("Eastern") Station, Nyugati ("Western") Station, and Déli ("Southern") Station. A century ago, the name of the station indicated which part of Europe it served. But these days, there's no correlation: Trains going to the east might leave from the Western Station, and vice-versa. Even more confusing, the station used by a particular train can change from year to year. Before departing from Budapest, it's essential to carefully confirm which station your train leaves from.

Keleti/Eastern Station and Nyugati/Western Station are both cavernous, slightly run-down, late-19th-century Erector-set masterpieces in Pest. Déli/Southern Station, behind Castle Hill in Buda, mingles its dinginess with modern flair.

All three stations are seedy and overdue for renovation. This makes them a bit intimidating—not the most pleasant first taste of Budapest. But once you get your bearings, they're easy to navigate. A few key words: *pénztár* is ticket window, *vágány* is track, *induló vonatok* is departures, and *érkező vonatok* is arrivals. At all stations, access to the tracks is monitored—you might have to show your ticket to reach the platforms (though this is very loosely enforced).

The taxi stands in front of each train station are notorious for ripping off tourists; it's better to call for a taxi. For tips on this—and on using the Metro system to connect into downtown Budapest—see "Getting Around Budapest" on page 44 in Orientation.

Here's the rundown, station by station:

Keleti/Eastern Station

Keleti train station (Keleti pu.) is just south of City Park, east of central Pest. On arrival, go to the front of long tracks 6–9 to reach the exits and services. Several travel agencies with *Tourist Information* signs cluster near the head of the tracks. None of these is an official TI, but all have a few helpful fliers. Along track 6, you'll find a left-luggage desk, an ATM (at K&H Bank), money-exchange

booths (avoid Interchange, which has bad rates), and a narrow passage marked *Exit*. Following this passage leads you to a broad, beautifully renovated hallway leading (to the left) to pay WCs and the Baross Restaurant (described later), and (to the right) to international information and ticket windows (look for *nemzetközi pénztár*, and take a number).

Back in the main hall, domestic ticket windows are across the tracks, near track 9. The big staircase at the head of the tracks leads down to more domestic ticket windows, WCs, telephones, more ATMs, and (a few minutes' walk straight ahead, through the open-air courtyard) a passageway to the Metro station entrance (M2/red line). If you go out the front door, you'll stumble over a cluster of suspicious-looking, unmarked taxis. You can try to negotiate with these goons—the fair rate to downtown is about 1,500 Ft—but it's far more reliable and less of a hassle to phone for a taxi (buy phone card at newsstand, go to the phone bank downstairs, call 266-6666 or 211-1111, tell the English-speaking dispatcher where you are, and go out front to meet your taxi).

Eating at Keleti Station: **Baross Restaurant,** at the head of track 6, captures some of the faded turn-of-the-20th-century gentility that this grand station once enjoyed. A time warp with dingy woodwork, chandeliers, and fake marble, they serve up tired Hungarian classics that are worth considering if you want a meal while waiting for your train (2,000–3,500-Ft main dishes, daily 8:00–20:00). Your other eating options inside the station are unappealing *döner kebab* stands.

Shopping near Keleti Station: Roughly across the street from the station is the brand-new **Arena Plaza** shopping mall (Mon–Sat 10:00–21:00, Sun 10:00–19:00, Kerepesi út 9, tel. 1/880-7000, www.arenaplaza.hu).

Nyugati/Western Station

Nyugati train station (Nyugati pu.) is the most central of Budapest's stations, on the northeast edge of downtown Pest. Most

international arrivals use tracks 1–9, which are set back from the main entrance. From the head of these tracks, exit straight ahead into a parking lot with taxis and buses, or use the stairs just inside the doors to reach an underpass and the Metro (M3/blue line). Note that the taxis here are often crooked—it's far better to call for your own cab (see instructions and phone numbers above).

Ticket windows are through an easy-to-miss door across the

tracks by platform 13 (marked *cassa* and *információ;* once you enter the ticket hall, international windows are in a second room at the far end—look for *nemzetközi,* daily 7:30–19:00).

From the head of tracks 10–13, exit straight ahead and you'll be on Teréz körút, the very busy Great Boulevard. (Váci utca, at the center of Pest, is dead ahead, about 20 min away by foot.) In front of the building is access to handy trams #4 and #6 (zipping all the way around Pest's great ring); to the right you'll find stairs leading to an underpass (use it to avoid crossing this busy intersection, or to reach the Metro's M3 line); and to the left you'll see the classiest Art Nouveau McDonald's on the planet. (Seriously. Take a look inside.)

Shopping near Nyugati Station: Next door is the huge, American-style **WestEnd City Center** mall (complete with a T.G.I. Friday's, daily 8:00–23:00, next to track 1, tel. 1/374-6573, www.westend.hu).

Déli/Southern Station

In the late 19th century, local newlyweds caught the train at Déli train station (Déli pu.) for their honeymoon in Venice. Renovated by the heavy-handed communists, today the station is dreary, dark-granite, smaller, and more modern-feeling than the others. It's tucked behind Castle Hill on the Buda side. From the tracks, go straight ahead into the vast, empty-feeling main hall, with well-marked domestic and international ticket windows at opposite ends. A left-luggage desk is outside, beyond track 1. If you head downstairs, you'll find several shops and eateries, and access to the very convenient M2/red Metro line, which connects you easily to several key points in town: Batthyány tér (on the Buda embankment, at the north end of the Víziváros neighborhood), Deák tér (the heart of Pest, with connections to other Metro lines), and Keleti train station.

Train Connections

There's no telling which station each train will use, especially since it can change from year to year—always confirm carefully which station your train leaves from. Remember, for specific schedules, check http://bahn.hafas.de/bin/query.exe/en or http://elvira.mav-start.hu.

From Budapest by Train to Destinations in Hungary: Eger (5/day direct, 2.5 hrs, more with transfer in Füzesabony, usually from Budapest's Keleti/Eastern Station), **Pécs** (8/day direct, 3 hrs; a few additional connections possible with transfer at the suburban Budapest-Kelenföld station), **Sopron** (7/day direct, 3 hrs, more with a transfer in Győr), **Visegrád** (trains arrive at Nagymaros-

Visegrád station, across the river—take shuttle boat to Visegrád; hourly, 40–60 min, usually from Budapest's Nyugati/Western Station), and **Esztergom** (hourly, 1.5 hrs, usually from Budapest's Nyugati/Western Station). Note that Nagymaros (the Visegrád station) and Esztergom are on opposite sides of the river—and on different train lines. To reach **Szentendre** and **Gödöllő**, you'll take the suburban HÉV line (see "By HÉV," below).

By Train to International Destinations: Bratislava (that's **Pozsony** in Hungarian, 5/day direct, 2.5 hrs; more with transfers), **Vienna** (that's **Bécs** in Hungarian, every 2 hrs direct, 3 hrs; more with transfers), **Prague** (4/day direct, 7–7.75 hrs, more with transfers in Győr and Vienna; plus 1 night train/day, 10.5 hrs), **Kraków** (1/day direct, 9.25 hrs; plus 1 direct night train/day, 10.5 hrs; otherwise transfer in Břeclav, Czech Republic), **Ljubljana** (1/day direct, plus 2/day with a transfer in Zagreb, 9.5 hrs; also possible in 8.5 hrs with changes at Vienna/Wien Meidling and Maribor; no convenient night train), **Munich** (1/day direct, 7.5 hrs; plus 1 direct night train/day, 10 hrs; otherwise transfer in Vienna and Salzburg), **Berlin** (1/day direct, 11.75 hrs), and **Zagreb** (3/day direct, 6–7.5 hrs).

By HÉV: Note that Budapest has its own suburban rail network, called HÉV. For tourists, this is mostly useful for reaching **Szentendre** (from M2: Batthyány tér) and **Gödöllő** (from M2: Örs vezér tere). For more on the HÉV system, see page 47.

BY BUS

Buses can be relatively inexpensive, but are typically slower and less convenient than trains. You can search bus schedules at the (Hungarian-only) website www.menetrendek.hu (click on "VOLÁN Menetrend"). Confusingly, several "bus stations" are scattered around Budapest. Each one sits next to a Metro stop of the same name. A few are particularly useful for tourists:

From the **Újpest-Városkapu** bus station (on the M3/blue line), buses depart about hourly to trace the Danube Bend around to **Szentendre** (30 min), **Visegrád** (1.25 hrs), and **Esztergom** (2 hrs).

The **Stadionok** bus station (on the M2/red line) serves **Eger** (hourly, 2–2.25 hrs).

The **Árpád híd** bus station (on the M3/blue line) has buses taking the overland route to **Esztergom** (1–2/hour, 1.25 hrs).

The **Népliget** bus station (on the M3/blue line) is mostly used by international buses (including **Bratislava:** 1/day, 4.25 hrs), as well as buses to **Pécs** (5/day direct, 3.5–4.5 hrs) and **Sopron** (2/day direct, 3.75 hrs).

BY PLANE

Budapest Ferihegy Airport

Budapest's airport is 10 miles southeast of the center (airport code: BUD, tel. 1/296-7000, www.bud.hu). The airport has two passenger terminals, which are about three miles from each other. Terminal 1 is used by the low-cost airlines. Terminal 2 has two adjacent parts: 2A is for flights from EU/Schengen countries (no passport control required), while 2B is for flights from other countries. (If you're flying out of Budapest, confirm which terminal your flight leaves from.) Both terminals have similar services, including ATMs and TI desks. There is no free bus between terminals. Bus #200E frequently connects Terminals 1, 2A, and 2B (covered by 290-Ft transit ticket at an automated machine, more expensive if purchased from driver), or you can connect between them with the airport shuttle minibus (700 Ft, described below).

From the Airport to Budapest: If you're using **Terminal 1,** consider taking the handy train that heads straight to Nyugati/ Western train station near downtown Pest (300 Ft, plus 520 Ft supplement for InterCity trains, 3–7/hr depending on the day and time, 25 min). Buy your ticket from the TI desk inside Terminal 1 before leaving the airport. Then, as you exit Terminal 1, bear left and follow signs to the train tracks (use colorful pedestrian overpass to reach the platform).

If you're using **Terminal 2A or 2B,** it's a hassle to get to Terminal 1 to catch the train (bus #200E to "Ferihegy 1" stop, go inside terminal to buy ticket from TI desk, then go back out to catch train). Instead, I'd consider one of these options (which also work from Terminal 1):

The fastest door-to-door option is to take a **taxi.** Zóna Taxi has a monopoly at the taxi stand out front, with a fixed off-meter price depending on where you're going (about 4,500–5,000 Ft to downtown, 1,000 Ft less from downtown to the airport, about 30 min, tel. 1/365-5555, www.zonataxi.eu). Note that you can also call any other taxi company to take you to or from the airport (see "Getting Around Budapest—By Taxi," page 49).

The **airport shuttle** minibus is cheaper for a solo traveler, but two people might as well take a taxi (2,600 Ft per person for minibus ride to any hotel in the city center, about 30–45 min depending on hotel location; they can also take you between terminals for 700 Ft; tel. 1/296-8555, www.airportshuttle.hu; if arranging a minibus transfer *to* the airport, call at least 24 hrs in advance). Because they prefer to take several people at once, you may have to wait a while for a quorum to show up (about 15 min in busy times, up to an hour when it's slow—they can give you an estimate).

Finally, the cheapest option is to take **public bus** #200E to the Kőbánya-Kispest station on the M3/blue Metro line, and then take the Metro all the way into town (allow about an hour total for the trip to the center).

To Eger: Eger makes an enjoyable small-town entry point in Hungary for getting over your jet lag. Unfortunately, there is no direct connection there from Budapest's airport. The easiest plan is to ride the airport shuttle minibus to Budapest's Keleti/Eastern Station, then catch the Eger-bound train from there. Or, to save a little money, you could take public bus #200E to Kőbánya-Kispest, ride the M3/blue Metro line to Deák tér, and transfer to the M2/red Metro line, which stops at both Keleti Station (for the train to Eger) and Stadionok (for the bus to Eger).

Flights from Budapest

Malév, the Hungarian national airline, offers the most connections from Budapest of any carrier (tel. 0640-212-121, from the US dial 011-36-1-235-3888, www.malev.com). While fares tend to be pricey, promotional deals on their website can allow you to connect affordably to other cities (for example, less than €200 round-trip to various European capitals).

As an alternative, low-cost airlines allow you to cheaply connect Budapest with several other European destinations. Budapest-based **Wizz Air** (www.wizzair .com)—which also has hubs in the Polish cities of Warsaw, Gdańsk, and Katowice (near Kraków)—is the first place to check. Also consider budget-carrier standbys **easyJet** (www.easyjet.com), **Ryanair** (www.ryanair.com), **germanwings** (www.germanwings.com), and **Air Berlin** (www.airberlin.com). To search several budget airlines at once, visit www.skyscanner.net.

If you're not finding the flight you want out of Budapest, consider flying out of Bratislava, Slovakia instead—just a three-hour train ride away (see Bratislava chapter). Bratislava is a hub for one of the biggest Central European budget airlines, **SkyEurope** (www.skyeurope.com). Vienna, Austria—also three hours from Budapest by train—has additional cheap flights on SkyEurope and germanwings.

Prices on these "no-frills" carriers are cheap, but there are some trade-offs: minimal customer service, nonrefundable tickets, and strict restrictions on the amount of baggage you're allowed to check without paying extra. In general, you'll be nickel-and-dimed every step of the way (no free drinks). Also note that you'll sometimes use less convenient, secondary airports. For example,

Wizz Air's flights to Kraków actually arrive at Katowice, 50 miles away. Finally, be warned that many budget airlines save money by scheduling flights on the same plane extremely close together—so they can pack more flights into one day. But this means that a delay early in the day can trickle down and cause major delays later.

BY CAR

To Drive or Not to Drive?

If you're focusing on Budapest, you definitely don't want a car. Even for side-trips into the countryside, virtually all of the attractions listed in this book (with the possible exception of Hollókő) are easily reachable by public transit. Even so, some areas—such as the Danube Bend or around Hollókő—can be done more efficiently by car. Instead of hassling with a car of your own, consider splurging by hiring a local guide (see page 50) or a driver (page 44).

For car-rental advice (including your insurance options), see "Car Rental," later in this chapter.

Driving Tips

Frankly, driving in Budapest is a nightmare. Especially during rush hour (7:00–9:00 and 16:00–18:00), congestion is maddening, and since the city has no expressway bypasses, any traffic going through the city has to go *through* the city—sharing the downtown streets with local commuters. If driving in the city, do not drive down roads marked with a red circle, or in lanes marked for buses; these can be monitored by automatic traffic cameras, and you could be mailed a ticket.

There are three concentric ring roads, all of them slow: the Small Boulevard (Kiskörút), Great Boulevard (Nagykörút), and outermost Hungária körút, from which highways and expressways spin off to other destinations. The new, desperately needed fourth ring—the M-0 expressway—is partly finished (south and east of downtown); when it's complete in a few years, it will have a huge impact on traffic, diverting freight trucks away from the city center and other ring roads.

Parking: Unless you're heading to an out-of-town sight (such as Memento Park), park the car at your hotel and take public transportation. Public parking costs 150–450 Ft per hour (pay in advance at machine and put ticket on dashboard—watch locals and imitate; free parking Mon–Fri after 18:00 and all day Sat–Sun—but you'll

DRIVING IN HUNGARY: DISTANCE AND TIME

Note: Your times may vary based on traffic, construction, and road conditions. It can take an additional 30-60 minutes to get out of Budapest's city center.

DANUBE BEND DETAIL
15m • .5h — Visegrád
Esztergom
25m • .75h — 15m .5h
Szentendre — 15m .5h
Budapest

TRANSPORTATION

have to pay all the time in tourist zones). Be careful to park within the lines—otherwise, your car is likely to get booted (I've seen more than one confused tourist puzzling over the giant red brace on their wheel). A guarded parking lot is safer, but more expensive (figure 3,000–4,000 Ft/day, ask your hotel or look for the blue *P*s on maps). As rental-car theft can be a problem, ask at your hotel for advice. For driving info in Budapest, visit www.fovinform.hu.

Toll Stickers: Hungary has a fine network of expressways, which always begin with "M" (e.g., the M-3 expressway runs east of Budapest toward Eger). To drive on Hungarian expressways, you'll need a toll sticker, or *autópálya matrica* (also called a "Vignette"; 1,170–1,530 Ft/4 days depending on season, 2,550 Ft/10 days, 4,200 Ft/month, www.motorway.hu). Ask about this when you rent your car (if it's not already included, you'll have to buy one). It's not uncommon to be pulled over at an on- or off-ramp to be checked for a toll sticker; those caught without one are subject to a hefty fine. If you dip into Slovakia or Austria, you'll also need to buy a toll sticker to drive on their highways (Slovakia—*úhrada*, 150 Sk/7 days; Austria—*Vignette*, €8/10 days, €22/2 months). Note that you don't need a toll sticker if you'll be dipping into the country on minor roads—only for major highways.

To Eger and Other Points East: Head out of the city center on Andrássy út, circling behind Heroes' Square to access Kós Károly sétány through the middle of City Park. You'll pass

Széchenyi Baths on the left, then (exiting the park) go over the Hungária körút ring road, before getting on M-3. This expressway zips you conveniently to Eger (exit #114 for Füzesabony; go north on road 33, then 3, then 25 into Eger). Between Budapest and Eger, M-3 also passes Gödöllő (with its Royal Palace) and to Hatvan (where you can exit for Hollókő).

To Bratislava, Vienna, and Other Points West: From central Pest, head over the Danube on the white, modern Elisabeth Bridge (Erzsébet híd). Once in Buda, the road becomes Hegyalja út; simply follow *Wien* signs to get on M-1.

To the Danube Bend: For tips on driving around the Danube Bend (Szentendre, Visegrád, and Esztergom), see page 289 in the Day Trips from Budapest chapter.

Car Rental

It's cheaper to arrange long-term car rentals in the US than in Europe. All of the big American companies have offices in Budapest. Comparison-shop on the Web to find the best deal (www.autoeurope.com is a consolidator with good rates), or ask your travel agent. Figure about $100 per day for a short-term rental of just a few days, or less per day for longer stretches. Be warned that dropping a car off in a different country—say, picking up in Budapest and dropping in Vienna—can be prohibitively expensive (depends on distance, but the extra fee averages a few hundred dollars).

If you want an automatic, reserve a car at least a month in advance and specifically request an automatic. You'll pay about 40 percent more to rent a car with an automatic instead of a manual transmission.

Be sure to bring along your valid US driver's license. Given the language barrier, it can also be helpful to get an International Driving Permit ahead of time at your local AAA office ($15 plus two passport-type photos, www.aaa.com).

As a rule, always tell your car-rental company up front exactly which countries you'll be entering. Some companies levy extra insurance fees for trips taken with certain types of cars (such as BMWs, Mercedes, and convertibles) in certain countries. Double-check with your rental agent that you have all the documentation you need before you drive off (especially if you're crossing borders into non-Schengen countries, such as Croatia or Romania, where you might need to present proof of insurance). For more on borders, see page 8.

When you pick up the car, check it thoroughly and make sure any damage is noted on your rental agreement. Find out how your car's lights, turn signals, wipers, and gas cap function. Be sure you know whether it takes diesel or unleaded fuel.

Learn the universal road signs. Seat belts are required. A new law makes it illegal to drink any alcohol at all before driving. More and more European countries require you to have your headlights on any time you're driving, even in broad daylight. The lights of many newer cars automatically turn on and off with the engine—ask when you pick up your car.

AND LEARN THESE ROAD SIGNS

Speed Limit (km/hr) · Yield · No Passing · End of No Passing Zone · One Way · Intersection · Main Road · Freeway · Danger · No Entry · No Entry for cars · All Vehicles Prohibited · Parking · No Parking · Customs · Peace

If you drop your car off early or keep it longer, you'll be credited or charged at a fair, prorated price. But always keep your receipts in case any questions arise about your billing.

Returning a car in a big city can be tricky; get precise details on the car drop-off location and hours. When you return the car, make sure the agent verifies its condition with you.

Car Insurance Options

When you rent a car, you are liable for a very high deductible, sometimes equal to the entire value of the car. You can limit your financial risk in case of an accident by choosing one of these three options: buy Collision Damage Waiver (CDW) coverage from the car-rental company, get coverage through your credit card (free, if your card automatically includes zero-deductible coverage), or buy coverage through Travel Guard.

CDW includes a very high deductible (typically $1,000–1,500). When you pick up the car, you'll be offered the chance to "buy down" the deductible to zero (for $10–30/day; this is often called "super CDW").

If you opt instead for credit-card coverage, there's a catch. You'll technically have to decline all coverage offered by the car-rental company, which means they can place a hold on your card for the full deductible amount. In case of damage, it can be time-consuming to resolve the charges with your credit-card company. Before you decide on this option, quiz your credit-card company about how it works and ask them to explain the worst-case scenario.

Buying CDW insurance (plus "super CDW") is the easier but

pricier option. Using the coverage that comes with your credit card saves money, but can involve more hassle.

Finally, you can buy CDW insurance from Travel Guard ($9/day plus a one-time $3 service fee covers you up to $35,000, $250 deductible, US tel. 800-826-4919, www.travelguard.com). It's valid nearly everywhere in Europe, except the Republic of Ireland and Italy. Oddly, residents of Washington State aren't allowed to buy this coverage.

For more fine print about car-rental insurance, see www.rick steves.com/cdw.

BY BOAT

In the summer, Mahart runs daily high-speed hydrofoils up the Danube to **Vienna.** It's not particularly scenic, and it's slower than the train, but it's a fun alternative for nautical types. The boat leaves Budapest late April through early October daily at 9:00 and arrives in Vienna at 15:30 (Vienna to Budapest: 9:00–14:30). The trip costs €89 one-way. On any of these boats, you can also stop in the Slovak capital, **Bratislava** (€79 one-way). To confirm times and prices, and to buy tickets, contact Mahart in Budapest (tel. 1/484-4010, www.mahartpassnave.hu) or DDSG Blue Danube in Vienna (tel. 01/58880, www.ddsg-blue-danube.at).

For details on taking the boat to **Danube Bend** towns (Szentendre, Visegrád, and Esztergom), see page 289 in the Day Trips from Budapest chapter.

DAY TRIPS FROM BUDAPEST

Gödöllő Palace • Hollókő • Szentendre • Visegrád • Esztergom

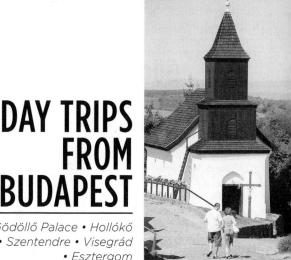

The most rewarding destinations outside Budapest are Eger, Pécs, Sopron, and Bratislava (Slovakia). But each of those (covered in their own chapters) is more than two hours away; for a shorter visit, the region immediately surrounding Budapest offers some enticing options for a break from the big city. Just outside Budapest, Gödöllő Palace is the best spot in Hungary to commune with its past Habsburg monarchs, the larger-than-life Franz Josef and Sisi. The tiny village of Hollókő, tucked in the hills northeast of Budapest, combines a living community with an open-air folk museum. And three river towns along the Danube Bend offer an easy escape: the charming town of Szentendre is an art colony with a colorful history to match; the castles of Visegrád boast a sweeping history and equally grand views over the Bend; and Esztergom is home to Hungary's top church.

Planning Your Time

Of this chapter's five attractions, Gödöllő Palace and Szentendre are the easiest to reach from Budapest (each one is a quick ride away on the suburban train, or HÉV). These sights—which are also the best attractions in this chapter—can be done in just a few hours each. The other sights (Hollókő, Visegrád, and Esztergom) are farther afield and less rewarding; do these only if you have extra time or they're on the way to your next stop.

For efficient sightseeing, you can cluster your visits to these sights strategically. If you have a car, Gödöllő Palace and Hollókő can be done in a day (round-trip from Budapest, or on a long day driving between Budapest and Eger; for details, see page 269). The Danube Bend sights (Szentendre, Visegrád, and Esztergom) also go well together if you have a car, and line up conveniently between Budapest and Bratislava or Vienna.

Gödöllő Palace

Holding court in an unassuming town on the outskirts of Budapest, Gödöllő Royal Palace (Gödöllői Királyi Kastély; pronounced roughly "GER-der-ler") is Hungary's most interesting royal interior to tour. Once the residence of Habsburg Emperor Franz Josef and his wife, Empress Elisabeth (known as Sisi), Gödöllő has recently been restored to its *"K und K"* (royal and imperial) splendor. The pink, U-shaped Baroque complex looks like just another mid-sized palace from the outside, but it's haunted by Habsburg ghosts...with an unmistakably Hungarian twist. Compared to other Habsburg properties, it's compact and pleasantly uncrowded. If you want a Habsburg fix and aren't going to Vienna (or if you're a Habsburg completist), Gödöllő is worth a half-day visit from Budapest.

ORIENTATION

Cost and Hours: 1,800 Ft; April–Oct daily 10:00–18:00; Nov–March Tue–Sun 10:00–17:00, closed Mon; last entry one hour before closing.

Getting There: Gödöllő Palace is an easy side-trip from Budapest, by HÉV suburban train or by car. By **public transit,** take the M2/red Metro line to the end of the line at Örs vezér tere, then cross the street to the HÉV suburban train green line and hop a train marked for Gödöllő (2/hr). Once in Gödöllő, get off at the Szabadság tér station (about an hour total from central Budapest). The palace is kitty-corner across the street from the station. **Drivers** will find the palace 17 miles east of Budapest, just off the M-3 expressway (on the way to Eger and other points east).

Information: Tel. 28/410-124, www.kiralyikastely.hu. There is a Gödöllő town TI inside the palace (down the hall from the ticket desk, tel. 28/415-402). No audioguide was available at the time of this writing (but ask if they have one now). English descriptions are posted in each room, and my self-guided tour (later in this chapter) covers the basics.

Time to Allow: By public transportation, figure an hour each way from central Budapest, plus another hour or so to tour the palace.

Starring: The royal and imperial couple, Franz Josef and Sisi.

Background

The palace was built in the 1740s by Count Antal Grassalkovich, a Hungarian aristocrat who was loyal to Habsburg Empress Maria Theresa (at a time when most Hungarians were chafing under her rule). When the Compromise of 1867 made Habsburg rulers Franz Josef and Sisi "king and queen of Hungary" (see page 278), the couple needed a summer home where they could relax in their Hungarian realm—and Gödöllő Palace was the place. Later it became the home of Admiral Miklós Horthy, who led Hungary as regent between the world wars. After falling into disrepair during the communist period (when it was a Soviet military barracks, then a nursing home), the palace was recently rehabilitated to Habsburg specifications and re-opened to the public. Renovations are ongoing, and more parts of the palace will open to the public in the coming years.

While many areas of the palace are available to rent for private receptions (including a Baroque theater and horse-riding arena), the tourist's palace has two wings: the Franz Josef wing (to the right as you enter) and the Sisi wing (to the left), which you'll visit in that order. Pleasant gardens stretch behind the palace.

Budapest Day Trips at a Glance

If you only have a day or two to venture outside of Budapest, this overview might help you decide where to go. I've listed these sights roughly in order of worthiness. Notice that each of the four top attractions is covered in its own, separate chapter.

▲▲▲**Eger** This appealing mid-sized town, packed with gorgeous Baroque architecture, has one of Hungary's most historic castles, some pleasantly quirky museums, excellent local wines, and fine thermal baths (including the excellent new Salt Hill Thermal Spa in the nearby countryside). Eger is the best look outside Budapest at workaday Hungary. Allow a full day or overnight. See Eger chapter.

▲▲▲**Pécs** A medium-sized city and the de facto capital of southern Hungary, Pécs features a rich history (typified by the unique mosque-turned-church on its main square), surprisingly top-notch museums, and beautiful buildings slathered with colorful local Zsolnay tiles. Allow a full day or overnight. See Pécs chapter.

▲▲**Bratislava, Slovakia** The Slovak capital—conveniently situated between Budapest and Vienna—is worth a look for its increasingly rejuvenated Old Town, taste of Slovak culture, and evocative sea of construction cranes, which are hard at work reinventing the city as an economic capital of the New Europe. Allow a half-day to a full day (most convenient on the way to Vienna). See Bratislava chapter.

▲▲**Sopron** A small-town alternative that's also between Budapest and Vienna, Sopron has a charmingly well-preserved Old Town peppered with dusty museum and historic buildings.

SELF-GUIDED TOUR

• *After buying your ticket, pick up the free floor plan and check out the model in the lobby to see how the palace was gradually expanded from its original U-shaped core.*

Head upstairs and go right, following the marked tourist route into the...

Franz Josef Wing

You'll walk down a long hallway and view a series of rooms celebrating the palace's construction and its original builders, the aristocratic **Grassalkovich family.** If this obscure blue blood doesn't thrill you, take the opportunity to simply appreciate the

Allow a half-day to a full day (most convenient on the way to Vienna). See Sopron chapter.

▲▲**Gödöllő Palace** This summer palace of the Habsburg monarchs is the best place in Hungary to get to know the "royal and imperial" couple, Franz Josef and Sisi. It's easy to see in a half-day from Budapest (or, by car, combine with Hollókő for a full day). See page 274 in this chapter.

▲▲**Szentendre** This colorful, Balkan-feeling artist colony is the easiest (and most touristy) small town to visit from Budapest. Allow a half-day from Budapest, or combine with a full-day trip around the Danube Bend. See page 290 in this chapter.

▲▲**Esztergom Basilica** Hungary's biggest and most important church, packed with history, looms above the Danube. Allow a full day combined with other Danube Bend sights (Szentendre and possibly Visegrád). See page 302 in this chapter.

▲**Hollókő** This intriguing village-meets-open-air folk museum hides in the middle of nowhere an hour and a half northeast of Budapest. Visit only if you have a car and are interested in Hungarian countryside culture and architecture. Allow a full day (by car, it can be combined with Gödöllő Palace for a full-day side-trip, or visited en route between Budapest and Eger). See page 281 in this chapter.

Visegrád The least engaging of the Danube Bend sights, Visegrád offers a small riverside palace museum and a dramatic hilltop castle with fine views over the Bend. Visit only if it's on the way of your Danube Bend day. See page 298 in this chapter.

opulent apartments. As in other palaces of the day, servants actually scurried around inside the walls like mice, serving their masters unseen and unheard. Look for "secret" access doors to these servant spaces, and notice that the stoves have no doors—they were fed from behind, inside the walls.

At the end of the Grassalkovich exhibit, the **oratory** gives you a peek into the chapel. This room allowed the royal couple to "attend" Mass without actually mingling with the rabble. Soon after the oratory, keep an eye out for the hideaway toilet and the access to the servants' crawlspace.

In the **coronation chamber,** we finally catch up with the Habsburgs. Look for the giant painting of Franz Josef being crowned at Matthias Church, on top of Buda's Castle Hill. (On

Franz Josef (1830-1916) and Sisi (1837-1898): Emperor and Empress of Austria, King and Queen of Hungary

In a unique power-sharing compromise, the emperor and empress of the Austrian realm were only the "king" and "queen" of Hungary. (This was known as *"K und K"* in German, for *König und Kaiser,* king and emperor...same guy.) From the beginning of this "K+K" arrangement in 1867 through the end of World War I, this "royal and imperial" couple was Franz Josef and Sisi.

Franz Josef I—who ruled for 68 years (1848-1916)—was the embodiment of the Habsburg Empire as it finished its six-century-long ride. Born in 1830, Franz Josef had a stern upbringing that instilled in him a powerful sense of duty and—like so many men of power—a love of all things military.

His uncle, Ferdinand I, suffered from profound epilepsy, which prevented him from effectively ruling. As the revolutions of 1848 (including Hungary's) were rattling royal families throughout Europe, the Habsburgs forced Ferdinand to abdicate, and put 18-year-old Franz Josef on the throne. Ironically, as one of his first acts as emperor, Franz Josef—whose wife would later become closely identified with Hungarian independence—marched into Budapest to put down the 1848 Revolution. He spent the beginning of his long reign understandably paranoid, as social discontent continued to simmer.

Franz Josef was very conservative. But worse, he wrongly believed that he was a talented military tactician, and led Austria into catastrophic battles. Wearing his uniform to the end, he couldn't see what a dinosaur his monarchy was becoming, and never thought it strange that the majority of his subjects didn't even speak German. Franz Josef had no interest in democracy and pointedly never set foot in Austria's parliament building. But, like Queen Victoria, his contemporary, he was the embodiment of his empire—old-fashioned but sacrosanct. His passion for low-grade paperwork earned him the nickname "Joe Bureaucrat." Mired in these petty details, he missed the big picture. In 1914, he helped start a Great War that ultimately ended the age of the divine monarchs.

Empress Elisabeth—Franz Josef's mysterious, narcissistic, and beautiful wife—has been compared to Princess Diana

the right side, hat in hand, is Count Andrássy, namesake of Pest's main drag and reputed lover of Franz Josef's wife Sisi—more on him later.) Across the room is a painting of another Franz Josef coronation, this time at today's Roosevelt tér in Pest. Back then, Buda and Pest were separate cities—so two coronations were required.

In the **study of Franz Josef,** we see a portrait of the emperor, with his trademark bushy 'stache and 'burns. The statue depicts

because of her beauty, bittersweet life, and tragic death.

Sisi, as she's lovingly called, was mostly silent. Her main goals in life seem to have been preserving her reputation as a beautiful empress, maintaining her Barbie-doll figure, and tending to her fairy-tale, ankle-length hair. In the 1860s, she was considered one of the most beautiful women in the world. But, in spite of severe dieting and fanatic exercise, age took its toll. After turning 30, she allowed no more portraits to be painted of her and was generally seen in public with a delicate fan covering her face (and bad teeth).

Complex and influential, Sisi was adored by Franz Josef, whom she respected. Although Franz Josef was supposed to marry her sister Helene (in an arranged diplomatic marriage), he fell in love with Sisi instead. It was one of the Habsburgs' few marriages for love. (The family was famously adept at strategic marriages.) Still, Sisi never felt fully accepted by her mother-in-law...which made the Hungarians—who also felt misunderstood and not taken seriously by the Habsburgs—like her even more.

Sisi's personal mission and political cause was promoting Hungary's bid for autonomy within the empire. While she was married to Emperor Franz Josef, she spent seven years in Budapest and at Gödöllő, enjoying horseback riding, the local cuisine...and the company of the dashing Count Gyula Andrássy. (For more on the Count, see page 153.) Hungarians, who call Sisi their "guardian angel," partly credit her for the Compromise of 1867, which elevated their status within the Habsburg Empire.

Sisi's personal tragedy was the death of her son Rudolf, the crown prince, in an apparent suicide (an incident often dramatized as "The Mayerling Affair"). Disliking Vienna and the confines of the court, Sisi traveled more and more frequently. As years passed, the restless Sisi and her hardworking husband became estranged. In 1898, while visiting Geneva, Switzerland, she was murdered by an Italian anarchist.

A final note: While for simplicity in this book I've referred to these figures as history knows them—"Emperor Franz Josef" and "Empress Sisi"—Hungarians might bristle at these imperial titles. After all, they (and *only* they) called the couple "King Franz Josef" and "Queen Sisi."

GÖDÖLLŐ PALACE

Franz Josef's great-great-nephew Otto von Habsburg, the Man Who Would Be Emperor, if the empire still existed. Otto, born in 1912, was an early proponent of the creation of the European Union (whose vision for a benevolent, multi-ethnic state bears eerie similarities to the Habsburg Empire of Franz Josef's time). Otto celebrated his 90th birthday here at Gödöllő Palace.

Franz Josef's salon (a.k.a. the reception room) displays a map of the Habsburg Empire at its peak, with all the different nationalities around the edge. Notice the very colorful reconstructed stove.

The lavishly chandeliered **grand ballroom** still hosts concerts. Above the main door, notice the screened-in loft where musicians could play—heard, but not seen.

• *At the far end of the grand ballroom, you enter the...*

Sisi Wing

This wing—where the red color scheme gives way to violet—is dedicated to the enigmatic figure that most people call "Empress Sisi," but whom the Hungarians call "our Queen Sisi." Sisi adored her Hungarian subjects, and they adored her; supposedly at certain times in her life, she spent more time here at Gödöllő Palace than in Vienna. While the Sisi-obsession is hardly unusual at Habsburg sights, notice that the exhibits here are particularly doting...and always drive home Sisi's Hungarian affinities.

In the **reception room,** along with the first of many Sisi portraits, you'll see the portrait of Count Gyula Andrássy. Sisi's enthusiasm for all things Hungarian reportedly extended to this dashing aristocrat, who taught Sisi how to handle horses...and supposedly sired her third daughter, Marie Valerie—nicknamed the "Little Hungarian Princess."

In Sisi's **study,** see the engagement portraits of the fresh-faced Franz Josef (age 23) and Sisi (age 16). While they supposedly married for love, Sisi is said to have later regretted joining the imperial family. The book by beloved Hungarian poet Sándor Petőfi, from Sisi's bedside, is a reminder that Sisi could read and enjoy the difficult Magyar tongue.

You'll then pass through Sisi's **dressing room** (with small family portraits) and **bedroom** (with a dress from one of her ladies-in-waiting), before reaching three more rooms with...more exhibits on Sisi. Look for the letter in Hungarian, written in Sisi's own hand; an invitation to her wedding; and a portrait of Ida Ferenczy, Sisi's elderly Hungarian lady-in-waiting who was particularly beloved by her countrymen and -women. There are also images of items throughout Hungary that are dedicated to Sisi (such as Budapest's Elisabeth Bridge).

On your way out, keep an eye out for the window into the little **stairwell,** which led from Sisi's study directly outside—allowing the famously reclusive empress/queen an easy escape in case of unwanted guests.

GÖDÖLLŐ PALACE

Hollókő

Remote, miniscule Hollókő (HOH-loh-ker), nestled in the hills a 1.5-hour drive from Budapest, survives as a time capsule of

Hungarian tradition. This proud village is half living hamlet, half open-air folk museum; unlike many such places around Europe, people actually reside in quite a few of Hollókő's old buildings. To retain its "real village" status, Hollókő has its own mayor, elementary school, general store, post office, and doctor (who visits twice a week). Hollókő is worth a visit for those who are interested in Hungarian folk culture, especially if you have a car. Note that most of the village shuts down off-season (mid-Oct–Easter) and on Mondays; at these times, skip Hollókő.

Getting There

Hollókő is in a distant valley about 60 miles northeast of Budapest. By **car,** it's about a 1.5-hour drive (assuming light traffic): Take the M-3 expressway east, exit at Hatvan (exit 55), and follow road #21 north toward Salgótarján. Keep an eye out (on the left) for the turn-off for Hollókő and Szécsény, then carefully track *Hollókő* signs. From Eger, figure about 1.5 hours (fastest via the M-3 expressway west, then follow the directions above).

In the summer, it's possible (but more time-consuming) to reach Hollókő by public transportation: A **bus** leaves from Budapest's Stadionok bus station once daily year-round (likely around 15:15), with a second bus daily in summer (likely around 8:30). Buses return to Budapest on a similar schedule (likely at 14:00 in summer, 16:00 year-round). The trip takes about 2.25 hours each way. Notice that this schedule makes a same-day round-trip from Budapest impossible outside of summer.

Planning Your Time

Hollókő deserves at least a couple of hours; a half-day is about right for most visitors. With a car, consider detouring to Hollókő between Budapest and Eger. Remember, Gödöllő Palace (which is also off the M-3 expressway) combines well with Hollókő; for example, see them both as a side-trip from Budapest, or on the way between Budapest and Eger.

The village is particularly worthwhile on festival days (listed on their website—www.holloko.hu). Again, don't bother on a

Monday or off-season, when nearly everything is closed.

If choosing what to visit at Hollókő, the Village Museum is the most worthwhile, followed by the Weaving House and Doll Museum. The others are skippable, but it's worth poking into several shops. Hike up to the castle only if you've got time and energy to burn.

ORIENTATION

Hollókő (total population: about 370) is a village squeezed into a dead-end valley overlooked by a castle. The hamlet is divided into two parts: the Old Village (with all the protected old houses, shops, and museums, and about 60 residents) and the New Village. The bus stop and big parking lot are just above the entry point to the Old Village. There's an ATM and a pay WC behind the pub that overlooks the entrance to the Old Village.

Tourist Information

Hollókő's useful TI is along the main street in the middle of the Old Village. They can give you a brochure and help you find a room (summer daily 8:00–18:00, sometimes until 20:00; winter Mon–Fri 8:00–16:00, Sat–Sun 10:00–16:00; Kossuth utca 68, tel. 32/579-011, www.holloko.hu).

Local Guide: Since English-speakers get little respect at Hollókő (only a few borrowable translations in some museums), you owe it to yourself to hire a local guide. **Ádám Kiss** is a young city-slicker who fell in love with Hollókő and moved here with his wife and kids to become part of the community. Ádám, who lived in Montana and speaks good English, will enthusiastically make your time here more meaningful, and he's a great value (5,000 Ft for a 2-hr tour, does not include entrance fees, mobile 0620-379-6132, kissadam@freemail.hu).

SELF-GUIDED TOUR

Hollókő's Old Village

The Old Village at Hollókő is a perfectly preserved enclave of folk architecture, dress, and traditions of the local Palóc culture. Because it's in a dead-end valley, Hollókő's folk traditions survived here well into the 20th century. (Only when villagers began commuting to other towns for work in the 1950s did they realize how "backward" they seemed to other Hungarians.)

It's free to enter the Old Village, but each sight inside has its own modest entry fee (generally around 250 Ft). Unless otherwise noted, sights here are open Easter–mid-Oct Tue–Sun 10:00–17:00, closed Mon; off-season, most places close entirely or are only open

Sat–Sun in good weather. Assume that no English is spoken, but at most places you can ask to borrow English translations.

• *Start at the entry point into the Old Village, which begins where the cobbles do. Get oriented with the big wooden map posted nearby. Across the street is the...*

Barnyard (Pajtakert): A local agency coordinates special events here for visiting groups. If you see the ladies in their color-

ful folk dresses (generally a few times each day in summer), feel free to gawk from over the fence. Hollókő's men, who tended to go elsewhere for work, abandoned their old-fashioned outfits earlier; but the women, who remained in the valley, kept wearing tradi-tional dress much longer. Their costume is marked by a big, round abdomen (a sign of fertility, created by layering many petticoats), an embroidered vest, and a colorful headdress.

HOLLÓKŐ

• *Now head down the village's main street. As you walk, don't be afraid to poke into any shop. (I'll mention only a few.) One of the best (on the right) is the...*

Handicraft Workshop: Here you can buy some local crafts, or English-speaking Tunde will teach you to make them yourself (same price, takes 5–30 min depending on craft, closed Mon–Tue).

On the left, the **Waxworks** (Panoptikum) is a tiny exhibit illustrating local legends (400 Ft, daily).

• *As you continue, take a closer look at the...*

Traditional Houses: The exteriors of these houses cannot be changed without permission, but interiors are modern (with plumbing, electricity, Internet access, phones, and so on). They

once had thatched roofs with no chimneys (to evade a chimney tax), but a devastating fire in 1909 compelled them to replace the thatch with tiles and add little chim-neys. The thick walls are made of a whitewashed, adobe-type mix of mud and dung (which keeps things cool in summer and warm in winter). Thick walls, small doors (watch your head), small windows...small people back then. The big, overhang-ing roof (nicknamed the house's "skirt") prevents rain from dam-aging this fragile composition. Most began as one simple house along the road; as children grew and needed homes of their own, a little family compound evolved around a central courtyard.

• *After passing two of the town's restaurants (on the right), you'll reach the **TI** on the left (see "Tourist Information" on page 282). On the right just before the fork is a...*

Forestry Museum: This cute museum has some exhibits about the local terrain and woodcarvings from a local artist (250 Ft, Fri–Sun 10:15–17:45, closed Mon–Thu).

• *At the fork in the road is Hollókő's...*

Church: A traveling priest says Mass here twice weekly. This is a popular wedding spot for Budapest urbanites charmed by its simplicity.

• *Take the fork to the right (Petőfi út) and wander past a few more shops until the road re-joins (at the town's third restaurant). Most tourists simply backtrack here, but poke a few more yards down the street. On the left, you'll see a* vár/castle *sign leading very steeply up to the town's castle (which is prominent overhead; for a more gradual approach, read on). Across the street is the...*

People and Landscape Museum: This little collection displays photos of Hollókő in the olden days—with thatched roofs and dirt roads...but otherwise looking much the same (250 Ft, closed Mon and Wed).

• *Head back up on the other road (Kossuth út). On the right, across from the restaurant, is the...*

Doll Museum: Step inside to see 160 dolls dressed in traditional costumes of the area. Each is labeled with the specific place of origin and a basic English description, allowing you to see the subtle changes from village to village (250 Ft, daily 10:00–17:00).

• *On the right is the...*

Weaving House: You can dip into the shop of locally made embroidery for free, and pay 300 Ft to watch a demonstration of two different looms (one more than a century old; closed Mon).

Farther up on the right, stop into **Grandma's Shop** to browse a wide range of locally produced Hungarian foods in jars—pickles, jams, honey, *pálinka* (schnapps), and more. Next door is a basket-maker's shop.

• *A few steps up on the right is the...*

Village Museum: The Old Village's highlight, this is the only house here with an authentic interior (250 Ft, March–Nov daily 10:00–18:00, closed Dec–Feb). Take a trip back 100 years as you stroll through the house.

You enter into the **kitchen.** Most of the family (including piles of kids) would sleep on the floor here, near the warmth of the stove. The doors on the back wall (behind the stove) lead to a smoker. Before the houses had chimneys, this very efficient design allowed them to heat the house, cook, bake, and smoke foods all at the same time.

Then head into the **main room** (to the left as you enter). Even today, many older Hungarians have a "nice room" where they keep

their most prized possessions and decorations. They let visitors peek in to see their treasures...then make them sit in the kitchen to socialize. In here you'll see plates and clocks proudly displayed. Looking around this room also gives you clues to the family's status. The pillows and linens piled on the bed (stored there during the day, as most family members bunked on the floor) indicate that this was a middle-class home. The matching furniture is delicately painted. The dresser is well-built and intricate, indicating that a carpenter was paid to make it (other furniture would have been more roughly built by the head of the household). All of these items (furniture and linens) were traditionally given by the bride's father as a dowry to the groom, allowing the couple to start their life together. The glass in the windows is not authentic; back then, they would have stretched pig bladders over the windows instead. Turn your attention to the ceiling: the rafters are painted blue, which was thought to ward off flies, and people would hang their boots (their most expensive item of clothing) up there to prevent mice from ruining them.

Now cross back over to the **third room,** used for storing tools and food. The matriarch of the house slept in here (on the uncomfortable-looking rope bed) and kept the key for this room, doling out the family's ration of food—so in many ways, Grandma was the head of the household. While the rest of the family slept elsewhere in the house, a young woman of courting age could meet a suitor in here. He'd sneak in through the window, but their social intercourse would be carefully monitored by Granny. (The Hungarians even have a verb for this concept—roughly, "storaging.") Find the crude crib, used to bring a baby along with adults

working the fields (notice it could be covered to protect from the sun's rays). In other parts of Hungary, peasants were known to partially bury their babies in the ground to prevent them from moving around while they worked. (These days, we use TV—is that really so much more humane?) Look up to find the bread rack suspended from the ceiling—again, to rescue the bread from those troublesome mice. Out back, you'll see the old wine press.

• *Continue up the street. A bit farther up on the right, look for the...*

Postal Museum: This shows off old postal uniforms, equipment, stamps, and currency (400 Ft).

• *A few more steps up, and you've completed your circle—you're back at the town church. There's one more sight in town. If you're up for a 15–20-minute uphill hike, consider going up to the...*

Castle: First hike up to the big parking lot; from there, follow the rough path marked *vár/castle* (a bit uphill at first, then mostly

level; in summer you can pay to hop on a tourist train to get there).

Hollókő's castle originally dates from the 13th century. By the 16th century, it was on the frontier between Habsburg-held Hungary and the Ottoman invaders (who eventually conquered the castle and used it for their own defense for a century and a half). After the Habsburgs had retaken Hungary, Emperor Leopold I destroyed the castle prophylactically (in 1711, just after the failed War of Independence) to ensure his Hungarian subjects wouldn't use it against him. It sat in ruins until 1966, when it underwent an extensive, 30-year-long renovation. There are only a few small exhibits to see inside, but it's enjoyable enough to hike around to ever-higher and better panoramas (600 Ft, daily 10:00–17:30, in winter on good-weather Sat–Sun only). Views over the Old Village give you a sense of how miniscule the town is. The nearby fields are used to graze Hollókő's livestock, which stay out at pasture at all times rather than being

stabled. The high hills on the horizon are across the border, in Slovakia.

The castle is also tied to the legend of how Hollókő ("Hill of the Ravens") got its name: Supposedly the owner of a castle that stood on the hill above this one once kidnapped a girl from the village. The girl's nanny, who was a witch, sent ravens to pick the castle apart, stone by stone.

SLEEPING

This is a very sleepy place to spend the night, but those who really want to delve into village Hungary might enjoy it (and its accommodations are far cheaper than other cities or towns in this book). The **TI** rents several rooms in nine traditional buildings right in the Old Village (figure Db-10,000 Ft including breakfast; see contact information under "Tourist Information" on page 282). **Tugári Vendégház,** run by local guide Ádám Kiss and his wife, has four rooms in a nicely restored old building in the New Village, a five-minute walk from the main sights (7,000–8,500 Ft depending on room size, breakfast-750 Ft, cheaper for stays of longer than 1 night, Rákóczi út 13, tel. 32/379-156, mobile 0620-379-6132, www .holloko-tugarivendeghaz.hu, tugarivendeghaz@gmail.com).

EATING

There are three restaurants in the Old Village of Hollókő, each one slinging traditional, well-priced Hungarian food: **Muskátli Restaurant** and **Katalin Csárda** (near the entrance to the village), and **Vár Restaurant** (at the bottom of the village). Be warned that all of these close early (by 18:00 or 19:00, just after the day-trippers go home), so don't wait too long for dinner. At the start of the village, you'll also see a **pub** (frequented by older locals) and a trendy **café** (favored by young locals). A humble **grocery store** is upstairs above the pub (Mon–Sat 7:30–15:30, closed Sun).

The Danube Bend

The Danube, which begins as a trickle in Germany's Black Forest, becomes the Mississippi River of Central Europe—connecting  10 countries and four capitals (Vienna, Bratislava, Budapest, Belgrade) as it flows southeast through the Balkan Peninsula toward the Black Sea. Just south of Bratislava, the river gets squeezed between mountain ranges, which force it to loop back on itself—creating the scenic "Danube Bend" (Dunakanyar). Here Hungarians sunbathe and swim along the banks of the Danube, or hike in the rugged hills that rise up from the river. Hungarian history hides around every turn of the Bend: For centuries, Hungarian kings ruled not

THE DANUBE BEND

from Buda or Pest, but from Visegrád and Esztergom. And during the Ottoman occupation of Hungary, this area was a buffer zone between Christian and Muslim Europe.

Today, three river towns north of Budapest on the Danube Bend offer a convenient day-trip getaway for urbanites who want to commune with nature. Closest to Budapest is Szentendre, whose colorful, storybook-cute Baroque center is packed with tourists. The ruins of a mighty castle high on a hill watch over the town of Visegrád. Esztergom, birthplace of Hungary's first Christian king, has the country's biggest and most important church. All of this is within a one-hour drive of the capital, and also reachable (up to a point) by public transportation.

Planning Your Time

Remember, Szentendre is the easiest Danube Bend destination—just a quick suburban-train (HÉV) ride away, it can be done in a few hours. Visegrád and Esztergom are more difficult to reach by public transportation; either one can require a substantial walk from the train or bus stop to the town's major sight.

By **public transportation,** don't try to see all three towns in one day; focus on one or two. (I'd skip Visegrád, whose fine castle is a headache to reach without a car.) If you want to do the whole shebang, take a tour, rent a car, or hire a driver (see page 44) or local guide (page 50).

With a **car,** try this ambitious one-day plan: 9:00–Leave Budapest; 9:30–Arrive at Szentendre and see the town; 12:00–Leave Szentendre; 12:30–Lunch in Visegrád; 13:30–Tour Visegrád Royal Palace and Citadel; 15:30–Leave Visegrád; 16:00–Visit Esztergom Basilica; 17:00–Head back to Budapest. With extra time, add a visit to the Hungarian Open-Air Folk Museum ("Skanzen") near Szentendre.

If you're driving between Budapest and Vienna (or Bratislava), the Danube Bend towns are a fine way to break up the journey, but seeing all three en route makes for a very long day—get an early start, or skip one.

Getting Around the Danube Bend

Going north from Budapest, the three towns line up along the same road on the west side of the Danube—Szentendre, Visegrád, Esztergom—each spaced about 15 miles apart.

By Car: It couldn't be easier. Get on road #11 going north out of Buda, which will take you through each of the three towns—the road bends with the Danube. As you approach Szentendre, watch for signs for *Centrum Szentendre* to branch off to the right, toward the old center and the river promenade. To return from Esztergom to Budapest, see "Route Tips for Drivers" at the end of this chapter.

By Boat: From early April to late October, Mahart runs boats from Budapest up the Danube Bend. The slower **riverboats** (1.5 hrs to Szentendre, 3.5 hrs to Visegrád, 5.5 hrs to Esztergom) run daily in the peak of the summer (June–Aug, sometimes also May and Sept) and weekends only (Sat–Sun) in the shoulder season. The faster **hydrofoils** (1 hr to Visegrád, 1.5 hrs to Esztergom, none to Szentendre) run only on weekends (Sat–Sun, maybe also Fri June–Aug). No boats run in winter (Nov–March). Check schedules and buy tickets at Mahart in Budapest (dock near Vigadó tér in Pest, tel. 1/484-4010, www.mahartpassnave.hu).

By Train: The three towns are on three separate train lines. Szentendre is truly handy by train, while Esztergom and Visegrád are less convenient.

Getting to **Szentendre** is a breeze by train—the HÉV, Budapest's suburban rail, zips you right there (catch train at Batthyány tér in Buda's Víziváros neighborhood, easy connection via M2/red Metro line; 4–7/hr, 40 min each way, last train returns from Szentendre around 23:00).

The nearest train station to **Visegrád** is actually across the river in Nagymaros (this station is called "Nagymaros-Visegrád";

don't get off at the station called simply "Nagymaros"). From the station, you'll walk five minutes to the river and take a ferry across to Visegrád (see "Arrival in Visegrád," page 299). Trains run hourly between Nagymaros-Visegrád and Nyugati/Western Station in Budapest (trip takes 40–60 min).

To **Esztergom,** trains run hourly from Budapest's Nyugati/Western Station (1.5 hrs), but the Esztergom train station is a 45-minute walk from the basilica.

By Bus: Without a car, buses are the best way to hop between the three towns. They're as quick as the train if you're coming from Budapest, but can be standing room only. There are two main routes. The **river route** runs from Budapest along the Danube through Szentendre (30 min) and Visegrád (1.25 hrs), then past Esztergom Basilica (2 hrs, Iskola Utca stop) to the Esztergom bus station (hourly, more frequent during weekday rush hours). This bus leaves from Budapest's Újpest-Városkapu bus station (at the M3/blue line Metro station of the same name). A different bus takes the **overland shortcut** (skipping Szentendre and Visegrád) to directly connect Budapest and Esztergom (1–2/hr, 1.25 hrs, departs from Budapest's Árpád híd station on the M3/blue Metro line). Buses make many stops en route, so you'll need to pay attention for your stop (ask driver or other passengers for help).

By Tour from Budapest: If you want to see all three towns in one day, don't have a car, and don't want to shell out for a private driver, a bus tour is the most convenient way to go. All of the companies are about the same (all three towns in about 10 hrs, including lunch and shopping stops, plus return by boat, for around 18,000 Ft); look for fliers at the TI or in your hotel's lobby.

Szentendre

The Old Town of Szentendre (SEHN-tehn-dreh, "St. Andrew" in English) rises gently from the Danube, a postcard-pretty village with a twisty Mediterranean street plan filled with Habsburg Baroque houses. Arguably the most "Balkan-feeling" town of Hungary—thanks to the immigrants who settled the community—Szentendre promises a taste of Hungarian village life without having to stray far from Budapest...but it sometimes feels like too many other people had

the same idea. Szentendre is where Budapesters bring their wives or girlfriends for that special weekend lunch. The town has a long tradition as an artists' colony, and it still has more than its share

SZENTENDRE

of museums and galleries. It's also packed with corny, gimmicky museums—some of which (such as the Micro Art exhibit) are actually pretty fun. But the best plan is this: Venture off the souvenir-choked, tourist-clogged main streets...and you'll soon have quiet back lanes under colorful Baroque steeples all to yourself.

ORIENTATION

(area code: 26)
Little Szentendre (pop. 23,000) is easy to navigate. It clusters along a mild incline rising from the Danube, culminating at the main square (Fő tér) at the foot of Church Hill (Templomdomb). From the embankment—where most tourists arrive—various streets lead up to Fő tér, none more touristy than the souvenir gauntlet of Bogdányi utca.

Tourist Information

The TI is along the tourist route between the station and the main square. Pick up the good town map, with sights and services well-marked (mid-June–Aug Mon–Fri 9:30–18:00, Sat–Sun 10:00–18:00; mid-March–mid-June and Sept–mid-Oct Mon–Fri 9:30–17:00, Sat–Sun 10:00–16:00; mid-Oct–mid-March Mon–Fri 9:30–16:30, Sat–Sun 10:00–14:00; Dumtsa Jenő utca 22, just by the bridge over the stream, tel. 26/317-965, www.szentendre program.hu).

Arrival in Szentendre

By Train or Bus: The combined **train/HÉV and bus station** is at the southern edge of town. To reach the town center from the station (about a 10-min walk), go through the pedestrian underpass at the head of the train tracks. (A handy map of town is posted by the head of the tracks.) The underpass funnels you onto the small Kossuth Lajos utca. After a long block, you'll pass the yellow Pozsarevacska Serbian Orthodox church, then cross the bridge; the TI is on the right, and the main square is three blocks straight ahead.

By Boat: Some boats arrive right near the main square, but most come to a pier about a 15-minute walk north of the center. After you get off the boat, take the first path to your left; stay on it, and it'll lead you straight into town.

By Car: Approaching on road #11 from Budapest, turn off at signs for *Centrum Szentendre,* then park anywhere along the embankment road. Look for a blue parking pay station (pay at meter, then put ticket in window—300 Ft/hr), or pay the parking attendant, if there is one. If you can't find parking here, continue on to the large bus parking lot near the boat dock. From the

A Taste of the Balkans: Szentendre's History

While it's in Hungary, Szentendre is hardly a Hungarian town. In fact, it's a melting pot for all the Balkans—built by Serbs, Greeks, and Dalmatians on the lam from the Ottomans.

After the Habsburgs succeeded in pushing the Ottomans out of Hungary in the late 17th century, the Ottomans began to claim lands farther south on the Balkan Peninsula. Especially after their successful 1690 siege of Belgrade, a flood of some 40,000 refugee families sought refuge up the Danube. Many settled here in Szentendre. Most were Serbs, but the diaspora also included Dalmatians (from today's Croatia) and Greeks.

At first, these Balkan transplants expected that their settle-ment here would be short-lived. They built temporary houses and shops, following the narrow-alley street plan of their homeland (where skinny streets protected pedestrians from the hot sun). They tended to settle in regional enclaves, each of which maintained its heritage and traditions: four neighborhoods representing different regions of Serbia, and two from other ethnic backgrounds (Greeks and Dalmatians). Each of the six neighborhoods had its own church. Add to that the original, medieval Catholic church, and Szentendre has seven very different houses of worship.

While they were waiting to return home, the Balkan refugees supported the Habsburgs (who were facing down the Hungarians in Ferenc Rákóczi's feisty War of Independence). This earned Szentendre the favor of the emperor, who rewarded the town with special trade privileges, including the right to make and sell wine—a tradition still evidenced by the vineyards blanketing the hillsides around town.

embankment, it's an easy uphill walk into town; all roads lead to the main square.

SIGHTS

Sightseeing in Szentendre is low-impact. While there are muse-ums and churches to visit, the best plan for most is to simply enjoy a stroll through town. Head off to the back streets, and you'll be surprised at how quickly you'll find yourself alone with Szentendre.

Gradually the Ottomans were forced out of the Balkans. But by this time, the Balkan settlers of Szentendre had decided to stick around. They benefited from the increased trade flowing up the Danube (from lands recently liberated from the Ottomans), and replaced their temporary houses and churches with permanent ones (but still following the same Mediterranean street plan)—mostly in the snazzy, colorful Baroque and Rococo styles popular in Habsburg lands at the time. This explains why so many churches in town look like any old Hungarian Baroque Catholic church from the outside, but have strikingly different Orthodox interiors.

The fortunes of the people here began to change in the 1770s, when the reformist Emperor Josef II took back the special rights Szentendre had enjoyed. The town's prominence declined, as commerce shifted down the Danube to Buda and Pest. The final nail in the coffin came with a phylloxera pest infestation in the 1880s, which devastated the town's vineyards.

By the late 19th century, Szentendre was a semi-ghost town, still populated by the now-poor descendants of those original Balkan immigrants. Artists began to discover the village, and were inspired by its colorful cultural pastiche, unusual-for-Hungary narrow lanes, low rents, and closeness to nature—all within close proximity to the bustling metropolis of Budapest. A "Szentendre School" of artists emerged, putting the town on the map of art history and luring art-loving Budapesters to come for a visit. Today Szentendre has six different museums dedicated to local artists, with many more starving art students who toil away, hoping to fill their own gallery someday. (While art-lovers can browse to their heart's content, the best single museum is Margit Kovács', described on page 294.)

Today's Szentendre remains a thriving art colony and tourist town, but also a bedroom community for wealthy Budapesters—near the big city, but still in a tranquil and beautiful setting.

▲Main Square (Fő Tér)

Szentendre's top sight is the town itself. Start at the main square (Fő tér). Take a close look at the **cross,** erected in 1763 to give thanks for surviving the plague. Notice the Cyrillic lettering at the monument's base. This is a reminder that in many ways, Szentendre is more of a Serbian town than a Hungarian one (see sidebar).

Face the cross and get oriented: Behind the cross, the square narrows as it curls

around Church Hill, with the hilltop Catholic church; just behind that is the Orthodox Cathedral. Through a narrow alley to the left (between the red and yellow houses) is the fun Micro Art Museum. The street to the left (Dumtsa Jenő utca) leads to the Marzipan Museum and TI. To the right, the church fronting the square is Orthodox (called Blagovestenszka); it's been closed for a lengthy restoration, but might re-open as a museum. And directly behind you (facing the cross) is the ticket office for Szentendre's top art collection, the Margit Kovács Museum. All of these sights are described in this chapter.

On or near Fő Tér

▲Margit Kovács Museum (Kovács Margit Múzeum)—The best of Szentendre's small art museums celebrates the local artist Margit Kovács, highly regarded for her whimsical, wide-eyed pottery sculptures (700 Ft, daily 10:00–18:00, www.pmmi.hu). First buy your tickets at the office at the bottom of Fő tér (at #2–5). Then, you might be able to pass directly into the museum, or you might have to go around the block to get there (jog down Görög utca and take your first right to Vastagh György utca 1).

Margit Kovács (1902–1977) was the first female Hungarian artist to be accepted as a major talent by critics and by her fellow artists. She came from a close-knit family, and had a religious upbringing, both themes that would appear frequently in her work. The down-to-earth Kovács, who never married, lived with her mother—her best friend and most constructive critic. This collection of her ceramic sculptures, displayed on several floors and explained in English, is organized by theme. You'll see Christian, mythological, and folkloric subjects depicted side-by-side; even in many biblical scenes, the subjects wear traditional Hungarian clothing. Look for the room of sorrowful statues dating from after her mother's death. On the top floor, in the replica of Kovács' study, find the gnarled tree stump. This tree, which once stood on Budapest's Margaret Island, had been struck by lightning, and its twisted forms inspired Kovács.

Micro Art Museum (Mikrocsodák Múzueuma)—This charming and genuinely fascinating exhibit, while a bit of a tourist trap, is worth a squint. Ukrainian artist Mikola "Howdedoodat" Szjadrisztij has crafted an array of literally microscopic art—a detailed chessboard on the head of a pin, a pyramid panorama in the eye of a needle, a swallow's nest in half a poppy seed, a golden lock on a single strand of hair, and even a miniscule portrait of Abe Lincoln. You'll go from microscope to microscope, peering at these remarkably detailed sculptures (500 Ft, English descriptions, daily 10:00–18:00, down the appropriately tiny alley called Török föz at Fő tér 18–19, tel. 26/313-651).

On Dumtsa Jenő Utca

This street, which leads away from Fő tér, is where you'll find the TI; nearby is the...

Marzipan Museum—This collection (attached to a popular candy and ice-cream store) features two floors of sculptures made of marzipan. Feast your eyes on Muppets, cartoon characters, Russian stacking dolls, an over-the-top wedding cake, a life-size Michael Jackson, and, of course, Hungarian patriotic symbols (the Parliament, the Turul bird, and so on). While fun for kids, this is skippable for adults (shop free, upper floor 400 Ft, daily April–Oct 9:00–19:00, Nov–March 10:00–18:00, Dumtsa Jenő utca 12, enter from Batthyány utca, tel. 26/311-931).

Church Hill Loop

For a representative look at Szentendre's seven churches, visit these two, connected with commentary.

• *Begin on the main square (Fő tér). Go a few steps up the street at the top of the square (behind the cross). Just before the white Town Hall, climb the stairs on your right, and work your way up to the hilltop park, called...*

Church Hill (Templomdomb)—This hill-capping perch offers

some of the best views over the jumbled, Mediterranean-style roofline of old Szentendre. (See how many steeples you can count in this church-packed town.) Looking down on Fő tér, you can see how the town's market square evolved at the place where its three trade roads converged.

• *The hill's centerpiece is...*

St. John Catholic Church (Keresztelő Szent János)—This was the first house of worship in Szentendre, around which the

Balkan settlers later built their own Orthodox churches. If it's open, step into the humble interior (free, sporadic hours, 100 Ft to take pictures). Pay special attention to the apse, which was colorfully painted by starving artists in the early 20th century.

• *Exiting the church, take the downhill lane toward the red-and-yellow steeple. Find the gate in the wall (along Alkotmány street) to enter the*

yard around this church. Pay a visit to the...

Belgrade Serbian Orthodox Cathedral (Belgrádi Székesegyház)—This offers perhaps Szentendre's best oppor-

tunity to dip into an Orthodox church (500 Ft, also includes museum; May–Sept Tue–Sun 10:00–18:00, closed Mon; Oct–Nov and March–April Tue–Sun 10:00–16:00, closed Mon; Dec–Feb Fri–Sun 10:00–16:00, closed Mon–Thu; during winter, go to the museum first, then they'll let you into the church).

Standing in the gorgeous **church interior,** ponder the Orthodox faith that dominates in most of the Balkan Peninsula (starting just south and east of the Hungarian border). Keep in mind

that these churches carry on the earliest traditions of the Christian faith. Notice the lack of pews—worshippers stand through the service, with men separate from women, as a sign of respect before God. The Orthodox Church uses essentially the same Bible as Catholics, but it's written in the Cyrillic alphabet (which you'll see displayed around any Orthodox church). Following Old Testament Judeo-Christian tradition, the Bible is kept on the altar behind the iconostasis—the big screen in the middle of the room covered with icons (golden paintings of saints), which separates the material world from the spiritual one.

Orthodox icons are typically not intended to be lifelike. Packed with intricate symbolism, and cast against a shimmering golden background, they're meant to remind viewers of the metaphysical nature of Jesus and the saints rather than their physical form. However, this church, which blends pure Orthodoxy with Catholic traditions of Hungary, features some Baroque-style statues that are unusually fluid and lifelike.

Orthodox services generally involve chanting (a dialogue that goes back and forth between the priest and the congregation), and the church is filled with the evocative aroma of incense. The incense, chanting, icons, and standing up are all intended to heighten the experience of worship. While many Catholic and Protestant services tend to be more of a theoretical and rote consideration of religious issues, Orthodox services are about creating an actual religious experience.

Don't miss the adjacent **museum,** covered by the same ticket. You'll see religious objects, paintings, vestments, and—upstairs— icons, with good English descriptions.

• *For a scenic back-streets stroll before returning to the tourist crush, go through the yard around the church, exit through the gate, and turn left up the little alley—which takes you through what was the Dalmatian neighborhood to charming Rab-Ráby tér. The lanes between here and the waterfront are among the most appealing and least crowded in Szentendre.*

Near Szentendre
Hungarian Open-Air Folk Museum (Szabadtéri Néprajzi Múzeum, a.k.a. Skanzen)—Three miles northwest of Szentendre is an open-air museum featuring examples of traditional Hungarian architecture from all over the country. As with similar museums throughout Europe, these aren't replicas—each building was taken apart at its original location, transported piece by piece, and reassembled here. The museum is huge and spread out, so a thorough visit could take several hours. The admission price includes a map in English, and the museum shop sells a good English guidebook for 1,000 Ft. Because it's so large, the museum is worth visiting only if you can give it the time it deserves. Skip it unless you can time your visit to coincide with one of their frequent special events (which are sometimes listed on their website). On those days, it costs 400 Ft extra—but it's well worth it (normally 1,000 Ft, April–Oct Tue–Sun 9:00–17:00, closed Mon and Nov–March, last entry 30 min before closing, Sztaravodai út, tel. 26/502-500, www.skanzen.hu).

Getting There: Buses from the Szentendre station leave for Skanzen (7/day direct, 12 min, departs from platform 7). A **taxi** from Szentendre to the museum should cost no more than 2,000 Ft; the TI can call one for you.

SLEEPING

(€1 = $1.40, 200 Ft = about $1, country code: 36, area code: 26)
I don't advise sleeping here if Budapest is your main interest. But if you must stay in Szentendre, these two places rent acceptable second-story rooms along the Danube embankment just north of the center (English is limited).

Centrum Panzió has eight pleasant rooms with a pink-and-red color scheme (Sb-€45, Db-€50–55, cheaper Sept–May, includes breakfast, cash only, air-con, on Dunakorzó, 2 blocks up from the small parking lot, tel. & fax 26/302-500, mobile 0620-482-1575, www.hotelcentrum.hu, hotel.centrum@t-online.hu).

Corner Panzió has six cozy, woody rooms with slanted ceilings above a restaurant (Sb/Db-11,000 Ft in July–Aug, 10,000 Ft in Sept–June, includes breakfast, cash only, air-con, Dunakorzó 4, tel. & fax 26/301-524, www.radoczy.hu, nikov@freemail.hu).

EATING

Interchangeable, touristy restaurants abound in Szentendre. I enjoy the ambience at **Promenade Vendéglő,** with charming courtyard or indoor seating. They serve Hungarian and Balkan cuisine with take-your-time service (2,000–3,000-Ft main dishes, daily 10:00–22:00, Futó utca 4, along the Dunakorzó embankment, tel. 26/312-626).

Visegrád

Visegrád (VEE-sheh-grahd, Slavic for "High Castle," pop. 1,600) is a small village next to the remains of two major-league castles: a hilltop citadel and a royal riverside palace. While this town disappoints many visitors, others enjoy the chance to be close to these two chapters of history.

The Romans were the first to fortify the steep hill overlooking the river. Later, Károly Róbert (Charles Robert), from the French/Neapolitan Anjou dynasty, became Hungary's first non-Magyar king in 1323. He was so unpopular with the nobles in Buda that he had to set up court in Visegrád, where he built a new residential palace down closer to the Danube. (For more on this king, see page 181.) Later, King Mátyás (Matthias) Corvinus—notorious for his penchant for Renaissance excess—ruled from Buda but made Visegrád his summer home, and turned the riverside palace into what some called a "paradise on earth." Matthias knew how to party; during his time here, red-marble fountains flowed with wine. (To commemorate these grand times, the town hosts a fairly corny Renaissance restaurant, with period cookware, food, costumed waitstaff, and live lute music—you can't miss it, by the palace and Hotel Vár.)

Today, both citadel and palace are but a shadow of their former splendor. The citadel was left to crumble after the Habsburg reoccupation of Hungary in 1686, while the palace was covered by a mudslide during the Ottoman occupation, and is still being excavated. The citadel is more interesting, but difficult to reach by public transport. Non-drivers who don't want to make the steep hike to the citadel are probably better off skipping this town.

ORIENTATION

The town of Visegrád is basically a wide spot in the riverside road, squeezed between the hills and the riverbank. At Visegrád's main intersection (coming from Szentendre/Budapest), the cross road leads to the left through the heart of the village, then hairpins up the hills to the citadel. To the right is the dock for the ferry to Nagymaros (home to the closest train station, called Nagymaros-Visegrád—see "Arrival in Visegrád," below).

The town has two sights. The less-interesting, riverside Royal Palace is a 15-minute walk downriver (towards Szentendre/Budapest) from the village center. The hilltop citadel, high above the village, is the focal point of a larger recreational area best explored by car.

Tourist Information

The town does not have an official TI. You can get information at the giant **Hotel Visegrád** complex, which caters to passing tour groups at the village crossroads. They answer basic questions, sell maps, and hand out a few free leaflets. In summer, check in at the **Visegrád Tours** travel agency (May–Oct daily 8:00–17:30, generally closed Nov–April, Rév utca 15, tel. 26/398-160, www.visegrad .hu); at other times, ask at the hotel reception desk (at the opposite end of the complex, through the unappealing Sirály restaurant).

Arrival in Visegrád

Train travelers arrive across the river at the Nagymaros-Visegrád station (don't get off at the station called simply "Nagymaros"). Walk five minutes to the river and catch the ferry to Visegrád, which lands near the village's main crossroads (hourly, usually in sync with the train, last ferry around 20:30). **Buses** to Visegrád make several stops: the Királyi Palota stop is most convenient for the Royal Palace near the entrance to town, while the Nagymarosi Rév stop is at the main crossroads in the heart of town.

SIGHTS

Visegrád Citadel (Fellegvár)

The remains of Visegrád's hilltop citadel, while nothing too exciting, can be fun to explore. Only a few exhibits have English labels, but some allow you to press a button to hear English information. Perhaps best of all, the upper levels of the citadel offer commanding views over the Danube Bend—which, of course, is exactly why they built it here.

Cost and Hours: 1,100 Ft, plus 300 Ft more for waxworks; flexible hours but generally April–mid-Oct daily 9:30–18:00;

mid-Oct–March Sat–Sun 10:00–15:00 in good weather only, usually closed Mon–Fri; last entry 30 min before closing, tel. 26/398-101.

Getting There: To **drive** to the citadel, follow *Fellegvár* signs down the village's main street and up into the hills. Otherwise, you have two options: Get a map at Visegrád Tours/Hotel and **hike** 45 steep minutes up from the village center; or take the **taxi service** misleadingly called "City Bus." This minivan trip costs 2,000 Ft one-way, no matter how many people ride along (ask at Visegrád Tours/Hotel, or call 26/397-372).

⊘ Self-Guided Tour: Buy your ticket and hike up the path toward the castle entry. On the way up, you can pay extra to try your hand with a bow and arrow, or pose with a bird of prey perched on your arm.

Belly up to the viewpoint for sweeping **Danube Bend views.** From here, you can see that the Danube actually does a double-bend—a smaller one (upstream), then a bigger one (downstream)—creating an S-shaped path before settling into its southward groove. It's easy to understand why the Danube, constricted between mountains, is forced to bend here. On this side of the Danube are the Pilis hills (glancing at a local map, you'll see many town names here begin with "Pilis-"), and across the river are the Börzsöny hills. The

river narrows as it passes through this gorge, then widens again below the castle, depositing sediment that becomes the islands just downstream. Just upstream from Visegrád, the strange half-lake on the riverbank is all that's left of an aborted communist-era dam project to tame the river.

Climb up to the top of the complex. In the **castle museum,** you'll see a replica of the Hungarian crown. The real one (now safely stored under the Parliament dome in Budapest) was actually kept here, off and on, for some 200 years, when this was Hungary's main castle.

Deeper into the complex, you reach the **waxworks** *(panop-tikum).* Here you can pay 300 Ft extra to see a scene from an important medieval banquet: In 1335, as Habsburg Austria was rising to the west, the kings of Hungary, Poland, and Bohemia converged here to strategize against this new threat. Centuries later, history repeated itself: In February of 1991, after the fall of the Iron Curtain, the heads of state of these same countries—Hungary, Poland, and Czechoslovakia—once again came together here, this time to compare notes about Westernization. To this day, these countries are still sometimes referred to collectively as the "Visegrád countries."

Continue up to the very top of the complex, the **inner castle.** Here you'll find a hunting exhibit (dioramas with piles of dead animals) and the armory (with a few weapons, and coats of arms of knights). To conquer the castle, climb up to the very top tower, where you can scramble along the ramparts.

Near the Citadel: Around the citadel is a recreational area that includes three restaurants, a picnic area, a luge and toboggan run, a network of hiking paths, a Waldorf school, and a children's nature-education center and campground.

Eating near the Citadel: Eating options in Visegrád are limited; most restaurants are big operations catering to tour groups. By the luge run (a lengthy-but-doable walk from the citadel), the **Nagyvillám restaurant** is elegant, with breathtaking views from the best tables (2,000–3,000-Ft main dishes, Mon–Thu 12:00–18:00, Fri–Sun 12:00–22:00, tel. 26/398-070). Only drivers can reach the **picnic area** (called Telgárthy-rét), in a shady valley with paths and waterfalls.

Royal Palace (Király Palota)

Under King Matthias Corvinus, this riverside ruin was one of

Europe's most elaborate Renaissance palaces. During the Ottoman occupation, it was deserted and eventually buried by a mudslide. For generations, the palace's existence faded into legend, so its rediscovery in 1934 was a surprise. Today, the partially excavated remains are tourable, though the sparse English descriptions are disappointing (1,000 Ft, Tue–Sun 9:00–17:00, closed Mon, tel. 26/398-026, www.visegradmuzeum.hu).

The palace courtyard, decorated with a red-marble fountain, evokes its Renaissance glory days. Upstairs, look for the giant green ceramic stoves, and at the top level, find the famous canopied fountain with lions. This "Hercules Fountain"—pictured on the back of the 1,000-Ft note—once had wine spouting from the lions' mouths, which Matthias used to ply visiting dignitaries to get the best results.

The small **tower** up the hill from

the Royal Palace once held a vampire...sort of. Vlad the Impaler, a nobleman who terrorized villagers in Transylvania (back when it was part of Hungary), was arrested and imprisoned here during the time of Matthias. Centuries later, Bram Stoker supposedly found inspiration in Vlad's story while writing his novel *Dracula*.

Esztergom

Esztergom (EHS-tehr-gohm, pop. 29,000) is an unassuming town

with a big Suzuki factory. You'd never guess it was the first capital of Hungary—until you see the towering 19th-century Esztergom Basilica, built on the site where István (Stephen) I, Hungary's first Christian king, was crowned in A.D. 1000.

Arrival in Esztergom

Esztergom's **boat dock** is more convenient to the basilica than the bus or train stations are (can't miss the basilica as you disembark—hike on up).

If arriving on the **riverside bus** from Visegrád, get off by the basilica (Iskola Utca stop)—not at the bus station.

If you're coming by **train,** or on the **overland bus** from Budapest, you're in for a longer walk. To reach the basilica on foot from the train station, allow at least 45 minutes. Continue in the same direction as the train tracks, and when the street forks, go straight along the residential Ady Endre utca. After a few minutes, you'll pass the bus station, from which it's 30 minutes farther to the basilica. Local buses run between the train station and the basilica roughly hourly. On Wednesdays and Fridays, an open-air market enlivens the street between the bus station and the center.

SIGHTS

▲▲Esztergom Basilica (Esztergomi Bazilika)

This basilica, on the site of a cathedral founded by Hungary's beloved St. István, commemorates Hungary's entry into the fold of Western Christendom. St. István was born in Esztergom, and on Christmas Day in the year 1000—shortly after marrying the daughter of the king of Bavaria and accepting Christianity—he was crowned here by a representative of the pope (for more on St. István, see page 178). Centuries later, after Esztergom had been

Cardinal József Mindszenty
(1892–1975)

József Mindszenty was a Hungarian priest who rose through the ranks to become Archbishop of Esztergom, cardinal, and head of the Hungarian Catholic Church. This outspoken cleric was arrested several times, by very different regimes: in 1919 for defying the early Hungarian communist leader Béla Kun; during World War II, for criticizing the Arrow Cross's deportation of Jews; and again in 1948, for speaking out against the communist regime.

Upon his arrest in 1948, Mindszenty was relentlessly tortured to extract a confession. He became the subject of a high-profile "show trial," and was convicted to life in prison. (An enraged Pope Pius XII excommunicated those who had tried and convicted Mindszenty.) Mindszenty's plight was dramatized in the 1955 film *The Prisoner,* starring Alec Guinness as the cardinal.

During the 1956 Uprising, Mindszenty was freed for a brief time. But when the uprising was put down with violence, he sought refuge in the US Embassy on Budapest's Szabadság tér—where he stayed for 15 years, unable to leave for fear of being recaptured. Many Catholic Americans who grew up during this time remember praying for Cardinal Mindszenty every day when they were kids. In 1971, he agreed to step down from his position, then fled to Austria.

On his deathbed in 1975, Mindszenty said that he did not want his body returned to Hungary as long as there was a single Russian soldier still stationed there. As the Iron Curtain was falling in 1989, Mindszenty emerged as an important hero to post-communist Hungarians, who wanted to bring his remains back to his homeland. But Mindszenty's secretary, in accordance with the cardinal's final wishes, literally locked himself to the coffin—refusing to let the body be transported as long as any Soviet soldier remained in Hungary. In May 1991, when only a few Russians were still in Hungary, Mindszenty's remains were finally brought to the crypt in the Esztergom Basilica.

re-taken from the retreating Ottomans, the Hungarians wanted

to built a "small Vatican" complex to celebrate the Hungarian Catholic Church and their triumphant return to the region. The Habsburgs who controlled the area at the time (and were also good Catholics) agreed, but did not want to be upstaged, so progress was sluggish. The

Neoclassical basilica was erected slowly between 1820 and 1869, on top of the remains of a ruined hilltop castle. With a 330-foot-tall dome, this is the tallest building in Hungary.

Cost and Hours: Basilica—free, daily April–mid-Oct 8:00–19:00, mid-Oct–March 8:00–16:00. Tower climb—250 Ft, same hours as basilica. Crypt—150 Ft, daily April–mid-Oct 9:00–16:30, mid-Oct–March 10:00–14:45. Treasury—600 Ft; March–Oct daily 9:00–16:30; Nov–Dec Tue–Fri 11:00–15:30, Sat–Sun 10:00–15:30, closed Mon; closed Jan-Feb.

◗ Self-Guided Tour: Approaching the church is like walking toward a mountain—it gets bigger and bigger, yet you never quite reach it. In front of the church is a **statue of Mary,** the "Head, Mother, and Patron" of the Hungarian Church.

Enter through the side door (on the left as you face the front of the basilica, under the arch). In the foyer, the stairway leading down to the right takes you to the **crypt.** This frigid space, with tree-trunk columns, culminates at the tomb of Cardinal József Mindszenty, revered and persecuted for standing up to the communist government (see sidebar on previous page). Also in the main chamber, look for original tombstones of 15th-century archbishops.

Back upstairs in the foyer, a stairway leads up to the church **tower,** which has fine views.

Enter the cavernous **nave.** Take in the enormity of the third-biggest church in Europe (by square footage). The lack of supporting pillars in the center of the church further exaggerates its vastness. This space was consecrated in 1856—before the entire building was finished—at a Mass with music composed by Franz Liszt.

As you face the altar, find the chapel on the left before the transept. This Renaissance **Bakócz Chapel** predates the basilica by 350 years. It was commissioned by the archbishop during King Matthias Corvinus' reign. The archbishop imported Italian marble-workers to create a fitting space to house his remains. Note the typically Renaissance red marble—the same marble that decorates Matthias' palace at Visegrád. When the basilica was built, the chapel was disassembled into 1,600 pieces and rebuilt inside the new structure. The heads around the chapel's altar were defaced by the Ottomans, who, as Muslims, believed that only God—not sculptors—can create man.

Continue to the **transept.** On the right transept wall, St. István offers the Hungarian crown to Mary. Mary is particularly important to Hungarians, because István—the first Christian king of Hungary—had no surviving male heir, so he appealed to Mary for help. (Eventually one of István's cousins, András I, took the crown and managed to keep his kingdom in the fold of Christianity.)

And one more tour-guide factoid: Above the **altar** is the biggest single-canvas painting in the world. (It's of the Assumption, by Michelangelo Grigoletti.)

Finish your visit with the **treasury,** to the right of the main altar (do this last, as you'll exit outside the building; no English descriptions—buy the 100-Ft illustrated listing at the entrance or, if they're out, at the gift shop at the end).

In the treasury's entry hall, examine the models of the church: a big one showing off the even more ambitious original plans for the basilica complex; smaller ones of the frames for the basilica's wooden nave and metal dome; and yet another showing what Esztergom looked like in the early 16th century (notice the more modest church that stood where this basilica is today).

Head up the spiral staircase to view the impressive collection. After a display of vestments, you'll wander a long hall tracing the evolution of ecclesiastical art styles: Gothic, Renaissance, Baroque, Rococo, and Modern. In the first (Gothic) section, find the giant drinking horns, used by kings at royal feasts. The second (Renaissance) section shows off some intricately decorated chalices. A close look at the vestments here shows that they're embroidered with 3-D scenes, and slathered with gold and pearls. In the case on the wall, find the collection's prized possession: an incredibly ornate cross showing Christ on the cross—but Jesus here bears an unmistakable likeness to King Matthias Corvinus. In the third (Baroque) and fourth (Rococo) sections, notice things getting frilly—and bigger and bigger, as the church got more money. The fifth (Modern) section displays an array of kissable bishop rings.

The exit takes you out to a **Danube-view terrace.** Walk downstream (right) to a recent statue of St. István being crowned, with grand views over the start of the Bend. That's Štúrovo, Slovakia, across the river, connected to Hungary by the Mária Valéria Bridge—destroyed in World War II and rebuilt only recently. Before its reconstruction, no bridges spanned the Danube between Budapest and Bratislava. When they rebuilt the bridge in 2001, they included border checkpoints; less than seven years later, these became obsolete, when in December of 2007 Hungary and Slovakia—fellow members of the open-borders Schengen Agreement—did away with passport

checks. If you have time, you can walk or drive across the bridge to Slovakia (for the best views back to this basilica) without even having to stop or flash your passport.

Near the Basilica

This hilltop was once heavily fortified, and some ruins of its castle survive—now part of a **museum** next to the basilica (opposite side from the István statue). Restorers recently discovered a fresco of the four virtues, likely by Sandro Botticelli. The complex also includes the chapel where St. István was supposedly born. Unfortunately, both of these areas are closed for restoration. For now, there's virtually nothing of interest to the casual tourist—lots of dusty old exhibits about arcane Hungarian history, from the Stone Age through the Ottoman period, with no English (800 Ft, summer Tue–Sun 10:00–18:00, winter Tue–Sun 10:00–16:00, closed Mon).

EATING

A few restaurants cluster near the basilica (including one built into the fortifications underneath the basilica), but these cater to tour groups and serve mediocre food. It's more interesting to venture down the hill to the **Víziváros** ("Water Town") neighborhood on the riverbank below the basilica. This area has a pleasant, old-town ambience and some fine local-style eateries. You can either walk down on the path from the basilica, or (in summer) catch a handy tourist train for 500 Ft.

TRANSPORTATION CONNECTIONS

By Bus

For connections, see "Getting Around the Danube Bend" on page 289. When choosing between the riverside bus and the direct, overland bus, note that the overland bus—while faster and offering different scenery—departs much farther from the basilica than the riverside bus.

Route Tips for Drivers: Returning from Esztergom to Budapest

The easiest choice is to retrace your route on road #11 around the Bend to Budapest. But to save substantial time and see different scenery, I prefer "cutting the Bend" and taking a shortcut through the Pilis hills (takes just over an hour total, depending on traffic).

To Cut the Bend: From the basilica in Esztergom, continue along the main road #11 (away from Budapest) to the roundabout with the round, yellow, Neoclassical church (built as a sort of practice before they started on the basilica). Here you can choose your exit: If you exit toward **Budapest/Dorog,** it'll take you back on road #11 for a while, then route you onto the busier road #10 (which can have heavy traffic—especially trucks—on weekdays). Better yet, if you head for **Dobogókő,** you'll follow a twistier but faster route via the town of Pilisszentkereszt to Budapest. After about 30 minutes on this road, in the town of Pomáz, follow signs to road #11 to the left, then turn right toward Budapest at the next fork to join road #11 into the city. (Don't follow signs at the Pomáz intersection for Budapest, which takes you along a more heavily trafficked road.)

EGER

Many travelers have never heard of Eger (EH-gehr). It's a county-seat town in northern Hungary, with about 60,000 people and a thriving teacher-training college. Among Hungarians, the town has various claims to fame. It's a bishopric whose powerful bishops have graced it with gorgeous churches. It has some of the best and most beloved spas in this hot-water-crazy country (including the excellent new Salt Hill Thermal Spa in the nearby countryside). And, perhaps most of all, Eger makes Hungarians proud as the town that, against all odds, successfully held off the Ottoman advance into Europe in 1552. This stirring history makes Eger the mecca of Hungarian school field trips. If the town is known internationally for anything, it's for the surrounding wine region (its best-known red wine is Bull's Blood, or Egri Bikavér).

And yet, refreshingly, enchanting Eger remains mostly off the tourist trail. Egerites go about their daily routines amidst lovely Baroque buildings, watched over by one of Hungary's most important castles. Everything in Eger is painted with vibrant colors, and even the communist apartment blocks seem quaint. The sights are few but fun, the ambience is great, and strolling is a must. It all comes together to make Eger an ideal introduction to small-town Hungary.

Planning Your Time

Mellow Eger is the best side-trip from Budapest. It's doable round-trip in a single day (2.5 hours by train each way), but it's much more satisfying and relaxing to spend the night.

A perfect day in Eger begins with a browse through the very local-feeling market and a low-key ramble on the castle ramparts. Then head to the college building called the Lyceum to visit the library and astronomy museum, and climb up to the thrillingly low-tech camera obscura. Take in the 11:30 organ concert in the cathedral across the street from the Lyceum (mid-May–mid-Oct only). In the afternoon, unwind on the square or, better yet, at a thermal bath (in Eger, or at Salt Hill Thermal Spa in nearby Egerszalók). If you need more to do, consider a drive into the countryside (including visits to local vintners—get details at TI). Round out your day with dinner on Little Dobó Square, or a visit to Eger's touristy wine caves in the Sirens' Valley.

ORIENTATION

(area code: 36)
Eger Castle sits at the top of the town, hovering over Dobó Square (Dobó István tér). This main square is divided in half by the Eger Creek, which bisects the town. Two blocks west of Dobó Square is the main pedestrian drag, Széchenyi utca, where you'll find the Lyceum and the cathedral. A few blocks due south from the castle (along Eger Creek) are Eger's various spas and baths.

EGER

Tourist Information

Eger's on-the-ball, eager-to-please TI (TourInform) is the most efficient place to get any Eger question answered. They give out a free brochure and town map, as well as piles of other brochures about the city and region. They can't book rooms, but they can help you find one—or anything else you're looking for (mid-June–mid-Sept Mon–Fri 9:00–18:00, Sat–Sun 9:00–13:00, possibly later; mid-Sept–mid-June Mon–Fri 9:00–17:00, Sat 9:00–13:00, closed Sun; Bajcsy-Zsilinszky utca 9, tel. 36/517-715, www.eger.hu). You can also get online here (200 Ft/30 min).

Arrival in Eger

By Train: Eger's tiny train station is a 20-minute walk south of the center. The closest ATM is at the Spar grocery store just up the street (turn left out of station, walk about 100 yards, and look for red-and-white supermarket on your right; ATM is around front). There's no official baggage storage, but sometimes workers at the train station can hold a bag for you—ask.

Taxis generally wait out front to take new arrivals into the center (1,000–1,400 Ft). Even in little Eger, it's always best to take a taxi with a company name and number posted.

To catch the **bus** toward the center, go straight out of the

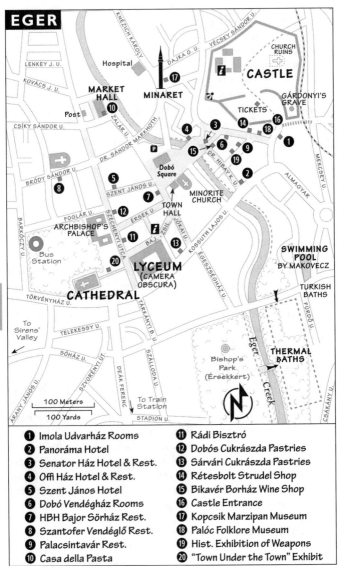

❶ Imola Udvarház Rooms	⓫ Rádi Bisztró
❷ Panoráma Hotel	⓬ Dobós Cukrászda Pastries
❸ Senator Ház Hotel & Rest.	⓭ Sárvári Cukrászda Pastries
❹ Offi Ház Hotel & Rest.	⓮ Rétesbolt Strudel Shop
❺ Szent János Hotel	⓯ Bikavér Borház Wine Shop
❻ Dobó Vendégház Rooms	⓰ Castle Entrance
❼ HBH Bajor Sörház Rest.	⓱ Kopcsik Marzipan Museum
❽ Szantofer Vendéglő Rest.	⓲ Palóc Folklore Museum
❾ Palacsintavár Rest.	⓳ Hist. Exhibition of Weapons
❿ Casa della Pasta	⓴ "Town Under the Town" Exhibit

station, and when the road you're on veers right, cross it to get to the bus stop (to the left) on the busier road above it. Buses #11, #12, and #14 cut about 10 minutes off the walk into town (220 Ft, buy ticket from driver; or 150 Ft if you buy it inside train station—ask for *helyijárat buszjegy*). Get off the bus when you reach the big yellow cathedral.

To **walk** all the way, leave the station straight ahead, turn right with the road, and then continue straight ahead (on busy Deák Ferenc utca) until you run into the cathedral. With your back to the cathedral entry, the main square is two blocks ahead of you, then a block to the left.

By Car: In this small town, most hotels will provide parking or help you find a lot. For a short visit, the most central lot is behind the department store on Dobó Square.

By Plane: Low-impact Eger is a pleasant place to get over jet lag. For tips on coming to Eger from Budapest's airport, see page 267.

Getting Around Eger

Everything of interest in Eger is within walking distance. But a taxi can be helpful to reach outlying sights, including the Sirens' Valley wine caves and the Salt Hill Thermal Spa in Egerszalók (taxi meter starts at 250 Ft, then around 250 Ft/km; try City Taxi, tel. 36/555-555).

Helpful Hints

Phoning and Faxing: Confusingly, Hungary's country code is the same as Eger's city code (36). This means that if you're calling from another country, you'll have to dial 36 twice. For example, to call my favorite Eger hotel from the US, I'd dial 011-36-36-411-711.

Blue Monday: Note that the castle museums and the Lyceum are closed on Mondays. But you can still visit the cathedral (and enjoy its organ concert), swim in the thermal bath, explore the market, see the castle grounds, and enjoy the local wine.

Organ Concert: Daily from mid-May to mid-October, Hungary's second-biggest organ booms out a glorious 30-minute concert in the cathedral (500 Ft, Mon–Sat at 11:30, Sun at 12:45).

Internet Access: The TI has one terminal (200 Ft/30 min; see "Tourist Information," earlier in this chapter). The town generally has other Internet cafés, but as these are prone to going out of business, ask the TI or your hotelier for current options.

Walking Tours: The TI offers an affordable town walking tour in English once weekly in summer (likely Sat at 10:00, early June–Sept only, price and schedule tend to change from year to year—confirm details at TI).

Tourist Train: A hokey little tourist train leaves the main square at the top of each hour. It does a circuit around town, then heads out to the Sirens' Valley wine caves (500 Ft, 50-min trip).

SIGHTS

▲▲Dobó Square (Dobó István Tér)

Dobó Square is the heart of Eger. In most towns this striking, the main square is packed with postcard stalls and other tourist traps. Refreshingly, Eger's square seems mostly packed with Egerites. Ringed by pretty Baroque buildings, decorated with vivid sculptures depicting the city's noble past, and

watched over by Eger's historic castle, this square is one of the most pleasant spots in Hungary.

The statue in the middle is **István Dobó** (EESHT-vahn DOH-boh), the square's namesake and Eger's greatest hero, who defended the city—and all of Hungary—from an Ottoman invasion in 1552 (see his story in the sidebar). Next to Dobó is his co-commander, István Mekcsey. And right at their side is one of the brave women of Eger—depicted here throwing a pot down onto the attackers.

Dominating the square is the exquisitely photogenic pink **Minorite Church**—often said to be the most beautiful Baroque

church in Hungary. The shabby interior (free entry) is less interesting, but has some appealing details. Notice that each of the hand-carved wooden pews has a different motif. Pay close attention to the side altars that flank the nave: The first set (left and right) are 3-D illustrations, painted to replicate the wood altars that burned in a fire; the next set are real. And looking up at the faded ceiling frescoes, you'll see (in the second one from the entrance) the church's patron: St. Anthony of Padua,

who's preaching God's word to the fishes after the townspeople refused to hear him.

Next to the Minorite Church is the Town Hall, then an old-fashioned pharmacy. The **monument** in front of the Town Hall also commemorates the 1552 defense of Eger: one Egerite against two Ottoman soldiers, reminding us of the townspeople's bravery despite the odds.

Use the square to orient yourself to the town. Behind the statue of Dobó is a bridge over the stream that bisects the city. Just before you reach that bridge, look to the left and you'll see the

István Dobó and the Siege of Eger

In the 16th century, Ottoman invaders swept into Hungary. They easily defeated a Hungarian army—in just two hours— at the Battle of Mohács in 1526. When Buda and Pest fell to the Ottomans in 1541, all of Europe looked to Eger as the last line of defense. István Dobó and his second-in-command, István Mekcsey, were put in charge of Eger's forces. They prepared the castle (which still overlooks the square) for a siege and waited.

On September 11, 1552— after a summer spent conquering more than 30 other Hungarian fortresses on their march northward—40,000 Ottomans arrived in Eger. Only about 2,000 Egerites (soldiers, their wives, and their children) remained to protect their town. The Ottomans expected an easy victory, but the siege dragged on for 39 days. Eger's soldiers fought valiantly, and the women of Eger also joined the fray, pouring hot tar down on the Ottomans...everyone pitched in. A Hungarian officer named Gergely Bornemissza, sent to reinforce the people of Eger, startled the Ottomans with all manner of clever and deadly explosives. One of his brilliant inventions was a "fire wheel"—a barrel of gunpowder studded with smaller jars of explosives, which they'd light and send rolling downhill to wreak havoc until the final, deadly explosion. Ultimately, the Ottomans left in shame, Eger was saved, and Dobó was a national hero.

The unfortunate epilogue: The Ottomans came back in 1596 and, this time, succeeded in conquering an Eger Castle guarded by unmotivated mercenaries. The Ottomans sacked the town and controlled the region for close to a century.

In 1897, a castle archaeologist named Géza Gárdonyi moved from Budapest to Eger, where tales of the siege captured his imagination. Gárdonyi wrote a book about István Dobó and the 1552 Siege of Eger called *Egri Csillagok* ("Stars of Eger," translated into English as *Eclipse of the Crescent Moon,* available at local bookstores and souvenir stands). The book—a favorite of many Hungarians—is taught in schools, keeping the legend of Eger's heroes alive today.

northernmost Ottoman **minaret** in Europe—once part of a mosque, it's now a tourist attraction. Across the bridge is the charming **Little Dobó Square** (Kis-Dobó tér), home to the town's best hotels, its outdoor dining zone, and a handy and atmospheric opportunity to sample local wines at the Bikavér Borház wine shop. Hovering above Little Dobó Square is Eger Castle; to get there, hang a right at the Senator Ház Hotel and go up Dobó utca. (All of these places are described in more detail later in this chapter.)

Now face in the opposite direction, with the castle at your back. On your right is a handy department store (with an ATM by the door). At the bottom end of this square, various pedestrian shopping lanes lead straight ahead two short blocks to Eger's main "walking street," Széchenyi utca (with the cathedral and the Lyceum at its left end). To reach the TI, jog left at the end of this square, then right onto Bajcsy-Zsilinszky utca (TI one block ahead on right). The market hall is in the opposite direction: Leave Dobó Square to the right (on Zalár József utca, with department store on your right-hand side; you'll see the market hall on the left).

Dobó Utca—The street called Dobó utca, which leads to the entrance of the castle (up the street to the right of Senator Ház Hotel), is lined with colorful shops and attractions. Don't miss the **wine-tasting courtyard** at #18. At the **Rétesbolt** strudel shop (#10), you can watch them make mouthwatering strudel (350 Ft, daily 10:00–17:00).

Also along this street are two small, underwhelming museums—worth considering only if it's a rainy day or you have a special interest. The tiny **Palóc Folklore Museum** displays a handful of traditional tools, textiles, ceramics, costumes, and pieces of furniture (200 Ft, borrow the skimpy English information, Easter–Sept Tue–Sun 9:00–17:00, closed Mon and Oct–Easter, Dobó utca 12). The **Historical Exhibition of Weapons** (Történeti Tárház) features centuries of Eger armaments: clubs, rifles, and everything in between (300 Ft, Tue–Sun 10:00–18:00, closed Mon, 450-Ft booklet labels weapons in English, 1,600-Ft English book gives more info, Dobó utca 9, actually just down Fazola Henrik utca).

▲Eger Castle (Egri Vár)

This castle is Hungary's Alamo, where István Dobó defended Eger from the Ottomans in 1552. These days, it's usually crawling with schoolchildren on field trips from all over the country.

The great St. István—Hungary's first Christian king—founded a church on this hill a thousand years ago. The church was destroyed by Tatars in the 13th century, and this fortress was built to repel another attack.

The castle grounds feature several small museums (including a history museum and a picture gallery), remains of a once-grand

cathedral and a smaller rotunda dating from the days of St. István (10th or 11th century), underground casements (tunnels through the castle walls), Heroes' Hall (with the symbolic grave of István Dobó), and temporary exhibits. For those of us who didn't grow up hearing the legend of István Dobó, the complex is hard to appreciate, and English information is sparse. Most visitors find that the most rewarding plan is to stroll up, wander around the grounds, enjoy the view overlooking the town (find the minaret and other landmarks), maybe pay a visit to the waxworks, and then head back into town past a gaggle of colorful shops.

Cost and Tours: A 600-Ft "walking ticket" gets you into the castle grounds only (free Nov–March). To go inside all the museums (except the privately run "Other Castle Sights," described below), buy the 1,200-Ft ticket. The underground casements and Heroes' Hall are only accessible by one-hour Hungarian tour, with some posted information in English (tours depart frequently in summer, sporadically off-season). Sometimes it's possible to join an English tour for 800 Ft extra (ask at information window when you arrive; most likely in June–Aug, but there's no set schedule).

Hours: The castle grounds are open April–Aug daily 8:00–20:00, Sept until 19:00, March and Oct until 18:00, Nov–Feb until 17:00. The castle museums are open March–Oct Tue–Sun 9:00–17:00 (last entry 40 min before closing). On Monday in March–Oct, and every day in Nov–Feb, all of the official castle museums are closed except the casements, which—as usual—you can visit only with a guided tour (since most sights are closed, you'll pay a reduced price of 1,000 Ft; some of the "Other Castle Sights" described next are open Mon). General castle info: tel. 36/312-744, www.div.iif.hu.

Other Castle Sights: In addition to the official castle museums, there are other privately run exhibits, each with its own sporadic hours and prices: an **archery** exhibit (look for archers just inside inner gate in summer, and pay them for the chance to shoot old-fashioned bows and crossbows—1 arrow/100 Ft, 5 arrows/400 Ft, 10 arrows/700 Ft); the **mint**, with a display of former currencies and a chance to make your own souvenir (entry-500 Ft, souvenirs

EGER

extra, in cellar of Gothic palace); **temporary exhibits** in the pink round tower; and the **waxworks,** or "Panoptikum" (500 Ft, daily April–Oct 9:00–18:00, Nov–March 9:00–16:00). Of these, only the waxworks is worth considering. You'll see a handful of eerily realistic heroes and villains from the siege of Eger (including István Dobó himself and the leader of the Ottomans sitting in his colorful tent). Notice the exaggerated Central Asian features of the Egerites—a reminder that the Magyars were more Asian than European. Sound

effects add to the fun...think of it as a very low-tech, walk-through *Ottomans of the Caribbean.* You'll also have the chance to scramble through a segment of the casements that run inside the castle walls.

Getting There: To reach the castle from Dobó Square, cross the bridge toward Senator Ház Hotel, then jog right around the hotel, turning right onto Dobó utca (with its own set of attractions, described on page 314). Take this street a few blocks until it swings down to the right; the ramp up to the castle is across the little park to your left.

On Széchenyi Utca

You'll find Eger's best sights along its main walking street, two blocks up from Dobó Square.

▲▲**Lyceum (Líceum)**—In the mid-18th century, Bishop Károly Eszterházy wanted a university in Eger, but Habsburg Emperor

Josef II refused to allow it. So instead, Eszterházy built the most impressive teacher-training college on the planet, and stocked it with the best books and astronomical equipment money could buy. The Lyceum still trains local teachers (enrollment: about 2,000). Since Eger is expensive by Hungarian standards, many families live in the surrounding countryside. The kids all come into Eger for school—and lots of teachers are needed. But the halls of the Lyceum are also roamed by tourists who have come to visit its classic old library (700 Ft), and its astronomy museum, with a fascinating camera obscura (covered by a separate 800-Ft ticket; both library and museum open March–mid-Oct Tue–Sun 9:30–15:30, closed Mon; mid-Oct–Feb

Sat–Sun only 9:30–13:30, closed Mon–Fri; last entry 30 min before closing, Eszterházy tér 1, at south end of Széchenyi utca at intersection with Kossuth utca, enter through main door across from cathedral and buy tickets just inside and to the left).

Library: First, visit the old-fashioned library one floor up (from main entry hall, cut through the middle of the courtyard, enter the

hall at the far end, turn right to find the staircase, head up one flight, then go left and look for room 223, marked *Bibliothek*). This library houses 50,000 books (here and in the two adjoining rooms, with several stacked two deep). Dr. Imre Surányi and his staff have spent the last decade cataloging these books. This is no easy task, since they're in over 100 languages—from Thai to Tagalog—and are shelved according to size, rather than topic. You'll likely meet Dr. Surányi's assistant, Dénes Szabó (if he's not away for a choral contest), or the resident tour guide, Katalin Bódi. Either of them will happily show you the library's pride and joy: a replica of a letter from Mozart. The shelves are adorned with golden seals depicting great minds of science, philosophy, and religion. Take some time to marvel at the gorgeous ceiling fresco, dating from 1778. If you want to thank the patron of this museum, say *köszönöm* to the guy in the second row up, to the right of the podium (second from left, not wearing a hat)—that's Bishop Károly Eszterházy. While the Lyceum now belongs to Eger, this library is still the property of the archbishop.

Astronomical Museum: Several flights above (continue up the same stairs you climbed to reach the library) is the **Astronomical Tower,** with some dusty old stargazing instruments, as well as a meridian line in the floor (the dot of sunlight dances along this line each day around noon). Across the hall is a fun, interactive **magic room,** where you can try out scientific experiments—such as using air pressure to make a ball levitate or sending a mini "hot-air balloon" up to the ceiling. Yet a few more flights up is the Lyceum's treasured **camera obscura.** You'll enter a dark room around a big, bowl-like canvas, and the guide will fly you around the streets of Eger (presentations about 2/hr, maybe more when busy). Fun as it is today, this camera must have astonished viewers when it was built in 1776—well before anyone had seen "moving pictures." It's a bit of a huff to get up here (nine flights of stairs, 302 steps)—but the camera obscura and the view of Eger from the outdoor terrace are worth it.

▲▲Eger Cathedral—Eger's 19th-century bishops peppered the city with beautiful buildings, including the second-biggest church

in Hungary (after Esztergom's—
see page 302). With a quirky,
sumptuous, Baroque-feeling
interior, Eger's cathedral is well
worth a visit (free entry, cathedral is the big, can't-miss-it yellow building at Pyrker János tér
1, just off Széchenyi utca).

Eger Cathedral was built in
the 1830s by an Austrian archbishop who had previously served in
Venice, and who thought Eger could use a little more class. The
colonnaded Neoclassical facade, painted a pretty Habsburg yellow, boasts some fine Italian sculpture. As you walk up the main
stairs, you'll pass saints István and László—Hungary's first two
Christian kings—and then the apostles Peter and Paul.

Enter the cathedral and walk to the first collection box,

partway down the nave. Then,
facing the door, look up at the
ornate **ceiling fresco:** On the
left, it shows Hungarians in
traditional dress, and on the
right, the country's most important historical figures. At the
bottom, you see this cathedral,
celestially connected with St.
Peter's in Rome (at the top).
This symbol of devotion to the Vatican was a brave statement when
it was painted in 1950. The communists were closing churches in
other small Hungarian towns, but the Eger archbishop had enough
clout to keep this one open.

Continue to the transept. A few years ago, the **stained-
glass windows** at either end were donated to the cathedral by a
rich Austrian couple to commemorate the 1,000th anniversary
of Hungary's conversion to Christianity—notice the dates 1000
(when St. István converted the Magyars to Christianity) and
2000.

As you leave, notice the enormous **organ**—Hungary's second-
largest—above the door. In the summer, try to catch one of the
cathedral's daily half-hour organ concerts (500 Ft, mid-May–mid-
Oct Mon–Sat at 11:30, Sun at 12:45, no concerts off-season).

If you walk up Széchenyi utca from here, you'll see the fancy
Archbishop's Palace on your left—still home to Eger's archbishop.

Just to the right of the steps leading up to the cathedral is the
entrance to the...

Town Under the Town (Város a Város Alatt)—Here you can
take a guided tour of the archbishop's former wine-cellar net-

work, which honeycombs the land behind the Archbishop's Palace (800 Ft, departs at the top of each hour, 5-person minimum, daily April–Sept 10:00–20:00, Oct–March 10:00–17:00, last tour departs 1 hr before closing, www.varosavarosalatt.hu).

North of Dobó Square

▲**Market Hall (Piaccsarnok)**—Wandering Eger's big indoor market will give you a taste of local life—and maybe some local

food, too. It's packed with Egerites choosing the very best of the fresh produce. Tomatoes and peppers of all colors and sizes are abundant—magic ingredients that give Hungarian food its kick. To reach the market, leave Dobó Square with the castle to your back; turn right on Zalár József utca, and you'll see the market on your left in two blocks, at the intersection with Dr. Sándor utca (June–Sept Mon–Fri 6:00–18:00, Sat 6:00–13:00, Sun 6:00–10:00; Oct–May Mon–Fri 6:00–17:00, Sat 6:00–13:00, Sun 6:00–10:00).

Minaret—Once part of a mosque, this slender, 130-foot-tall minaret represents the century of Ottoman rule that left its mark on Eger and all of Hungary. The little cross at the top symbolizes the eventual Christian victory over Hungary's Ottoman invaders. You can climb the minaret's 97 steps for fine views of Eger, but it's not for those scared of heights or tight spaces (200 Ft, April–Oct daily 10:00–18:00, closed Nov–March; if it's locked, ask for the key at nearby Hotel Minaret).

▲**Kopcsik Marzipan Museum (Kopcsik Marcipánia)**—Lajos Kopcsik is a master sculptor who's found his medium: marzipan. Kopcsik can make this delicate mixture of sugar and ground almonds take virtually any form. In this surprisingly engaging little museum, you'll see several remarkable, colorful examples of Kopcsik's skill: sword, minaret, gigantic wine bottle, suitcase, Russian stacking dolls, old-timey phonograph, grandfather clock, giant bell...and paintings galore (including Van Gogh's sunflowers and Picasso's musicians). The list literally goes on for four pages. Who'd have thought you could do so much with candy? You'll also see a video showing the master at work, and a new "Baroque room" that's furnished and decorated entirely in marzipan (400 Ft, ask for printed English information; Easter–Oct daily 10:00–18:00;

Nov–Easter Tue–Sun 10:00–17:00, closed Mon; Harangöntő utca 4, tel. 36/412-626.)

EXPERIENCES

Aqua Eger

Swimming and water sports are as important to Egerites as good wine. They're proud that many of Hungary's Olympic medalists in aquatic events have come from this county. The men's water polo team took the gold for Hungary at each of the last three Olympics, and swimmer László Cseh might have been a multiple gold medal-winner at Beijing in 2008 if he hadn't been swimming next to Michael Phelps. The town's Bitskey Aladár swimming pool—arguably the most striking building in this part of Hungary—is practically a temple to water sports.

Eger also has two of the most appealing thermal bath complexes outside of Budapest: one right in town, and the other a few miles away (near the village of Egerszalók). Budapest offers classier bath experiences, but the Eger options are more modern and a bit more accessible, and allow you to save Budapest time for big-city sights. Before you go, be sure to read the Thermal Baths chapter on page 87.

In Eger

Note that you can't rent a swimsuit or a towel at either of these places; bring both with you, along with shower sandals for the locker room (if you've got them).

Bitskey Aladár Pool—This striking swimming pool was designed by Imre Makovecz, the father of Hungary's Organic architectural style. Some Eger taxpayers resented the pool's big price tag, but it left the city with a truly distinctive building befitting its love of water sports. You don't need to be an architecture student to know that the pool is special. It's worth the five-minute walk from Dobó Square just to take a look. Oh, and you can swim in  it, too (750 Ft; Mon–Fri 6:00–20:00; until 21:00 on Mon, Wed, and Fri; Sat 8:00–20:00, Sun 8:00–18:00; follow Eger Creek south from Dobó Square to Frank Tivadar utca, tel. 36/511-810).

▲**Eger Thermal Bath (Eger Thermálfürdő)**—For a refreshing break from the sightseeing grind, consider a splash at the spa. This is a fine opportunity to try a Hungarian bath: relatively accessible (men and women are clothed and together most of the time), but

Hungary's Organic Architecture

In recent years, a unique, eye-catching style of architecture has caught on in Hungary: Organic. The Hungarian brand of Organic was developed and championed by Imre Makovecz. After being blackballed by the communists for his nationalistic politics, Makovecz was denied access to building materials, so he taught himself to make impressive structures with nothing more than sticks and rocks. Makovecz was inspired by Transylvanian village architecture: whitewashed walls with large, overhanging mansard roofs to maximize attic space (resembling a big mushroom).

Now that the regime is dead and Makovecz is Hungary's premier architect, he still keeps things simple. He believes that a building should be a product of its environment, rather than a cookie-cutter copy. Organic buildings use indigenous materials (especially wood) and take on unusual forms—often inspired by animals or plants—that blend in with the landscape. Organic buildings look like they're rising up out of the ground, rather than plopped down on top of it. You generally won't find this back-to-nature style in big cities like Budapest; Makovecz prefers to work in small communities such as Eger (see photo on previous page), instead of working for corporations.

Organic architecture has become *the* post-communist style in Hungary. Even big supermarket chains are now imitating Makovecz—a sure sign of architectural success.

frequented mostly by locals.

Cost, Hours, Location: 1,250 Ft, adventure bath included Sept–April but 700 Ft extra (and worth it) May–Aug. Open May–Sept Mon–Fri 6:00–19:30, Sat–Sun 8:00–19:00, may be open until 23:00 Thu–Sat in summer; Oct–April daily 9:00–18:30. It's at Petőfi tér 2, tel. 36/314-142, www.egertermal.hu.

Getting There: It's easy to reach, within a 10-minute walk of most hotels. From Dobó Square, follow the stream four blocks south (signs for *Strand*). You'll come first to the main entrance (on the left after crossing busy street, roughly facing the fancy swimming-pool building on Petőfi tér). However, as this entrance is a bit more confusing and farther from the best pools, I'd use the side entrance instead: Continue following the stream as it runs along the side of a park (to the right of the main entrance building). Soon you'll

see the side entrance to the bath on your left over a bridge.

Entry Procedure: You'll enter and be given a little barcode bracelet, which acts as your ticket (keep it on until you leave). If you use the main entrance, you can change in the blocky white buildings just inside the entry (get a hanger from the desk, change in one of the free little cabins, then bring your clothes-laden hanger back for them to store it, 400 Ft extra to use safe-deposit box). At the better side entrance, you'll show your ticket/bracelet to get a key to a locker (1,000-Ft deposit per key, which will be refunded; private changing cabins available in the locker room for no extra charge). After you change and stow your stuff, put the key around your wrist, then join the fun.

Taking the Waters: There's a sprawling array of different pools, each one thoughtfully described in English and labeled with the depth and temperature. From the main entrance, you'll see them in this order: big and small warm pools, a very hot sulfur pool (where Egerites sit peacefully, ignore the slight stink, and supposedly feel their arthritis ebb away), the adventure bath, a kids' pool with splashy slide fun, and a lap pool (some of these are closed off-season). The best part is the green-domed, indoor-outdoor adventure bath, right at the side entrance. Its cascades, jets, bubbles, geysers, and powerful current pool will make you feel like a kid again.

Near Eger, in Egerszálok

▲▲**Salt Hill Thermal Spa**—This brand-new spa complex, in the hills about four miles outside of Eger, is the most modern and accessible thermal bath I've vis-

ited in Hungary. While it lacks the old-fashioned class of the Budapest options, it trumps them in user-friendliness and overall soggy fun.

For decades, Egerites would come to the "salt hill" (a natural terraced formation caused by mineral-rich springwater running down the hillside) in the middle of nowhere and cram together to baste in pools of hot water. Then the developers arrived. Today, those same simple pools are still used by local purists, but a giant new hotel and spa complex has been built nearby. With 12 indoor pools and five outdoor ones—many cleverly overlapping each other on several levels—these cutting-edge baths are worth the trip outside of Eger.

Ideal for kids but fun for anyone, the complex has pools with mineral water as well as plain old swimming-pool water. And the high-tech admission system is wonderfully simple: You pay and are

given a watch-like bracelet to wear around your wrist, which serves as your ticket, locker key, and credit card. Press it against a nearby computer screen to find out which locker you've been assigned. Find that locker in the common locker room (you can change in one of the private cabins), stow your stuff there, and have fun. Take some time to explore the sprawling complex. Everything is labeled in English, and each pool is clearly marked with the depth and temperature (in Celsius). You can buy food or drinks with the bracelet, too—it's keeping tabs so you can be charged when you leave.

Cost and Hours: 2,400 Ft for up to three hours, or 1,500 Ft after 17:00 on Mon–Thu, 1,000 Ft extra to access "sauna world" with five different saunas, 700 Ft for towel rental, massages and other treatments also available. Open June–Aug daily 9:00–20:00; Sept–May Mon–Fri 10:00–18:00, Sat–Sun 10:00–20:00 (as it's a new facility, these hours are subject to change—call ahead). Tel. 36/688-500, www.egerszalokfurdo.hu.

Getting There: It's about a mile outside the village of Egerszalók, which is itself about three miles from Eger. You can take a public **bus** from Eger's bus station to the baths (take bus going toward Demjén, you want the *Egerszalók Gyógyfürdő* stop—tell the bus driver "EH-gehr-sah-lohk FEWR-dur"—just after leaving the town of Egerszalók, 9/day Mon–Fri, 2/day Sat, 1/day Sun, 17-min trip, 200 Ft). Check the return bus information carefully (especially on weekends, when frequency plummets). Or you can take a **taxi** from Eger (about 2,500 Ft; tel. 36/787-761 for a return taxi from Egerszalók). A fun and very hedonistic afternoon plan: Take the bus or taxi to the spa, taxi back to Eger's Sirens' Valley for some wine-cave hopping, then taxi back to your Eger hotel.

Note: The humble little baths beside the parking lot are a whole other story—fun but very traditional (just sitting in hot water). Don't mistake these for the new complex. To find the big one, continue walking about five minutes beyond the parking lot to the hotel.

Eger Wine

Eger is at the heart of one of Hungary's best-known wine regions, internationally famous for its **Bull's Blood** (Egri Bikavér). You'll likely hear various stories as to how Bull's Blood got its name during the Ottoman siege of Eger. My favorite version: The Ottomans were amazed at the ferocity displayed by the Egerites, and wondered what they were drinking that boiled their blood and stained their beards so red...it must be potent stuff. Local merchants, knowing that the Ottomans were Muslim and couldn't drink alcohol, told them it was bull's blood. The merchants made a buck, and the name stuck.

Creative as these stories are, they're all bunk—the term dates only from 1851. Egri Bikavér is a blend (everyone has their own recipe), so you generally won't find it at small producers. Cabernet Sauvignon, Merlot, Kékfránkos, and Kékoportó are the most commonly used grapes.

Of course, there's so much more to Hungarian wines than Bull's Blood—and the Eger region produces many fine options. For all the details, see "Hungarian Wines" on page 223.

While it would be enjoyable to drive around the Hungarian countryside visiting wineries, the most accessible way to get a quick taste of local wine is at a wine shop in town. I like the Kenyeres family's **Bikavér Borház,** right on Little Dobó Square (across from Offi Ház Hotel). In addition to a well-stocked (if slightly overpriced) wine shop, they have a wine bar with indoor and outdoor seating (six tastings and two cheeses for less than 2,000 Ft, or wine by the glass, some English spoken, menu lists basic English description for each wine, daily 10:00–22:00, Kis-Dobó tér 10, tel. 36/413-262).

Sirens' Valley (Szépasszony-völgy)—When the Ottoman invaders first occupied Eger, residents moved into the valley next door, living in caves dug into the hillside. Eventually the Ottomans were driven out, the Egerites moved back to town, and the caves became wine cellars. (Most Eger families who can afford it have at least a modest vineyard in the countryside.) There are more than 300 such caves in the valley to the southwest of Eger, several of which are open for visitors.

The best selection of these caves (about 50) is in the Sirens' Valley (sometimes also translated as "Valley of the Beautiful Women"—or, on local directional signs, the less poetic "Nice Woman Valley"). It's a fun scene—locals showing off their latest vintage, with picnic tables and tipsy tourists spilling out into the street. At some places, you'll be offered free samples; others have a menu for tastes or glasses of wine. While you're not expected to buy a bottle, it's a nice gesture to buy one if you've spent a while at one cave (and it's usually very cheap). Most caves offer something light to eat with the wine, and you'll also see lots of non-cave, full-service restaurants. Some of the caves are fancy and finished, staffed by multilingual waiters in period costume. Others feel like a dank basement, with grandpa leaning on his moped out front and a monolingual granny pouring the wine inside. (The really local places—where the decor is cement, bottles don't have labels, and food consists of potato chips and buttered Wonder Bread—can be the most fun.) This experience is a strange mix of touristy and local, but not entirely accessible to non-Hungarian-speakers—it works best with a bunch of friends and an easygoing, social attitude. Hopping from cave to musky cave can make for an enjoyable evening, but be sure to wander around a bit to see the options before you dive in. Caves #2 (Bíró Borozó), #34, #43, and the one called "Kiss" have a particularly good reputation (cellars generally open 10:00–22:00 in summer, best June–Aug after 19:00 and good-weather weekends in the shoulder season; it's much quieter off-season, when only a handful of cellars remain open for shorter hours).

Getting to the Sirens' Valley: The valley is a 25-minute walk southwest of Eger. Figure no more than 1,000 Ft for a **taxi** between your hotel and the caves. During the summer, you can take the 500-Ft **tourist train** from Eger's main square to the caves (see "Helpful Hints," page 311), then catch a later one back. To **walk,** leave the pedestrian zone on the street next to the cathedral (Törvényház utca), with the cathedral on your right-hand side. Take the first left just after the back end of the cathedral (onto Trinitárius utca), go one long block, then take the first right (onto Király utca). At the fork, bear to the left. You'll stay straight on this road—crossing busy Koháry István utca—for several blocks, through some nondescript residential areas (on Szépasszony-völgy utca). When you crest the hill and emerge from the houses, you'll see the caves (and tour buses) below you on the left—go left (downhill) at the fork to get there. First you'll come to a stretch of touristy non-cave restaurants; keep going past these, and eventually you'll see a big loop of caves on your left.

NIGHTLIFE

Things quiet down pretty early in this sedate town. Youthful student bars and hangouts cluster along the main "walking street," Széchenyi utca. Older travelers feel more at home on Little Dobó Square, with schmaltzy live music until 21:00 or 22:00 in summer, or exploring the Sirens' Valley wine caves.

SLEEPING

Eger is a good overnight stop, and a couple of quaint, well-located hotels in particular—Senator Ház and Offi Ház—are well worth booking in advance. The TI can help you find a room; if you're stumped, the area behind the castle has a sprinkling of cheap guesthouses *(vendégház)*. Elevators are rare (except at Panoráma)—expect to climb one or two flights of stairs to reach your room. A tax of 310 Ft per person will be added to your bill (not included in the prices listed here).

Sleep Code

(200 Ft = about $1, country code: 36, area code: 36)
S = Single, **D** = Double/Twin, **T** = Triple, **Q** = Quad, **b** = bathroom.
Unless otherwise noted, English is spoken, breakfast is included, and credit cards are accepted.

To help you sort easily through these listings, I've divided the rooms into three categories, based on the price for a standard double room with bath:

$$$ Higher Priced—Most rooms 20,000 Ft or more.
$$ Moderately Priced—Most rooms between 15,000-20,000 Ft.
$ Lower Priced—Most rooms 15,000 Ft or less.

Phone Tip: Remember, if calling or faxing Eger internationally, you'll have to dial 36 twice (once for the country code, again for the area code).

EGER

$$$ Imola Udvarház rents six spacious apartments—with kitchen, living room, bedroom, and bathroom—all decorated in modern Scandinavian style (read: Ikea). They're pricey, but roomy and well-maintained, with a great location near the castle entrance (July–Aug: Sb-19,000 Ft, Db-22,000 Ft, Tb-24,000 Ft, Qb-26,000 Ft; each room 2,000 Ft less April–June and Sept–Oct and 4,000 Ft less Nov–March; air-con, free Wi-Fi, enter through restaurant courtyard at Dózsa György tér 4, tel. & fax 36/516-180, udvarhaz @imolanet.hu).

$$$ Panoráma Hotel is a good big-hotel option, still close to Dobó Square. You'll miss the quaintness of some of the other listings—its 38 faded, overpriced rooms are all business—but you get free access to its "Unicornis Thermarium" spa facility (Sb-21,500 Ft, Db-25,500 Ft, Tb-30,500 Ft, 15 percent cheaper Nov–March, apartments also available, air-con, elevator, fee for Wi-Fi, free parking, Dr. Hibay K. utca 2, tel. 36/412-886, fax 36/410-136, www.panoramahotels.hu, hoteleger@panoramahotels.hu).

$$ Senator Ház Hotel is one of my favorite small, family-run hotels in all of Eastern Europe. Though the 11 rooms are a bit worn, this place is cozy and well-run by András Cseh and his right-hand man, Viktor. With oodles of character, all the right quirks, and a picture-perfect location just under the castle on Little

Dobó Square, it's a winner (July–Aug: Sb-14,200 Ft, Db-19,000 Ft; May–June and Sept–Oct: Sb-13,700 Ft, Db-18,300 Ft; cheaper Nov–April, extra bed-6,000 Ft, air-con, free Internet access and Wi-Fi, Dobó István tér 11, tel. & fax 36/411-711, www.senator haz.hu, senator@enternet.hu). The Cseh family also runs **Pátria Vendégház**—two doubles (same prices as main hotel) and four apartments (Db-20,000 Ft, Tb-27,000 Ft) with luxurious decor around a courtyard in a nearby building (same contact info as Senator Ház Hotel).

$$ Offi Ház Hotel shares Little Dobó Square with Senator Ház. Its five rooms are classy and romantic (Sb-13,500 Ft, Db-15,500 Ft, Db suite-18,500 Ft, Tb suite-23,000 Ft, extra bed-4,500 Ft, 15 percent cheaper Nov–March, non-smoking, air-con, free cable Internet, Dobó István tér 5, tel. & fax 36/518-210, www .offihaz.hu, offihaz@t-online.hu, Offenbächer family).

$$ Szent János Hotel, less charming and more business-like than the Senator Ház and Offi Ház, offers a good but less atmospheric location, 11 straitlaced rooms, and a pleasant winter garden to relax in (Sb-12,000 Ft, Db-17,500 Ft, extra bed-4,000 Ft, 15 percent cheaper Nov–April, non-smoking rooms, air-con, free cable Internet, McDonald's walk-up window across the street can be noisy at night—especially weekends—so request a quiet back room, a long block off Dobó Square at Szent János utca 3, tel. 36/510-350, fax 36/517-101, www.hotelszentjanos.hu, hotelszent janos@hotelszentjanos.hu).

$ Dobó Vendégház, run by warm Mariann Kleszo, has seven basic but colorful rooms just off Dobó Square. Mariann speaks nothing but Hungarian, but gets simple reservation emails and faxes translated by a friend (Sb-8,500 Ft, Db-12,500 Ft, Tb-16,000 Ft, Qb-20,000 Ft, cash only, some rooms have air-con, Wi-Fi, Dobó utca 19, tel. 36/421-407, fax 36/515-715, www.dobovendeghaz .hu, dobovh@t-online.hu).

EATING

Bajor Sörház (known to locals as "HBH" for the brand of beer on tap) is favored by tourists and locals alike for its excellent Hungarian cuisine. Everything's good here. You could make a meal of the giant 750-Ft bowl of their spicy *gulyás leves* soup (that's *real* Hungarian goulash, described on page 220)—but it's fun to supplement it with some other well-prepared Hungarian dishes. This is a good place for two or more people to split several dishes. They also feature some Bavarian specialties...but with a Hungarian accent (most main dishes 1,500–3,000 Ft, daily 11:30–22:00, outdoor tables in summer, right at the bottom of Dobó Square at Bajcsy-Zsilinszky utca 19, tel. 36/515-516). If you're lucky, you may

EGER

get to meet animated István "Call Me Steve Miller" Molnár, one of my favorite Hungarians.

The recommended hotels **Senator Ház** and **Offi Ház** both have restaurants at the top end of Dobó Square that are open long hours daily (both are listed under "Sleeping"). These places have fine Hungarian and international food (most main dishes 1,500–2,500 Ft) and postcard-perfect outdoor seating that shares Little Dobó Square with a gazebo featuring cheesy live music on summer evenings. This low-key scene is fun and memorable.

Szantofer Vendéglő serves traditional Hungarian food at local prices to both Egerites and tourists. The good, unpretentious, fill-the-tank grub is presented with an artistic flourish, and the creatively translated menu is good for a laugh (most main dishes 1,400–2,100 Ft, daily 11:30–22:00, Bródy Sándor utca 3, tel. 36/517-298).

Palacsintavár ("Pancake Castle"), near the ramp leading up to the castle, isn't your hometown IHOP. This cellar bar serves up inventive, artfully presented crêpe-wrapped main courses to a mostly students clientele. It's decorated with old cigarette boxes, and cutting-edge rock music plays on the soundtrack (most main dishes 1,300–1,500 Ft, daily 12:00–22:00, Dobó utca 9).

Casa della Pasta, above the market hall, has a pleasant treehouse ambience. Sit indoors or enjoy covered terrace seating that's delightful in warm weather. The menu is mostly Italian, with pasta and pizzas (900–1,400 Ft) and main dishes (1,600–2,000 Ft), and a few Hungarian standbys thrown in (1,600–2,000 Ft; daily 12:00–23:00, Katona István tér 2, tel. 36/412-452).

Fast and Cheap: **Rádi Bisztró** is a popular student hangout and a convenient spot for 200-Ft pastries and inexpensive, premade 400-Ft sandwiches (Mon–Fri 7:00–19:00, Sat 7:00–18:00, Sun 9:00–18:00, just down the street from the Lyceum at Széchenyi utca 2).

Dessert: Cukrászda (pastry shops) line the streets of Eger. For deluxe, super-decadent pastries of every kind imaginable—most for less than 450 Ft—drop by **Dobós Cukrászda** (daily 9:30–21:00, point to what you want inside and they'll bring it out to your table, Széchenyi utca 6, tel. 36/413-335). For a more local scene, find the tiny **Sárvári Cukrászda,** a block behind the Lyceum. Their pastries are good, but Egerites line up here after a big Sunday lunch for their homemade gelato (150 Ft/scoop, Mon–Fri 7:00–19:00, Sat–Sun 10:00–19:00, Kossuth utca 1, between Jókai utca and Fellner utca).

EGER

TRANSPORTATION CONNECTIONS

By Train

The only major destination you'll get to directly from Eger's train station is **Budapest** (5/day direct to Budapest's Keleti/Eastern Station, 2.5 hrs; more frequent and faster with a change in Füzesabony—see next). For most other destinations, you'll connect through Füzesabony or Budapest.

Eger is not as well-connected as the smaller, nearby junction town of **Füzesabony** (FOO-zesh-ah-boyn). Eger is connected to Füzesabony by frequent trains (13/day, 17 min). The very rustic Füzesabony station does not have lockers, but—oddly enough—does have a modest museum of local artifacts. There is no ATM at the station—exit straight from the station and walk about two blocks, and you'll find an ATM on your right.

In Füzesabony, you can transfer to Budapest (including some speedy InterCity trains—with a 900-Ft supplement—that get you to Budapest in 2 hours total).

Night Train to Kraków: If you're connecting to Poland, it's sometimes possible to use a night train between Budapest and Kraków that stops at Füzesabony. If you want to start (or end) your Hungarian trip in Eger, this allows you to sleep into (or out of) Eger with a handy change at Füzesabony, rather than backtracking to Budapest. However, recently this train has run sporadically (summer only, or maybe not at all); sometimes the Budapest–Kraków night train goes through the Czech Republic instead. If this option intrigues you, investigate your options carefully at http://bahn.hafas.de/bin/query.exe/en.

By Bus

From Eger to Budapest: Since Eger's bus station is more central than its train station, some travelers prefer the direct bus to **Budapest** (hourly, 2–2.25 hrs). The bus station is a five-minute uphill walk behind Eger's cathedral and Archbishop's Palace: Go behind the cathedral and through the park, and look for the modern, green, circular building. Blue electronic boards in the center of the bus station complex show upcoming departures. This bus leaves you near Budapest's Stadionok bus station (on the M2/red Metro line).

To Salt Hill Thermal Spa: Buses from the same station also connect Eger to the Salt Hill Thermal Spa near Egerszalók (see "Getting There" on page 323). However, buses marked for Egerszalók do not actually go to the spa; instead, you need a bus going *beyond* Egerszalók, marked for Demjén.

PÉCS

An established town for nearly 2,000 years, Pécs (pronounced "paych") is a historic, museum-packed, and oh-so-pretty town near Hungary's southern frontier. Cheerful, inviting Pécs, with colorful buildings dripping with lavish Zsolnay porcelain decoration, feels unusually proud and prosperous.

Pécs' position as the major city of southern Hungary has placed it at the crossroads of cultures. Owing to its illustrious history, Pécs offers surprisingly engaging sightseeing for a city of its size; museum-going is fun and enlightening here. You'll gradually peel back the many layers of Pécs' past: Walk in the footsteps of Romans through ancient crypts, stroll the medieval trade-town street plan, explore some rare surviving artifacts of the Ottoman occupation, ogle colorful Baroque and Art Nouveau buildings... and enjoy the energetic bustle of one of Hungary's leading cities. The city's symbol—a mosque-turned-church—says it all.

The Mecsek Hills gently cradle the city, protecting it from the colder northern weather. Pécs' mild Mediterranean climate is closer to Croatia's than to Budapest's. It's no surprise that this bright and invigorating city has earned a reputation as a leading art colony. Its streets are lined with museums devoted to local artists both obscure and well-known (including Vasarely and Csontváry, considered the two great figures of Hungarian art). Students love it, too. Hungary's first university was founded here in 1367, and today's U. of Pécs rivals Budapest's ELTE as the country's biggest university. More than 30,000 students give Pécs a youthful buzz.

The city's rich tradition of history and culture is ramping up for its status as a European City of Culture in 2010. Busloads of tourists are about to bust out of the Budapest rut and discover this charming city. Beat them to it.

Planning Your Time

One full day is enough to get your fill of Pécs. Like Eger, it's a long day trip from Budapest (3 hours each way by train), so it's worth spending the night. With the better part of a day in Pécs, go for a walk through town following my self-guided commentary in the "Sights" section, dipping into the museums that appeal to you.

ORIENTATION

(area code: 72)

With about 170,000 people, Pécs is Hungary's fifth-largest city. But it feels like a small town, right down to the convivial strolling atmosphere that combusts along its pedestrian zone. The Belváros, or Inner Town, is hemmed in by a ring road (the site of the former town wall, some of which still stands). You can walk from one end of this central tourist zone to the other in about 15 minutes. All roads lead to the main square, Széchenyi tér, marked by the palatial yellow Town Hall and giant mosque/church. Because Pécs is nestled up against a gentle hillside, you'll go gradually uphill as you head north.

Tourist Information

The Pécs TI is right on the main square, in the ornately decorated County Hall building (mid-June–mid-Sept Mon–Fri 8:00–17:30, Sat 9:00–14:00, closed Sun; May–mid-June and mid-Sept–Oct Mon–Fri 8:00–17:30, closed Sat–Sun; Nov–April Mon–Fri 8:00–16:00, closed Sat–Sun; Széchenyi tér 9, tel. 72/213-315, www .pecs.hu).

Arrival in Pécs

By Train: The Pécs train station is three-quarters of a mile due south of the city center's Széchenyi tér. Inside, the station is long but straightforward (with ATM, lockers, and all the usual amenities). The fastest way downtown is to take the **bus:** As you exit the station, head down to the left end of the bus stops, and hop on bus #30, #32, or #33 (buy 280-Ft ticket from driver and validate in red box—stick ticket in slot, then pull the slot itself toward you; ride it three stops in about 10 minutes to Boldogságház, just after you see the giant green-domed mosque/church on the main square). You can also **walk** there in about 15 minutes: Exit straight ahead from the station and walk up the tree-lined, slightly angled Jókai út, which funnels you directly to the main Széchenyi square. A **taxi** to any of my recommended hotels should cost no more than 1,000 Ft.

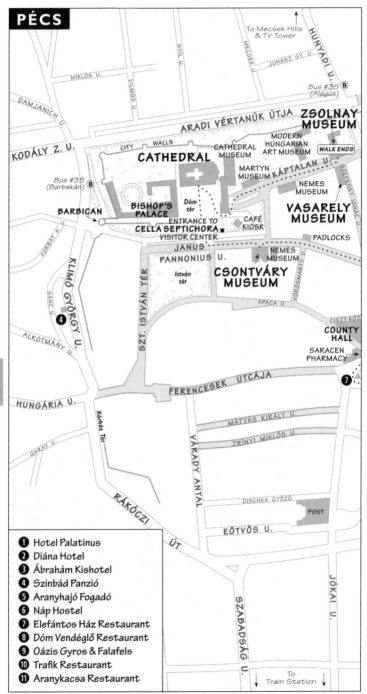

PÉCS

To Mecsek Hills & TV Tower

HUNYADI U.

MECSEK U.

JUHÁSZ GY. U.

NYIL U.

VILMOS U.

MIKLÓS U.

Bus #35 (Alagút)

DAMJANICH U.

ARADI VÉRTANÚK ÚTJA

ZSOLNAY MUSEUM

KODÁLY Z. U.

CITY WALLS

CATHEDRAL

CATHEDRAL MUSEUM

MODERN HUNGARIAN ART MUSEUM

WALK ENDS

MARTYN MUSEUM

KÁPTALAN U.

SZEPESSY IGNÁC U.

NEMES MUSEUM

Bus #35 (Barbakán)

BARBICAN

BISHOP'S PALACE

Dóm tér

CAFÉ KIOSK

VASARELY MUSEUM

ENTRANCE TO **CELLA SEPTICHORA** VISITOR CENTER

PADLOCKS

FORBÁT A. U.

SÁNC U.

KLIMÓ GYÖRGY U.

JANUS PANNONIUS U.

István tér

NEMES MUSEUM

CSONTVÁRY MUSEUM

VÖRÖSMARTY U.

APÁCA U.

CISZT KÖZ

COUNTY HALL

❹

ALKOTMÁNY U.

SZT. ISTVÁN TÉR

SARACEN PHARMACY

❼

HUNGÁRIA U.

FERENCESEK UTCÁJA

Kórház Tér

MÁTYÁS KIRÁLY U.

ZRÍNYI MIKLÓS U.

GARAY U.

VÁRADY ANTAL U.

RÁKÓCZI ÚT

DISCHKA GYŐZŐ

POST

EÖTVÖS U.

JÓKAI U.

SZABADSÁG U.

To Train Station

❶ Hotel Palatinus
❷ Diána Hotel
❸ Ábrahám Kishotel
❹ Szinbád Panzió
❺ Aranyhajó Fogadó
❻ Náp Hostel
❼ Elefántos Ház Restaurant
❽ Dóm Vendéglő Restaurant
❾ Oázis Gyros & Falafels
❿ Trafik Restaurant
⓫ Aranykacsa Restaurant

PÉCS

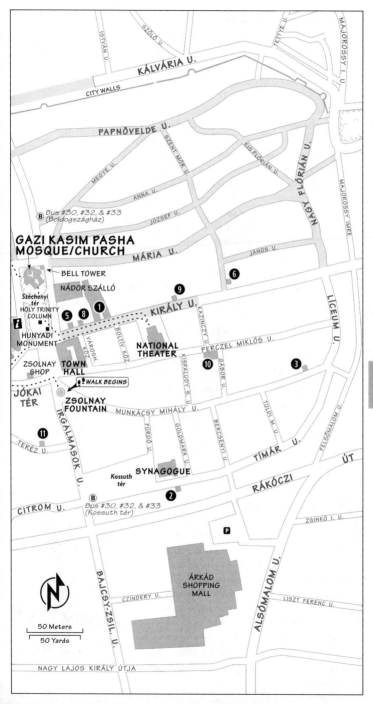

Getting Around Pécs

You probably won't need to use public transit in Pécs, except for getting into town from the train station or heading up into the hills. A single ticket is 210 Ft when purchased in advance at a kiosk, or 280 Ft when bought on the bus.

Helpful Hints

Internet Access: Internet cafés with long hours and fair prices are easy to find and well-signed from the main walking zone.

Shopping: The giant, American-style **Árkád** shopping mall, with a supermarket, food court, and lots more, is just a block beyond the synagogue and Kossuth tér, at the southern edge of the Inner Town (Mon–Sat 7:00–21:00, Fri until 22:00, Sun 8:00–19:00, Bajcsy-Zsilinszky utca 11, www.arkadpecs.hu).

Tourist Train: A hokey tourist train does a 40-minute loop through the city center (1,000 Ft, departs from bottom of Széchenyi tér, May–Sept only).

Local Guide: Brigitta Gombos is a knowledgeable guide who leads good tours of her hometown (12,000 Ft/3 hrs, mobile 0670-505-3531, gerluc@freemail.hu).

SIGHTS

I've arranged these sights roughly in the order of a handy self-guided orientation walk through town. Note that most museums in Pécs (except the cathedral and the Roman crypts) have similar hours, and are covered by a single 2,000-Ft day ticket *(napijegy)*. This is a good deal only if you see at least three museums (which you likely will—the Csontváry, Vasarely, and Zsolnay museums are all highly recommended). Simply buy the day pass at the first museum you visit.

• *Begin in front of the little church next to the Town Hall, at the...*

▲Zsolnay Fountain (Zsolnay-kút)

This fountain, an icon of Pécs, was a gift from the beloved local Zsolnay (ZHOL-nay) family. Their innovation of a type of ceramics called pyrogranite allowed colorful, delicate-seeming porcelain to be made frostproof and hard as steel—ideal for external building decoration. The ox heads—modeled after an ancient drinking vessel found in Pécs—are specially glazed with another Zsolnay invention, eosin. Notice how eosin glaze glimmers

PÉCS

with a unique range of colors. (Since the eosin glaze compromises the pyrogranite, the fountain must be covered in winter.) Above the oxen heads are traditional symbols of Pécs. One is the shield with five tall churches, dating from the Middle Ages. (Germans still call the town Fünfkirchen.) This seal was appropriated by the Zsolnay family as a symbol of their porcelain. The other seal is Pécs' coat of arms: a walled city under vineyard-strewn hills.

This is the first of many gorgeous Zsolnay decorations we'll see all over town. But Pécs is just the beginning. In the late 19th and early 20th centuries, Budapest and cities all over Europe covered their finest buildings with decorations from this city's Zsolnay Porcelain Manufacture. (For all the details, see the "Zsolnay Porcelain" sidebar on page 346.)

• *Across the wide street is the entrance to an enjoyable pedestrian zone called...*

Jókai Tér

As you enter the traffic-free area, notice the **chessboards** on top of the little pillars. When this street was renovated in 2000—with funky benches and other playful elements—the designers wanted to remind locals to take time to relax.

On the right (at #2), notice the **Zsolnay porcelain shop.** Although the company was reduced to an industrial supplier under the communists, today Zsolnay is proudly reclaiming its role as a maker of fine art. Dipping into the shop, notice that some of the decorative items use the same distinctive eosin glaze as the fountain's oxen heads...and are priced accordingly.

Continuing to the corner, look down the pedestrian street called **Ferencesek utcája.** When Pécs was a walled market town, this street—and Király utca, also now pedestrianized—made up the main east–west road. At the house at the corner, notice the elephant. This used to be a grocery store, which likely imported exotic Eastern goods, symbolized by the then-mysterious pachyderm. (Now it's a recommended Italian restaurant, Elefántos Ház—see "Eating," page 351.)

Hang a right around the elephant house, noticing the former tram tracks preserved in the street. Imagine how unappealing this drag was when it was choked with tram and car traffic. On the left, look for the old-time **Saracen Pharmacy** (marked with the words *Sipöcz István* over the door). Its interior—with gorgeous woodwork, little porcelain medicine pots, and a gorgeous Zsolnay fountain—is protected and open to tourists (free, Mon–Fri 9:00–18:00, Sat 9:00–12:00, closed Sun, Apáca 1).

• *Continuing up the street, you'll emerge into...*

▲The Main Square: Széchenyi Tér

In the Middle Ages, Pécs was a major stop on a Byzantine trade route. At the intersection of the city's original north–south and east–west thoroughfares, Széchenyi tér was a natural meeting point and market zone. Today the market is gone, but no fewer than 12 streets converge here, and it remains the bustling city center. This is where both political demonstrations and the annual New Year's Eve festivities percolate.

Let's get oriented. Face the green-domed **Gazi Kasim Pasha Mosque** at the top of the square (described in detail on next page). On the right, the giant yellow-and-white building with the tower is the **Town Hall** (Városház, 1908), strategically located here since the olden days to watch over the market activities. The Town Hall's tower plays laid-back organ ditties throughout the

day. Across the square (on the left) is the gorgeous, red-roofed **County Hall** (Megyháza, 1898) frosted like a wedding cake with sumptuous Zsolnay decorations (and a TI on the far corner). Because it was origi-nally a bank, it's adorned with beehives (one at the very peak of the building, and two more between the top-floor windows)—industrious bees, who carefully collect and store away their golden deposits, are a common symbol for banking. Farther up the square on the right is the pink **Nádor Szálló.** In the early 20th century, this hotel was a popular gathering place for artists and intellectuals (but now it's awaiting a massive renovation).

The square has two monuments. On the right is an equestrian statue of **János Hunyadi,** the war hero who fended off the Ottoman invaders at the 1456 Battle of Belgrade (described on page 183). Later those Ottomans took Pécs and built the mosque at the top of the square. But Hunyadi gets the last laugh: If you position yourself just right in front of the Town Hall, it appears that Hunyadi's club is smashing the crescent at the top of the mosque. This statue is a popular meeting point: Locals say, "I'll meet you under the horse's...tail." With perhaps unintended irony, Hunyadi—who died of the plague soon after that battle—shares the square with the **Holy Trinity Plague Column,** built to give thanks to God for surviving a nasty bout of the plague in the late 17th century. Around its base are three saints known for protecting against disease or injury: Sebastian, who was killed by arrows (on left); Rocco, with a nasty leg wound (on right); and Anthony of Padua, who offers help recovering that which is lost—including health (behind the pillar).

• *We'll visit the mosque/church soon. But first, head down the street branching off to the right, next to the Town Hall...*

▲▲The Walking Street: Király Utca

This vibrant Technicolor people zone—combined with Jókai tér and Ferencesek utcája, across the square—bisects the city center. Király utca ("Royal Street") is lined with shops, several recommended restaurants (see "Eating," page 351), and gorgeous facades that continue the architectural cancan from out on the square.

A few steps down the street on the right, the big green building marked **Bazár** was the Zsolnay family home, before they moved closer to their porcelain factory just outside town. Just beyond (on the left) is the gorgeous horseshoe-shaped **Hotel Palatinus.** Step into the lobby for a taste of genteel Secession (see "Sleeping," page 349).

A few more steps take you to the square in front of the **National Theater,** built (along with most of the other houses on

this square) for the Hungarian millennial celebrations of 1896 (see page 40). The decorations on the theater—including the stone-like statues—are all made of Zsolnay pyrogranite. This is a popular venue in this city of culture, including sometimes for the local philharmonic (duck into the box office to see what's showing while you're in town).

While this part of Pécs appears wealthy and manicured, the region is struggling. In the early 1950s, Pécs had only about 50,000 residents. Coal and uranium mines kick-started the economy, causing the population to more than triple over the last 50 years. However, both mines have since closed. While the university and business center of Pécs continues to thrive, outlying communities are grappling with 30 percent unemployment.

• *Head back to Széchenyi tér to visit the...*

▲▲Gazi Kasim Pasha Mosque (Gázi Kászim Pasa Dzsámija)/Inner Town Parish Church

It's rare to find such a well-preserved Ottoman structure in Hungary. The Ottomans—who began their 150-year stay in Pécs in 1543—lived here in the Inner Town, while the dwindling Hungarian population moved to the outskirts. The Ottomans tore down the church that had stood on this spot and used the stones to build the structure you see today. After the Ottomans were forced out, the Catholic Church reclaimed this building and turned it into a church—which is why it's still intact today. Despite renovations over the year, it remains an offbeat hybrid of Islamic and Christian faiths.

Cost and Hours: Free but donations are requested—consider buying a postcard or booklet; mid-April–mid-Oct Mon–Sat 10:00–16:00, Sun 11:30–16:00; mid-Oct–mid-April Mon–Sat 10:00–12:00, Sun 11:30–14:00.

◔ Self-Guided Tour: From the **outside,** notice the crescent moon of Islam capping the dome—but it's topped by the victorious Christian cross. The only decorations on the austere facade are the striped ogee arches over the windows. Before entering, notice the fig trees; locals are proud that their mild climate can support these heat-seekers.

Go **inside** and let your eyes adjust to the low light. Are you

in a church, or a mosque... or both? The striped arches over the windows are inside as well. Notice the colorful Islamic-style stalactite decorations at the tops of the corners. The painting on the underside of the dome seems to combine Christian

figures with the geometric designs of Islam. To the right of the main altar is a verse from the Quran translated into Hungarian and used for Christian worship (a reminder that Islam and Christianity are founded on many of the same principles). Look for gray patches with faint Arabic script peeking through—most were whitewashed during the church-ification.

Looking back to where you entered, you'll see a large **prayer niche** (mihrab) next to the door. This niche, which faces Mecca (southeast from here), indicated to Muslim worshippers where they had to face to pray. The holy water basin in the niche and the crucifix suspended above it make it clear who's in charge now.

Mentally erase these and other Christian elements, and go back in time to the Ottoman period. There were no pews, and carpets covered the floor. Worshippers—men in front, women segregated in back—stood and knelt as they prayed toward the mihrab. A step-stair pulpit, called a mimber, likely stood off to one side of the mihrab.

When the Christians reclaimed this building, they flipped it around, putting an altar where the entrance was, and vice versa. Much later, in 1939, they added the giant **apse** (semi-circular area behind the altar). As you explore this area, in the corners you'll see small stone basins. These once stood outside the building, where the Ottoman worshippers performed their ablution, or ritual washing before prayer. The modern paintings depict Bible scenes and events in Hungary's Christian history. And the giant organ is an Angster (made by a local Hungarian organ-maker).

Exiting the building, head around back to find the latest addition to this constantly evolving structure: the modern **bell tower** and a concrete footprint that recalls the original church that preceded this mosque. The statue depicts St. Bartholomew, the patron of this church. Depicted (as he always is) with his skin peeling away, he steps on a serpent, representing victory over evil (Islam?). Every day at 12:00 and 19:00, the bell tower rises up 40 feet in the air to play a tune.

• *While interesting, this is not Pécs' main church. To see that (and a lot more), go down the street at the upper-left corner of the square...*

Janus Pannonius Utca

About a block down this street, watch (on the right) for a railing that's completely covered in **padlocks.** Nobody knows for sure how this local tradition began, back in the 1980s. Some say it was a clever way for graduating students to get rid of the padlocks from their lockers. These days, the padlocks mostly belong to lovers who want to pledge themselves to each other. You can see that many of the locks are marked (or even engraved) with couples' names. (If you're interested in early retirement, set up a padlock shop here.) Farther down the same block, the tradition continues at the padlock-covered gate.

• *Continue along the street until you emerge into the little square. In the pretty off-white building on the left (with the grey roof), you'll find Pécs' best art museum...*

Tivadar Csontváry Kosztka
(1853–1919)

Adored by Hungarians, but virtually unknown outside his home-land, Tivadar Csontváry Kosztka had a life as interesting as his paintings. Because of the time in which he lived and his struggles with mental illness (schizophrenia)—if not for his talent—Csontváry (CHONT-vah-ree) is often compared to Van Gogh. While that's a bit of a stretch, viewing Csontváry's works give you a glimpse into the Hungarian psyche, and into his own fractured mind.

Tivadar Kosztka was born to an upper-class family, seemingly bound for a humdrum lot in life. He didn't pick up a paintbrush until his 27th year. Then one day, while idly sketching sleeping oxen, he had a revelation (or, perhaps, a psychotic episode): A voice told him that he was destined to become "the world's greatest *plein air* painter, greater even than Raphael."

He adopted the pseudonym Csontváry and became driven by an almost pathological compulsion to prepare himself for what he believed to be his destiny. He figured it would take him 20 years, working as a pharmacist to finance his quest. At 41, he had saved enough to attend art school (in Munich and in Paris). Seeking the ideal subjects for his outdoor style, he traveled extensively around Europe and the Middle East: Italy, Croatia, Bosnia-

▲Csontváry Museum (Csontváry Múzeum)

This small but good collection showcases the works of beloved Hungarian painter Tivadar Csontváry Kosztka. Csontváry produced only 100 paintings and 20 drawings, of which about half are collected here. For a crash course in this enigmatic painter, read the sidebar above before visiting (700 Ft, covered by 2,000-Ft day ticket, borrow the English information sheet, April–Oct Tue–Sun 10:00–18:00, Nov–March Tue–Sun 10:00–17:00, closed Mon year-round, Janus Pannonius utca 11, tel. 72/224-255).

The museum is divided into five rooms. In Room 1, see Csontváry's art-school sketches that capture people at unguarded moments. Room 2 shows mostly scenes from around Hungary. *Storm on the Great Hortobágy* is a dynamic snapshot of life on the Great Hungarian Plain, where cowherds attend to longhorn cattle. A storm brews on the horizon as a horseman races across the bridge. Notice the balance between movement and stillness, and between the yellow sky and the deep blue clouds. In Room 3, Csontváry's

Herzegovina, Greece, Egypt, Lebanon, Jerusalem, and the Tatra Mountains of his own homeland. By the time he began painting in earnest, he had only six productive years (1903–1909).

Csontváry's rough, autodidactic (self-taught) style reveals his untrained origins, but contains a depth of meaning and of composition that exceeded his technical skill. While classified as a Post-Impressionist, Csontváry forged a style all his own. Like his contemporary Marc Chagall, he worked in almost childlike bright colors and often reverted to big, bold themes. His most common subjects are the destinations he traveled to that inspired him.

After exhibitions in 1909 and 1910 failed to win him the praise he so desperately sought, he became consumed by his schizophrenia and created only bizarre, surrealistic works. He died in obscurity in 1919.

After Csontváry's death, his family planned to sell his works to wagon-makers, who wanted the valuable canvas to stretch over their wagons. Fortunately a Budapest art collector bought them instead, preserving the legacy of this important figure in Hungarian art history.

Csontváry remained largely unappreciated until the 1960s, when art-lovers began to take notice. But one discerning eye for talent knew greatness when he saw it, before many others did: Pablo Picasso reportedly discovered Csontváry's canvases at a 1949 exhibition, and proceeded to lock himself in the room with them for an hour. Finally emerging, he told his friend Marc Chagall that Chagall could never produce a work half as good as Csontváry's.

most acclaimed work, *The Lonely Cedar*, depicts a windblown tree on a ridge above the sea. The tree seems boldly independent even as it longs for companionship. Rooms 3 and 4 are filled with other "postcards" of Csontváry's far-flung travels, where he found inspiration in the Middle East (Baalbek, Jerusalem, Nazareth) and Europe (France, Sicily, Croatia, Bosnia-Herzegovina, Greece). The last room (5) displays Csontváry's final major painting, *Riders on the Seashore*. This haunting valedictory canvas, with an equestrian party pausing by an eerily deep-blue cove, hints at the troubled depths of Csontváry's own psyche. Other works in this room date from Csontváry's final days, when—in his worsening mental state—he sketched large-scale, absurdist scenes.

• *Continue down Janus Pannonius utca, along the tree-lined path. Soon you'll see a beautiful **yellow kiosk** (on the right)—an inviting place for a coffee break. Just below and to the left of that, look for the modern entrance to the...*

▲▲Cella Septichora Visitor Center (Roman Crypts)

This unique, modern, well-presented museum allows visitors to take a peek inside some remarkably preserved Roman crypts.

Cost and Hours: 1,200 Ft, April–Oct Tue–Sun 10:00–18:00, Nov–March Tue–Sun 10:00–16:00, always closed Mon, Dóm tér, tel. 72/224-755. A "joint ticket" for an extra 300 Ft gets you into another, smaller tomb nearby (at the base of the stairs up to the cathedral). It's basically more of the same, plus a marble sarcophagus.

Tours: For 300 Ft extra, you can join a 45-minute English tour. These English tours run regularly, but not according to a set schedule. If the sight isn't too busy, a guide might be able to give you a private tour; or you might have to wait up to 30 minutes in summer or 60 minutes in winter. Taking the tour is worthwhile if you really want to appreciate all the details, so consider calling ahead to check the schedule (tel. 72/224-755). For a brief visit, my self-guided tour (below)—and the good posted English descriptions—will guide you through the basics.

Background: There was a Roman settlement in today's Pécs from the year A.D. 30, and by the second century it was a provincial capital called Sopinae. During that time, this part of town was a vast cemetery, which included the graves of Christian martyrs. Later, after Christianity became the state religion in the early fourth century, the tombs of these martyrs attracted pilgrims from afar. Wealthy Christian families were now free to build a double-decker  structure to hold the remains of their relatives: a sealed crypt below ground (painted with Bible scenes and floral motifs), with a chapel directly above for remembering and praying for the dead. About a century later, Rome fell. Nomadic invaders would live in the chapels and raid the crypts (then carefully re-cover them). Today the remains of some of these crypt-chapels have been discovered, excavated, and opened to visitors.

➲ Self-Guided Tour: Buy your ticket and head into the first area, the foundation of a **giant chapel with seven apses.** (The exhibit is named for this—Cella Septichora means "seven-apsed chapel.") Experts believe that the crypt of a different martyr would have been placed in each apse, and pilgrims would come here to worship. However, the structure was never finished.

Head up the stairs and go down the hall on the left. After passing a stone sarcophagus, you'll go down a steep set of stairs and through a long corridor. Unlike Rome's famous catacombs, these crypts were not originally connected underground; modern archaeologists built this tunnel to allow visitors easier access to all the tombs.

You'll emerge at the **Wine Pitcher Burial Chamber.** The model shows the two-tiered structure. Peer through the window to see the paintings that decorate the crypt.

Its nickname comes from the wine jug and glass painted in the niche above the body. Romans used wine to toast to the memory of the departed (the Roman version of "pour one out for the homies who ain't here"). Climb up the stairs to what was ground level, where you can view the foundation of the chapel and look down into the crypt. From here, you'll see other paintings (representing paradise), as well as the drain at the bottom of the sarcophagus. The Romans, ever clever engineers, provided drainage so that accumulating groundwater would not defile the body.

Retrace your steps, then follow signs to the Peter and Paul crypt. Along the way, you'll pass through an area with several **smaller crypts.** Notice that these didn't have large chapels up top; rather, worshippers would kneel and look inside a small decorative chapel. In one, a hole in the floor of the chapel indicates where tomb raiders broke in to search for valuables. Turn right into the **octagonal chapel,** which—like the seven-apsed chapel—was likely designed to be a pilgrim church. Finally you'll pass another small crypt that's more intact, showing the barrel vaulting that once covered all of these.

At the **Peter and Paul Burial Chamber,** kneel down to see Sts. Peter and Paul above the sarcophagus, flanking the Christogram (an ancient Christian symbol). Then head down the spiral stairs to an area below the crypt, where you can look up through Plexiglas to see more decorations. The side walls are painted with biblical scenes, while the ceiling features another Christogram, four portraits (possibly the Four Evangelists), and more nature motifs—plants and birds. (An artist's rendering of the original version is nearby.) Notice the little window above the body. Experts believe that a ribbon tied to the sarcophagus led through this window up into the chapel, so the faithful could have a tangible connection to the dead.

Retracing your steps on your way out, you'll pass through even more crypts (they've unearthed more than 20), as well as some simple brick sarcophagi used by poorer families to bury their dead.

• *Exiting the exhibit, turn right and continue down Janus Pannonius utca, which deposits you at...*

István Tér and Dóm Tér

These two squares—the lower István Square, which belonged to the people, and the upper Cathedral Square, which was the bish-

op's—used to be separated by a wall and moat. But then the enlightened **Bishop Szepesy** turned them into one big park. In the statue that dominates the square, he's stepping down from the pulpit clutching a Bible—a reminder that he's believed to have been the first priest to use Hungarian.

Walk up the stairs and take a closer look at Cathedral Square. The brown, Neo-Renaissance building on the left (with a yellow Baroque addition) is the Bishop's Palace. At the corner of this

building, notice the engaging statue of **Franz Liszt** by popular 20th-century sculptor Imre Varga (see page 84). Liszt was a friend of the bishop, and Liszt's visit here in 1846 is still the stuff of legends.

• *Now turn your attention to the massive, four-towered....*

▲▲Cathedral

St. István established a bishopric in Pécs in the year 1009, and this church building grew in fits and starts from then on. By the 14th

century, it had roughly the same floor plan as today, and gradually morphed with the styles of the day: Romanesque, Gothic, Renaissance. The Ottomans used it as a stable, grain store, and library, and even turned one small chapel into a mosque and erected a minaret. Later, when it became the cathedral again, it got a Baroque

overhaul. Finally in the 1880s, a bishop (likely hoping to be remembered as a visionary) grew tired of the architectural hodge-podge, gutted the place, and turned it into the Neo-Romanesque fortress of God before you today. The 12 apostles stand along the roofline, and the four distinctive corner towers anchor and fortify the massive structure.

Cost and Hours: 800 Ft, 300 Ft more to also visit cathedral museum and bishop's wine cellar for a tasting; April–mid-Oct Mon–Sat 9:00–17:00, Sun 13:00–17:00; mid-Oct–March Mon–Sat

10:00–16:00, Sun 13:00–16:00; can be closed for weddings Sat afternoons—especially in summer, tel. 72/513-030.

Ø Self-Guided Tour: Get close to the entrance and inspect the highly symbolic **bronze gate** from 2000. The vines, grapes, and branches are all connected, as we are all connected to God. If you look closely, you'll find animals representing good (birds) and evil (snake, scorpion, frog). The sculpture on the left depicts St. István giving Pécs to the first bishop; on the right, Jesus offers his hand to St. Peter.

Go to church. Stepping inside, it's clear that the renovating bishop did not subscribe to the "less is more" school of church decoration. Like the Matthias Church in Budapest (see page 58)—renovated at about the same time—every square inch is covered by a thick layer of colorful paint. Along the **nave** are paintings depicting the lives of the church's patrons, Sts. Peter and Paul. Above the arches are biblical scenes. The coffered ceiling of the nave depicts the 12 apostles and (near the organ) John the Baptist.

The **altar,** with its richly decorated canopy, is a replica of the 13th-century original. The mosaic on the apse dome (behind the altar, not entirely visible from here) features Jesus flanked by Peter and Paul (on the right) and, on the left, István and Mary (the patron saint of Hungary).

To the right of the organ is the **bishop's treasury,** in the Chapel of Mary. (This is the only one of the cathedral's four such chapels open to tourists.) The vestments, goblets, and monstrances are surrounded by paintings of events from the Christian history of Hungary. At the far end of the chapel is a remarkably detailed 16th-century alabaster sculpture, done by a Dutch sculptor for an Italian family who didn't want it after all (so the Pécs bishop bought it instead).

Back in the main church, to the right of the altar are the stairs

down to the **crypt.** This 11th-century forest of columns (redecorated like the rest of the church) is part of the original church building on this site. The bust at the back depicts the bishop who decided to renovate the church.

• *From in front of the cathedral, if you want to take a look at part of the* old **city wall,** *you can go down the stairs and turn right at the wide path, which will take you to a barbican (round tower) that helped fortify*

PÉCS

Zsolnay Porcelain

Because of the pioneering Zsolnay (ZHOL-nay) family of Pécs, buildings all over Hungary are slathered with gorgeously colorful porcelain.

Miklós Zsolnay (1800–1880) opened a porcelain factory in Pécs in 1853. But the real breakthrough came at the hands of his innovative son, Vilmos Zsolnay (1828–1900), who experimented with glazes and additives, and revolutionized the use of porcelain in building materials. He invented a type of ceramic called pyrogranite to create porcelain decorative elements that were as resilient as steel and weatherproof, but could still be deli-

cately sculpted and painted any color of the rainbow. Zsolnay pyrogranite made a splash at the 1873 World Exhibition in Vienna, winning an avalanche of orders from all over Europe. The twists and curves that Zsolnay porcelain allowed for were a perfect fit for the slinky, organic Art Nouveau style of the day. Exhibits at further

world fairs added to the Zsolnay family's renown and wealth.

In 1893, Vilmos Zsolnay unveiled his latest innovation: eosin, a shimmering—almost metallic—iridescent glaze. Named for the Greek word for "dawn," it has an otherworldly way of making porcelain resemble light striking a precious stone or the surface of a soap bubble. This eosin technique is exemplified by Pécs' Zsolnay Fountain (described on page 334).

Boom time for the Zsolnays also coincided with the 1896

---

the walls. (For more on these walls, see page 348.)

Otherwise, exiting the cathedral, you can turn left, pass through the archway, walk over the glassed-in Roman ruins, and walk down…

Káptalan Utca: Pécs' "Museum Row"

A cluster of museums line tranquil Káptalan Street ("Chapterhouse Street," where priests once lived), just east of the cathedral. A few of the smaller museums are skippable, but the Zsolnay and Vasarely museums are worthwhile. Remember, all of these are covered by the same 2,000-Ft day ticket described on page 334. The website for all is www.jpm.hu. These are listed roughly in the order you reach them, coming from the cathedral.

▲**Viktor Vasarely Museum (Vasarely Múzeum)**—You might not know Viktor Vasarely (1908–1997), but you know his work. Think optical illusions, and the dizzying Op Art that inspired the millennial celebrations in Budapest (see page 40). The city's architects, who had ample resources and imagination, were striving to create a unique Hungarian national style. Many of them adopted colorful pyrogranite tiles and other decorations  as an integral part of that style. In Budapest alone, the Great Market Hall, Matthias Church and National Archives on Castle Hill, and Ödön Lechner's Postal Savings Bank and Museum of Applied Arts are roofed with Zsolnay pyrogranite tiles. Zsolnay decorative elements also adorn the Hungarian Parliament, Gellért Baths, and many other buildings. To this day, Zsolnay tiles are synonymous with Budapest (and Hungarian) architecture.

All of that porcelain generated a lot of work for the Pécs factory. By the time World War I broke out, the Zsolnay family business was the Austro-Hungarian Empire's biggest company. But the stripped-down modern styles that emerged in the 20th century had little use for the fanciful Zsolnay decorations. The factory was nationalized by the communists, the Zsolnay name was abandoned, and quality plummeted.

In the 1990s, private investors took over and have made great strides toward rehabilitating the Zsolnay name. All over Hungary, you'll see shops selling beautiful Zsolnay tableware, some with designs as innovative as ever. But to keep up with our modern economy, Zsolnay also creates everyday items. In fact, they recently signed a big deal to make dishes for Ikea.

psychedelic 1960s. Here in his hometown, you can see a museum of Vasarely's eye-popping creations. Inspired by nature, Vasarely discovered that the repetition and slight variation of lines and forms can play with the viewer's brain to create illusions of depth and movement. In other words, black-and-white lines undulating across a canvas are trippy, baby. It's easy to get lost in Vasarely's mind-bending designs—such as, in the first room, a pair of carpets with zebras—which make you go cross-eyed before you stumble up the stairs to see him add more color to the mix (700 Ft, covered by 2,000-Ft day ticket, borrow the English information, April–Oct Tue–Sun 10:00–18:00, Nov–March Tue–Sun 10:00–17:00, closed Mon, Káptalan utca 3, tel. 72/514-040).

Modern Hungarian Art Museum (Modern Magyar Képtár)— While Hungarian art has its fans, this museum—featuring work from the late 1800s through the 1940s—feels like a house of rip-offs of better-known French artists. Most visitors will enjoy a more focused visit at the museums dedicated to two specific artists, Vasarely and Csontváry (460 Ft, covered by 2,000-Ft day ticket, borrow the English information, April–Oct Tue–Sun 12:00–18:00, Nov–March Tue–Sun 12:00–16:00, closed Mon, Káptalan utca 4, tel. 72/514-040).

▲**Zsolnay Porcelain Museum (Zsolnay Múzeum)**—This museum, situated in the former mansion of the Zsolnay family, is as much a shrine to the family as a showcase of their work. (For more on the family and their legacy, see the "Zsolnay Porcelain" sidebar, previous page.) The collection is divided into two parts: architectural elements and decorative ware. In the architectural elements section, you'll see impressively detailed and colorful decorations for the many buildings the Zsolnays were involved in renovating (including Budapest's Matthias Church and Parliament). You'll also see a playful duck fountain, and some beautiful pieces of the destroyed István Stove that once warmed Budapest's Royal Palace. The decorative-ware collection displays vases, sculptures, and other objects that demonstrate the evolution of porcelain style. Watch how trends came and went over time. A spinning table allows you to inspect each place setting of Zsolnay dinnerware (700 Ft, covered by 2,000-Ft day ticket, everything well-described in English, April–Oct Tue–Sun 10:00–18:00, Nov–March Tue–Sun 10:00–17:00, closed Mon, Káptalan utca 4, tel. 72/514-040).

Other Museums—Nearby are museums that showcase the work of yet two more local artists, Ferenc Martyn and Endre Nemes.

• *From Káptalan utca, you're just a block above the main square and our starting point. If you have more time, consider some of these sights...*

Elsewhere in Pécs

City Walls—Several segments of the city walls around the northern part of Pécs are still standing (most notably around the cathedral area). Built after the Tatar invasions of the 13th century, and beefed up in the 15th century, the walls were no match for the Ottoman invaders who took the town in 1543. Still standing just west of the cathedral area is

the round, stout barbican defensive gate, which you can actually climb.

Synagogue (Zsinagóga)—Just south of the old center, overlooking Kossuth tér, is Pécs' colorful synagogue. Dating from the 1860s, but recently restored, this building is a powerful reminder of Pécs' Jewish heritage. The city had a thriving population of

4,000 Jews, of whom only a few hundred survived the Holocaust (500 Ft, May–Sept Sun–Fri 10:00–17:00, closed Sat and Oct–April, Kossuth tér, tel. 72/315-881).

Mecsek Hills—Pécs is picturesquely nestled in the Mecsek (MEH-chek) Hills, a popular place to go for a hike. To get an aerial view of Pécs, ride bus #35 about 30 minutes up to the TV tower overlooking the city and surrounding region (catch this bus at the train station, or at the northern entrance to city center). Ascend the 580-foot-tall TV tower for views over the town and region (650 Ft, daily 9:00–20:00).

SLEEPING

Most of Pécs' city-center accommodations seem to follow a similar pattern: affordable pensions with simple but sleepable rooms. Some are called *kishotel* ("small hotel"). Elevators are rare.

$$$ Hotel Palatinus is your big-hotel option, perfectly located right on the main walking street. You'll rarely find a more impressive facade, lobby, and breakfast room; the showpiece building has been painstakingly restored to its turn-of-the-20th-century glory. But many of the 100 rooms have not been renovated to a similar standard. While this makes it a bit overpriced, the location and public areas help compensate (Sb-16,000–23,000 Ft, Db-19,000–25,000 Ft, price depends on type of room— more for air-con or more recently renovated rooms, elevator, fee for Wi-Fi, Király utca 5, tel. 72/889-400, www

.danubiushotels.com/palatinus, palatinus.reservation@danubius hotels.com).

$$ Diána Hotel has 20 rooms just up the street from the synagogue, between the town center and the Árkád shopping mall (Sb-10,000 Ft, Db-14,000 Ft, 1,500 Ft more for bigger "deluxe" rooms, rates about 1,000 Ft cheaper if you pay cash, air-con-1,600 Ft, some street noise, Wi-Fi, Tímár utca 4a, tel. 72/328-594, www .hoteldiana.hu, rikopecs0275@t-online.hu).

$$ Ábrahám Kishotel is a Jewish-themed pension with a blue-and-white color scheme in its five tidy rooms. Ilona, who has a big personality and a little dog, doesn't speak English, but has an

Sleep Code

(200 Ft = about $1, country code: 36, area code: 72)

S = Single, **D** = Double/Twin, **T** = Triple, **Q** = Quad, **b** = bathroom. Unless otherwise noted, English is spoken, breakfast is included, and credit cards are accepted. The hotel tax (350 Ft per person, per night) is not included in these rates.

To help you sort easily through these listings, I've divided the rooms into three categories, based on the price for a standard double room with bath:

$$$ Higher Priced—Most rooms 15,000 Ft or more.

$$ Moderately Priced—Most rooms between 10,000–15,000 Ft.

$ Lower Priced—Most rooms 10,000 Ft or less.

English-speaking helper in the busy summer months (Sb-8,100 Ft, Db-11,000 Ft, Tb-13,000 Ft, 1,000 Ft extra when air-con is turned on during hot weather—typically June–Aug, one room has private bathroom across the hall, Wi-Fi, Munkácsy Mihály utca 41, tel. 72/510-422, www.abrahamhotel.hu, abrahamhotel@invitel.hu).

$$ Szinbád Panzió is on a busy street in a dull urban area just outside the city wall. But it feels more hotelesque than the other mid-range options in town: Its public areas are classy, the 27 rooms are nice, and it's a short walk from the cathedral area (Sb-8,900 Ft, Db-11,300 Ft, Tb-14,200 Ft, request quieter courtyard room, fee for Internet access, free Wi-Fi in some rooms, Klimó György utca 9, tel. 72/221-110, www.szinbadpanzio.hu, szinbadpanzio @freemail.hu).

$$ Aranyhajó Fogadó ("Golden Ship Inn"), a lesser value, is ideally situated at the start of the Király utca pedestrian zone. In operation since the 18th century, the 18 rooms are old and a bit musty, with once-classy furniture (Sb-11,250 Ft, Db-14,600 Ft, Tb-17,850 Ft, pedestrian street out front can be noisy after hours—ask for quieter room in back, Király utca 3, tel. 72/210-685, www .aranyhajo.hu, hotel@aranyhajo.hu).

$ Náp Hostel ("Sun") is a colorful new hostel well-run by Tamás. Hiding upstairs in an apartment building on the main walking street, its four bedrooms share three WCs and two show-ers (D-11,000 Ft, bunk in 8-bed dorm-3,000 Ft, in 6-bed dorm-3,500 Ft, in 6-bed dorm with balcony-4,000 Ft, includes breakfast, Internet access and Wi-Fi, kitchen, laundry service, Király utca 23-25, tel. 72/950-684, www.naphostel.com).

PÉCS

EATING

On the Pedestrian Drag

The walking streets branching off from the main square (Király utca and Ferencesek utcája) are lined with restaurants and cafés that feature outdoor tables with ideal people-watching. Window-shop for your favorite, or try one of these.

Elefántos Ház ("House at the Elephant") features good Italian fare in its ho-hum interior or outdoors at inviting tables on a delightful shopping square in the town center (1,000–1,500-Ft pizzas and pastas, 2,000–3,000-Ft meat dishes, daily 11:30–23:30, Jókai tér 6, tel. 72/216-055).

Dóm Vendéglő, wonderfully located at the head of Király utca just off the main square, serves traditional Hungarian cuisine along with pizzas and other international dishes with indoor and outdoor seating (1,500–2,000-Ft main dishes, 1,000–1,500-Ft pizzas, 3,000-Ft steaks, daily 11:00–23:00, Király utca 3, tel. 72/210-088).

Oázis is the place for a simple, cheap, fast, and good gyro or falafel. Grab one to go, or enjoy it at their outdoor tables on the main walking street (600-Ft sandwiches, daily 10:00–23:00, Király utca 17).

Elsewhere in Pécs

Trafik, in the ground floor of the Apollo art-house cinema, offers international fare with an Italian flair, in a cool and trendy bar atmosphere (1,000–2,000-Ft main dishes, Mon–Fri 12:00–24:00, Sat 18:00–24:00, closed Sun, Perczel Miklós utca 22, tel. 72/212-672).

Aranykacsa ("Golden Duck") is in all the guidebooks thanks to its well-respected, traditional Hungarian fare, specializing in duck (1,000–2,000-Ft main dishes, pricier duck specialties, Tue–Sat 11:30–22:00, Sun 11:30–15:30, closed Mon, Teréz utca 4, tel. 72/518-860).

TRANSPORTATION CONNECTIONS

From Pécs by Train: For most destinations in this book (including **Eger, Sopron,** and **Bratislava**), you'll first have to change trains in Budapest. Direct trains connect Pécs and **Budapest** (8/day, 3 hrs, a few additional connections possible with a transfer at the suburban Budapest-Kelenföld station). One handy train each afternoon follows a different route, near the Croatian border, connecting Pécs directly to **Sopron** (4.75 hrs), then **Vienna** (6 hrs).

SOPRON

Sopron (SHOH-prohn), nestled in the foothills of the Alps a stone's throw from Austria, is a picture-perfect little Baroque town jam-packed with historic buildings. Its square—watched over by the town's symbol, the Fire Tower—is one of the most romantic in Hungary. Because Austrians flock over the border to sightsee, sample the local wine, and get dental work done (at a fraction of the cost back home), the town's streets are lined with modest museums and dentist's offices.

Sopron, populated since Roman times, was a stop on the Amber Route of trade between the Adriatic and Baltic Seas. As a Hungarian backwater of Austria's Vienna, the town has long been a unique, bilingual mix of Hungarian and Germanic culture. But it's always remained true to Hungary, most famously after World War I, when residents voted to stick with the Magyars rather than becoming part of Austria—giving it the nickname "the most loyal city." Even so, its proximity to Austria keeps Sopron in touch with its Germanic heritage. Today Sopron caters almost entirely to its German-speaking tourists (while English is in short supply).

Sopron is sleepy...maybe *too* sleepy. After dark, the Main Square is magical—but deserted. Museum attendants react to your visit as though they've never seen a tourist before. With a little more restoration and liveliness in the Old Town, it could become a major draw. For now, this not-quite-ready-for-prime-time Hungarian burg is a delightful hidden secret.

Planning Your Time

Sopron deserves a half-day. A few hours is more than enough time to exhaust its sightseeing options, and its sleepiness makes the initial "Oh, wow!" wear off quickly. It fits perfectly on a trip between Budapest and Vienna (adding about an hour to your total train time). Consider arriving at midday, spending the afternoon here, then either taking a late train out, or spending the night and leaving the next morning.

On a brief visit, check your bag at the station and do a spin through the Old Town. With a little more time, explore the Ikva neighborhood northeast of town. If you're here for a while, head into the Lővér Hills.

ORIENTATION

(area code: 99)

Sopron, with about 60,000 inhabitants, is a manageable small city. The compact tourist zone of the Old Town (Belváros) contains most of Sopron's attractions, and you can walk from one end to the other in less than 10 minutes. A ring road (Várkerület) that follows the former outer walls sur-

rounds the Old Town, and the gently rolling Lővér Hills embrace the entire city.

Tourist Information

Sopron's TI hands out maps and brochures about the town. There are two branches: The main one is in the big, yellow Franz Liszt Cultural Center at the southwest corner of the Old Town (Liszt Ferenc utca 1), and another office is at the long park called Deák tér, halfway between the Old Town and the train station (both open June–Sept Mon–Fri 9:00–17:00, Sat–Sun 9:00–14:00; Oct–May Mon–Fri 9:00–17:00, Sat 9:00–12:00, closed Sun; tel. 99/517-560, www.sopron.hu). The main office has information on and sells tickets for local cultural events.

Arrival in Sopron

By Train: Sopron's compact little train station is situated an easy half-mile walk south of the Old Town. A left-luggage office is inside the station (per bag: 150 Ft/6 hrs, 300 Ft/day, same hours as station—3:00 in the morning until 24:00). Domestic ticket windows line the main wall; the international ticket window is to the left as you face the exit (near the taxi sign, look for *nemzetközi jegypénztár/internazionale kasse*). There are bus stops in front of the station (#1 and #2 take you into the Lővér Hills) and (to the right) a giant Spar supermarket with an ATM.

It's a 10-minute **walk** into the Old Town—just go straight out of the station and head up Mátyás király utca ("King Matthias Street") toward the big yellow building in the distance. After two blocks, you'll cross the long, skinny park called Deák tér; a TI branch is on your right. Go two blocks farther to Széchenyi tér, cross into this park, turn left at the flagpole (commemorating Hungarian uprisings throughout history), and look for the big, yellow building on the right (the Franz Liszt Cultural Center). The main TI is here, and the street next to it—Templom utca ("Church Street")—is the main drag through the Old Town.

Getting Around Sopron

If you're staying at one of my recommended accommodations, you probably won't need to use a bus (200 Ft, 175 Ft in advance from kiosk). A taxi ride from the Old Town to the Lőver Hills (the farthest any tourist is likely to go) shouldn't cost more than 700 Ft (taxi tel. 99/333-333).

SIGHTS

Old Town (Belváros)

Sopron's Old Town is peppered with museums, but only a few are worthwhile (if tight on time or money, visit the Storno House and climb the Fire Tower, but skip the rest). Notice that these sights are listed in order of a handy orientation walk (which begins where the "Arrival in Sopron" directions, above, leave off).

• *Begin exploring the town in front of the TI and the yellow...*

Franz Liszt Cultural Center—The huge building is boldly marked with the words *Magyar Művelődés Háza* ("House of Hungarian Culture") to show up their Germanic rivals. Its current name honors the composer who performed his first-ever public concert here in Sopron in 1820, when he was only nine years old. You'll see "Liszt played here" signs all over town.

• *Now head into the Old Town on...*

Templom Utca ("Church Street")—This was where important local bigwigs lived: mayors, lawyers, and intelligentsia. The town's sturdy wall spared it from being devastated by the Tatar and Ottoman invaders that reshaped much of Hungary. However, a fire, quickly spread by the strong winds that blow through this valley, consumed the town in 1676. Sopron was rebuilt in Baroque style (often over earlier Gothic cellars), which has left it colorful and tidy-looking. You'll notice that every other building has a *MŰEMLÉK* ("historical monument") plaque. Although lots of locally important people and events have graced Sopron, very little of it is meaningful to visitors. Don't worry about the nitty-gritty of the town's history—just enjoy its ambience.

Near the end of the block, at #12 (on the left), go into the

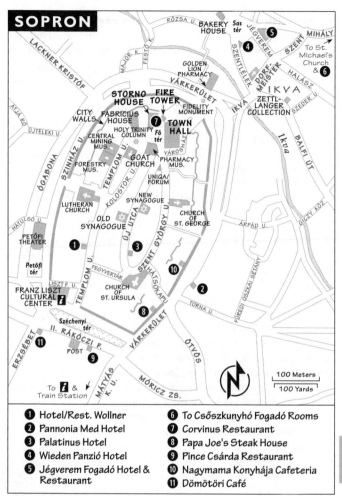

SOPRON

1. Hotel/Rest. Wollner
2. Pannonia Med Hotel
3. Palatinus Hotel
4. Wieden Panzió Hotel
5. Jégverem Fogadó Hotel & Restaurant
6. To Csőszkunyhó Fogadó Rooms
7. Corvinus Restaurant
8. Papa Joe's Steak House
9. Pince Csárda Restaurant
10. Nagymama Konyhája Cafeteria
11. Dömötöri Café

Gothic passage, which leads into a little courtyard with a Renaissance/Baroque porch, showing the evolution of the local architecture.

Back on the main street and a few steps down, the big church on the left is Lutheran. Because the local mayor protected the rights of religious minorities, Sopron was unusually tolerant, attracting groups who were persecuted elsewhere (such as Lutherans at the time of the Reformation).

• *When the road forks at the green building, take the left fork. In the next block on the left are two very modest museums, dedicated to Sopron's major industries. First, at #4, is the...*

Forestry Museum (Erdészeti Gyűjtemény)—While most of Hungary's geography consists of rolling plains and farmland, the area around Sopron is heavily wooded. This museum, part of the local Forestry College, celebrates that heritage, but has virtually no English information and is worthwhile only if you have a special interest (400 Ft, May–Oct Thu–Tue 13:00–17:00, Nov–April Thu–Tue 10:00–13:00, closed Wed, Templom utca 4, tel. 99/338-870). After the 1956 Uprising, there was an exodus of teachers and students from Sopron's Forestry College to Vancouver, British Columbia. To this day, Hungarians play a major role in the Canadian timber industry.

• *Next door at #2 is the town's slightly more interesting...*

Central Mining Museum (Központi Bányászati Múzeum)—Displayed around a courtyard in the beautiful town house of a powerful local family, this museum explains the lives of miners and the history of Hungarian mining and coinage, and features a life-size replica of a mine and small-scale working models of mining equipment. Collections include decorative items made of metal, and rock and mineral samples. Look for the little dioramas-in-bottles, created by miners (500 Ft, April–Oct Tue–Sun 10:00–18:00, Nov–March Tue–Sun 10:00–16:00, closed Mon, Templom utca 2, tel. 99/312-667).

• *At the end of the block, the street opens into the main square. Before exploring the square, visit the Gothic church on the right...*

Goat Church (Kecske Templom)—So nicknamed for the goat on the coat of arms over its door, this prominent Benedictine church is a Sopron landmark (free, summer daily 7:00–21:00, winter daily 8:00–18:00). While much of the rest of Hungary was occupied by the Ottomans, this region remained in Hungarian hands—and this church was actually used for a few royal coronations and parliament sessions. The humble Gothic interior is adorned with wood-carved Baroque altars and a Rococo pulpit. On the right, find the plaque listing the ancestors of István Széchenyi who are buried here. (Széchenyi was a powerful 18th-century aristocrat who championed  the rights of the poor and built, among other things, Budapest's Chain Bridge.) The door to the right leads around a little cloister to the chapter hall (free but donation requested; April–Sept Tue–Sun 10:00–12:00 & 13:00–18:00, Thu until 17:00, closed Mon; Oct–March Tue–Sun 10:00–12:00 & 13:00–15:00, closed Mon). Borrow the English descriptions, which explain that the carvings that top the columns represent human sins.

• *Leaving the church, you're in the middle of Sopron's...*

▲▲**Main Square (Fő Tér)**—One of the most appealing Old World squares in Hungary, this area is dominated by the giant

Holy Trinity Column, erected in 1701 to commemorate a plague that had occurred six years earlier. The wealthy local couple who commissioned the column kneel at its base. Above them, the column corkscrews up to heaven, marked by Jesus, God the Father, and a dove representing the Holy Spirit. Gleeful cherubs ride back down the column like a waterslide.

Grand buildings surround the column. Orient yourself with the Goat Church to your back: On the left is the big, white Neoclassical County Hall. To the right of it are three historic houses, two of which house museums.

The tall Fire Tower is the town's main landmark. Next to it is the vast, yellow 19th-century Town Hall, in the eye-pleasing Historicist style of the day. (Those interested in ancient history can walk behind the Town Hall to see fragments of Roman-era Sopron, with posted English information.) Across from the Town Hall, the little yellow building sticking out into the square houses a very small **Pharmacy Museum** (Patika-Ház), which was a working pharmacy from 1642 to 1967 (you can see most everything from the door with a sweep of your head, or pay 400 Ft to examine the exhibits; April–Sept Tue–Sun 10:00–18:00, Oct–March Tue–Sun 14:00–18:00, closed Mon). In the early 16th century, local officials wanted to tear down this house to enlarge the square. But the king, who had visited Sopron earlier and enjoyed the square the way it was, decreed that it not be touched...making it Hungary's first government-protected building.

• *If you're ready for some museum-going, consider the two museums along the top of the square. The pretty Baroque house with the corner turret is the...*

▲▲**Storno House (Storno-Ház)**—This prime real estate is marked with plaques celebrating visits by two big-league Hungarians: King Mátyás (Matthias) Corvinus and Franz Liszt. Today the building houses two exhibits: the Storno Collection and the Local History Exhibition (1,000 Ft for both, April–Sept Tue–Sun 10:00–18:00, Oct–March Tue–Sun 14:00–18:00, closed Mon, Fő tér 8, tel. 99/311-327).

Sopron's best museum is the **Storno Collection** (Storno-Gyűjtemény). Franz Storno, the son of a poor 19th-century Swiss family of chimney sweeps, showed prodigious talent as an artist at a young age. He eventually moved here to Sopron, married a chimney-sweep master's widow, and became a restorer of buildings

for the Habsburg Empire. Today, in his creaky old house, attendants direct visitors through a series of jam-packed rooms to look at a random but fun grab-bag of paintings, decorative items, and other bric-a-brac that Franz collected in his renovation work. Take some time to look around and take in all the little details (borrow the English descriptions or rent the 200-Ft audioguide). In the first room, check out the panorama painting of 18th-century Sopron (high up on the wall). In the dining room, examine the painted leather chair. The balcony room boasts a gorgeously painted, light-filled alcove with table and chairs (as well as more paintings of old Sopron). The old iron box here has a complicated secret-locking system. Passing through the painted door into the bedroom, look for the Biedermeier paintings on the walls, and notice the grotesque little faces carved into the backs of the chairs. The antler chandelier shows a 3-D version of the family seal: chimney-sweeping brush in one hand, compass (for restoration work) in the other. Even after the family became wealthy, Storno's sons trained in both restoration work and the family business of chimney sweeping.

Downstairs is the **Local History Exhibition** (Helytörténeti Kiállítás), which traces the history of Sopron (no English information). Find the exhibit about the post–World War I referendum in which Sopron elected to remain part of Hungary instead of Austria. The referendum, which took place December 14–16, 1921, asked citizens to vote with color-coded ballots whether they would join Austria or Hungary. As you can see from the bilingual posters announcing the results, Hungary won 15,334 votes to Austria's 8,227. This cemented Sopron's already-established reputation as being the "most loyal town." (Maybe it was because other Austrians would never let them live down the town's German name, Ödenburg, which roughly means "Dullsville.") Nearby, you'll see propaganda trying to convince locals to vote one way or another—such as the unsettling poster of the skeleton, clad in traditional Hungarian folk costume, menacingly serenading the town on his violin.

• *Two buildings to the left of the Storno House is the...*

Fabricius House (Fabricius-Ház)—This historic mansion, once belonging to Sopron's most beloved mayor, is home to a pair of dull, skippable museums (700 Ft apiece, or 1,400 Ft for both, both open April–Sept Tue–Sun 10:00–18:00, Oct–March Tue–Sun 10:00–14:00, closed Mon, Fő tér 6). The **Civic Apartments** (Polgári

Lakások), basically a collection of old furniture, will appeal only to antique-lovers. The **Archaeological Exhibit** (Régészet-Kőtár) is a very dry overview of the history of Sopron, especially relating to the Amber Road trade route that put the town on the map. The best part is the Roman Lapidarium in the cellar (same ticket)—a collection of Roman tombstones unearthed here, as well as the shattered fragments of three larger-than-life Roman statues.

• *Dominating the Main Square is Sopron's symbol, the...*

Fire Tower (Tűztorony)—A Roman watchtower once stood here, but the current version was gradually expanded from the 13th to the 18th centuries. Fire watchmen would survey the town from the top of the tower, then mark the direction of a fire with colorful flags (by day) or a bright light (at night) to warn townspeople. Just above the passage through the gate is a stone carving depicting Hungária, the female embodiment of Hungary—given to the city to thank them for choosing Hungary during the 1921 referendum.

Buy your ticket and climb the 120 steps to the top (700 Ft; May–mid-Sept daily 10:00–20:00; April and mid-Sept–Oct Tue–Sun 10:00–18:00, closed Mon; closed Nov–March, Fő tér 1). On the way up, pause at the landings to check out the exhibits. There are historic photos and drawings of the tower, and the original double-headed Habsburg eagle—with an "L" for the Emperor Leopold—that topped the tower's spire.

At the top, do a clockwise spin: First is a great view over the rooftops of the Old Town; beyond that, you can see the Lőver

Hills, Sopron's playground. (While the name sounds romantic, *lőver* refers to master archers who defended the border from Tatar invasions in the 13th century.) Continuing around the tower and looking down, you'll see remains of the city wall defining the Old Town; an outer wall was once located on the outside of today's ring road. Beyond the stadium lights is Austria. A bit farther to the right, the big steeple in the distance is St. Michael's, one of Sopron's historic churches. Farther to the right, the oddly shaped bulbous tower on the hill is a windmill missing its blades. This was used to garrison Habsburg troops after the 1848 Revolution.

• *Descending from the tower, continue through the gateway.*

Outside the Walls—Just on the other side of the tower, look for the giant **key monument** on the left, commemorating a "key" event in this loyal town's history. After presenting the Hungarian king with the key to their city when his rival was planning an invasion, Sopron was rewarded with free royal town status, which came with special privileges (in 1277). Just beyond is the entrance to the **City Wall Walk** (Várfal Sétány), where you can walk along part of the course of the surviving wall (not particularly scenic since it's outside the wall rather than on top of it; free, Mon–Fri 9:00–20:00, Sat–Sun 9:00–18:00).

Continue toward the ring road, and look (on your left) for a modern **sculpture** with three figures, each one representing a time when Sopron demonstrated its fidelity: 1277, when the town sided with the Hungarian king (described above); 1921, when they voted to remain part of Hungary; and 1989, when the Iron Curtain fell (symbolized by the woman breaking the barbed wire). In August of that fateful year—before the communists had officially given up the ghost—the "Pan-European Picnic" took place in the hills near Sopron. Residents of various Central European countries—East Germany, Austria, and Hungary—came together for the first time in decades, offering a tantalizing taste of freedom.

Across the busy ring road from this sculpture, look for the **Golden Lion Pharmacy** (*Gyógyszertár Apotheke* sign), which has beautiful Art Nouveau Zsolnay porcelain decorations.

Looking back toward the Old Town, notice the **colorful little shops** that cling like baby animals to the protective town walls.

• *From here, you can backtrack to the Main Square and head down New Street to a pair of other sights (described next). Or keep going beyond the walls into the Ikva neighborhood (described in the "Ikva Neighborhood" section on next page).*

New Street (Új Utca)—This misnamed street is actually one of the oldest in town. At the start of the street (a few steps down from the Main Square), the **Uniqa insurance office** is the unlikely home of a museum. Stepping into the lobby, you'll see a Roman column extending below ground level. Buy a ticket at the desk and head down into the cellar to see remains from the forum (main square) of Sopron's Roman settlement (300 Ft, no English info, Mon–Thu 8:00–17:00, Fri 8:00–13:30, closed Sat–Sun, Új utca 1, tel. 99/321-804).

Continue down New Street—which used to be called "**Jewish Street**" (Zsidó utca) until the Jews were kicked out in 1526. After the 1848 Revolution, they finally returned...but for less than a century. When the Nazis took control of Hungary, they walled off both ends of this street and turned it into a ghetto. Some 1,840 Sopron Jews were eventually sent to concentration camps...where 1,650 of them died. Along the street are two synagogues. The first is the **New Synagogue** (Új Zsinagóga), in a modern office on the left at #11. It's not a museum, but if the door is open you can peek inside.

A few steps down, on the right at #22, is the **Old Synagogue** (Ó Zsinagóga), dating from the early 14th century (600 Ft, borrow English descriptions, May–Oct Tue–Sun 10:00–18:00, closed Mon and Nov–April, Új utca 22, tel. 99/311-327). Rediscovered in 1968, it has been renovated but still retains a few of its original elements (such as the Torah holder). Notice the two adjacent rooms, separated by narrow windows: Men worshipped in the main room, with the women in the smaller room. In the courtyard is a reconstruction of a ritual bath.

• *New Street ends at Ursula Square (Orsolya tér), watched over by the Church of St. Ursula and a statue of Mary that stands in the center of the square. If you double back to the left, you can head up the third of old Sopron's three parallel streets...*

St. George's Street (Szent György Utca)—This street is named for the red-and-white **Church of St. George** (free, daily 8:00–18:00). The beautiful, stuccoed Baroque interior hosted Lutheran services for a time, but the Lutherans were evicted during the Counter-Reformation. Head across the street and into the fine Renaissance courtyard at #12, where the Lutherans were forced to worship al fresco. Notice the stone pulpit carved into the upper balcony, and the metal rings used to secure a tarp that covered the service in bad weather.

• *St. George's Street will take you right back up to the Main Square, where—if you haven't already—you can head into...*

The Ikva Neighborhood, Northeast of the Old Town

With a little more time, venture into the workaday streets northeast of the Old Town—beyond the ring road and the Ikva brook (hidden here beneath the road). While lacking the storybook charm of the Old Town, this area is also historic. Back when wealthy

SOPRON

aristocrats populated the Old Town, farmers and craftsmen lived here—giving it a rustic, lived-in ambience that's fun to explore. (It's also home to several recommended accommodations, and the good Jégverem restaurant—see "Sleeping" and "Eating," later in this chapter.)

The main drag changes names as it twists through this neighborhood (first called Ikva híd, then Dorfmeister utca, then Szent Mihály utca). Eventually it leads up a hill to **St. Michael's Church** (Szent Mihály Templom) and the adjacent little Romanesque chapel. The church complex is surrounded by a cemetery.

• *Closer to the Old Town, just up Bécsi út from Sas tér, is the adorable...*

▲**Bakery House (Pék-Ház)**—This modest but strangely fascinating little museum shows off the living quarters, bakehouse, and shop of Sopron's baker, dating from the 19th century. While most surviving European homes from this era are posh and snooty, the baker lived a simple life, with rough wooden-beam floors, humble furniture, and a Seven-Dwarves charm. Over one bed is a wedding portrait from 1887. Out in the courtyard, look for the pulley that brought up water from the well. In the bakehouse, you'll see the ovens and tools used to make bread and other edibles (such as molds for chocolate or marzipan). Dough was placed in the long cabinet to rise, and then kneaded on top of it. It's easy to imagine making bread today using this same gear. The shop, which was later converted into a sweet shop, has little tables where people could sit and socialize—not unlike the cafés of today. The animated monolingual grannies who eagerly show off the exhibits add to its appeal (400 Ft, not a word of English, April–Sept Tue–Sun 14:00–18:00, closed Mon and Oct–March, Bécsi utca 5).

• *Closer to the Belváros, but still in the Ikva neighborhood, is one final Sopron sight...*

Zettl-Langer Collection (Zettl-Langer Gyűjtemény)—This eclectic private collection includes furniture, porcelain, paintings, an armory collection, and more (500 Ft; April–Oct Tue–Sun 10:00–12:00, closed Mon; Nov–Jan and March, Fri–Sun 10:00–12:00, closed Mon–Thu; closed Feb; Balfi utca 11, tel. 99/311-136).

Hiking

With its forested hillsides and fresh air, Sopron is popular with hikers. To get to the best trailhead, take bus #1 or #2 from the Old Town to Lővér Körút, and get off at the giant domed bath complex. From here, several trails lead through the hills. Before setting out, get advice from the TI (they can give you a free map, or sell you a better one).

SLEEPING

Few places have air-conditioning; even fewer have an elevator (I've noted those that do).

In or near the Old Town

You'll pay a bit extra to be right in the Old Town. But it's worth it—not for the convenience, but for the romance of calling those floodlit cobbles home after dark.

$$$ Hotel Wollner, clearly the top option in Sopron, is pure class. This 300-year-old Baroque townhouse on the Old Town's main street was thoroughly renovated in 2000 and has 18 tastefully appointed rooms. A good restaurant and an inviting terraced garden out back round out its appeal (Sb-15,900 Ft, Db-18,600 Ft, Tb-23,800 Ft, entirely non-smoking, Templom utca 20, tel. 99/524-400, www.wollner.hu, wollner@fullnet.hu).

$$$ Pannonia Med Hotel, a Best Western, rents 62 rooms on the ring road just across from the Old Town. As you're paying a premium for its big-hotel services, it's a bit overpriced (Sb-18,900 Ft, smaller "classic" Db with older furnishings-20,900 Ft, bigger and newer "comfort" Db with air-con-28,900 Ft, "antique suite" with fancy old furniture-31,900 Ft, elevator, free Internet access, fee for Wi-Fi, street noise—ask for quieter room, Várkerület 75, tel. 99/312-180, www.pannoniahotel.com, sopron@pannonia hotel.com).

SOPRON

$$ Palatinus Hotel is a soulless, tour-oriented place with 31 rooms. But it's well-priced and ideally located in the heart of the Old Town. I'd splurge and pay extra for the new-feeling "superior" rooms, which are much nicer than the rickety old "standard" rooms (Sb-8,100 Ft, Db-11,400 Ft, about 1,100 Ft/person extra for "superior" rooms, three floors with no elevator, non-smoking rooms, fee for Wi-Fi, Új utca 23, tel. 99/523-816, www.palatinussopron.com, info@palatinussopron.com).

Northeast of the Old Town

These three accommodations are just outside the ring road. While not as romantic as the Old Town, this appealing residential zone is also historic. The first two places are a five-minute, slightly uphill walk from the Old Town, while the third is about five minutes farther up.

$$ Wieden Panzió has 15 crisp, newly renovated rooms (Sb-8,000 Ft, Db-11,000 Ft, Tb-14,000 Ft, some very large rooms also available, free Wi-Fi, some street noise, Sas tér 13, tel. 99/523-222, www.wieden.hu, wieden@fullnet.hu).

$ Jégverem Fogadó ("Ice House Inn"), also listed under "Eating," rents five cheap, simple rooms above its busy restaurant. While the beds are an afterthought to the food, they plan to build a pension nearby soon (Sb-7,000 Ft, Db-9,000 Ft, extra bed-2,000 Ft, breakfast extra—most options around 500 Ft, cash only, Jégverem utca 1, tel. 99/510-113, www.jegverem.hu).

$ Csőszkunyhó Fogadó ("Field Guard's Shelter") sits across the street from St. Michael's Church, on a small hill near the Old Town. Above this local restaurant are two beautiful, spacious, woody rooms—the nicest I saw in Sopron in this price range (Sb-6,200 Ft, Db-8,900 Ft, Tb-12,600 Ft, cash only, limited English, Szent Mihály utca 35, tel. 99/506-588, www.csoszkunyho.atw.hu, csoszkunyho@gmail.com).

EATING

You might notice lots of bean dishes on the menu in Sopron. The thrifty Germans—who were responsible for most of the wine-making in the surrounding hills—would plant beans in the earth between their rows of vines. In fact, in local dialect, German residents are called "bean farmers."

Jégverem Fogadó ("Ice House Inn") serves up heaping plates of reliably tasty Hungarian food from a clever, descriptive menu. It's worth the five-minute walk outside the Old Town (near several recommended accommodations). The circular table in the middle of the cozy dining room peers down into a pit where ice was stored

SOPRON

to be sold through the hot summer months. In good weather, sit out on the inviting terrace. This eatery has earned its place in all the guidebooks for its good food at a good price. The half-portions are plenty for most eaters (1,000–2,000-Ft meals, daily 11:00–23:00, Jégverem utca 1, tel. 99/510-113).

Corvinus, across from the City Hall and in the shadow of the Fire Tower, is a no-brainer for a romantic al fresco dinner on the Main Square. The place sprawls into a wine cellar and its sister restaurant next door, the Generális café (1,000–2,000-Ft Hungarian and international dishes, also indoor seating, daily 11:30-22:00, Fő tér 7–8, tel. 99/505-035).

Hotel Wollner, also listed under "Sleeping," offers Hungarian fare and a long wine list. Choose to sit either in the tasteful dining room or out in the courtyard (2,000–3,000-Ft main dishes, daily 7:00–22:00, Templom utca 20, tel. 99/524-400).

Papa Joe's, an American-style steakhouse, had my travel sensibilities crying, "No!"—but my stomach saying, "Hmmmm... maybe." Here's your chance to experience the Old West through Hungarian eyes. Done up to the nines like a cowboy saloon (including six shooter–handle doorknobs and saddle barstools), this theme restaurant grills up steaks and other Tex-Mex dishes (such as baked beans). When Hungarians want a break from Hungarian food, they go here (1,000–3,000-Ft steaks, 1,500–2,000-Ft main dishes, daily 11:00–24:00, Várkerület 108, tel. 99/340-933).

Pince Csárda ("Csárda Cellar") is the place for cheap, unpretentious, stick-to-your-ribs Hungarian grub, served in a straightforward cellar with not a tourist in sight, just across Széchenyi tér from the Old Town (1,000–1,500-Ft main dishes, daily lunch specials get you a full meal and drink for less than 1,000 Ft, daily 11:00–22:00, Széchenyi tér 5, tel. 99/319-023).

Fast and Cheap: **Nagymama Konyhája** ("Grandma's Kitchen") is your best option for a quick, no-frills meal. This small self-service cafeteria, filled with locals, specializes in savory and sweet crêpes (*palacsinta,* see English menu, 500–600 Ft), but you can also get traditional Hungarian food—just point to what you want (700–800 Ft for most meals, Mon–Sat 10:00–21:00, Sun 12:00–21:00, Várkerület 104, mobile 0620-315-8730).

Coffee and Cake: **Dömötöri** is a pastry and coffee shop slinging a wide array of cakes—with seating in a classy interior, and out on a pretty square across from the big, yellow Franz Liszt Center. It's where locals satisfy their sweet tooth (Mon–Thu 7:00–22:00, Fri–Sat 7:00–23:00, Sun 8:00–22:00, 300-Ft desserts, Széchenyi tér 13, tel. 99/506-623).

TRANSPORTATION CONNECTIONS

From Sopron by Train to: Budapest (7/day direct, 3 hrs, more with a transfer in Győr), **Eger** (about every 2 hrs, 5–6 hrs, transfer in Budapest and sometimes also in Füzesabony), **Pécs** (1/day direct, 4.75 hrs; otherwise about every 2 hrs, 6.5 hrs, most transfer at Budapest's suburban Kelenföld station), **Bratislava,** Slovakia (at least hourly, 2.5 hrs, transfer at Vienna's Südbahnhof), **Vienna,** Austria (1–2/hr, 1.25 hrs).

BRATISLAVA, SLOVAKIA

Pozsony/Pressburg

Bratislava, long a drab lesson in the failings of the communist system, is turning things around...fast. A decade ago, the city center was grim, deserted, and dangerous—a place where only thieves and fools dared to tread. Today it's downright charming, bursting with colorfully restored facades, lively outdoor cafés, swanky boutiques, in-love-with-life locals, and (on sunny days) an almost Mediterranean ambience.

The rejuvenation doesn't end in the Old Town. The ramshackle quarter to the east is gradually being flattened and redeveloped into a new forest of skyscrapers. Bratislava is working together with its neighbor Vienna to forge a new super-capital for trade and commerce, bridging the former Western Europe and the former Eastern Europe. The hilltop castle is getting a facelift. And even the glum commie suburb of Petržalka is getting a Technicolor makeover. Before our eyes, Bratislava is becoming the quintessential post-communist Central European city...what can happen when government and business leaders make a concerted effort to jump-start a failing city.

You get the feeling that workaday Bratislavans—who strike some visitors as gruff—are being pulled to the cutting edge of the 21st century kicking and screaming. But many Slovaks embrace the changes, and fancy themselves as the yang to Vienna's yin: If Vienna is a staid, elderly aristocrat sipping coffee, then Bratislava is a vivacious young professional jet-setting around Europe.

Bratislava is not worth going far out of your way for. But its priceless location—on the Danube (and the tourist circuit) smack-dab between Budapest and Vienna—makes it worth considering as an illuminating "on the way" destination. Frankly, the city used to leave me cold. But all the new changes are positively inspiring. See Bratislava now...in a few years, it'll be a different city.

Welcome to Slovakia

In many ways, Slovakia is the "West Virginia of Europe"—poor and relatively undeveloped, but spectacularly beautiful in its own rustic way. Sitting quietly in the very center of Central Europe, wedged between bigger and stronger nations (Hungary, Austria, the Czech Republic, and Poland), Slovakia was brutally disfigured by the communists, then overshadowed by the Czechs. But in recent years, this fledgling republic has begun to find its wings.

With about 5.4 million people in a country of 19,000 square miles (similar to Massachusetts and New Hampshire combined), Slovakia is one of Europe's smallest nations. Recent economic reforms are causing two very different Slovakias to emerge: the modern, industrialized, flat, affluent west, centered on the capital of Bratislava; and the remote, poorer, mountainous, "backwards" east, with high unemployment and traditional lifestyles. Slovakia is quite ethnically diverse: In addition to the Slavic Slovaks, there are Hungarians (about 10 percent of the population, "stranded" here when Hungary lost this land after World War I) and Roma (Gypsies, also about 10 percent). Slovakia has struggled to incorporate both of these large and often-mistreated minority groups.

Slovakia has spent most of its history as someone else's backyard. For centuries, Slovakia was ruled from Budapest and known as "Upper Hungary." At other times, it was an important chunk of the Habsburg Empire, ruled from neighboring Vienna. But most people think first of another era: the 75 years that Slovakia was joined with the Czech Republic as the country of "Czechoslovakia." From its start in the aftermath of World War I, this union of the Czechs and Slovaks was troubled; some Slovaks

Planning Your Time

A few hours is enough to get the gist of Bratislava. Head straight for the Old Town and follow my self-guided walk, dropping into your choice of museums. With more time, ascend to the "UFO" observation deck atop the funky suspension bridge. Or hike up to the castle, which offers great views over town (even though its interior is closed for renovation). Spend the night if you like, but I find hotel values and evening fun better in Budapest and Vienna.

chafed at being ruled from Prague, while many Czechs resented the financial burden of their poorer neighbors to the east.

After they gained their freedom from the communists during 1989's peaceful "Velvet Revolution," the Czechs and Slovaks began to think of the future. The Slovaks wanted to rename the country Czecho-Slovakia, and to redistribute powers to give themselves more autonomy within the union. The Czechs balked, relations gradually deteriorated, and the Slovak nationalist candidate Vladimír Mečiar fared surprisingly well in the 1992 elections. Taking it as a sign that the two peoples wanted to part ways, politicians pushed through (in just three months) the peaceful separation of the now-independent Czech and Slovak Republics. (The people in both countries never actually voted on the change, and most opposed it.) The "Velvet Divorce" became official on January 1, 1993.

At first the Slovaks struggled. Communist rule had been particularly unkind to them, and their economy was in a shambles. Visionary leaders set forth bold solutions, including the 2003 implementation of a Steve Forbes–style flat tax (19 percent), followed by EU membership in 2004. And before long, a funny thing started happening...major international corporations began to notice the same thing the communists had: This is a great place to build stuff, thanks to a magnificent location, low labor costs, and a well-trained workforce. Multiple foreign automakers have built plants here, making the country the world's biggest car producer (per capita) and leading the *New York Times* to dub Slovakia "the European Detroit."

While the flat tax is not without its critics—especially in the very impoverished eastern half of the country, where poor people feel they're becoming even poorer—there's no doubt it has been a boon for middle-class areas in the west. In 2007, Slovakia had Europe's fastest-growing economy (10.4 percent). And in 2009, Slovakia became the first former Warsaw Pact country to adopt the euro currency.

ORIENTATION

(area code: 02)

Bratislava, with nearly half a million residents, is Slovakia's capital and biggest city. It has a small, colorful Old Town (Staré Mesto), with the castle on the hill above it. This small area is surrounded by a vast construction zone of new buildings and a few colorized communist suburbs (including Petržalka, across the river). The north and west of the city is hilly and cool (these "Little Carpathians" are draped with vineyards), while the south and east is flat and warmer.

Tourist Information

The TI has two branches in the heart of the city. There's a small window in the **train station** (June–Oct Mon–Fri 8:00–19:00, Sat–Sun 9:00–17:00; Nov–May Mon–Fri 9:00–17:00, Sat–Sun 9:00–14:00; tel. 02/5249-5906), and a main branch on **Primate's Square** behind the Old Town Hall (June–Sept Mon–Fri 8:30–19:00, Sat 9:00–17:00, Sun 10:00–17:00; Oct–May Mon–Fri 8:30–18:00, Sat 9:00–16:00, Sun 10:00–15:00; Klobučnícka 2, tel. 02/5443-3715, www.bkis.sk and www.bratislava.sk). There are also TI windows at the airport and passenger boat terminals.

At any TI, pick up the free *Bratislava Guide* (with map) and browse their brochures. They can help you find a room for a modest fee. The **Bratislava City Card,** which includes free transit and sightseeing discounts, is worthwhile only if you're doing the Old Town walking tour (see "Tours," later in this section; €10/day, includes walking tour April–Oct, 50 percent discount on tour Nov–March, sold at TI).

Arrival in Bratislava

By Train: Bratislava's Main Train Station, called Bratislava Hlavná Stanica, is about a half-mile north of the Old Town. The city plans to tear down most of the station and start from scratch in the next few years (to accommodate, among other things, a new high-speed rail line connecting Bratislava to Paris). Therefore, these arrival instructions are likely to change; just look for signs or ask the TI for help.

As you emerge from the tracks, the TI is down the hall to your left, and the left-luggage desk is to your right (€1–2, depending on size; look for *ú schovňa batožín;* there are no lockers, and the check desk usually closes for 30-min lunch and dinner breaks—try to confirm that they'll be there when you get back if you'll be rushing to catch a train).

It's an easy 15-minute **walk** to the town center. Leave straight ahead and walk to the busy cross street. Take the overpass across the street, and continue straight on Štefánikova. This formerly elegant old boulevard is lined with rotting facades from Bratislava's high-on-the-hog Habsburg era. After about 10 minutes, you'll pass the nicely manicured presidential gardens on your left, then the Grassalkovich Palace, Slovakia's "White House." Continue straight through the busy intersection onto Súche Mýho, and head for the green onion-domed steeple (get there by taking the narrow street next to the mod, green, white-capped Alizé restaurant). This is St. Michael's Gate, at the start of the Old Town (and my self-guided walk, described later in this chapter).

If you want to shave a few minutes off the trip, you can go part of the way by **tram** (from train station's main hall, with tracks at your back, look for signs to *električky* on left; take escalator down, buy a €0.60/30-minute ticket from the machine, hop on tram #13, ride it to Poštová, then walk straight down Obchodná street).

The Main Train Station described above is the most convenient place to arrive. But if you wind up instead at Bratislava's other major train station (called "ŽST Petržalka"), in the **Petržalka** suburb, you can take bus #80, #93, #94, or #N93 to the Zochova stop (near St. Michael's Gate), or bus #91 or #191 to the Nový Most stop (at the Old Town end of the New Bridge). Buses #93 (by day) and #N93 (by night) also connect the two stations.

By Boat or Plane: For information on Bratislava's riverboats and airport, see "Transportation Connections," at the end of this chapter.

Helpful Hints

Money: Slovakia officially adopted the euro currency in January of 2009 (€1 = about $1.40). You'll find ATMs at the train stations and airport. For more on this currency, see page 11. You might still see references to the old currency, the Slovak *koruna* (30 Sk = about €1).

Language: While many people in Bratislava speak English, the official language is Slovak (closely related to Czech and Polish). The local "ciao"—used informally for both "hi" and "bye"—is easy to remember: *ahoj* (pronounced "AH-hoy," like a pirate). "Please" is *prosím* (PROH-seem), "thank you" is *ďakujem* (DYAH-koo-yehm), and "Cheers!" is *Na zdravie!* (nah ZDRAH-vyeh).

Phone Tips: Slovakia's phone system works differently from Hungary's. When calling locally (such as within Bratislava), dial the number without the area code. To make a long-distance call within Slovakia, start with the area code (which begins with 0). Slovakia's country code is 421. To call from Hungary to Slovakia, you'd dial 00-421, then the area code minus the initial zero, then the number (from the US, dial 011-421-area code minus zero, then the number). To call from Slovakia to Hungary, you'd dial 00-36, then the complete area code and number.

Internet Access: You'll see signs advertising Internet cafés around the Old Town. If you have a laptop with Wi-Fi, you can get online free at the three main squares in the Old Town (Old Town Square, Primate's Square, and Hviezdoslav Square).

Local Guidebook: For in-depth suggestions on Bratislava sightseeing, dining, and more, look for the excellent and eye-pleasing *Bratislava Active* guidebook by Martin Sloboda (see "Tours," next; around €10, sold at every postcard rack).

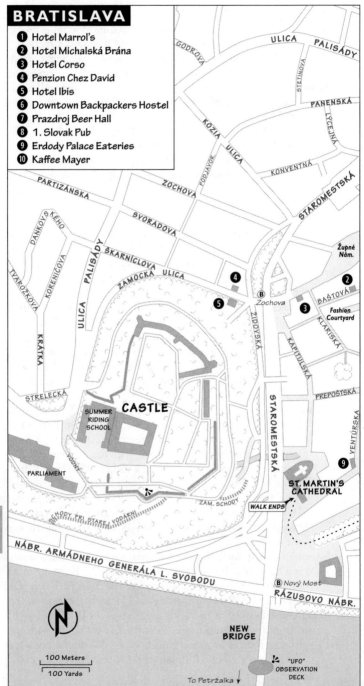

BRATISLAVA

1. Hotel Marrol's
2. Hotel Michalská Brána
3. Hotel Corso
4. Penzion Chez David
5. Hotel Ibis
6. Downtown Backpackers Hostel
7. Prazdroj Beer Hall
8. 1. Slovak Pub
9. Erdody Palace Eateries
10. Kaffee Mayer

ULICA PALISÁDY

GODROVA

ŠTETINOVA

PANENSKÁ

LYCEJNÁ

KOZIA ULICA

PODJAVOR

KONVENTNÁ

STAROMESTSKÁ

PARTIZÁNSKA

ZOCHOVA

DANKOVSKÉHO

TVARÓŽKOVA

KORENILCOVA

ULICA PALISÁDY

SVORADOVA

ŠKARNICLOVA

Žúpné Nám.

ZÁMOCKÁ ULICA

4

2

BAŠTOVÁ

B Zochova

3

Fashion Courtyard

5

ŽIDOVSKÁ

KLARISKA

KRÁTKA

KAPITULSKÁ

PREPOŠTSKÁ

STRELECKÁ

CASTLE

SUMMER RIDING SCHOOL

VODNY

STAROMESTSKÁ

VENTÚRSKA

9

PARLIAMENT

ST. MARTIN'S CATHEDRAL

ZAM. SCHODY

WALK ENDS

SCHODY PRI STAREJ VODÁRNI

NÁBR. ARMÁDNEHO GENERÁLA L. SVOBODU

B Nový Most

RÁZUSOVO NÁBR.

N

100 Meters
100 Yards

NEW BRIDGE

"UFO" OBSERVATION DECK

To Petržalka ↓

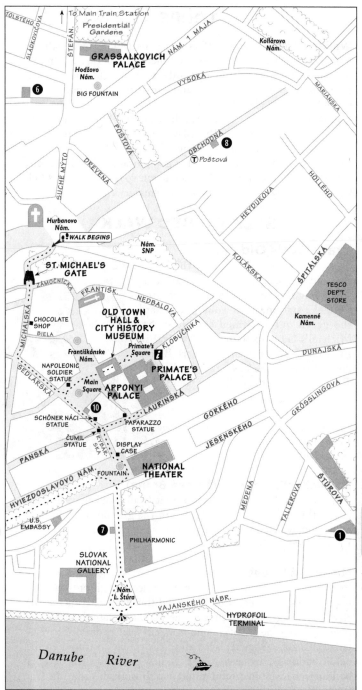

TOURS

Walking Tour—The TI offers a one-hour Old Town walking tour in English every day in the summer at 14:00 (€12.50, free or discounted with Bratislava City Card—see page 370; runs sporadically based on demand Nov–March—call ahead to confirm, tel. 02/5443-4059, guides@bkis.sk).

Local Guide—MS Agency, run by **Martin Sloboda** (a can-do entrepreneur and tireless Bratislava booster, and author of the great local guidebook described under "Helpful Hints," earlier in this chapter), can set you up with a good local guide (€120/3 hrs, €150/4 hrs), and can help you track down your Slovak roots (tel. 02/5464-1467, www.msagency.sk, info@msagency.sk).

SELF-GUIDED WALK

Bratislava's Old Town

This orientation walk through the heart of delightfully traffic-free old Bratislava takes about an hour (not including stops). If you're coming from the station, make your way toward the green onion-domed steeple of St. Michael's Gate (explained in "Arrival in Bratislava," earlier in this chapter). Before going through the passage into the Old Town, peek over the railing on your left to the inviting garden below—once part of the city moat.

• *Step through the first gate, walk along the passageway, and pause as you come through the onion-domed...*

St. Michael's Gate (Michalská Brána)

This is the last surviving tower of the city wall. Just below the gate, notice the "kilometer zero" plaque in the ground, marking the point from which distances in Slovakia are measured.

• *You're at the head of...*

Michalská Street

Pretty as it is now, the Old Town was a decrepit ghost town during the communist era. Locals avoided this desolate corner of the city, preferring to spend time in the Petržalka suburb across the river. But after the fall of communism, city leaders decided to revitalize this zone. They replaced all of the cobbles, spruced up the public buildings, and encouraged the new private owners of other buildings to invest in careful restoration. It worked: Today the Old

Town is gleaming, and packed with locals and tourists alike.

The cafés and restaurants that line this street are inviting, especially in summer. But if you don't look beyond the facades and outdoor tables, you'll miss much of Bratislava's charm. Courtyards and galleries—most of them open to the public—burrow through the city's buildings. For example, a half-block down on the right, the gallery at #7 is home to several fashion designers.

Speaking of fashion...are you noticing a lot of skin? Tight jeans? Low-cut tops? Slovak women are known for their provocative dress. When pressed for a reason for this, local men smirk and say, "That's just the way it is."

On the left (at #6), the **Čokoládovňa pod Michalom** chocolate shop is highly regarded among locals for its delicious, creamy truffles (Mon–Fri 9:00–21:00, Sat–Sun 10:00–21:00, tel. 02/5443-3945).

Look over the shop's entrance and find the **cannonball** embedded in the wall above the seal. This commemorates Napoleon's two sieges of Bratislava, which together caused massive devastation—even worse than the city suffered during World War II. Keep an eye out for these cannonballs all over town...somber reminders of one of Bratislava's darkest times.

• *Two blocks down from St. Michael's Gate, the name of this main drag changes to Ventúrska, the street jogs to the right, and the café scene continues. At the jog, detour left (along Sedlárska) and head for the...*

Main Square (Hlavné Námestie)

This is the bustling centerpiece of Old World Bratislava. Virtually every building around this square dates from a different architectural period, from Gothic (the yellow tower) to Art Nouveau (the fancy facade facing it from across the square). When these buildings were restored a few years ago, great pains were taken to achieve authenticity—each one matches the color most likely used when  it was originally built. Extremely atmospheric cafés line the bottom of the square. **Kaffee Mayer** is the classic choice (described on page 387), but you can't miss along here. Choose the ambience you like best (indoors or out) and nurse a drink with arguably Slovakia's best urban view.

Peering over one of the benches is a cartoonish statue of a **Napoleonic officer** (notice the French flag marking the embassy right behind him). With bare feet and a hat pulled over his eyes,

City of Three Cultures:
Pressburg, Pozsony, Bratislava

Historically a Hungarian and Austrian city as much as a Slovak one, Bratislava has always been a Central European melting pot. The Hungarians used Pozsony (as they called it) as their capital during the century and a half that Buda and Pest were occupied by Ottoman invaders. Later, the city was a favorite retreat of Habsburg Empress Maria Theresa (who used its German name, Pressburg). Everyone from Hans Christian Andersen to Casanova sang the wonders of this bustling burg on the Danube.

By its late-19th-century glory days, the city was a rich intersection of cultures. Shop clerks had to be able to greet customers in German, Hungarian, and Slovak. It was said that the mornings belonged to the Slovaks (farmers who came into the city to sell their wares at market), the afternoons to the Hungarians (diplomats and office-workers filling the cafés), and the evenings to the Austrians (wine-producers who ran convivial neighborhood wine pubs where all three groups would gather). In those wine pubs, the vintner would listen to which language his customers used, then automatically bring them the correct size glass: 0.3 liters for Hungarians, 0.25 liters for Austrians, and 0.2 liters for Slovaks (a distinction that still exists today). Jews (one-tenth of the population), Romanians, and Roma (Gypsies) rounded out the city's ethnic brew.

When the new nation of Czechoslovakia was formed from the rubble of World War I, the city shed its German and Hungarian names, proudly taking the new Slavic name Bratislava. The Slovak population—which had been at only about 10 percent—was on the rise, but the city remained tri-cultural.

World War II changed all of that. With the dissolution of Czechoslovakia, Slovakia became an "independent" country under the thumb of the Nazis—who decimated the Jewish popu-

it's hardly a flattering portrait—you could call it the Slovaks' revenge for the difficulties they faced at Napoleon's hands.

At the top of the Main Square is the impressive **Old Town Hall** (Stará Radnica), marked by a bold yellow tower. Near the bottom of the tower (to the left of the window), notice the cannonball embedded in the facade— yet another reminder of Napoleon's impact on Bratislava. Over time, the Old Town Hall gradually grew, annexing the buildings next to it— creating a mishmash of architectural

lation. Then, at the end of the war, in retribution for Hitler's misdeeds, a reunited Czechoslovakia expelled people of Germanic descent (including all of those Austrians). And finally, a "mutual exchange of populations" sent the city's Hungarians back to Hungary.

Bratislava suffered terribly under the communists. It became the textbook example of a historic city whose multilayered charm and delicate cultural fabric were ripped apart, then shrouded in gray by the communist regime. For example, the communists were more proud of their ultramodern New Bridge than of the historic Jewish quarter they razed to make way for it. Now the bridge and its highway slice through the center of the Old Town, and the heavy traffic rattles the stained-glass windows of St. Martin's Cathedral.

But Bratislava's most recent chapter is one of great success. Over the last decade, the city has gone from gloomy victim of communism to thriving economic center and social hub. Its population of 450,000 includes some 70,000 students (at the city's six universities), creating an atmosphere of youthful energy and optimism. Its remarkable position on the Danube, a short commute from Vienna, is prompting its redevelopment as one of Europe's most up-and-coming cities.

Bratislava and Vienna have realized it's in both cities' interest to work together to bring the Slovak capital up to snuff. They're cooperating as a new "twin city" commerce super-zone...and things are happening at an astonishing pace. In the coming years, foreign investors plan to erect a skyline of 600-foot-tall skyscrapers and a clutch of glittering new mega-malls. You'd never have guessed it a few years ago, but today calling Bratislava "the next Berlin on a smaller scale" is only a bit of a stretch.

styles along this side of the square. (A few steps down the street to the right are the historic apartments and wine museum at the Apponyi House—see "Sights" on page 380.)

Step through the passageway into the Old Town Hall's gorgeously restored **courtyard,** with its Renaissance arcades. (If the City History Museum is open, its entrance is here—see "Sights.")

Then, to see another fine old square, continue through the other end of the courtyard into **Primate's Square** (Primaciálne Námestie). The pink mansion on the right is the Primate's Palace, with a fine interior decorated with six English tapestries (see "Sights"). Do you see a lot of people using laptops? In a progressive move befitting its status as an emerging business center of Europe, Bratislava provides free Wi-Fi on three squares in the Old Town. The huge student population (not to mention tourists) happily surfs in this beautiful setting. At the far end of this square is the main branch of the TI.

• *Backtrack to the Main Square. With your back to the Old Town Hall, go to the end of the square and follow the street to the left (Rybárska Brána). Soon you'll pass a pair of...*

Whimsical Statues

Several playful statues (such as the Napoleonic officer we met earlier) dot Bratislava's Old Town. Most of these date from the late 1990s, when city leaders wanted to entice locals back into the newly prettied-up Old Town.

A half-block down this street (on the left), you'll come to a jovial chap doffing his top hat. This is a statue of **Schöner Náci,**

who lived in Bratislava until the 1960s. This eccentric old man, a poor carpet cleaner, would dress up in his one black suit and top hat, and go strolling through the city, offering gifts to the women he fancied. (He'd often whisper *"schön"*—German for "pretty"—to the women, which is how he got his nickname.) After spending his life cheering up the gloomy streets of communist Bratislava, Schöner Náci now gets to spend eternity greeting visitors in front of his favorite café, Kaffee Mayer.

As a sad epilogue, Schöner Náci's arm was broken off recently by a bunch of drunks. As Prague gets more expensive, Bratislava is becoming the cheaper alternative for weekend "stag parties," popular with Brits lured here by cheap flights and cheap beer. Locals hope this is a short-lived trend, and that those rowdy louts will move farther east before long.

• *Continue down Rybárska.*

At the end of this block, at the intersection with Panská,

watch out on the right for **Čumil** ("the Peeper"), grinning at passersby from a manhole. This was the first and is still the favorite Bratislava statue. There's no story behind this one—the artist simply wanted to create a fun icon and let the townspeople make up their own tales. Čumil has survived being driven over by a truck—twice—and he's still grinning.

For a peek at a third statue—a nosy **Paparazzo**—you can turn left up Panská and go one block, watching the corner on the left.

• *Continuing straight past Čumil, you'll reach the long, skinny square called...*

Hviezdoslav Square (Hviezdoslavovo Námestie)

This square, named for a beloved Slovak poet, is yet another part of Bratislava that has undergone a much-needed sprucing-up. The landscaped park in the center is particularly inviting. At this end of the square is the impressive, silver-topped Slovak National Theater

(Slovenské Národné Divadlo). Beyond that, the opulent yellow building that seems to be melting is the Philharmonic. The prominence of these two venues is evidence of Bratislava's strong performing arts tradition.

Right in front of the theater (by the McDonald's), look down into the glass **display case** to see the foundation of the one-time Fishermen's Gate into the city. Surrounding the base of the gate is water. This entire square was once a tributary of the Danube, and the Carlton Hotel across the way was a series of inns on different islands. The buildings along the Old Town side of the square mark where the city wall once stood.

• *From here, it's just a block to the Danube—passing the **Slovak National Gallery**, for those curious about local art (lime-green building on the corner with a modern annex). Once at the Danube, cross the street and belly up to the railing.*

The Danube (Dunaj)

Here you get a good look at the communists' pride and joy, the **New Bridge** (Nový Most, a.k.a. Most SNP). As with most Soviet-era landmarks in former communist countries, locals aren't crazy about this structure—not only for the questionable starship *Enterprise* design, but also because of

the oppressive regime it represents. However, the restaurant and observation deck up top—long a stale holdover from communist times—was recently renovated into a posh eatery called (appropriately enough) "UFO." You can visit for the views, a drink, or a full meal (see page 383).

• *Backtrack to the silver-topped National Theater at Hviezdoslav Square. Follow this square to the left, passing some fun public art: a statue of the square's namesake; the heavily fortified US Embassy (on the left); a glass pavilion (popular venue for summer concerts); and, on the right near the end, a statue of Hans Christian Andersen (the Danish storyteller, who enjoyed his visit to Bratislava).*

Reaching the end of the square (at the column with the big highway behind it), jog right and head for the big...

St. Martin's Cathedral (Dóm Sv. Martina)

This historic church isn't looking too sharp these days—and the highway thundering a few feet in front of its door (courtesy of the

Soviets) doesn't help matters. If it were any closer, the off-ramp would go through the nave. Sad as it is now, the cathedral has been party to some pretty important history. While Buda and Pest were occupied by Ottomans for a century and a half, Bratislava was the capital of Hungary. A total of 19 Hungarian kings and queens were crowned in this church—more than have been crowned anywhere in Hungary. A replica of the Hungarian crown still tops the steeple.

• *Our walk is finished. From here, you have some sightseeing options (described in detail under "Sights," next). To reach the castle, take the underpass beneath the highway, go up the stairs on the right (marked by* Hrad/Castle *sign), then turn left up the stepped lane marked* Zámocké Schody. *Or, to get to the New Bridge's "UFO" view platform, turn left, walk toward the Danube, then walk the length of the bridge (pedestrian walkway on lower level) to reach the tower's entrance at the far end.*

SIGHTS

It seems that all of Bratislava's sights have just reopened after a renovation...or are about to undergo one. In any event, most of Bratislava's charm is in its streets, not its museums. But these sights are fine for a rainy day or for "extra credit."

On or near the Old Town's Main Square

These three museums cluster within a few steps of the Main Square.

City History Museum (Mestské Múzeum)—This museum, in the Old Town Hall, will likely be closed through 2010 for a long-overdue renovation. When open, it offers an exhibit on town history (including torture equipment, or "feudal justice") and a chance to climb the Old Town Hall tower for a view of the square (if open, likely €3, Tue–Fri 10:00–17:00, Sat–Sun 11:00–18:00, closed Mon, enter through courtyard of Old Town Hall, tel. 02/5920-5130, www.muzeum.bratislava.sk).

▲**Apponyi House (Apponyiho Palác)**—This brand-new museum, which reopened in 2008 in the gorgeously restored mansion of a Hungarian aristocrat, comes in two parts. The cellar holds an interesting exhibit on the vineyards of the nearby "Little Carpathian" hills, with historic presses and barrels, and a replica of an old-time wine-pub table. Upstairs are two floors of urban apartments from old Bratislava: The first floor up shows off the 18th-century Rococo-style rooms of the nobility, while the second floor up (with lower ceilings and simpler wall decorations) illustrates 19th-century bourgeois/middle-class lifestyles, including some fine Empire-style furniture (€7, Tue–Fri 10:00–17:00, Sat–Sun 11:00–18:00, closed Mon, Radničná ulica 1, tel. 02/5920-5135).

▲**Primate's Palace (Primaciálny Palác)**—Probably Bratislava's most interesting museum, this tastefully restored French-

Neoclassical mansion (formerly the residence of the archbishop, or "primate") dates from 1781. The smaller rooms were the archbishop's private quarters, now decorated with Dutch, Flemish, German, and Italian paintings. You'll peer from a bay window down into the archbishop's own, private marble chapel. When the archbishop became too ill to walk down to Mass, this window was built for him to take part in the service. The larger rooms were public...designed to impress. Among these is the Mirror Hall, used for concerts, city council meetings, and other important events.

But the museum's highlight is its series of six English tapestries, illustrating the ancient Greek myth of the tragic love between Hero and Leander. The tapestries—the only complete cycle of their kind in existence—were woven in England by Flemish weavers for the court of King Charles I (in the 1630s). After the king was deposed and beheaded, the tapestries disappeared. Centuries later, in 1903, restorers broke through a false wall in this mansion and discovered the six tapestries, neatly folded and perfectly preserved. Nobody knows how they got there (perhaps they were squirreled away during the Napoleonic invasion, and whoever hid them didn't survive). The archbishop—who had just sold the palace to the city, but emptied it of furniture before he left—cried foul and tried to get the tapestries back...but the city said, a deal's a deal (€2, Tue–Fri 10:00–17:00, Sat–Sun 11:00–18:00, closed Mon, Primaciálne Námestie 3, tel. 02/5935-6394).

Bratislava Castle (Bratislavský Hrad)

This imposing fortress, nicknamed the "upside-down table," is the city's most prominent landmark. There surely has been a castle

on this spot for centuries, but the oldest surviving chunk is the 13th-century Romanesque watchtower (the one slightly taller than the other three). When Habsburg Empress Maria Theresa took a liking to Bratislava in the 18th century, she transformed the castle from a military fortress to a royal residence suitable for holding court. She added a summer riding school (the U-shaped complex next to the castle), an enclosed winter riding school out back, and lots more...and painted the whole thing yellow. Maria Theresa's favorite daughter, Maria Christina, lived here with her husband Albert when they were newlyweds. Locals nicknamed the place "little Schönbrunn," in reference to the Habsburgs' summer palace on the outskirts of Vienna.

But M.T.'s castle burned to the ground in an 1811 fire, and it was left as a ruin for a century and a half—not reconstructed until 1953. Unfortunately, the communist rebuild was drab and uninviting; the inner courtyard felt like a prison exercise yard.

The good news is that the city is in the midst of a five-year renovation project to rehabilitate the castle from top to bottom. They've already reconstructed the summer riding school, and plan to rebuild the winter riding school and terraced French gardens out back...as well as paint the whole thing that pretty "Habsburg yellow" once again. The bad news is that during the restoration, the castle interior is closed to visitors. But more good news: The interior

was never appealing anyway, so the main reason to visit—for up-close views of the castle, over the rooftops of the Old Town, and across the Danube to Petržalka—remains the same (and free).

For details on the best way to hike up to the castle, see the end of my self-guided walk that begins on page 374.

The "UFO" at New Bridge (Nový Most)

The bizarre, flying-saucer-capped bridge near the Old Town—completed in 1972 in heavy-handed communist style—has been

reclaimed by capitalists. It's been spruced up and turned into an overpriced café/restaurant, with an observation deck that allows visitors sweeping 360-degree views of Bratislava from about 300 feet above the Danube. Think of it as the "Slovak Space Needle."

Cost and Hours: €7, daily 10:00–23:00, elevator free if you have a meal reservation—main courses steeply priced at €25–30, tel. 02/6252-0300, www.u-f-o.sk/en.

Getting There: Just walk across the New Bridge from the Old Town—the elevator entrance is underneath the tower on the Petržalka side.

◆ Self-Guided Tour: The "elevator" that takes you up is actually a funicular—you'll notice you're moving at an angle. At the top, walk up the stairs to the observation deck.

Begin by viewing the **castle** and **Old Town.** Notice, to the right of the Old Town, the massive construction zone. If you set

up a time-lapse camera here over the next few years, you'd watch skyscrapers pop up like dandelions. International investors are throwing many billions of euros at Bratislava, before rents skyrocket. (Imagine having so much prime, undeveloped real estate available downtown in the capital of an emerging European economic power...just an hour down the road from Vienna, no less.) Most of the development is taking place along the banks of the Danube. In a decade, this will be a futuristic city.

The huge, pointy monument back toward the train station (behind the Old Town) is **Slavín,** where more than 6,800 Soviet soldiers who fought to liberate Bratislava from the Nazis are buried. A nearby church had to take down its steeple so as not to draw attention

away from the huge Soviet soldier on top of the monument.

Now turn 180 degrees to face **Petržalka,** a planned communist suburb that sprouted here in the 1970s. The site was once occupied by a village, and the various districts of modern Petržalka still carry their original names (which now seem ironic): "Meadows" *(Háje),* "Woods" *(Lúky),* and "Courtyards" *(Dvory).* The ambitious Soviet planners envisioned a city laced with Venetian-style canals to help drain the marshy land, but the plans were abandoned after the harsh crackdown on the 1968 Prague Spring uprising. Today, one in four Bratislavans lives in Petržalka. A few years ago, this was a grim and decaying sea of miserable communist apartment *panelák* ("panel buildings," so called because they're made of huge prefab concrete panels that were built elsewhere, then brought here to assemble on-site). But things are changing fast. Many of the *panelák* are being retrofitted with new layers of insulation, and the apartments inside are being updated. And, like Dorothy opening the door to Oz, the formerly drab buildings are being splashed with bright new colors. Far from being a slum, Petržalka is a popular neighborhood for Bratislavan yuppies who can't yet afford to build their dream house. Locals read the Czech-language home-improvement magazine *Panel Plus* for ideas on how to give their *panelák* apartments some style (www.panelplus.cz).

Still facing Petržalka, notice that new construction is also happening along this riverbank (such as the supermall down below). But there's still history here. The **park** called Sad Janka Kráľa, a.k.a. "Aupark"—just downriver from the bridge—was technically the first public park in Europe, and is still a popular place for locals to relax and court.

Scanning the **horizon** beyond Petržalka, two things stick out: on the left, the old communist refinery (which has been fully updated); and on the right, a sea of modern windmills. These are just over the border, in Austria...and Bratislava is sure to grow in that direction quickly.

Before you leave, consider nursing a drink at the café (€3 coffee or beer, €5–15 cocktails). If nothing else, be sure to use the memorable WCs.

Sleep Code

(€1 = about $1.40, country code: 421, area code: 02)
S = Single, **D** = Double/Twin, **T** = Triple, **Q** = Quad, **b** = bathroom.
English is spoken at each place. Unless otherwise noted,
breakfast is included and you can pay by credit card.

To help you sort easily through these listings, I've divided
the rooms into three categories, based on the price for a
standard double room with bath:

$$$ **Higher Priced**—Most rooms €100 or more.
$$ **Moderately Priced**—Most rooms between €50–100.
$ **Lower Priced**—Most rooms €50 or less.

SLEEPING

A few years ago, there were no sleepable hotels near Bratislava's
Old Town. But new accommodations open every year, so the scene
is rapidly improving. Hotel values here still aren't great. I'd rather
sleep in Budapest or Vienna. But if the city entices you to stay longer than a day trip, these options are all inside or within a short
walk of the Old Town. Business-oriented places charge more on
weekdays (Mon–Thu) than on weekends (Fri–Sun).

$$$ Hotel Marrol's is the town's most enticing splurge.
Although it's in a drab urban neighborhood, it's a five-minute walk
from the Old Town, and the 54 rooms are luxurious and taste-
fully appointed Old World country-style. While pricey, the rates
drop to temping lows on weekends (Mon–Thu: Sb-€227, Db-€255;
Fri–Sun: Sb-€134, Db-€153; air-con, non-smoking, free cable
Internet, gorgeous lounge, Tobrucká ulica 4, tel. 02/5778-4600,
www.hotelmarrols.sk, rec@hotelmarrols.sk).

$$$ Hotel Michalská Brána is a charming boutique hotel
hiding down a tight, atmospheric little lane just inside St. Michael's
Gate in the Old Town. The 14 rooms are sleek, mod, and classy
(Mon–Thu: Sb-€150, Db-€160; Fri–Sun: Sb-€125, Db-€135; pricier suites also available, air-con, non-smoking, free cable Internet,
elevator, Baštová 4, tel. 02/5930-7200, www.michalskabrana.com,
michalskabrana@gmail.com).

$$ Hotel Corso has four rooms at the top floor of an office
building right on the edge of the Old Town (Sb-€69, Db-€81,
Tb-€104, cash only, elevator and some stairs, free Wi-Fi, some
tram noise, Kapucínska 7, tel. 02/5441-6450, www.bratislava
hotel.sk).

$$ Penzion Chez David is a simple, Jewish-themed hotel
with 10 budget rooms just outside the Old Town (Mon–Thu:

Sb-€64, Db-€88; Fri–Sun: Sb-€54, Db-€78; fee for Wi-Fi, some street noise from busy road and tram—request quieter room, Zámocká 13, tel. 02/5441-3824, www.chezdavid.sk, recepcia@chez david.sk).

$$ Hotel Ibis, part of the cookie-cutter chain, offers 120 rooms overlooking a busy tram junction across the street from Penzion Chez David (Mon–Thu: Sb/Db-€94; Fri–Sun: Sb/Db-€79; rates flex with demand, optional breakfast-€10 per person, Zámocká 38, tel. 02/5929-2000, fax 02/5929-2111, www.ibishotel.com, h3566@accor.com).

$ Downtown Backpackers Hostel is Bratislava's best hostel option. Funky but well-run, it's near the Grassalkovich (presidential) Palace about a five-minute walk from the Old Town (61 beds in 12 rooms, Db-€70, D-€55, bunk in Qb-€25, bunk in 7–8-bed dorm-€20, bunk in 10-bed dorm-€18, Panenská 31, tel. 02/5464-1191, www.backpackers.sk, info@backpackers.sk).

EATING

Slovak cuisine shows some Hungarian influence, but it's closer to Czech cuisine—with lots of starches and gravy, and plenty of pork, cabbage, and potatoes. Keep an eye out for Slovakia's national dish, *bryndzové halušky* (small potato dumplings with sheep's cheese and bits of bacon). Like the Czechs, the Slovaks produce excellent beer (*pivo*, PEE-voh). One of the top brands is Zlatý Bažant ("Golden Pheasant"). Bratislava is packed with inviting new eateries. In addition to the heavy Slovak staples, you'll find trendy new bars and bistros, and a wide range of ethnic offerings. The best plan may be to stroll the Old Town and keep your eyes open for the setting and cuisine that appeals to you most. Or consider one of these options.

Prazdroj ("Urquell") is a Czech-style beer hall with lively ambience and good traditional food. It sprawls through several rooms of a building just off Hviezdoslav Square at the edge of the Old Town (€7–10 main dishes, Mon–Fri 10:00–24:00, Sat–Sun 11:00–24:00, Mostová 8, tel. 02/5441-1108).

1. Slovak Pub (as in "the first") is the Slovak equivalent of Prazdroj, attracting a younger crowd. Enter from a bustling modern shopping street just outside the Old Town, and climb the stairs into a vast warren of rustic old countryside-style pub rooms. While enjoying the lively, loud, almost chaotic ambience, you'll dine on affordable and truly authentic Slovak fare, made with products from the pub's own farm. This is a good place to try the

Slovak specialty, *bryndzové halušky* (€6–9 main dishes, Mon–Sat 10:00–24:00, Sun 12:00–24:00, Obchodná 62, tel. 02/5292-6367).

Erdody Palace, a newly renovated mansion in the center of the Old Town at Ventúrska 1, is a great place to splurge at one of two eateries with an Andy Warhol theme (after all, he was Slovak). As the owner is a huge Warhol fan, original Warhols hang in each restaurant, named for the theme of the works: **Flowers** dishes up Mediterranean fare in a bright, covered courtyard (€7–14 pastas, €15–25 main dishes, daily 11:30–1:00 in the morning, tel. 02/2092-2733); the stuffier **Camouflage** features nouvelle cuisine in a somewhat snooty white-minimalist setting (€15–30 main dishes, Mon–Sat 11:30–1:00 in the morning, closed Sun, reservations smart, tel. 02/2092-2711). Even if you're not eating here, peek in the window at Camouflage to see Warhol enjoying the place.

Fast and Cheap: A local chain called **Coffee & Co,** with branches throughout the Old Town and beyond, serves up good €3–4 sandwiches—ideal for a bite on the run (various locations, all open long hours daily).

Classic Coffee House: The venerable **Kaffee Mayer,** at the corner of the main square, is an institution—they've been selling coffee and cakes to a genteel clientele since 1873. You can enjoy your pick-me-up in the swanky old interior, or out on the square (€2–3 cakes, Mon–Fri 9:30–22:00, Sat–Sun 9:30–23:00, Hlavné Námestie 4, tel. 02/5441-1741).

TRANSPORTATION CONNECTIONS

By Train

Bratislava has two major train stations. The Main Train Station (Hlavná Stanica, abbreviated "Bratislava hl. st." on schedules) is closer to the Old Town, while the Petržalka station (ŽST Petržalka), in the suburb across the river, can be more convenient for some connections. When checking schedules (http://bahn .hafas.de/bin/query.exe/en is helpful), pay attention to which station your train uses. Bus #93 connects these two Bratislava stations (5–12/hr, 10 min; or use bus #N93 at night).

From Bratislava by Train to: **Budapest** (5/day direct, 2.5 hrs; more with transfers), **Sopron** (at least hourly, 2.5 hrs, transfer at Vienna's Südbahnhof), **Vienna** (2–3/hr, 1 hr), **Prague** (3/day direct, 4.25–5.5 hrs). For more Hungarian destinations (such as **Eger** or **Pécs**), you'll connect through Budapest.

By Boat

Riverboats connect Bratislava to the nearby capitals of Budapest and Vienna. Conveniently, these boats dock right along the Danube in front of Bratislava's Old Town. While they are more expensive, less frequent, and slower than the train, some travelers enjoy getting out on the Danube.

To Budapest: For details on the Mahart boats to and from Budapest, see page 272 in the Transportation Connections chapter.

To Vienna: The Vienna-based DDSG line offers several daily boat trips between Bratislava and Vienna's Schwedenplatz (where Vienna's town center hits the canal; €28 each way, €17 at less convenient times, €2 more on weekends, 1.25-hr trip; daily April–Oct only, Austrian tel. 01/58880, www.ddsg-blue-danube.at). The Budapest-based Mahart boat connects Bratislava to Vienna's Reichsbrücke dock once daily (€29 one-way, €39 round-trip, 1.5–2 hrs, daily late April–early Oct only; for more details, see page 272 of Transportation Connections).

Bratislava Airport (Letisko Bratislava)

Bratislava Airport (airport code: BTS, www.letiskobratislava .sk) is six miles northeast of downtown Bratislava. The low-cost carriers who fly here (including SkyEurope) sometimes market it as "Vienna–Bratislava," thanks to its proximity to both capitals. The airport is officially named for Milan Rastislav Štefánik, who worked toward the creation of Czechoslovakia at the end of World War I. It's compact and manageable, with all the usual amenities (including ATMs).

To Downtown Bratislava: The airport has easy **public bus** connections to Bratislava's Main Train Station (€0.60, plus €0.30 ticket for each big bag, bus #61, 6/hr in peak times, 3/hr in slow times, trip takes 30 min). To reach the bus stop, exit straight out of the arrivals hall, cross the street, buy a ticket at the kiosk, and look for the bus stop on your right. For directions from the train station into the Old Town, see "Arrival in Bratislava," page 370. A **taxi** from the airport into central Bratislava should cost less than €20.

To Budapest: Take the bus or taxi to Bratislava's train station (described above), then hop a train to Budapest.

To Vienna: A slow option is to connect through Bratislava's train station (described above). More direct and still affordable, you can take a Eurolines bus from Bratislava Airport to the Erdberg stop of Vienna's U-3 subway line (9/day, €10, trip takes about an hour, book in advance, www.gratislava.at). A taxi from Bratislava Airport directly to Vienna costs €60–90 (depending on whether you use a cheaper Slovak or more expensive Austrian cab).

HUNGARY: PAST AND PRESENT

The Hungarian story—essentially the tale of a people finding their home—is as epic as any in Europe. Over the course of a millennium, a troublesome nomadic tribe that was the scourge of Europe gradually assimilated with its neighbors and—through stubbornness, tenacity, and diplomacy—found itself controlling a vast swath of Central and Eastern Europe. Since arriving in Europe in 896, the Hungarians adopted Christianity; fended off Tatars and Turks; lost, regained, then lost again two-thirds of their land; and built one of the world's great 19th-century cities. Today, the Hungarians still perplex and amuse their neighbors with their bizarre Asian language, lovably quirky customs, and spicy cuisine. And yet, despite their mysterious origins and idiosyncrasies, the Hungarians have carved out a unique and vital niche in European life. Hungary is a place worth grappling with, and the persistent reap grand rewards here. Locals toss around the names of great historical figures such as Kossuth, Széchenyi, and Nagy as if they're talking about old friends. Take this crash-course so you can keep up.

The story begins long, long ago and far, far away...

Welcome to Europe

The land we call Hungary today has long been considered the place—culturally, if not geographically—where the West (Europe) meets the East (Asia). The Roman province of Pannonia extended to the final foothills of the Alps that constitute the Buda Hills, on the west side of the Danube. Across the river, Rome ended and the barbarian wilds began. From here, the Great Hungarian Plain stretches in a long, flat expanse all the way to Asia—hemmed in to the north by the Carpathian Mountains. (Geologists consider this prairie-like plain to be the westernmost steppe in Europe—

Who Were the Magyars?

The ancestors of today's Hungarians, the Magyars, are a mysterious lot. Of all the Asian invaders of Europe, they were arguably the most successful—integrating more or less smoothly with the Europeans, and thriving well into the 21st century. Centuries after the Huns, Tatars, and Ottomans retreated east, leaving behind only fragments of their culture, the Hungarians remain a fixture in contemporary Europe.

The history of the Magyars before they arrived in Europe in A.D. 896 is hotly contested. Because their language is related only to Finnish and Estonian, it's presumed that these three peoples were once a single group, which likely originated east of the Ural Mountains (in the steppes of present-day Asian Russia).

After the Magyars' ancestors spent some time in Siberia, climatic change pushed them south and west, eventually (likely around the fifth century A.D.) crossing the Ural Mountains and officially entering Europe. They settled near the Don River (in today's southwestern Russia) before local warfare pushed them farther and farther west. The Magyars began raiding European lands, eventually setting up camp in the Carpathian Basin—today's Hungary—in A.D. 896.

resembling the terrain that covers much of Central Asia.) After Rome collapsed and Europe fell into the Dark Ages, Hungary became the territory of Celts, Vandals, Huns, and Avars...until some out-of-towners moved into the neighborhood.

The seven Magyar tribes, led by the mighty Árpád (and, according to legend, by the mythical Turul bird), thundered into

the Carpathian Basin in A.D. 896. They were a rough-and-tumble nomadic people from Central Asia who didn't like to settle down in one place. (For more on this mysterious clan, see "Who Were the Magyars?" above.) And yet, after their long and winding westward odyssey, the Great Hungarian Plain felt comfortingly like home to the Magyars—reminiscent of the Asian steppes of their ancestors.

After the Magyars settled down and began to intermarry with Germans, Slavs, and other European peoples, their Asian features and customs mostly faded away. But the Europeans also took on some elements of the Hungarian language and culture ("Magyarization"). Hungary became Central Europe's melting pot. After all these centuries, most Hungarians have lost track of the many tangled strains of their personal family history. In fact, a recent genetic study found that Hungarians are the most ethnically diverse nationality on the planet.

But even though certain aspects of their Magyar heritage have been lost to time, the Hungarians have done a remarkable job of clinging on to their Asian roots. They still do things their own way, making Hungary subtly but unmistakably different from its neighboring countries. And people of German-Hungarian, Slavic-Hungarian, and Jewish-Hungarian descent still speak a language that's not too far removed from the Asian tongue spoken by those original Magyars.

Were the Hungarians (Magyars) descended from the Huns, a similarly violent nomadic tribe that lived in the same area centuries earlier? It has long been a popular romantic notion—for historians, but also in legends and among everyday people—to speculate a tie between these two groups. But modern historians strongly doubt that the two ever had anything to do with each other. Even so, many Hungarians still take pride in the legendary link to the Huns...and Attila remains a popular name even today.

The Magyars would camp out in today's Hungary in the winters, and in the summers, they'd go on raids throughout Europe. They were notorious as incredibly swift horsemen, whose use of stirrups (an eastern innovation largely unknown in Europe at the time) allowed them to easily outmaneuver foes and victims. Italy, France, Germany's Rhine, the Spanish Pyrenees, all the way to Constantinople (modern-day Istanbul)—the Magyars had the run of the Continent.

For half a century, the Magyars ranked with the Vikings as the most feared people in Europe. To Europeans, this must have struck a chord of queasy familiarity: a mysterious and dangerous eastern tribe running roughshod over Europe, speaking a gibberish language and employing strange, terrifying, relentless battle techniques. No wonder they called the new arrivals "Hun-garians."

Now planted in the center of Europe, the Hungarians effectively drove a wedge in the middle of the sprawling Slavic populations of the Great Moravian Kingdom (basically today's "Eastern Europe"). The Slavs were split into two splinter groups, north and south—a division that persists today: Czechs, Slovaks, and Poles to the north; and Croats, Serbs, and Bosniaks to the south. (You can still hear the division caused by the Magyars in the language: While Czechs and Russians call a castle *hrad*, the Croats and Serbs call it *grad*.)

After decades of terrorizing Europe, the Magyars were finally defeated by a German and Czech army at the Battle of Augsburg in 955. The Magyars' King Géza—realizing that if they were to survive, his people had to put down roots and get along with their neighbors—made a fateful decision that would forever shape Hungary's future: He adopted Christianity, baptized his son, Vajk, and married him to a Bavarian princess at a young age.

On Christmas Day in the year 1000, Vajk changed his name to István (Stephen) and was symbolically crowned by the pope (for more on István, see page 178). The domestication of the nomadic Magyars was difficult, thanks largely to the resistance of István's uncles, but was ultimately successful. Hungary became a legitimate Christian kingdom, welcomed by its neighbors. Under kings such as László I, Kálmán "the Book-Lover," and András II, Hungary entered a period of prosperity. (For more on these three kings, see pages 179–180.)

The Tatars, the Ottomans, and Other Outsiders (A.D. 1000–1686)

One of Hungary's earliest challenges came at the hands of fellow invaders from Central Asia. Through the first half of the 13th century, the Tatars—initially led by Genghis Khan—swept into Eastern Europe from Mongolia. In the summer of 1241, Genghis Khan's son and successor, Ögedei Khan, broke into Hungarian territory. The Tatars sacked and plundered Hungarian towns, laying waste to the kingdom. It was only Ögedei Khan's death in early 1242—and the ensuing dispute about succession—that saved the Hungarians, as Tatar armies rushed home and the Mongolian Empire contracted. The Hungarian king at the time, Béla IV, was left to rebuild his ruined kingdom from the rubble—creating for the first time many of the stout hilltop castles that still line the Danube. (For more on Béla IV, see page 181.)

Each of Béla's successors left his own mark on Hungary, as the Magyar kingdom flourished. They barely skipped a beat when the original Árpád dynasty died out in 1301, as they imported French kings (from the Naples-based Anjou, or Angevin, dynasty) to continue building their young realm. King Károly Róbert (Charles Robert) won over the Magyars, and his son Nagy Lajos (Louis the Great) expanded Hungarian holdings (for more on these two, see pages 181 and 182).

This was a period of flux for all of Central and Eastern Europe, as the nearby Czech and Polish kingdoms also saw their longstanding dynasties expire. For a time, royal intermarriages juggled the crowns of the region between various ruling families. Most notably, for 50 years (1387–1437) Hungary was ruled by Holy Roman Emperor Sigismund of Luxembourg, whose holdings also included the Czech lands, parts of Italy, much of Croatia, and more.

For more than 150 years, Hungary did not have a Hungarian-blooded king. This changed in the late 15th century, when a shortage

of foreign kings led to the ascension to the throne of the enlightened King Mátyás (Matthias) Corvinus. The son of popular military hero János Hunyadi, King Matthias fostered the arts, sparked a mini-Renaissance, and successfully balanced foreign threats to Hungarian sovereignty (the Habsburgs to the north and west, and the Ottomans to the south and east). Under Matthias, Hungarian culture and political power reached a peak. (For more on this great Hungarian king, see page 183.)

But even before the reign of "good king Matthias," the Ottomans (from today's Turkey) had already begun slicing their way through the Balkan Peninsula toward Central Europe. (It's ironic that the two greatest threats to the Magyar kingdom came in the form of fellow Asian invaders: Tatars and Turks. Or maybe it's not surprising, as these groups all found the steppes of Hungary so familiar and inviting.) In 1526, the Ottomans entered Hungary when Sultan Süleyman the Magnificent killed Hungary's King Lajos II at the Battle of Mohács. By 1541, they took Buda. The Ottomans would dominate Hungarian life (and history) until the 1680s—nearly a century and a half.

The Ottoman invasion divided Hungary into thirds: Ottoman-occupied "Lower Hungary" (more or less today's Hungary); rump "Upper Hungary" (basically today's Slovakia), with its capital at Bratislava (which they called "Pozsony"); and the loosely independent territories of Transylvania (in today's Romania), ruled by Hungarian dukes. During this era, the Ottomans built many of the thermal baths that you'll still find throughout Hungary.

Ottoman-occupied Hungary became severely depopulated,

and many of its towns and cities fell into ruins. While it was advantageous for a Hungarian subject to adopt Islam (for lower taxes and other privileges), the Ottomans rarely resorted to forced conversion—unlike the arguably more oppressive Catholics who controlled other parts of Europe at the time (such as the monarchs of Spain, who expelled the Jews and conducted the Spanish Inquisition). Ottoman rule meant that Hungary took a different course than other parts of Europe during this time. The nation fully enjoyed the Renaissance, but missed out on other major

European historical events—both good (the Age of Discovery and Age of Reason) and bad (the devastating Catholic-versus-Protestant wars that plagued the rest of Central Europe).

Crippled by the Ottomans and lacking power and options, Hungarian nobles desperately offered their crown to the Austrian Habsburg Empire, in exchange for salvation from the invasion. The Habsburgs instead used Hungary as a kind of "buffer zone" between the Ottoman advance and Vienna. And that was only the beginning of a very troubled relationship between the Hungarians and the Austrians.

Habsburg Rule, Hungarian National Revival, and Revolution (1686–1867)

In the late 17th century, the Habsburg army, starting from Vienna, began a sustained campaign to push the Ottomans out of Hungary in about 15 years. They finally wrested Buda and Pest from the Ottomans in 1686. The Habsburgs repopulated Buda and Pest with Germans, while Magyars reclaimed the countryside. Even 25 years after the Ottomans were kicked out, the combined population of Buda and Pest was less than 20,000—and most of them were Germans from other parts of the Habsburg Empire. As recently as the early 19th century, Hungary was considered practically beyond Europe; Vienna marked the end of the "civilized" European world. But that would soon change. The population of Buda and Pest grew nearly tenfold from the beginning to the end of the 19th century. The new Austrian rulers rebuilt Hungary in their favored colorful, frilly Baroque style. Even today, it seems every Hungarian town has a cheerfully painted church with a Habsburg-style onion dome.

The Habsburgs governed the country as an outpost of Austria. The Hungarians—who'd had enough of foreign rule—fought them tooth and nail. Countless streets, squares, and buildings throughout the country are named Rákóczi, Széchenyi, or Kossuth—the

Top 10 Dates That Changed Hungary

A.D. 896—The nomadic Magyars (a tribe from Central Asia) arrive in the Carpathian Basin and begin to terrorize Europe.

1000—King István (Stephen) accepts Christianity, marking the domestication of the Magyars.

1541—Invading Ottomans take Buda and Pest...and build thermal baths.

1686—The Austrian Habsburgs drive out the Ottomans, making Hungary part of their extensive empire (despite occasional rebellions from nationalistic Hungarians).

1867—A Golden Age begins, as Hungary gains semi-autonomy from Austria; Budapest, the new co-capital of a vast empire, booms.

1920—A loser in World War I, Hungary is stripped of two-thirds its territory and half its population in the Treaty of Trianon...and they're still angry about it.

1945—After World War II, the Soviet Union "liberates" the country and establishes a communist state.

1956—Hungarians bravely revolt. A massive invasion of Soviet tanks and soldiers brutally suppresses the rebellion, killing 2,500.

1989—Hungary is the first Soviet satellite to open its borders to the West, sparking similar reforms throughout the Eastern Bloc.

2004—Hungary joins the European Union.

"big three" Hungarian patriots who resisted the Habsburgs during this time.

Transylvanian prince Ferenc Rákóczi led Hungarians in the first major rebellion against the Habsburgs, the War of

Independence (1703–1711). While Rákóczi initially enjoyed great territorial gains, his war ultimately failed, he went into exile in the Ottoman Empire, and Habsburg rule continued. (For more on Rákóczi, see page 184.)

The early 19th century saw a thawing of Habsburg oppression. Here as throughout Europe, "backwards" country traditions began to trickle into the cities, gaining more respect and prominence. It was during this time of reforms that Hungarian (rather than German) became the official language. It also coincided with a Romantic Age of poets and writers (such as Mihály Vörösmarty and Sándor Petőfi) who began to use the Hungarian tongue to create literature for the first time. By around 1825, the Hungarian National Revival was underway, as the people began to embrace the culture and traditions of their Magyar ancestors. Like people across Europe—from Ireland to Italy, and from Germany to Scandinavia—the Hungarians were becoming aware of what made them a unique people.

In Hungary, the movement was spearheaded by Count István Széchenyi, who had a compelling vision of a resurgent Hungarian nation...and the wealth and influence to make it happen. Széchenyi funded grand structures in Budapest (such as the iconic Chain Bridge) to give his Magyar countrymen something to take pride in. But even as Széchenyi spurred Hungarian patriotism, he was savvy enough not to push for total Hungarian independence—knowing that the volatile combination of strong Habsburg rule and a complicated ethnic mix would make an independent Hungarian state unlikely. Rather, he sought some degree of autonomy within the empire. And it began to work, as the Habsburgs gave in to some Hungarian demands.

And yet, despite the "Reform Age" that was already brewing, the gradual progress was too little, too late for many Hungarians. In March of 1848, a wave of Enlightenment-fueled nationalism that began in Paris spread like wildfire across Europe, igniting a revolutionary spirit in cities such as Vienna, Milan...and Budapest.

In Hungary, it inspired a revolt against the Habsburgs. Széchenyi's slowly-but-surely patriotism was eclipsed by the militarism of popular orator Lajos Kossuth (pictured) and patriotic poet Sándor Petőfi. On March 15, the Revolution of 1848 began on the steps of the National Museum in Pest (see page 70).

For several tense months, the uprising led to little more than diplomatic wrangling (as the Habsburgs were distracted elsewhere). Meanwhile, minority groups inside Hungarian territory—most notably the Croats, led by Josip Jelačić—began to rise up against the Hungarians. That winter, Habsburg Emperor Ferdinand I abdicated, replaced by his young and dynamic nephew, Franz Josef. One of his first acts was to officially condemn Hungarian independence.

In the spring of 1849, the Hungarians mounted a bloody but successful offensive to take over a wide swath of territory, including Buda and Pest. But in June, Franz Josef enlisted the aid of his fellow divine monarch, the Russian czar, who did not want the Magyars to provide an example for his own independence-minded subjects. Some 200,000 Russian reinforcements flooded into Hungary, crushing the revolution by August. After the final battle, the Habsburgs executed 13 Hungarian generals, then celebrated by clinking mugs of beer. To this very day, clinking beer mugs is, for many traditional Hungarians, just bad style.

For a while, the Habsburgs cracked down on their unruly Hungarian subjects. It was a time of shame for Hungary. Lajos Kossuth, now in exile, traveled the world to convince foreign leaders to take an interest in Hungary's plight (for more on him, see page 185). The now-forgotten Count Széchenyi spent his final years in a mental hospital, before committing suicide in 1860. The poet Sándor Petőfi disappeared while participating in an 1849 battle, and is presumed to have been killed in the fighting.

In the 1860s, a clever elder statesman named Ferenc Deák—in an attempt to seize on the spirit of reform and liberalization of the time—began to advocate for a power-sharing arrangement with the Habsburgs. Deák believed that diplomacy, rather than unilateral military action, could be most effective. Deák's often-repeated motto: "Quiet persistence can succeed where violence fails." (In some ways, this could be the slogan for the whole of Hungarian history.)

After an important military loss to Bismarck's Prussia in 1866, Austria began to agree that it couldn't control its rebellious Slavic holdings all by itself. The Habsburgs found themselves governing a vast, sprawling empire in which their own ethnic/linguistic group—Germans—were a tiny minority. In order to balance out the huge Slav population, they took Deák's advice and teamed up with the Hungarians.

And so, just 18 years after crushing the Hungarians in a war, the Habsburgs handed them the reins. With the Compromise *(Ausgleich)* of 1867, Austria granted Budapest the authority over the eastern half of their lands, creating the so-called Dual Monarchy of the Austro-Hungarian Empire. Hungary was granted their much-prized "home rule," where most matters (except finance, foreign policy, and the military) were administered from Budapest rather than Vienna. The Habsburg emperor, Franz Josef, agreed to a unique "king and emperor" *(König und Kaiser)* arrangement, where he was emperor of Austria, but only king of Hungary. In 1867, he was crowned as Hungarian king in both Buda (at Matthias Church) and Pest (on today's Roosevelt tér). Today, the insignia "K+K" *(König und Kaiser,* king and emperor) evokes these grand days. (For more on Franz Josef and his wife Sisi, see page 278.)

Budapest's Golden Age (1867–1918)

The *Ausgleich* marked an enormous turning point for the Hungarians, who once again governed their traditional holdings: large parts of today's Slovakia, Serbia, and Transylvania (northwest Romania), and smaller parts of today's Croatia, Slovenia, Ukraine, and Austria. To better govern their sprawling realm, in 1873, the cities of Buda, Pest, and Óbuda merged into one megametropolis: Budapest. But each part retained (and still retains) its unique character. Buda, which was more Germanic, Catholic, and pro-Habsburg, remains the traditional, conservative part of town. And Pest (with three times Buda's population), which was a hotbed of Magyar pride and the crucible of the uprisings of the mid-19th century, remains the more liberal, youthful, forward-looking part of town.

Serendipitously, Budapest's new prominence coincided with the 1,000th anniversary of the Hungarians' ancestors, the Magyars, arriving in Europe...one more excuse to dress things up. Budapest's longstanding rivalry with Vienna only spurred them to build bigger and better. The year 1896 saw an over-the-top millennial celebration, for which many of today's greatest structures were created (see page 40).

It was clearly Budapest's Golden Age. No European city grew faster in the second half of the 19th century than Budapest; in the last quarter of the 19th century alone, Budapest doubled in size, building on the foundation laid by Széchenyi and other patriots. By 1900, the city was larger than Rome, Madrid, or Amsterdam. During this time, among other claims to fame, Budapest was the world's biggest mill city—grinding grains from across Hungary and throughout the Balkans. The speedy expansion of the city garnered comparisons with Chicago, another boomtown of that era.

Budapest's most characteristic and most impressive architecture dates from this era. Today's palatial mansions and administrative buildings—whether sooty and crumbling, or newly restored and gleaming—hint at this era of unbridled prosperity. Compelled to adopt the trends of the Habsburgs, but eager to distinguish their own, uniquely Hungarian style, local architects made creative use of  Historicism—borrowing bits and pieces of past styles, injecting a healthy dose of bigger-is-better modernity, and finishing it all off with striking, unique flourishes. Miklós Ybl and Ödön Lechner were two of the most prominent architects of this era, designing banks, museums, churches, and municipal buildings around

Budapest. It was during this time that many buildings were first decorated with the colorful Zsolnay tiles—pretty as porcelain but hard as stone—invented in the city of Pécs (see page 346). To this day, these colorful adornments are a defining characteristic of Hungarian architecture.

It was also a period of great artistic and creative achievement. Composers Franz Liszt (more Germanic than Magyar) and (later) Béla Bartók and Zoltán Kodály incorporated the folk and Roma (Gypsy) songs of the Hungarian and Transylvanian countryside into their music. As Magyar culture thrived, the traditions of the countryside flowed into the music salons of Budapest. (For more on these great musicians, see "Hungarian Music" on page 252.)

Observers at the time saw Hungarians as characterized by a strange combination of pessimism and optimism: pessimistic about their future, especially relating to the Habsburgs; and optimistic (or maybe even chauvinistic) about the influence of their culture—which, while thriving, remained on the fringe of mainstream Europe. Hungarian historians proposed outrageous boasts about Magyar heritage (including suggesting that Adam and Eve must have been Magyars, and "proving" connections between the Magyars and the Huns and ancient Greeks).

During its time of plenty, Hungary—which had for so long been an oppressed minority under the Habsburgs—became known for disrespecting its own minorities' rights. (Only a little more than half of the people in Hungarian territory were ethnic Hungarians.) Most signs were in Hungarian only, and the Magyar tongue was taught in every school in the realm. Minorities—who were given virtually no say in government—staged uprisings and revolts, and in 1868 Croatia was even granted semi-autonomy. (It wasn't enough—as early as 1890, Croats began grumbling with Serbs and other South Slavs to create their own Yugo-Slavia.)

However, this did have the intended effect of "Magyarization"—people from all ethnic backgrounds adopted the Hungarian language and culture, giving it an uncanny persistence for something so very foreign and so very old. Germans and Jews adapted their names to Hungarian. For example, the Hungarian communist leader Belá Kun was born Aaron Kohn.

Before long, the optimist in every Hungarian would be proven very wrong indeed—as the Golden Age came crashing to an end, and Hungary plunged into its darkest period.

The Crisis of Trianon (1918–1939)

World War I marked the end of the age of divine monarchs, as the Romanovs of Russia, the Ottomans of Asia Minor, and, yes, the Habsburgs of Austria-Hungary saw their empires break apart. Hungary, which had been riding the Habsburgs' coattails to power

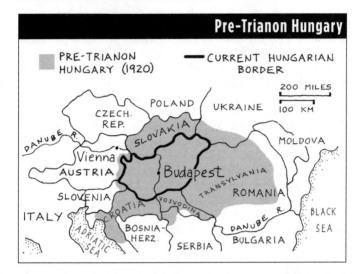

Pre-Trianon Hungary

PRE-TRIANON HUNGARY (1920)

━━ CURRENT HUNGARIAN BORDER

200 MILES / 100 KM

POLAND · UKRAINE · CZECH. REP. · DANUBE R. · SLOVAKIA · MOLDOVA · Vienna · AUSTRIA · Budapest · TRANSYLVANIA · ROMANIA · SLOVENIA · CROATIA · VOJVODINA · ITALY · ADRIATIC SEA · BOSNIA-HERZ. · DANUBE R. · BLACK SEA · SERBIA · BULGARIA

and prominence for the past half-century, now paid the price. As retribution for their role on the losing side of World War I, the 1920 Treaty of Trianon (named for the palace on the grounds of Versailles where it was signed) reassigned two-thirds of Hungary's former territory and half of its population to Romania, Ukraine, Czechoslovakia, and Yugoslavia (Slovenia, Croatia, and Serbia).

It is impossible to overstate the impact of the Treaty of Trianon on the Hungarian psyche—and on Hungarian history. Not unlike the overnight construction of the Berlin Wall, towns along the new Hungarian borders were suddenly divided down the middle. Many Hungarians found themselves unable to visit relatives or commute to jobs that were in the same country the day before. This sent hundreds of thousands of Hungarian refugees—now "foreigners" in their own towns—into Budapest, sparking an enormous but bittersweet boom in the capital.

To this day, the Treaty of Trianon is regarded as one of the greatest tragedies of Hungarian history. Like the Basques and the Serbs, the Hungarians feel separated from each other by circumstances outside their control. Today, more than two million ethnic Hungarians live outside Hungary (mostly in Romania)—and many Hungarians claim that these lands still belong to the Magyars. The sizeable Magyar minorities in neighboring countries have often been mistreated—particularly in Romania (under Ceaușescu), Yugoslavia (under Milošević), and Slovakia (under Mečiar). You'll see maps, posters, and bumper stickers with the distinctive shape of a much larger, pre-WWI Hungary...patriotically displayed by Magyars who feel as strongly about Trianon as if it happened yesterday. Some Hungarians see the enlargement of the European

Union as a happy ending in the big-picture sense: They have finally been reunited with Slovakia and Romania.

After Trianon, the newly shrunken Kingdom of Hungary had to reinvent itself. The Hungarian crown sat unworn in the Royal Palace, as if waiting for someone worthy to claim it. The WWI hero Admiral Miklós Horthy had won many battles with the Austro-Hungarian navy. Though the new Hungary had no sea and no navy, Horthy retained his rank and ruled the country as a regent. A popular joke points out that during this time, Hungary was a "kingdom without a king" and a landlocked country ruled by a sea admiral. This sense of compounded deficiency pretty much sums up the morose attitude Hungarians have about those gloomy post-Trianon days.

Adding insult to injury, in the mid-1940s Hungary's currency (the *pengő*) underwent the worst inflation in the history of money. At the lowest point of the crisis, the government issued a 100,000,000,000,000,000,000-*pengő* note. Their plan for a 1,000,000,000,000,000,000,000-*pengő* bill fell through when the note became worthless after they printed it, but before they had a chance to circulate it.

The mounting financial crisis, and lingering resentment about the strict post-WWI reparations, made Hungary fertile ground for some bold new fascist ideas.

World War II and the Arrow Cross (1939–1945)

As Adolf Hitler rose to power, some countries that had felt unfairly treated in the aftermath of World War I—including Hungary—saw Nazi Germany as a vehicle to greater independence. Admiral Horthy joined forces with the Nazis with the hope that they might help Hungary regain the crippling territorial losses of Trianon. In 1941, Hungary (reluctantly) declared war on the Soviet Union in June—and against the US and Britain in December.

Being an ally to the Nazis, rather than an occupied state, also allowed Hungary a certain degree of self-determination through the war—temporarily saving its sizeable Jewish population from immediate deportation. Winning back chunks of Slovakia, Transylvania, and Croatia in the early days of World War II also bolstered the Nazis' acceptance in Hungary.

As Nazism took hold in Germany, the Hungarian fascist movement—spearheaded by the Arrow Cross Party (Nyilaskeresztes Párt)—gained popularity within Hungary. As Germany increased its demands for Hungarian soldiers and food, Admiral Horthy resisted...until Hitler's patience wore thin. In March of 1944, the Nazis invaded and installed the Arrow Cross in power. The Arrow Cross made up for lost time, immediately

beginning a savage campaign of executing Hungary's Jews—not only sending them to death camps, but butchering them in the streets. Almost 600,000 Hungarian Jews were murdered. (For more on this dark era of Hungarian history, see "The Jewish Story of Budapest" sidebar, page 72.)

The Soviet Army eventually "liberated" Hungary, but at the expense of Budapest: A months-long siege, from Christmas of 1944 to mid-February of 1945, reduced the proud city to rubble. One in 10 Hungarian citizens perished in the war.

Communism...with a Pinch of Paprika (1945–1989)

After World War II, Hungary was gradually compelled to adopt Moscow's system of government. The Soviet-puppet hardliner Mátyás Rákosi ruled Hungary with an iron fist. Everyday people were terrorized by the KGB-style secret police, called the ÁVO and ÁVH, to accept the new regime. Non-Hungarians were deported, potential and actual dissidents disappeared into the horrifying gulag system of Siberia, food shortages were epidemic, people were compelled to spy on their friends and families, and countless lives were ruined. Coming on the heels of Trianon and two devastating world wars, communist rule was a blow that Hungary is still recovering from. (For much more on life in Soviet-controlled Hungary, see the House of Terror Tour on page 159.)

Beginning on October 23, 1956, the Hungarians courageously staged a monumental uprising, led by Communist Party reformer Imre Nagy. Initially, it appeared that one of the cells on the Soviet Bloc might win itself the right to semi-autonomy. But Moscow couldn't let that happen. In a Tiananmen Square–style crackdown, the Soviets sent in tanks to brutally put down the uprising and occupy the city. When the dust settled, 2,500 Hungarians were dead, and 200,000 fled to the West. (If you know any Hungarians in the US, their families more than likely fled there in 1956.) Nagy was arrested, given a sham trial, and executed in 1958. For more on these events, see the "1956" sidebar on page 120.

The Hungarians were devastated, in every sense. They were frustrated that the Suez Canal crisis distracted the world from their uprising. Many felt betrayed that the US—which spoke so boldly against the Soviet Union—did not offer them military support (contrary to the promises of the US-based Radio Free Europe). While the US and its Western allies understandably did not want to turn the Cold War hot, the Hungarians (also understandably) felt abandoned.

Weeks after the uprising came the so-called "Blood in the Water" match at the Melbourne Olympics. Soviet satellite states were often ordered to "throw" matches to allow the USSR's athletes to prevail. On December 6, 1956, Moscow issued such a decree to the Hungarian men's water polo team in their semifinal against the Soviet Union. The Hungarians refused and played their hearts out, much to the delight of their fans (and the rest of the world). The game turned violent, and in one indelible image, a Hungarian athlete emerged from the pool with blood pouring from a gash above his right eye. The Hungarians won, 4-0, and went on to take the gold.

After the uprising, the USSR installed János Kádár—a colleague of Nagy's who was also loyal to Moscow—to lead Hungary.

For a few years, things were bleak, as the secret police ratcheted up their efforts against potential dissidents. But in the 1960s, Kádár's reformist tendencies began to cautiously emerge. Seeking to gain the support of his subjects (and avoid further uprisings), Kádár adopted the optimistic motto, "If you are not against us, you are with us." While still mostly cooperating with Moscow, Kádár gradually allowed the people of Hungary more freedom than citizens of neighboring countries had—a system dubbed "goulash communism." The "New Economic Mechanism" of 1968 partly opened Hungary to foreign trade. People from other Warsaw Pact countries—Czechs, Slovaks, and Poles—flocked to Budapest's Váci utca to experience "Western evils" unavailable to them back home, such as Adidas sneakers and Big Macs. People half-joked that Hungary was the happiest barrack in the communist camp.

In the late 1980s, the Eastern Bloc began to thaw. And Hungary—which was always skeptical of the Soviets (or any foreign rule)—was one of the first satellite states that implemented real change. In February of 1989, the Hungarian communist parliament, with little fanfare, essentially voted to put an expiration date on their own regime. There were three benchmarks in that fateful year: May 2, when Hungary was the first Soviet Bloc country to effectively open its borders to the West (by removing its border fence with Austria); June 16, when communist reformer Imre Nagy and his comrades were given a proper, ceremonial reburial on Heroes' Square; and August 19, when, in the first tentative steps toward the reunification of Europe, Hungarians and Austrians came together in a field near the town of Sopron for the so-called "Pan-European Picnic." (Some 900 East Germans seized this opportunity to make a run for the border...and slipped into the West while Hungarian border guards refused their orders to shoot defectors.) On October 23—the anniversary of the 1956 Uprising—the truly democratic Republic of Hungary triumphantly replaced the People's Republic of Hungary.

Hungary's first post-communist president, Árpád Göncz, was a protestor from the 1950s who was famous for learning English while in prison...a skill that later came in handy when he translated *The Lord of the Rings* into Hungarian. Fantasy was becoming a reality in Hungary. Change was in the air.

Hungary Today (1989–Present)

The transition from communism to capitalism has been rocky in Hungary. While many Hungarians were eager for the freedom to travel and pursue the interests that democracy allowed them, many others struggled to cope with the sudden reduction of government-provided services. Hungary seems to have had an even more difficult transition than some of its neighbors, as post-communist governments have attempted to preserve as many social services as possible while stepping down taxation—leaving Hungary with rampant inflation unmatched in Europe (and bringing back unpleasant memories of the *pengő* debacle of the 1940s).

The process of privatization (handing property once seized by the communist government back over to private owners) has been messy. When possible, the government attempted to find the original owners of the property, and allow them to purchase it at a low price. But it was often difficult, or impossible, to find someone who owned a property before World War II (especially considering that one in 10 Hungarians did not survive that war). And so, in other cases, people were simply given the opportunity to purchase the apartment or house where they were living on the day of the transition. If you had a good apartment, this was good news; if not, you were out of luck.

The transition has manifested itself in sometimes surprising ways. For example, under communism, the medical profession was prestigious but not very lucrative. In the new capitalist era, things have not changed much, and Hungarians carry on an unusual (to us) tradition: It's expected that a patient will tip his or her doctor after the appointment. While this is a largely unspoken agreement, it follows a carefully proscribed routine: The money, always cash, is

PAST AND PRESENT

What Do Stephen Colbert, Chuck Norris, and Miklós Zrínyi Have in Common?

In 2006, the Hungarian government announced an online contest to choose a name for a new bridge in northern Budapest. While Hungarians tend to be proud of their rich history, a spirit of irreverence permeated this particular contest. The name "Chuck Norris Bridge"—for the American action star, popularized in a series of campy Hungarian ads—shot out to an early lead. The government, nervous about the unexpected irreverence, lobbied hard to win votes for the name "Miklós Zrínyi Bridge," for a 17th-century Croatian military leader who defended Hungary from invading Ottomans.

But then, on August 11, American television satirist Stephen Colbert implored his viewers to visit the website to name the bridge for himself. When the voting was complete a week and a half later, Colbert had trounced his competitors with 17 million votes—that's seven million more than the entire population of Hungary—with Zrínyi finishing a distant second with two million votes. The Hungarian ambassador to the US was a good sport, appearing on Colbert's show to tell him he'd won, but was ineligible (since he neither spoke Hungarian nor was deceased).

A few weeks later, the bridge was unimaginatively christened "Megyeri Bridge," since it connects two suburbs called Megyer (Káposztásmegyer and Békásmegyer)—a name that hadn't even been in the running. Today it's a crucial link in Budapest's new M-0 beltway. If nothing else, the bridge-naming contest demonstrated that democracy and the Internet don't always combine for serious results.

inserted into a blank white envelope and handed to the doctor at the end of the session. The amount that's expected varies by procedure, which can cause a lot of anxiety for a patient who doesn't know how much to pay (as if going to the doctor weren't stressful enough).

In 2004, Hungary took the monumental step of joining the European Union (along with nine other, mostly former-communist nations). Many of the new members demonstrated great ambivalence about joining the EU, fearing that they would lose their hard-fought autonomy. And EU membership has come with its share of heavy-handed regulation and convoluted bureaucracy. But even the most ardent Euroskeptics now agree that the EU has done more good than harm.

Still, the EU hasn't solved all of Hungary's problems. Hungary's leaders continue to struggle with how to afford the generous social-welfare network its people have come to expect.

The Hungarian Socialist Party, which took control of parliament in 2002, stubbornly maintained and even extended some social programs, prompting experts to worry that the mounting public debt would bankrupt the country.

Hungary made international headlines in 2006, when Prime Minister Ferenc Gyurcsány gave a secret speech to the party's leaders after his Hungarian Socialist Party won re-election in April. The intent of his shockingly frank remarks was to give his colleagues a wake-up call. But Gyurcsány's method—ranting on and on about how badly they'd fouled things up (and using very colorful language)—was ill-advised. Someone in the meeting recorded the whole thing, waited a few months, then turned the audio tape over to the press.

On September 17, 2006, Hungarians turned on their TVs to hear their prime minister detailing the ways he and his party had driven their country to the brink of ruin, and then shamelessly lied about it to stay in power: "We have screwed up. Not a little but a lot. No country in Europe has screwed up as much as we have...We did not actually do anything for four years. Nothing...We lied morning, noon, and night."

The following night, demonstrators (many of them members of fringe political groups—and even, according to local scuttlebutt, known gangs of soccer hooligans) showed up at two strategic squares in downtown Budapest, demanding Gyurcsány's resignation. Riot police were sent in to subdue the looters with water cannons and tear gas. The violence was quickly put down, but the unrest continued to simmer for several months. Gyurcsány refused to resign, but Hungary's politicians learned a valuable lesson about dealing with a fragile new democracy.

Hungary continues to struggle with rampant inflation, which has postponed its adoption of the euro currency. In late 2008, with Gyurcsány warning of "state bankruptcy" and a currency collapse, Hungary received a $25 billion bailout package from the EU, International Monetary Fund, and World Bank.

Fortunately, tourists visiting today's Hungary are scarcely aware of its economic woes. The Hungarian people—relieved to be free of oppression, and allowed to pursue their lovably quirky customs with a renewed vigor—enthusiastically welcome and charm visitors. It's been a long road for the Hungarians from those distant, windblown steppes of Central Asia...but today they seem to be doing better than ever.

APPENDIX

CONTENTS

RESOURCES

Tourist Information Offices

The **Hungarian National Tourist Office** is a wealth of information. Before your trip, request the free *Budapest Guide* and any specifics you may want (such as brochures about specific regions or topics). Call 212/695-1221 or visit www.gotohungary.com (info @gotohungary.com).

Once in Hungary, **local tourist offices**—which all belong to a large government agency—are called "TourInform," and are marked by a white *i* in a green rectangle (www.tourinform.hu). These vary in quality; those in some of the smaller towns (including Eger's) can be excellent, while Budapest's are hit-or-miss (locations listed on page 39 of the Orientation chapter). Note that tourist information offices are abbreviated "**TI**" in this book.

Resources from Rick
Guidebooks and Online Updates

I've done my best to make sure that the information in this book is up-to-date—but things change. For the very latest, visit www.ricksteves.com/update. Also at my website, you'll find a valuable list of reports and experiences—good and bad—from fellow travelers who have used this book (www.ricksteves.com/feedback).

Rick Steves' Budapest is one of more than 30 titles in my series on European travel, which includes country guidebooks (including

Eastern Europe), city and regional guidebooks (including Prague & the Czech Republic and Vienna, Salzburg & Tirol), and my budget-travel skills handbook, *Rick Steves' Europe Through the Back Door.* My phrase books—for German, French, Italian, Spanish, and Portuguese—are practical and budget-oriented. My other books are *Europe 101* (a crash course on art and history, newly expanded and in full color), *European Christmas* (on traditional and modern-day celebrations), and *Postcards from Europe* (a fun memoir of my travels over 25 years). For a complete list of my books, see the inside of the last page of this book.

Public Television and Radio Shows

My TV series, *Rick Steves' Europe,* covers European destinations in 80 shows, including one on Budapest. My weekly public radio show, *Travel with Rick Steves,* features interviews with travel experts from around the world. All the TV scripts and radio shows (which include interviews from over a hundred hour-long programs, and are easy and free to download to an iPod or other MP3 player) are at www.ricksteves.com.

Maps

The black-and-white maps in this book, designed by my well-traveled staff, are concise and simple. The maps are intended to help you locate recommended places and get to local TIs, where you can pick up a more in-depth map of the city or region (usually free).

Better maps are sold at newsstands and bookstores all over Hungary—take a look before you buy to be sure the map has the level of detail you want. The Hungarian-produced maps by Cartographia are best (www.cartographiaonline.com). Train travelers can usually manage fine with the freebies they get at the local tourist offices. Hikers will find no shortage of excellent, very

Begin Your Trip at www.ricksteves.com

At our travel website, you'll find a wealth of free information on European destinations, including fresh monthly news and helpful tips from thousands of fellow travelers.

Our **online Travel Store** offers travel bags and accessories specially designed by Rick Steves to help you travel smarter and lighter. These include Rick's popular carry-on bags (wheeled and rucksack versions), money belts, totes, toiletries kits, adapters, other accessories, and a wide selection of guidebooks, planning maps, and DVDs.

Choosing the right **railpass** for your trip—amidst hundreds of options—can drive you nutty. We'll help you choose the best pass for your needs, plus give you a bunch of free extras.

Rick Steves' Europe Through the Back Door travel company offers **tours** with more than two-dozen itineraries and about 450 departures reaching the best destinations in this book...and beyond. We offer a 17-day Best of Eastern Europe tour that visits Budapest and Eger, along with highlights of the Czech Republic, Poland, Croatia, and Slovenia. You'll enjoy great guides, a fun bunch of travel partners (with small groups of around 26), and plenty of room to spread out in a big, comfy bus. You'll find European adventures to fit every vacation length. For all the details, and to get our Tour Catalog and a free Rick Steves Tour Experience DVD (filmed on location during an actual tour), visit www.ricksteves.com or call the Tour Department at 425/608-4217.

detailed maps locally. For drivers, I'd recommend a 1:450,000-scale map of Hungary.

Other Guidebooks

Especially if you'll be exploring beyond my recommended destinations, you may want some supplemental information. Considering the improvements that they'll make in your $4,000 vacation, $40 for extra maps and books is money well-spent. One budget tip can easily justify the price of an extra guidebook. Note that none of the following books is updated annually; check the publication date before you buy.

The Rough Guides are packed with historical and cultural insight. The Lonely Planet guides are similar, but are designed more for travelers than for intellectuals. Both of these publish books on Hungary and on Budapest. If choosing between competing books by these two companies, I buy the one that was published most recently.

Students, backpackers, and nightlife-seekers should consider the Let's Go guides (by Harvard students, with the best hostel listings, look for their *Eastern Europe* title). Dorling Kindersley (DK) publishes snazzy Eyewitness Guides on Budapest and on Hungary. While pretty to look at, these guides weigh a ton and are skimpy on actual content.

In Your Pocket publishes a regularly updated magazine on Budapest. This handy guide is especially good for its up-to-date hotel, restaurant, and nightlife recommendations (available locally, usually for a few dollars, but often free; condensed version available free online at www.inyourpocket.com).

For more extensive coverage of Hungary's neighboring countries, consider *Rick Steves' Eastern Europe; Rick Steves' Vienna, Salzburg & Tirol; Rick Steves' Prague & the Czech Republic;* and *Rick Steves' Croatia & Slovenia.*

Recommended Books and Movies

To get the feel of Hungary past and present, consider these books and films:

Non-Fiction

Lonnie Johnson's *Central Europe: Enemies, Neighbors, Friends* is the best history overview of Hungary and the surrounding nations. John Lukacs' *Budapest 1900* is a scholarly but readable cultural study that captures Budapest at its turn-of-the-20th-century zenith. Patrick Leigh Fermor's *Between the Woods and the Water* is the vividly recounted memoir of a young man who traveled by foot and on horseback across the Balkan Peninsula (including Hungary) in 1933. András Török's irreverent *Budapest: A Critical*

Guide, while technically a guidebook, offers more local insight (and wit) than any other source. Timothy Garton Ash has written several good "eyewitness account" books analyzing the transition in Central and Eastern Europe over the last two decades, including *History of the Present* and *The Magic Lantern.* Tina Rosenberg's dense but thought-provoking *The Haunted Land* asks how individuals who actively supported communist regimes should be treated in the post-communist age. For information on Eastern European Roma (Gypsies), consider the textbook-style *We Are the Romani People* by Ian Hancock, and the more literary *Bury Me Standing* by Isabel Fonseca. And for a look at life during communist times—albeit not in Hungary—Croatian journalist Slavenka Drakulić has written a pair of insightful essay collections from a woman's perspective: *Café Europa: Life After Communism* and *How We Survived Communism and Even Laughed.*

Fiction

Imre Kertész, a Hungarian-Jewish Auschwitz survivor who won the Nobel Prize for Literature in 2002, is best known for his semi-autobiographical novel *Fatelessness (Sorstalanság),* which chronicles the experience of a young concentration-camp prisoner. Arthur Phillips' confusingly titled novel *Prague* tells the story of American expats negotiating young-adult life in post-communist Budapest, where they often feel one-upped by their compatriots doing the same in the Czech capital (hence the title). Joseph Roth's *The Radetzky March* details the decline of an aristocratic family in the Austro-Hungarian Empire. The Newbery Honor book *Zlateh the Goat* (Isaac Bashevis Singer) includes seven folktales of Jewish Eastern Europe.

Films

One of the more accessible films for an introduction to Budapest is *Sunshine* (1999, starring Ralph Fiennes, directed by István Szabó; not to be confused with Danny Boyle's excellent but very different 2007 film of the same name). Tracing three generations of an aristocratic Jewish family in Budapest—from the Golden Age, through the Holocaust, to the Cold War—*Sunshine* is an enlightening if somewhat melodramatic look at recent Hungarian history.

For Hungarian-language films, one of the biggest crossover hits of recent years is the surreal dark comedy *Kontroll* (2003), about ticket inspectors on the Budapest Metro whose lives are turned upside-down by a serial killer lurking in the shadows. *Fateless,* the 2005 adaptation of Imre Kertész's Nobel Prize–winning novel about a young man in a concentration camp, was scripted by Kertész himself. The 1998 Oscar-winning documentary *The Last Days* chronicles the fate of Jews when the Nazis took over Hungary in 1944. *The Witness (A Tanú,* a.k.a. *Without a Trace,* 1969), a cult classic about a simple man who mysteriously wins the favor of communist bigwigs, is a biting satire of the darkest days of Soviet rule. *Time Stands Still (Megáll Az Idö),* a hit at the 1982 Cannes Film Festival, tells the story of young Hungarians in the 1960s. *Children of Glory (Szabadság, Szerelem,* 2006), which has seen only limited release in the US, dramatizes the true story of the Hungarian water polo team that defiantly trounced the Soviets at the Olympics just after the 1956 Uprising.

Many American studios have taken advantage of Hungary's low prices to film would-be blockbusters in Budapest (such as the 2002 Eddie Murphy/Owen Wilson action-comedy *I Spy*—a terrible film that makes wonderful use of many real Budapest settings). More often, Budapest stands in for other cities—for example, as Buenos Aires in Madonna's 1996 film *Evita,* and as various European cities in Stephen Spielberg's 2005 film *Munich.*

Two recent German movies—while not about Hungary—are still excellent for their insight into the surreal and paranoid days of the Soviet Bloc. The Oscar-winning *The Lives of Others* (2006) chronicles the constant surveillance that the communist regime employed to keep potential dissidents in line. For a funny and nostalgic look at post-communist Europe's fitful transition to capitalism, *Good Bye Lenin!* (2003) can't be beat.

TELEPHONES, EMAIL, AND MAIL

Telephones

Smart travelers learn the phone system and use it daily to reserve or reconfirm rooms, get tourist information, reserve restaurants, confirm tour times, or phone home.

Types of Phones

You'll encounter various kinds of phones on your trip:

Card-operated phones, in which you insert a locally bought phone card into a public pay phone, are available in Hungary.

Coin-operated phones, the original kind of pay phone (but now increasingly rare), require you to have enough change to complete your call.

Hotel room phones are sometimes cheap for local calls (confirm at the front desk first), but can be a rip-off for long-distance calls (more details later in this section).

American mobile phones work in Europe if they're GSM-based, tri-band or quad-band, and on a calling plan that includes international calls. They're convenient, but pricey. For example, if you're roaming with a T-Mobile phone in Hungary, you'll pay $1 per minute for calls and about $0.35 per text message.

Hurdling the Language Barrier

The language barrier in Hungary is no bigger than elsewhere in Europe. In fact, as a monolingual visitor, I find that it's actually easier to communicate in Hungary than in places such as Italy or Spain. Since Hungary is small and not politically powerful, the people here realize that it's unreasonable to expect visitors to learn Hungarian (which has only 12 million speakers worldwide). It's essential for them to find a common language with the rest of the world—so they learn English early and well. You'll find that most people in the tourist industry—and virtually all young people—speak fine English.

Of course, not *everyone* speaks English. You'll run into the most substantial language barriers in situations when you need to deal with a lesser-educated clerk or service person (train stations and post-office counters, maids, museum guards, bakers, and so on)—especially outside of Budapest. Be reasonable in your expectations. Museum ticket-sellers in Hungary are every bit as friendly and multilingual as they are in the US.

Luckily, it's relatively easy to get your point across in these places. I've often bought a train ticket simply by writing out the name of my destination; the time I want to travel (using the 24-hour clock); and the date I want to leave (year first, then month, then day). Here's an example of what I'd show a ticket-seller at a train station: "Eger, 10:30, 2009.8.15."

Hungarians, realizing that their language intimidates Americans, often invent easier nicknames for themselves—so András becomes "Andrew," Erzsébet goes by "Elisabeth," and István tells you, "Call me Steve."

There are certain universal English words all Hungarians know: "hello," "please," "thank you," "super," "pardon," "stop," "menu," "problem," and "no problem." Still, while Hungarians don't expect you to be fluent in their tongue, they definitely appreciate it when they can tell you're making an effort to pronounce Hungarian words correctly or use the local pleasantries. For pronunciation tips, see page 24. For survival phrases in Hungarian, see page 425.

Don't be afraid to interact with locals. Hungarians might initially seem shy or even brusque—a holdover from the closed communist society—but often a simple smile is the only icebreaker you need to make a new friend. You'll find that doors open a little more quickly when you know a few words of the language. Give it your best shot. The locals will appreciate your efforts.

European mobile phones run about $75–90 (for the most basic models) and come without contracts. These phones are loaded with prepaid calling time that you can recharge as you use up the minutes. As long as you're not "roaming" outside the phone's home country, incoming calls are free. If you're traveling to multiple countries within Europe, make sure the phone is electronically "unlocked," so that you can swap out its SIM card (a fingernail-sized chip that holds the phone's information) for a new one in other countries. For more information on mobile phones, see www.ricksteves.com/phones.

Using Phone Cards

Get a phone card for your calls. Prepaid phone cards come in two types: insertable and international.

Insertable phone cards are a convenient way to pay for calls from public pay phones. Buy these cards at post offices, tobacco shops, newsstands, post offices, and train stations (sold in several denominations starting at 1,000 Ft). Simply take the phone off the hook, insert the prepaid card, wait for a dial tone, and dial away. The price of the call (local or international) is automatically deducted while you talk. Insertable phone cards are a good deal for calling within Europe, but calling the US can be more expensive (at least $0.50/min) than if you use an international phone card. Each European country has its own insertable phone card—so your Hungarian card won't work in a Slovak phone. Be aware that with the prevalence of mobile phones, public phones are getting harder to find.

Prepaid **international phone cards,** which are popular and easy to buy in some parts of Europe, are still relatively rare (and more expensive) in Hungary. Look for fliers advertising long-distance rates, or ask about the cards at Internet cafés, newsstands, souvenir shops, youth hostels, and post offices. If you can snare one of these cards, your calls to the US will generally cost around $0.25–0.50 cents per minute (and they also work for domestic calls).

Before buying a card, make sure the access number you dial is toll-free, not a local number (or else you'll be paying for a local call *and* deducting time from your calling card). These cards usually work only in the country where you buy them, but some brands work internationally. Buy a lower denomination in case the card is a dud.

To use a card, scratch off the back to reveal your code. After you dial the access phone number, the message tells you to enter your code and then dial the phone number you want to call. A voice may announce how much is left in your account before you dial. Usually you can select English, but if the prompts are in another language, experiment: Dial your code, followed by the pound sign (#), then the number, then pound again, and so on, until it works. For tips on dialing, see "How to Dial," below.

Using Hotel-Room Phones, VoIP, or US Calling Cards

Calling from the phone in your **hotel room** is convenient...but expensive. While incoming calls (made by folks back home) can be the cheapest way to keep in touch, charges for *outgoing* calls can be a very unpleasant surprise. Before you dial, get a clear explanation from the hotel staff of the charges, even for local and (supposedly) toll-free calls. I find hotel room phones handy for making local calls.

If your family has an inexpensive way to call Europe, either through a long-distance plan or prepaid calling card, have them call you in your hotel room. Give them a list of your hotels' phone numbers before you go. Then, as you travel, send them an email or mobile-phone text message, or make a quick pay-phone call, to set up a time for them to give you a ring.

If you're traveling with a laptop, consider trying **VoIP (Voice over Internet Protocol).** With VoIP, two computers act as the phones, allowing for a free Internet-based call. The major providers are Skype (www.skype.com) and Google Talk (www.google .com/talk).

US Calling Cards (such as the ones offered by AT&T, MCI, and Sprint) are the worst option. You'll nearly always save a lot of money by paying with a phone card (see above).

How to Dial

Calling from the US to Europe, or vice versa, is simple—once you break the code. The European calling chart on page 416 will walk you through it.

Dialing Domestic Calls

Like many things in Hungary, making domestic calls is uniquely confusing. You must dial different codes depending on whether you're calling locally or long distance within the country.

To dial a number in the same city, simply dial direct, with no area code.

To dial long-distance within Hungary, you have to add the prefix 06, followed by the area code (e.g., Budapest's area code is 1, so you dial 06-1, then the rest of the number).

For example, to call a hotel in Eger, I'd dial 411-711 if I'm calling from within Eger; but from Budapest, I'd have to dial 06, then 36 (Eger's area code), then 411-711.

APPENDIX

European Calling Chart

Just smile and dial, using this key:
AC = Area Code, LN = Local Number.

European Country	Calling long distance within ...	Calling from the US or Canada to ...	Calling from a European country to ...
Austria	AC + LN	011 + 43 + AC (without the initial zero) + LN	00 + 43 + AC (without the initial zero) + LN
Belgium	LN	011 + 32 + LN (without initial zero)	00 + 32 + LN (without initial zero)
Bosnia-Herzegovina	AC + LN	011 + 387 + AC (without initial zero) + LN	00 + 387 + AC (without initial zero) + LN
Britain	AC + LN	011 + 44 + AC (without initial zero) + LN	00 + 44 + AC (without initial zero) + LN
Croatia	AC + LN	011 + 385 + AC (without initial zero) + LN	00 + 385 + AC (without initial zero) + LN
Czech Republic	LN	011 + 420 + LN	00 + 420 + LN
Denmark	LN	011 + 45 + LN	00 + 45 + LN
Estonia	LN	011 + 372 + LN	00 + 372 + LN
Finland	AC + LN	011 + 358 + AC (without initial zero) + LN	999 + 358 + AC (without initial zero) + LN
France	LN	011 + 33 + LN (without initial zero)	00 + 33 + LN (without initial zero)
Germany	AC + LN	011 + 49 + AC (without initial zero) + LN	00 + 49 + AC (without initial zero) + LN
Greece	LN	011 + 30 + LN	00 + 30 + LN
Hungary	06 + AC + LN	011 + 36 + AC + LN	00 + 36 + AC + LN
Ireland	AC + LN	011 + 353 + AC (without initial zero) + LN	00 + 353 + AC (without initial zero) + LN

European Country	Calling long distance within ...	Calling from the US or Canada to ...	Calling from a European country to ...
Italy	LN	011 + 39 + LN	00 + 39 + LN
Montenegro	AC + LN	011 + 382 + AC (without initial zero) + LN	00 + 382 + AC (without initial zero) + LN
Netherlands	AC + LN	011 + 31 + AC (without initial zero) + LN	00 + 31 + AC (without initial zero) + LN
Norway	LN	011 + 47 + LN	00 + 47 + LN
Poland	LN	011 + 48 + LN (without initial zero)	00 + 48 + LN (without initial zero)
Portugal	LN	011 + 351 + LN	00 + 351 + LN
Slovakia	AC + LN	011 + 421 + AC (without initial zero) + LN	00 + 421 + AC (without initial zero) + LN
Slovenia	AC + LN	011 + 386 + AC (without initial zero) + LN	00 + 386 + AC (without initial zero) + LN
Spain	LN	011 + 34 + LN	00 + 34 + LN
Sweden	AC + LN	011 + 46 + AC (without initial zero) + LN	00 + 46 + AC (without initial zero) + LN
Switzerland	LN	011 + 41 + LN (without initial zero)	00 + 41 + LN (without initial zero)
Turkey	AC (if no initial zero is included, add one) + LN	011 + 90 + AC (without initial zero) + LN	00 + 90 + AC (without initial zero) + LN

- The instructions above apply whether you're calling a land line or mobile phone.
- The international access codes (the first numbers you dial when making an international call) are 011 if you're calling from the US or Canada, or 00 if you're calling from virtually anywhere in Europe (except Finland, where it's 999).
- To call the US or Canada from Europe, dial 00, then 1 (the country code for the US and Canada), then the area code and number. In short, 00 + 1 + AC + LN = Hi, Mom!

Dialing Internationally

To make an international call **to Hungary,** start with the international access code (00 if calling from Europe, 011 from the United States or Canada), then Hungary's country code (36), then the area code (but not the 06) and number.

To make an international call **from Hungary,** dial 00, the country code of the country you're calling (see chart on page 416), the area code if applicable (many countries requires dropping the initial zero), and the local number.

So, to call my office in Edmonds, Washington, from Hungary, I dial 00 (Europe's international access code), 1 (the US country code), 425 (Edmonds' area code), and 771-8303.

Europeans often write their phone numbers with + at the front—it's just a placeholder for the international access code (again, that's 011 from the US or Canada, 00 from Europe).

Dialing Mobile Phones and Other Unusual Numbers

Certain Hungarian phone numbers are particularly tricky to dial. Numbers beginning with 0620, 0630, or 0670 are mobile phones; those beginning with 0680 are toll-free; and 0681 and 0690 are expensive toll lines.

To call these numbers **from within Hungary,** simply dial direct, as they appear in this book.

To dial them **from outside Hungary,** you need to replace the initial 06 with 011-36 (from the US) or 00-36 (from Europe). So, to call my favorite Budapest guide from inside Hungary, you'd dial 0620-926-0557; from North America, you'd dial 011-36-20-926-0557; and from another European country, you'd dial 00-36-20-926-0557.

Useful Phone Numbers
Emergencies
Any Emergency: Dial 112.
Police: Dial 107.
Ambulance: Dial 104.
Fire: Dial 105.
Directory Assistance: Dial 198.

Embassies in Budapest
United States: Tel. 1/475-4164, after-hours (17:00–8:00) emergency tel. 1/475-4703 or 1/475-4924 (Mon–Thu 13:00–16:00, Fri 9:00–12:00 & 13:00–16:00, closed Sat–Sun, Szabadság tér 12, district V, www.usembassy.hu).
Canada: Tel. 1/392-3360 (Mon–Thu 8:00–16:30, Fri 8:00–13:30, closed Sat–Sun, Ganz utca 12–14, district II).

Embassies in Bratislava, Slovakia

United States: Tel. 02/5443-0861 (Mon–Fri 8:00–11:45 & 14:00–15:15, closed Sat–Sun, Hviezdoslavovo Námestie 4, http://slovakia .usembassy.gov).
Canada: Tel. 02/5920-4031 (Mon–Fri 8:30–12:00 & 13:30–16:30, closed Sat–Sun, Mostová 2).

Email and Mail

Email: Many travelers set up a free email account with Yahoo, Microsoft (Hotmail), or Google (Gmail). Internet cafés are easy to find in Budapest, and in some smaller towns. Look for the places listed in this book, or ask the local TI, computer store, or your hotelier. If you have your own laptop, some cafés offer free Wi-Fi for paying customers.

Some hotels have a dedicated computer for guests' email needs—sometimes free, sometimes for a fee. Small places with no guest computer or Wi-Fi are accustomed to letting clients (who've asked politely) sit at their desk for a few minutes just to check their email.

Internet access for laptop users is becoming commonplace at most hotels and B&Bs. Most hotels that offer this do so for free, but some (especially fancier chain hotels) charge by the minute. You'll either access the hotel's wireless Internet (Wi-Fi, sometimes called "WLAN" in Europe), sometimes using a password provided by the hotelier; or plug your computer directly into an Internet wall socket (they can usually loan you a cable). I've noted this in each listing. If I say "Internet access," there's a public terminal in the lobby for guests to use. If I say "Wi-Fi" or "cable Internet," you can access it in your room, but only if you have your own laptop.

Mail: Get stamps at the neighborhood post office, newsstands within fancy hotels, and some mini-marts and card shops. While you can arrange for mail delivery to your hotel (allow 10 days for a letter to arrive), phoning and emailing are so easy that I've dispensed with mail stops altogether.

HOLIDAYS AND FESTIVALS

This is a partial list of holidays and festivals. While Hungary is a nominally Catholic country, most people are not very devout. Catholic holidays (such as Epiphany, Ascension, Corpus Christi, and the Assumption of Mary) are observed, but with less impact than in some other countries. Many of Budapest's top festivals share a website: www.fesztivalvaros.hu. I've listed websites for some of the other festivals below; for information on these or other activities, contact the Hungarian National Tourist Office (listed at the beginning of this chapter).

Jan 1	New Year's Day
Jan 6	Epiphany
March 15	National Day (celebrates 1848 Revolution)
Late March	Budapest Spring Festival (2 weeks, March 20–April 5 in 2009)
Early April	Budapest Fringe Festival (last weekend of Spring Festival, April 3–5 in 2009)
Easter	(April 12 in 2009, April 4 in 2010)
May 1	Labor Day (and anniversary of joining the EU)
Ascension	(May 21 in 2009, May 13 in 2010)
Pentecost	("Whitsunday"; May 31 in 2009, May 23 in 2010)
Whitmonday	(June 1 in 2009, May 24 in 2010)
Corpus Christi	(June 11 in 2009, June 3 in 2010)
June–July	Outdoor Festival, Pécs (outdoor performances in the evenings, www.pecs iszabadteri.hu)
Late June–late Aug	Summer on the Chain Bridge, Budapest (bridge is closed to traffic on weekends, lined with food stalls and performers)
Late June–late Aug	Szentendre Summer Festival, Szentendre (art festival with theater, concerts, film, activities)
Late June	Early Music Days, Sopron (1 week, June 20–27 in 2009, www.filharmoniabp.hu)
Early Aug	Sziget Festival, Budapest (1 week, rock and pop music, www.sziget.hu)
Aug 15	Assumption of Mary
Aug 20	St. István's Day (fireworks, celebrations)
Late Aug	Formula 1 races, Budapest (Aug 24–26 in 2009, www.hungaroinfo.com/formel1)
Late Aug–early Sept	Jewish Summer Festival, Budapest (2 weeks, www.jewishfestival.hu)

Oct 23	National Day (remembrances of 1956 Uprising)
Mid-Oct	Budapest Autumn Festival (1 week, music)
Nov 1	All Saints' Day/Remembrance Day (religious festival, some closures)
Dec 24–25	Christmas Eve and Christmas Day
Dec 26	Boxing Day

CONVERSIONS AND CLIMATE

Numbers and Stumblers

- Europeans write a few of their numbers differently than we do. 1 = $\mathcal{1}$, 4 = $\mathcal{4}$, 7 = $\mathcal{7}$.
- In Hungary, dates appear as year/month/day, so Christmas is 2010/12/25 (or sometimes using dots: 2010.12.25).
- Commas are decimal points and decimals commas. A dollar and a half is 1,50, and there are 5.280 feet in a mile.
- Remember, Hungarians usually list their surname first (for example, Bartók Béla instead of Béla Bartók).
- When counting with fingers, start with your thumb. If you hold up your first finger to request one item, you'll probably get two.
- What Americans call the second floor of a building is the first floor in Europe.
- On escalators and moving sidewalks, Europeans keep the left "lane" open for passing. Keep to the right.

Metric Conversions (approximate)

1 foot = 0.3 meter	1 square yard = 0.8 square meter
1 yard = 0.9 meter	1 square mile = 2.6 square kilometers
1 mile = 1.6 kilometers	1 ounce = 28 grams
1 centimeter = 0.4 inch	1 quart = 0.95 liter
1 meter = 39.4 inches	1 kilogram = 2.2 pounds
1 kilometer = 0.62 mile	32°F = 0°C

Climate

The first line is the average daily high; the second line, the average daily low. The third line shows the average number of rainy days. For more detailed weather statistics for destinations in this book (as well as the rest of the world), check www.worldclimate.com.

	J	F	M	A	M	J	J	A	S	O	N	D
HUNGARY • Budapest												
	34°	39°	50°	62°	71°	78°	82°	81°	74°	61°	47°	39°
	25°	28°	35°	44°	52°	58°	62°	60°	53°	44°	38°	30°
	13	12	11	11	13	13	10	9	7	10	14	13

Temperature Conversion: Fahrenheit and Celsius

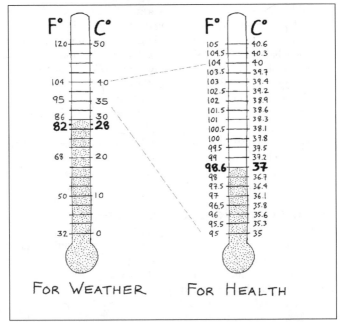

FOR WEATHER   FOR HEALTH

Europe takes its temperature using the Celsius scale, while we opt for Fahrenheit. For a rough conversion from Celsius to Fahrenheit, double the number and add 30. For weather, remember that 28°C is 82°F—perfect. For health, 37°C is just right.

Essential Packing Checklist

Whether you're traveling for five days or five weeks, here's what you'll need to bring. Remember to pack light to enjoy the sweet freedom of true mobility. Happy travels!

- ❏ 5 shirts
- ❏ 1 sweater or lightweight fleece jacket
- ❏ 2 pairs pants
- ❏ 1 pair shorts
- ❏ 1 swimsuit (women only—men can use shorts)
- ❏ 5 pairs underwear and socks
- ❏ 1 pair shoes
- ❏ 1 rainproof jacket
- ❏ Tie or scarf
- ❏ Money belt
- ❏ Money—your mix of:
  - ❏ Debit card for ATM withdrawals
  - ❏ Credit card
  - ❏ Hard cash in US dollars
- ❏ Documents (and back-up photocopies)
- ❏ Passport
- ❏ Airplane ticket
- ❏ Driver's license
- ❏ Student ID and hostel card
- ❏ Railpass/car rental voucher
- ❏ Insurance details
- ❏ Daypack
- ❏ Sealable plastic baggies
- ❏ Camera and related gear
- ❏ Empty water bottle
- ❏ Wristwatch and alarm clock
- ❏ Earplugs
- ❏ First-aid kit
- ❏ Medicine (labeled)
- ❏ Extra glasses/contacts and prescriptions
- ❏ Sunscreen and sunglasses
- ❏ Toiletries kit
- ❏ Soap
- ❏ Laundry soap (if liquid and carry-on, limit to 3 oz.)
- ❏ Clothesline
- ❏ Small towel
- ❏ Sewing kit
- ❏ Travel information
- ❏ Necessary map(s)
- ❏ Address list (email and mailing addresses)
- ❏ Postcards and photos from home
- ❏ Notepad and pen
- ❏ Journal

Hotel Reservation

To: _____   _____
              hotel   email or fax

From: _____   _____
               name   email or fax

Today's date: _____ /_____ /_____
                  day   month   year

Dear Hotel _____ ,
Please make this reservation for me:

Name: _____

Total # of people: _____   # of rooms: _____   # of nights: _____

Arriving: _____ /_____ /_____   My time of arrival (24-hr clock): _____
              day   month   year   (I will telephone if I will be late)

Departing: ____ /____ /_____
               day   month   year

Room(s): Single___   Double ___   Twin ___   Triple ___   Quad___

With: Toilet ____   Shower ____   Bath ____   Sink only ___

Special needs: View___ Quiet___ Cheapest___ Ground Floor___

Please email or fax confirmation of my reservation, along with the type of room reserved and the price. Please also inform me of your cancellation policy. After I hear from you, I will quickly send my credit-card information as a deposit to hold the room. Thank you.

_____
Name

_____
Address

_____
City   *State*   *Zip Code*   *Country*

Before hoteliers can make your reservation, they want to know the information listed above. You can use this form as the basis for your email, or you can photocopy this page, fill in the information, and send it as a fax (also available online at www.ricksteves.com/reservation).

Hungarian Survival Phrases

Remember, the letter *a* is pronounced "aw," while *á* is a brighter "ah."
In the phonetics, *dj* is pronounced like the j in "jeans."

English	Hungarian	Pronunciation
Hello. (formal)	Jó napot kívánok.	yoh NAH-pot KEE-vah-nohk
Hi. / Bye. (informal)	Szia. or Hello.	SEE-yaw, "Hello"
Do you speak English?	Beszél angolul?	BEH-sayl AWN-goh-lool
Yes. / No.	Igen. / Nem.	EE-gehn / nehm
I (don't) understand.	(Nem) értem.	(nehm) AYR-tehm
Please.	Kérem.	KAY-rehm
You're welcome.	Szívesen.	SEE-veh-shehn
Thank you (very much).	Köszönöm (szépen).	KUR-sur-nurm (SAY-pehn)
Excuse me. / I'm sorry.	Bocsánat.	BOH-chah-nawt
No problem.	Semmi gond.	SHEH-mee gohnd
Good.	Jól.	yohl
Goodbye.	Viszontlátásra.	VEE-sohnt-lah-tahsh-raw
one / two	egy / kettő	edj / KEH-tur
three / four	három / négy	HAH-rohm / naydj
five / six	öt / hat	urt / hawt
seven / eight	hét / nyolc	hayt / nyolts
nine / ten	kilenc / tíz	KEE-lehnts / teez
hundred / thousand	száz / ezer	sahz / EH-zehr
How much?	Mennyi?	MEHN-yee
local currency	forint (Ft)	FOH-reent
Where is it?	Hol van?	hohl vawn
Is it free (no charge)?	Ingyen van?	een-JEHN vawn
Is it included?	Benne van az árban?	BEH-neh vawn oz AHR-bawn
Where can I find / buy...?	Hol találok / vehetek...?	hohl TAW-lah-lohk / VEH-heh-tehk
I'd like...	Kérnék...	KAYR-nayk
We'd like...	Kérnénk...	KAYR-naynk
...a room	...egy szobát	edj SOH-baht
...a ticket (to ___)	...egy jegyet (___-ig)	edj YEHDJ-eht (___-ig)
Is it possible?	Lehet?	leh-HEHT
Where is the...?	Hol van a...?	hohl vawn aw
big train station (in Budapest)	pályaudvar	PAH-yood-vawr
small train station (elsewhere)	vasútállomás	VAW-shoot-ah-loh-mahsh
bus station	buszpályaudvar	BOOS-pah-yood-vawr
tourist information office	turista információ	TOO-reesh-taw EEN-for-maht-see-yoh
toilet	toalet or WC	TOH-aw-leht, VAYT-say
men	férfi	FAYR-fee
women	női	NUR-ee
left / right	bal / jobb	bawl / yohb
straight	egyenesen or előre	EDJ-eh-neh-shehn, EH-lew-reh
At what time...	Mikor...	MEE-kohr
...does this open / close?	...nyit / zár?	nyit / zahr
Just a moment.	Egy pillanat.	edj PEE-law-nawt
now / soon / later	most / hamarosan / később	mohsht / HAW-maw-roh-shawn / KAY-shurb
today / tomorrow	ma / holnap	maw / HOHL-nawp

In the Restaurant

English	Hungarian	Pronunciation
I'd like to reserve a table for one / two people.	Szeretnék foglalni egy asztalt egy / két fő részére.	SEH-reht-nayk FOG-lawl-nee edj AWS-tawlt edj / kayt few RAY-say-reh
Non-smoking.	Nem dohányzó.	nehm DOH-hayn-zoh
Is this table free?	Ez az asztal szabad?	ehz oz AWS-tawl saw-BAWD
Can I help you?	Tessék.	TEHSH-shayk
The menu (in English), please.	Kérem az (angol) étlapot.	KAY-rehm oz (AWN-gohl) AYT-law-poht
service (not) included	a számla a felszolgálási díjat (nem) tartalmazza	aw SAHM-law aw FEHL-sohl-gah-lah-shee DEE-yawt (nehm) TAWR-tawl-maw-zaw
cover charge	belépő	BEH-lay-pur
"to go"	elvitelre	EHL-vee-tehl-reh
with / without	___-val / nélkül	___-vawl / NAYL-kewl
and / or	és / vagy	aysh / vawdj
fixed-price meal (of the day)	(napi) menü	(NAW-pee) MEH-new
specialty of the house	a ház specialitása	aw hahz SHPEHT-see-aw-lee-tah-shaw
half portion	fél adag	fayl AW-dawg
daily special	napi ajánlat	NAW-pee AW-yahn-lawt
fixed-price meal (for tourists)	(turista) menü	(TOO-reesh-taw) MEH-new
main courses	főételek	FUR-ay-teh-lehk
appetizers	előételek	EH-lur-ay-teh-lehk
bread / cheese	kenyér / sajt	KEHN-yayr / shayt
sandwich	szendvics	SEND-veech
soup / salad	leves / saláta	LEH-vehsh / SHAW-lah-taw
meat / poultry	hús / szárnyasok	hoosh / SAHR-nyaw-shohk
fish	halak	HAW-lawk
seafood	tengeri halak	TEHN-geh-ree HAW-lawk
fruit	gyümölcs	JEWM-urlch
vegetables	zöldség	ZULRD-shayg
dessert	desszert	DEH-sehrt
vegetarian	vegetáriánus	VEH-geh-tah-ree-ah-noosh
(tap) water	(csap) víz	(chawp) veez
mineral water	ásványvíz	ASH-vawn-veez
milk	tej	TAYee
(orange) juice	(narancs) lé	(NAW-rawnch) lay
coffee / tea	kávé / tea	KAH-vay / TEH-aw
beer / wine	sör / bor	shohr / bohr
red / white	vörös / fehér	VUR-rursh / FEH-hayr
sweet / dry / semi-dry	édes / száraz / félszáraz	AY-dehsh / SAH-rawz / FAYL-sah-rawz
glass / bottle	pohár / üveg	POH-hahr / EW-vehg
Cheers!	Egészségedre!	EH-gehs-shay-geh-dreh
More. / Another.	Még. / Másikat.	mayg / MAH-shee-kawt
The same.	Ugyanazt.	OODJ-aw-nawst
Bill, please. (literally, "I'll pay.")	Fizetek.	FEE-zeh-tehk
tip	borravaló	BOH-raw-vaw-loh
Bon appétit!	Jó étvágyat!	yoh AYT-vah-yawt
Delicious!	Finom!	FEE-nohm

INDEX

Rick Steves®

EUROPEAN TOURS

Experience Europe the Rick Steves
way, with great guides,
small groups...and no grumps!

See 30 itineraries at ricksteves.com

▸ Plan Your Trip

Browse thousands of articles and a wealth of money-saving tips for planning your dream trip. You'll find up-to-date information on Europe's best destinations, packing smart, getting around, finding rooms, staying healthy, avoiding scams and more.

▸ Eurail Passes

Find out, step-by-step, if a rail pass makes sense for your trip—and how to avoid buying more than you need. Get a bunch of free extras!

▸ Graffiti Wall & Travelers' Helpline

Learn, ask, share—our online community of savvy travelers is a great resource for first-time travelers to Europe, as well as seasoned pros.

Rick Steves

www.ricksteves.com

TRAVEL SKILLS
Europe Through the Back Door

EUROPE GUIDES
Best of Europe
Eastern Europe
Europe 101
European Christmas
Postcards from Europe

COUNTRY GUIDES
Croatia & Slovenia
England
France
Germany
Great Britain
Ireland
Italy
Portugal
Scandinavia
Spain
Switzerland

CITY & REGIONAL GUIDES
Amsterdam, Bruges & Brussels
Athens & The Peloponnese NEW IN 2009
Budapest NEW IN 2009
Florence & Tuscany
Istanbul
London
Paris
Prague & The Czech Republic
Provence & The French Riviera
Rome
Venice
Vienna, Salzburg & Tirol NEW IN 2009

PHRASE BOOKS & DICTIONARIES
French
French, Italian & German
German
Italian
Portuguese
Spanish

RICK STEVES' EUROPE DVDs
Austria & The Alps
Eastern Europe
England
Europe
France & Benelux
Germany & Scandinavia
Greece, Turkey, Israel & Egypt
Ireland & Scotland
Italy's Cities
Italy's Countryside
Rick Steves' European Christmas
Spain & Portugal
Travel Skills & "The Making Of"

PLANNING MAPS
Britain, Ireland & London
Europe
France & Paris
Germany, Austria & Switzerland
Italy
Spain & Portugal

JOURNALS
Rick Steves' Pocket Travel Journal
Rick Steves' Travel Journal

CREDITS

Contributor
Gene Openshaw

Gene is the co-author of seven Rick Steves books. For this book, he wrote material on Europe's art, history, and contemporary culture. When not traveling, Gene enjoys composing music, recovering from his 1973 trip to Europe with Rick, and living everyday life with his daughter.

Special Thanks
Many thanks to our Hungarian friends for sharing their invaluable insights: **Péter Pölczman, Andrea Makkay,** and **Elemér Boreczky.** *Köszönjük szépen!*

Hotel Pilvax

Pilvax Köz 1-3

06 1 266 7660

Rick Steves' Guidebook Series

Country Guides

Rick Steves' Best of Europe
Rick Steves' Croatia & Slovenia
Rick Steves' Eastern Europe
Rick Steves' England
Rick Steves' France
Rick Steves' Germany
Rick Steves' Great Britain
Rick Steves' Ireland
Rick Steves' Italy
Rick Steves' Portugal
Rick Steves' Scandinavia
Rick Steves' Spain
Rick Steves' Switzerland

City and Regional Guides

Rick Steves' Amsterdam, Bruges & Brussels
Rick Steves' Athens & the Peloponnese (new in 2009)
Rick Steves' Budapest (new in 2009)
Rick Steves' Florence & Tuscany
Rick Steves' Istanbul
Rick Steves' London
Rick Steves' Paris
Rick Steves' Prague & the Czech Republic
Rick Steves' Provence & the French Riviera
Rick Steves' Rome
Rick Steves' Venice
Rick Steves' Vienna, Salzburg & Tirol (new in 2009)

Rick Steves' Phrase Books

French
German
Italian
Spanish
Portuguese
French/Italian/German

Other Books

Rick Steves' Europe Through the Back Door
Rick Steves' Europe 101: History and Art for the Traveler
Rick Steves' Postcards from Europe
Rick Steves' European Christmas

(Avalon Travel)

Avalon Travel
a member of the Perseus Books Group
1700 Fourth Street
Berkeley, CA 94710

Text © 2009 by Rick Steves
Cover © 2009 by Avalon Travel. All rights reserved.
Maps © 2009 by Europe Through the Back Door
Printed in the USA by Worzalla. First printing March 2009.

Portions of this book were originally published in *Rick Steves' Eastern Europe* © 2008, 2007, 2006, 2005, 2004 by Rick Steves and Cameron Hewitt.

For the latest on Rick Steves' lectures, guidebooks, tours, public radio show, and public television series, contact Europe Through the Back Door, Box 2009, Edmonds, WA 98020, tel. 425/771-8303, fax 425/771-0833, www.ricksteves.com, rick@ricksteves.com.

ISBN (13) 978-1-59880-217-7
ISSN 1946-6161

Europe Through the Back Door Lead Editor: Cameron Hewitt
ETBD Senior Editor: Jennifer Madison Davis
ETBD Managing Editor: Risa Laib
ETBD Editors: Tom Griffin, Sarah McCormic, Cathy McDonald
Avalon Travel Senior Editor and Series Manager: Madhu Prasher
Avalon Travel Project Editor: Kelly Lydick
Copy Editor: Ellie Behrstock
Proofreader: Janet Walden
Indexer: Stephen Callahan
Production & Typesetting: McGuire Barber Design
Cover Design: Kimberly Glyder Design
Graphic Content Director: Laura VanDeventer
Maps & Graphics: David C. Hoerlein, Laura VanDeventer, Lauren Mills, Barb Geisler, Brice Ticen, Mike Morgenfeld
Photography: Cameron Hewitt, Rick Steves, Gretchen Strauch
Front Matter Color Photo: page i: Royal Palace © Cameron Hewitt
Cover Photo: Fishermen's Bastion © Cameron Hewitt

Distributed to the book trade by Publishers Group West, Berkeley, California